# U.S. NAVAL POWER IN THE 21st CENTURY

# U.S. NAVAL POWER IN THE 21ST CENTURY

## A NEW STRATEGY FOR FACING THE CHINESE AND RUSSIAN THREAT

## BRENT DROSTE SADLER

### FOREWORD BY J. WILLIAM MIDDENDORF II

Naval Institute Press
Annapolis, Maryland

Naval Institute Press
291 Wood Road
Annapolis, MD 21402

ISBN: 978-1-68247-777-9 (hardcover)
ISBN: 978-1-68247-811-0 (eBook)

**Library of Congress Cataloging-in-Publication Data is available.**
♾ Print editions meet the requirements of ANSI/NISO z39.48–1992
(Permanence of Paper).
Printed in the United States of America.

31 30 29 28 27 26 25 24 23      9 8 7 6 5 4 3 2 1
First printing

*All charts, tables, and maps were provided by and used with the permission of the
Heritage Foundation.*

THIS BOOK IS DEDICATED TO MY LATE GRANDFATHER,
William C. Sadler (an engineering duty officer and naval attaché whose
wartime photos are included in this book), and late grandmother,
Rowena B. Sadler (a wartime naval communications officer), whose naval
careers and many sea stories across wartime Asia and Cold War Philippines
served as inspiration for my naval career. I would not have been able to
dedicate the time needed for this book without the support of my family:
William and Connie Sadler; Christine Berry; my wife Yulia and daughters
Sophia and Vivienne. Finally, I would like to express my appreciation for
the editorial support I received from Thomas McArdle and the
intellectual insights and guidance from Dr. Bernard D. Cole,
whose mentoring has been so important.

# CONTENTS

# CONTENTS

# ILLUSTRATIONS

## PHOTOS

## TABLES

# FOREWORD

T he collapse of the Soviet Union in December 1991 was a seminal event in world history that inspired hope for relief from the long and dangerous conventional military and nuclear standoff with Moscow and its satellites during decades of Cold War.

Yet that relief and a new era of peace did not materialize. Today's world remains more dangerous than ever, with Russia invading Ukraine and China threatening Taiwan. The nation and our leaders confront new challenges with a coming war in space, cyberattacks, and information, economic, and financial warfare. The Hong Kong protest that began in 2019 continues to escalate, and it may be only a matter of time before China eliminates the "one country, two systems" approach.

Our military has been stretched to its limits, making do with aging ships, planes, tanks, and weapons systems. The threats we face have grown increasingly sophisticated, with cyber-war, artificial intelligence, and space weapons for which we have no defense. The best way to prepare for war is to be prepared to win it. We need to stop underfunding the military, especially in areas of research, space, cyber-war, and artificial intelligence. War is changing and we need to change with it. We cannot expect success fighting tomorrow's conflicts with yesterday's weapons.

During my tenure as Secretary of the Navy from 1974 to 1977, some of the most important weapons systems were built and deployed. They included the *Ohio*-class ballistic missile submarine fleet and Trident missiles that remain the backbone of the U.S. strategic nuclear deterrent. We also developed an advanced fleet of Aegis battle management system–equipped warships and the F/A-18 warplane.

Defense and national security in the twenty-first century require both new technologies and improved weapons systems. My book *The Great Nightfall: How We Win the New Cold War* assesses the threats from China, Russia, North Korea, and Iran. It warns that the current weapons and strategies for using them urgently need updating. My concern is that the current administration is not taking the danger seriously. Defense spending is not a top priority, and the main interests seem to be pursuing social equity and reducing carbon emissions.

Brent Sadler provides a fresh look in his book *U.S. Naval Power in the 21st Century*, which lays out a compelling, new strategic approach on how the nation can compete during these dangerous times. The central premise of his book is that new statecraft is required. While similar in scale and scope to Cold War "containment" strategies against the Soviets, *U.S. Naval Power in the 21st Century* is so much more. It has to be. China is integrated into global supply chains and wields significant financial heft.

The author provides a unique vision for competing with two global competitors—China and Russia. Rather than simply calling for better-coordinated U.S. diplomacy, military operations, and economic statecraft, he lays out a vision for integrating these levers of national power coherently and sustainably. His approach is strengthened by a long career rich in working with various agencies of government, foreign militaries, including hostile ones, and our allies. It is an approach imminently appropriate to our times but comes with a realization that the nation is not ready for the competition it faces from China and Russia.

Several critical investments are needed to achieve the goal of peaceful competition with China and Russia. First is the need to focus limited national power on decisive theaters key to our competitors' theories of victory. The second is shoring up our economy to eliminate Chinese and Russian influence and prevent intellectual theft while building the capacity to sustain a wartime economy should it be inevitable. Third is building a new model fleet designed for great power competition, which incorporates new concepts, classes of warships, and naval leaders attuned to the rigors of this new era. *U.S. Naval Power in the 21st Century* details the investments needed and the costs associated in detail.

The nation may face a dark future by not heeding the dangers before us and not following Brent Sadler's recommendations. He refuses to subscribe to the notion that the United States cannot afford military superiority over our combined most dangerous adversaries, China and Russia. The alternative to not meeting these challenges exposes our nation to the whims of those who do not share our values and covet our prosperity. That course of action would surely lead to a great nightfall on humanity.

The universal goal of freedom-loving people in America and throughout the world remains unchanged. We see it now as most nations condemn the Russian invasion of Ukraine and supply military and humanitarian aid to the embattled country. We must take advantage of a revitalized NATO and unite with nations around the world as they finally recognize the threats from Russia and China.

Brent Sadler shows us how in his rare and valuable contribution to the national debate over how best to respond to China's rise and Russia's expansion plans. It is an essential work to understand where we are and where we must go to preserve our way of life.

J. WILLIAM MIDDENDORF II
Secretary of the Navy, 1974–77

# PREFACE

*The Navy has both a tradition and a future—and we look with pride and confidence in both directions.*

—Adm. George Anderson, Chief of
Naval Operations, August 1, 1961

The world is on the cusp of a dangerous decade, and whether it becomes a violent peace or worse is a function of how we as a nation choose to respond. Already Russia has invaded Ukraine, and the danger of similar aggressions is growing. Time is in short supply, and the Navy has been unable to grow to meet these challenges fast enough—so conventional thinking must change.

At congressional hearings in March 2021, the then-current Indo-Pacific commander, Adm. Philip Davidson, and the then-future commander, Adm. John Aquilino, both testified that China is preparing for conflict by 2027. Hopes to mitigate tensions are slim, however, since 2019 the "one country, two systems" construct for a peaceful resolution of China's unresolved civil war has collapsed and could very likely draw the United States into major conflict over Taiwan. At the same time, Russia has transitioned from strategic agitator to outright aggressor under the leadership of Vladimir Putin.

Yet, despite congressional mandates and presidential advocacy, the Navy has been unable to break through a glass ceiling of 300 ships and get on track to meet a 2016 congressionally mandated goal of 355 warships by 2034. Meanwhile, Russia's navy is maintaining a dangerous submarine fleet and has armed its smaller warships with lethal long-range cruise missiles, and China's navy has grown and modernized at an astounding rate. China in 2021 has 360 warships and is on track to reach more than 425 by 2030.

An active strategy is needed, one with its theory of victory based on a Navy able both to field a war-winning fleet and compete aggressively in peace. This will place a premium on forward presence and new roles incorporating developmental economics in its execution. Time is of the essence.

The nation is beyond a so-called inflection point, the strategic initiative must be seized in a new approach. This requires enhancing our and like-minded nations' strengths while leveraging the weaknesses of our competitors China and Russia. As a consequence, naval operations must be conceptualized in a wider diplomatic and economic context. As China and Russia blur distinctions of war and peace and execute strategies that blend military, economic, informational, and legal activities, the nation must rethink its own statecraft. This book provides a novel approach to do this called "naval statecraft," defined as the synthesis of naval power in a comprehensive strategic competitive framework. This new statecraft, as I will show, will require new organizing structures as well as new naval capabilities optimized for this era of great power competition.

The war in Ukraine should make clear to all the new era we live in, but earlier events in Hong Kong galvanized me to begin this project. Beginning in 2019, a series of protests and riots began in Hong Kong over an extradition law the Chinese Communist Party (CCP) had wanted enacted. This and subsequent actions by the CCP were clearly abrogating the 1984 Sino-British Joint Declaration, specifically by invalidating the pledge to leave intact Hong Kong's democratic and capitalist way of life till 2047. This added to my sense of urgency given Russia's 2014 annexation of Crimea— the first unilateral territorial change in Europe since World War II. It was clear that long-standing constructs keeping the peace were fast eroding and a new approach was urgently needed.

The foundational theme of this book is naval statecraft, a concept I first committed to writing in 2010 while a student at the National War College. This was three years before the CCP would announce its Belt and Road Initiative, aiming to bind countries along a maritime silk road to China's economic and security interests. As I progressed the project, called "The Fulcrum of Wealth," I periodically briefed then–Chief of Naval Operations Adm. Gary Roughead, who was considering a rebalance of naval forces to the Asia-Pacific. Those discussions would both shape and reinforce the need for creative new thinking on maritime strategy and concepts of naval operations.

An early finding, but by no means remarkable, was the importance of enlisting and treating like-minded allies and partner nations as strong assets in great power competition with China and Russia. I saw the value of allies time and again from 1999 to 2001 while a flag lieutenant (a personal assistant) to Commander Seventh Fleet in Yokosuka, Japan. Again later, as an Olmsted Scholar in Tokyo, Japan, from 2004 to 2007, I saw it when I dug deeper into the mechanics and legal constraints of modernizing key alliances. The insights and relationships built during those years studying at Keio University, Jochi University, and a short stint at the United Nations University proved invaluable to this book.

Harder to articulate, and a topic on which there is limited research, was something I witnessed growing up on navy bases in Guam and Japan: an interesting but commonsensical tendency for communities in once war-torn areas to grow and prosper around military bases. The relationship between base and community would not always be placid, a point made by Alexander Cooley, who called this "base politics" in his similarly named 2008 book. However, there was evidence for "mutual benefit—bases for projecting security and in turn economic input to the community." The effort to turn this into a basis for sustainable forward naval presence would form a unique element of naval statecraft.

After graduating from National War College in 2011, I joined Bryan Clark and Kristen Gunness on Adm. Jonathan Greenert's personal staff (known as N00Z) shortly after he became Chief of Naval Operations (CNO). My task was to help him, and thereby the Navy, develop regionally informed approaches to compete with China. This was an exciting time as I pulled from my operational experiences in the Pacific as a submarine officer and past research to inform policies and initiatives the Navy implemented as part of a national effort. During this time I found myself involved in a project that had the president's attention, culminating with publication of the 2012 Defense Strategic Guidance—otherwise known as the Rebalance to the Asia-Pacific.

Perhaps partly due to my role on N00Z and development of the Rebalance, I was sent to U.S. Pacific Command in Hawaii. While there I supported Adm. Samuel Locklear in executing the Rebalance to the Asia-Pacific in concert with a whole-of-government effort. This resulted in many 2 a.m. meetings and long working weekends to prepare for countless briefings and decision meetings with the deputy secretary of defense. In what would be called "rebalance initiatives," I along with partners John Dutoit and Rick Cartwright crafted and then secured over $12 billion in an effort that actualized the rebalance. The lessons from the many budget knife fights and debates on future presence operations animates this book, especially the later chapters, which focus on how to turn strategy into action.

As the Rebalance was prematurely winding down in 2014, I returned to Tokyo for four months as a Council on Foreign Relations international affairs fellow. At the time, I was also a special assistant at the request of the Office of the Secretary of Defense to help modernize our military alliance with Japan. This would be done by revising the bilateral Defense Guidelines at the behest of Prime Minister Abe's government in Tokyo. This revision would see several key changes—a standing national policy coordination body called the Alliance Mechanism, and the development of the Alliance Enterprise to coordinate military-capacity-building activities. This was a heady time that saw the president in 2014 acknowledge Japan's administrative control of the Senkaku Islands, signaling to the Chinese that any attack there would trigger the alliance—specifically U.S. intervention. The importance of shared national interest, and personal connections, also find their way into naval statecraft's long-term goal of building enduring economic-military bridges to partner nations.

On returning to Hawaii in August 2014, I would have one last mission at Pacific Command and a new role as lead for Maritime Strategy and Policy. While still in Tokyo, I watched the secretary of defense deliver a speech in June 2014 at the Shangri-La Dialogue in Singapore. In it he directed Admiral Locklear, my boss, to host an Association of Southeast Asian Nations (ASEAN) maritime domain awareness event within a year; it would become my task to bring together senior policy-makers and enable their own consensus and action. The approach I took was unorthodox, but it worked and facilitated the establishment of the $500 million Maritime Security Initiative to improve Southeast Asian maritime domain awareness and bring together policy-makers from Malaysia, Indonesia, and the Philippines for what later would become the Trilateral Cooperative Agreement to jointly patrol pirate-infested waters of the Sulu Sea. A key takeaway from this experience was that forcing a commitment from partner nations up front is more likely to be counterproductive: after all, these countries have to balance precarious economic and security interests. A pragmatic and regionally informed approach worked, and it animates the diplomatic and soft-power aspects of naval statecraft.

Two weeks after hosting ASEAN nations to a maritime domain awareness workshop, and after a short vacation, I was once again working for Admiral Greenert at N00Z. This time my focus would be supporting the development of Navy's part of what Deputy Secretary of Defense Bob Work called a Third Offset. It was thrilling to use my background in robotics and artificial intelligence in imaginative new ways, all the while cognizant of the strategic imperative to compete with China's growing aggressiveness and Russian adventurism. It turned out to be an education in future force design and the important fact that timelines in delivering a new fleet must remain cognizant of evolving threats. This knowledge is what informs an accelerated shipbuilding program in this book.

In one of my last assignments before retiring from the Navy, I was honored to be the defense attaché in Malaysia. It turned out to be a remarkable time to be in Kuala Lumpur, from coordinating responses to the destroyer *McCain* (DDG-56) collision in August 2017, and opening several politically sensitive ports and airfields to U.S. forces, to witnessing the historic May 2018 national elections ushering in an opposition party for the first time since Malaysia's independence. But notable for this book was the approach the Malaysian chief of navy, Adm. Kamarul Badaruddin, took to secure funding to grow his navy. He relayed to me personally his economic argument: he pointed out that securing Malaysian fishing fleets would prevent the loss of $6 million in fishing revenues, and that he could secure this revenue at a cost of $4 million. It was a compelling argument that worked for him and fit into a broader "Blue Ocean" strategy of the prime minister—a strategy that avoids competition by seeking new markets at low cost while creating new demand. For me it was remarkable how similar this was to what I had learned at National War College. This experience further informed the economic foundations of a naval statecraft approach.

All said, this book represents the culmination of a decade of theoretical and hands-on testing of naval statecraft. The book opens by making the case that a maritime strategy is appropriate and that there is urgency to act as China and Russia contest the maritime rules-based order. The discussion then shifts to detail the forces (natural and man-made) shaping the maritime rules-based order and where national interests will gravitate in the long run to 2050. Later chapters focus on building and operating a "new model navy" to execute this strategy and the associated costs through 2035. The book concludes in the final chapters with an action plan that anticipates Chinese and Russian countermoves, and the need to mentor maritime leaders for this new era.

This book is intended to spark new thinking about our current strategic predicament, and provide solutions. Sadly, conventional thinking has not delivered the results or the forces needed to effectively compete with China and Russia for too long. Perhaps taking a naval statecraft approach can change that.

# ABBREVIATIONS

| | |
|---|---|
| AI | artificial intelligence |
| APEC | Asia Pacific Economic Cooperation |
| ARG | Amphibious Ready Group |
| ASEAN | Association of Southeast Asian Nations |
| ASW | antisubmarine warfare |
| BRAC | Base Realignment and Closure |
| CCG | China Coast Guard |
| CCP | Chinese Communist Party |
| CLC | fleet command ship |
| CNO | Chief of Naval Operations |
| COFA | compact of free association |
| CONOPs | concepts of operations |
| CSBA | Center for Strategic and Budgetary Assessments |
| CSG | Carrier Strike Group |
| CSI | Container Security Initiative |
| CVNE | light aircraft carrier |
| CVS | scout carrier |
| DARPA | Defense Advanced Research Projects Agency |
| DDC | corvette |
| DDG | destroyer |
| DFC | U.S. International Development Finance Corporation |
| DHS | U.S. Department of Homeland Security |
| DMO | Distributed Maritime Operations |
| DoD | U.S. Department of Defense |

| | |
|---|---|
| DoS | U.S. Department of State |
| EABO | Expeditionary Advanced Base Operations |
| EDA | excess defense articles |
| EEZ | exclusive economic zone |
| ERC | Exercise Related Construction |
| ESG | Expeditionary Strike Group |
| EU | European Union |
| eVTOL | electric vertical takeoff and landing craft |
| FAO | Foreign Area Officer |
| FFG | guided missile frigate |
| FLC | fleet logistic center |
| FONOP | freedom of navigation operation |
| FPDA | Five Powers Defense Arrangement |
| FRCs | fast-response cutters |
| FSM | Federated States of Micronesia |
| GDP | gross domestic product |
| GFM | Global Force Management |
| GRU | Russia's Main Intelligence Directorate |
| INDOPACOM | U.S. Indo-Pacific Command |
| JADC2 | Joint All-Domain Command and Control |
| JIATF | Joint Interagency Task Force |
| LAWs | Light Amphibious Warships |
| LCS | littoral combat ship |
| LNG | liquified natural gas |
| LOCE | Littoral Operations in a Contested Environment |
| LPD | landing helicopter assault ship |
| LSE | Large-Scale Exercise |
| LUSV | large unmanned surface vehicle |
| MARA | U.S. Maritime Administration |
| MOTR | Maritime Operational Threat Response |
| MSI | Maritime Security Initiative |
| MSP | Maritime Security Program |
| NASA | National Air and Space Administration |

| | |
|---|---|
| NATO | North Atlantic Treaty Organization |
| NAVSEA | Naval Sea Systems Command |
| NMCB | Naval Mobile Construction Battalions |
| NOAA | National Oceanic and Atmospheric Administration |
| NORAD | North American Defense Command |
| NSC | National Security Council |
| OCS | outer continental shelf |
| OFRP | Optimized Fleet Response Plan |
| PLA | People's Liberation Army (China) |
| PLAN | People's Liberation Army Navy |
| PMC | private military company |
| PSI | Proliferation Security Initiative |
| REEs | rare earth elements |
| RMI | Republic of the Marshall Islands |
| SIOP | Shipyard Infrastructure Optimization Program |
| SMA | Special Measures Agreement |
| SPP | State Partnership Program |
| SSBN | strategic ballistic missile submarine |
| T-AKM | munitions logistic ship for VLS reload |
| UNCLOS | United Nations Convention on the Law of the Sea |
| USAID | U.S. Agency for International Development |
| USCG | U.S. Coast Guard |
| VLS | vertical launch systems |
| XLUUV | extra-large unmanned undersea vehicle |

# Introduction
## Acting beyond the Inflection Point

*Sir Walter Raleigh declared in the early seventeenth century that "whoever commands the sea, commands the trade; whosoever commands the trade of the world commands the riches of the world, and consequently the world itself."*

—Fleet Adm. Chester W. Nimitz, USN, on his
day of departure from the Navy Department
as Chief of Naval Operations in 1948.

G reat nations have great navies, and diminish without them, a fact borne out time and again throughout history. On this point, Alfred Thayer Mahan's seminal 1889 book *The Influence of Sea Power upon History* remains relevant. Today less than 1 percent of America's maritime trade is conducted using American merchant ships, amid a rapidly maturing Chinese and Russian maritime threat. The United States has been here before, in the lead-up to World War I, when only 8.7 percent of its trade was on U.S. merchant ships defended by 224 warships. Mahan made this particularly important observation about the Seven Years' War (1756–63) between France and England: "The one nation that gained in this war was that which used the sea in peace to earn its wealth, and ruled it in war." This point is especially important in the great power competition of today; simply having a large Navy is not enough to assure the nation's prosperity and security.

The United States would be wise to heed the lessons of the Ming dynasty, as the Chinese Communist Party is certainly doing. For a time, the Ming dynasty ruled the seas of the Indo-Pacific, but in 1433 it shunned its navy, turning instead to domestic political intrigues and internal control. Burning its own fleet set in motion a remarkable turn of events and began the once-dominant global power's rapid decline. The absence of the

1

Ming fleet opened the door to European domination of global sea routes by the mid-1500s. It was a war over the opium trade with Britain in 1839, however, that began China's century of humiliation—a national tragedy that evokes sharp emotions and a commitment to avoid a repeat by today's CCP, which as of 2016 has the world's largest navy.

While China has been building a world-class navy with a vengeance, Western nations have been heading in the opposite direction. It is imperative for the free world to meet this challenge in a way that deters war, ensures freedom of commerce, bolsters maritime security, and anchors a rules-based order that respects the rights of large and small nations alike. Failing this, it could be the United States and the free world that endures one hundred years of humiliation.

Doing this requires embracing the new reality, a multipolar world in which U.S. diplomatic, social, economic, and military power can no longer influence events by fiat. The United States is already being provoked in every domain as its relative strengths wane in every element of national power. The world crossed the so-called inflection point in 2015 following Russia's annexation of Crimea and China's establishment of an archipelago of man-made island garrisons in the South China Sea. We are now in a new post–Cold War world, and in 2022 the United States is still coming to grips with today's great power competition.

It is a triangular competition over global influence and power chiefly between the CCP, Russia's oligarchy, and the United States. Like China, Russia under Vladimir Putin has become increasingly aggressive as it asserts a newfound confidence, having recovered from its recent era of humiliation that began with the 1991 dissolution of the Soviet Union. Yet another feature of the present era's great power competition is the blurring of peace and warfare across military and commercial tools of statecraft—reminiscent of the past rivalries recounted in Mahan's *Influence of Seapower.*

Moreover, the longtime global soft-power dominance of U.S. entertainment media has receded and been subsumed by the CCP through pursuit of profit in Chinese markets. Examples include Dreamworks' *Abominable*, a children's movie that included controversial Chinese "nine-dash line"

## Map 1. Steaming Times to Areas of Vital U.S. National Interest

Steam times are approximate based on an average speed of 15 knots.

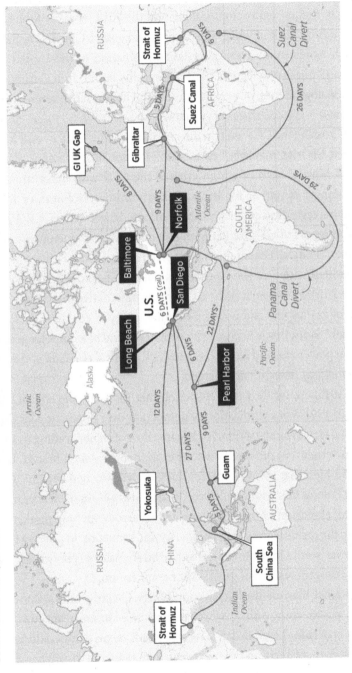

* Assumes no delay in passage through the Panama Canal.

**SOURCE:** Heritage Foundation research.

claims to the South China Sea;[1] the removal of the Taiwan flag from the *Top Gun* sequel lead actor's jacket;[2] and the 2012 remake of the Cold War movie *Red Dawn* in which the original antagonist, China, is replaced with North Korea in an even more fanciful invasion of the United States to please Chinese moviegoers.[3] This new reality has no Iron Curtain separating ideological foes, or oceans offering the nation sanctuary—the threat is here and it is sometimes very personal.

Crossing the CCP even in the heartland carries a price—ask Roy Jones, a fired Marriot manager,[4] or former Houston Rockets general manager Daryl Morey,[5] both of whom crossed the CCP with unfortunate tweets. The danger is starker for Russian expats who cross Putin, or for ethnic Chinese, regardless of citizenship, deemed a danger to the CCP. A Freedom House report titled "Out of Sight, Not out of Reach" documents countless cases of political assassination and forced repatriation. Putin's government is credited with 7 of the 26 overseas political assassinations documented since 2014. However, it is the CCP that is most active in overseas suppression of its diaspora and political enemies, guilty of 214 cases, or 35 percent overall.[6] Sadly, this is likely a symptom of the end of a unipolar geopolitical global power era, and a new one in which political coercion and economic and military statecraft are merged.

At this point it's worth reflecting that for some the end of the Cold War in 1991 was a vindication of democracy over dogmatic Marxist ideology—a victory underwritten by the free flow of capital leading to sustained improvements in prosperity wherever capitalism was embraced. Euphoria was so high that by 1992 ideologically driven war had become a relic, or what Francis Fukuyama called the "end of history."[7] In the few years following, an explosion of freely moving capital across opening markets underwrote the greatest growth of prosperity and reduction in poverty the world had ever seen. Unfortunately, that period in history is now over, replaced with the stark realism of great power competition.

Rather than an ideological contest between governing systems, today's great power competition is over control of economies and the underlying global rules-based order: state capitalism versus democratic capitalism. The stakes are high and democracy alone does not guarantee success in this strategic competition. As Seva Gunitsky states in his book *Aftershocks*,

"Material success . . . often creates its own legitimacy: regimes become morally appealing simply by virtue of their triumph."[8]

In this contest, China's economic success and cynicism of democracy are potently captured in the words of Hu Xijin, editor-in-chief of the state newspaper *Global Times*. Accompanying a photo of Beijing's latest mobile intercontinental ballistic missile, the DF-41, Hu tweeted, "China was just fine forgoing the 'good stuff' of electoral democracy on display in 'Haiti, Libya, Iraq, and Ukraine.'"[9] A consequence of this, as World Bank president Jim Yong Kim stated in September 2018, is the rate of historic reductions in poverty since the Cold War is slowing. This and a potential reversal in poverty trends are concomitant with the return to great power competition and incipient fracturing of global markets and common rules-based discourse along evolving modern spheres of influence. The challenge for democratic capitalism led by the United States is to regain global economic dynamism. Failure could usher in a new era of what Francis Fukuyama labeled an "age of pessimism," blinding many to the inherent weaknesses of totalitarianism.[10]

In this unfolding age of pessimism, the United States and its key security partners are rethinking their foreign policies. The role of hard power is ascendant and with it comes risk to destructive demagoguery in place of reasoned strategy, as Kurt Campbell and Jake Sullivan argue in their 2019 essay "Competition without Catastrophe."[11] In this new reality our competitors, namely Russia and China, will constrain approaches and have a vote on outcomes. As Mark Miles and Charles Miller have argued in "Global Risks and Opportunities," this new era of great power competition will likely follow historical precedent, being global in scale and comprehensive in scope of national power as opportunistic competitors seek any advantage.[12] The acknowledgment of this reality has been long in coming.

Since the Cold War's end, assumptions based on the preeminence of U.S. military and economic power have encouraged generally passive or reactive national security policies. The 2017 National Security Strategy and 2018 National Defense Strategy indicate that assumptions of U.S. supremacy no longer inform competitive approaches to China and Russia. Likewise, in contemplating a *New Cold War* it's instructive to weigh the opportunity costs, as Derek Leebaert's book *The Fifty Year Wound* does for the Cold War.[13] He postulates what medical advances, technological discoveries, or betterment of the human condition might have been achieved sooner absent the demands of deterring communist expansionism for fifty years. Based on such insights, great power competition today, specifically with China, will certainly have opportunity costs. It is a challenge, however, that has come to the United States and requires a comprehensive, coherent approach for success. Or, as Patrick Cronin and Ryan Neuhard argue, it is total competition, encompassing economic, legal, psychological, military, and information spheres.[14] The challenge is to minimize such opportunity costs while actualizing an approach that can be executed and sustained by our democratic system and open free-market economy. Amid these issues, the geopolitical realities are changing nowhere more than in Asia.

In Asia, long-standing assumptions and security constructs are being questioned and overturned. Japan, faced with myriad challenges and uncertainty about U.S. security and diplomatic assurances, has under Prime Minister Abe shaken off pacifism for a proactive comprehensive regional strategy. Monthslong protests against CCP diktats in Hong Kong challenged the "one country, two systems" premise for peaceful unification between China and Taiwan. In this environment, Taiwan's January 2020 national elections returning President Tsai Ing-wen for a second term further agitated Beijing's suspicions that her government would abandon the long-term goal of unification. It is an objective the Chinese Communist Party would prefer be settled well below the threshold of war with the United States. This approach channels Chinese strategic culture as stated by the eminent Sun Tzu: "Hence to fight and conquer in all your battles is not supreme excellence; supreme excellence consists in breaking the enemy's resistance without fighting."[15]

In this global contest, mobility and ability to apply sustained force rapidly makes the Navy an asymmetric challenge to Chinese and Russian theories of victory. This advantage must be pressed, but to do this the Navy must recover from decades of slim and often inconsistent budgets that have dangerously reduced its capacity. The Navy of today is still largely the legacy of decades of Cold War investment—especially the Reagan-era naval buildup to the so-called six-hundred-ship navy. Since the fall of the Berlin Wall in 1989, however, the United States has cashed in on its Cold

War success and has been slow to adjust to the rapid rise of China and the methodical modernization of Russia's navy. To quantify the Navy's peace dividend contribution from 1989 to 2020, if the Navy budget only grew with actual inflation compared with executed budgets, the Navy saved over $1.2 trillion, reduced ship numbers (from 592 down to 296), divested infrastructure (the closing of four shipyards), and cashiered manpower (from 605,802 down to 347,487). Such sustained cuts have instilled in the Navy an organizational mindset predicated on pursuit of cost efficiencies even when domestic politics and security threats necessitate a mission first priority—a say/do gap that has grown since 2018's National Defense Strategy. New thinking and investments are required to reverse this decades-long divestment and recover the forward presence that has been foundational to U.S. security and diplomacy. But there have been some positive developments.

In a remarkable series of deployments beginning in May 2020, as a Taiwan president despised by the CCP took office, the U.S. Navy increased its forward presence. Most notably, the U.S. naval presence in the South China Sea grew to include two aircraft carrier strike groups in the area for the first time in more than a decade. Beijing, though not happy about the deployment, offered only a muted response; it had its hands full with COVID pandemic recovery, escalating border tensions after a deadly clash with India, and growing international condemnation of the CCP's suppression and genocide of its Uyghur population. The heightened U.S. naval presence not only dampened Chinese intimidation toward Taiwan but also had salubrious effects elsewhere . . . for a while. For example, Chinese ships had been harassing a survey ship, the *West Capella*, chartered by the Malaysian government for an oil exploration job in its own economic exclusive waters; that behavior diminished once U.S. ships entered the scene. The lessons of this event will be explored in more detail in later chapters, including the insights it gives into the CCP's strategic calculus.

Drawing on a broad array of academic and historical research, a naval-based strategy is the best fit for great power competition of the day. Such an approach can better assure U.S. interests and future prosperity, and can secure the peace relative to revisionist powers dead set on undermining the U.S. democratic system, its economy, and global network of trade and military partnerships. A naval-centered national strategy can best secure our global network of partners and trade, while leveraging positional advantage by avoiding being locked into fixed land competitions. Determining the design of such naval forces and timelines for its deployment in furthering such a global strategy necessitates a deep understanding of the main competitors, China and Russia, and the forces at play across the world's existing and new maritime technologies.

Elbridge Colby laid out the challenge during a hearing on the 2018 National Defense Strategy before the Senate Armed Service Committee in January 2019, paying particular attention to China and Russia. These two superpowers, Colby asserted, pose a particularly dangerous threat to the United States and its allies because of plausible theories of victory that weave together subversion, advanced area denial weapons, nuclear deterrence, and "gray-zone" actions.[16] Using similar approaches China and Russia have changed the realities on the ground and national borders in Ukraine and the South China Sea without triggering a war. It is the potential for an attempted fait accompli by Russia against a member of the North Atlantic Treaty Organization (NATO), or China against Taiwan, however, that poses the greatest risk for major war. Deterring such a move requires relevant military forces nearby at so-called flashpoints. Or, as Jerry Hendrix describes it, the future fleet must be designed to preserve the peace, sustain the liberal capitalist order, and when need be, win in war.[17] Both China and Russia are aware of this and have sought to break out from a naval cordon with a growing array of overseas bases beginning in Syria and Djibouti. Their approaches are born in weakness, however . . . for now.

Typical of autocracies, both China and Russia are externally risk-averse, since they must also contend with dangerous domestic challenges; the CCP spends almost 20 percent more on internal defense than on external national defense.[18] Because of this, they attempt to change realities on the ground and at sea without direct confrontation via so-called hybrid or gray-zone operations. Backed by active influence campaigns, economic largess, and military presence, their theory of victory is to alienate the United States from its allies and partners, elbow out market influence and access, and depict the rules-based order as hypocritical and only serving

U.S. interests. Their goal is to position themselves to dictate or accomplish via fait accompli their strategic economic, political, and military goals.

Great power competition with China and Russia will require a modern synthesis of the theoretical work of naval luminaries Alfred Thayer Mahan and Julian Corbett. Mahan, as I already mentioned, focused on the influence naval power has on comprehensive national power and the importance of protecting economic connections over the seas.[19] Corbett saw naval rivalries as the only situation where limited war was possible and disagreed with Mahan on the importance of massed naval power, focusing instead on the role of naval forces in defeating an enemy's political objectives.[20] Importantly, this is not a Navy-only game. The development of long-range shore-based antiship cruise missiles and antiair missiles provides an opportunity for land forces to play in maritime great power competition in new ways. Such land forces fit both Mahan's and Corbett's conceptualizations of naval warfare in attacking an adversary's naval forces and securing critical logistic and economic nodes. Such forces will likewise have a limited but real economic impact on overseas communities and trade. Naval statecraft attempts a modern synthesis of these naval luminaries' thinking as it applies to the modern spectrum of rivalry with China and Russia.

At this point it is worth pausing to define what is meant by statecraft. In his book *Foreign Affairs Strategy*, Terry L. Deibel defined statecraft as the synthesis of strategic objectives with the instruments of national power to form a course of action.[21] Inherent in this definition is the constraining effect of organizational structures on the most effective employment of resources. Graham Allison's 1969 analysis of the Cuban Missile Crisis provides examples of how "standard operating procedures" prevented the most effective courses of action—a dynamic still bedeviling our institutions adjusting to this new era.[22] Naval statecraft, while adhering to Deibel's definition, goes further and recommends optimizing organizational structures for great power competition. As will be seen, there is an urgent need for such an adjustment.

Since the Scarborough Shoal crisis between China and the Philippines in 2012, and Russia's annexation of Crimea in 2014, the Department of Defense (DoD) and the Navy have recognized the need to compete below

**Table 1. Naval Fleet Design**

| | Starting Point | Recommendation | | | Navy Plan (Dec. 2020) | | Range per Future Naval |
|---|---|---|---|---|---|---|---|
| | Jan. 2021 | 2023 | 2028 | 2035 | 2023 | 2035 | Force Study |
| Unmanned (LUSV, MUSV, XLUUV) | 0 | 9 | 48 | 136 | 2 | 110 | 143 to 242 |
| Aircraft Carriers (CVN, CVNE, CVS) | 11 | 11 | 12 | 15 | 11 | 11 | 8 to 17 |
| Large Surface Combatant | 91 | 103 | 111 | 94 | 92 | 86 | 73 to 88 |
| Small Surface Combatant | 30 | 32 | 38 | 56 | 37 | 58 | 60 to 67 |
| Logistics and Support Vessels | 63 | 71 | 98 | 135 | 70 | 96 | 96 to 117 |
| Submarines (SSBN, SSGN, SSN) | 68 | 78 | 77 | 82 | 72 | 74 | 84 to 90 |
| Amphibious Warships | 33 | 34 | 42 | 57 | 28 | 52 | 61 to 67 |
| Total Without Unmanned | 296 | 329 | 378 | 439 | 310 | 377 | 382 to 446 |
| Total | 296 | 338 | 426 | 575 | 312 | 487 | 525 to 688 |

SOURCES: U.S. Navy, Office of the Chief of Naval Operations, Deputy Chief of Naval Operations (Warfighting Requirements and Capabilities–OPNAV N9), *Report to Congress on the Annual Long-Range Plan for Construction of Naval Vessels*, December 9, 2020, https://media.defense.gov/2020/Dec/10/2002549918/-1/-1/1/SHIPBUILDING%20PLAN%20DEC%20 20_NAVY_OSD_OMB_FINAL.PDF (accessed August 19, 2021), and Heritage Foundation research.

the threshold of conflict, in a gray zone, to confound Xi's and Putin's strategic calculus. Actualizing that recognition has been too long in coming. To deny China and Russia victories without firing a shot, the Navy will need to build and employ a larger fleet with new competencies to keep competitors in Beijing and Moscow unsure of the correlation of forces. Attempts to counter Chinese and Russian campaigns have been mixed, with failures in the South China Sea, Ukraine, and Georgia pointing to an inability of today's military to preempt fait accompli operations.

The United States cannot wish away those who view its prosperity and democratic principles as an impediment to their designs. Reluctantly, the nation has awoken to a new era of great power competition, which is about to enter a dangerous new phase. To slacken resolve and vigilance now would make conflict more likely and costly. Yet the United States cannot, and should not, try to counter every Russian and Chinese coercive act; this would be a mistake that would overtax limited diplomatic capital and stretched military resources.

The pages to follow will identify where the nation's enduring maritime interests lie, where the risks are greatest between now and 2035 from China and Russia, and how best to respond in decisive theaters while targeting competitors' weaknesses, and it concludes with a plan for action. To deter the growing Chinese armada arrayed against us requires more than matching numbers in arsenals and fleets; we must grow our fleet while also rethinking naval operations in a wider diplomatic and economic context. We need a new naval statecraft: one that leverages and enables naval presence while demonstrating the economic benefits of a Free and Open Indo-Pacific.

A successful strategy must include diplomatic efforts to attract and bolster like-minded partner nations. In the competition with China partners such as India, Vietnam, Indonesia, the Philippines, and Malaysia will be key. But soft power alone will not dissuade Beijing, nor will it alone attract the partners we need. China's intentions are not likely to change if the United States and its allies do nothing to complicate or slow Beijing's gray-zone strategy; inaction risks ceding the global commons of maritime Asia. Inaction would also encourage China to push harder while misjudging U.S. commitments, thereby increasing the risk of conflict.

A strong Navy has been a bedrock of America's security and will be critical in a naval statecraft approach that also assures prosperity by securing trade in a free and open maritime order. To ensure that this remains the case, the nation urgently needs to build, train, and sustain a Navy that can compete effectively in peacetime and win in war. For the past forty years, the Navy has maintained approximately one hundred warships at sea, and as the overall size of the fleet has dwindled, this has meant longer deployments and greater operational demands on both ships and personnel. Each sailor and officer represents a significant investment in capital and time for effective operation of the fleet—an investment that must not be squandered and, if lost, cannot easily be replaced.

At the same time, China has assiduously studied the United States and built up a global economic and military machine. Russia is different but has likewise studied the United States and built a niche capacity to play global spoiler to Western interests, increasingly in concert with China. By the late 1990s the military challenge from China had been recognized by a few academics and some in the DoD and Congress. At a March 2021 hearing before the House Armed Services and Foreign Affairs Committees, witnesses described a maritime Asia at a tipping point. It's a complicated situation of overlapping maritime claims, domestic politics, and economics.[23] In fact, the growth of the People's Liberation Army Navy (PLAN) has exceeded all analysts' expectations, and the PLAN's remarkable modernization is likely to continue.[24]

Against such challenges, the United States will need to employ its limited but comprehensive power to greatest effect. Yet the challenge to secure access to emerging markets amid diverging perceptions of rights pertaining to the maritime commons will continue to require traditional naval missions. At the same time, budget constraints will make building naval alliances a necessity. Expanding trade can sustain prosperity for the United States, while providing the means for emerging markets to peacefully rise free of Chinese and Russian malign influence. Free and open market competition, it is hoped, will lead to improved governance and stability as populations realize that their needs and their aspirations for a more prosperous life are best met through trade.

Compounding the Navy's strategic and operational challenges is a loss of confidence caused by a series of events. The never-ending "Fat Leonard" influence-peddling scandal, a series of serious collisions in 2017, and frequent senior leadership changes in 2019 and 2020 have taken their toll on morale and effectiveness.[25] At a time when the Navy desperately needs visionary leadership, turmoil in the most senior ranks began with the last-minute withdrawal of prospective CNO Adm. William Moran in August 2019. Then came the firing of the Secretary of the Navy in November 2019, followed by the acting Secretary of the Navy's departure in April 2020. In addition, the lack of an accessible and coherent maritime vision for great power competition contributed to the takeover in mid-2020 of the Navy's future-fleet-building plan—the Integrated Naval Force Structure Assessment (INFSA)—by the secretary of defense. Failure to meet these challenges head-on will cede the maritime domain and its associated rules-based order to China and Russia. They will not allow the Navy the luxury of a time-out to sort out either its culture or its seamanship. Real action, propelled by leadership with a vision and the fire to drive the Navy forward, is needed *today*.

Specifically, in order to regain its leading role, the Navy must

- Restore public confidence in its professionalism and seamanship while competing more effectively in the peacetime day-to-day contest over the principles of a maritime rules-based order.
- Develop, build, and sustain a fleet that can win wars and be reconstituted quickly both in war and between wars.

Today's need for a reconceptualized and larger Navy is driven largely by the tremendous growth in China's navy and the steady improvement of Russia's naval forces. Although this point enjoys wide recognition in 2022, it has yet to be matched by a vision of how and with what forces the Navy is to compete in great power competition. Without a clear and accessible vision of "the Navy the nation needs," the effort to expand and train the future Navy for this competition will falter.

# CHAPTER 1

# Naval Statecraft

*I think the world is sadly mistaken when it supposes that battles are won by this or that kind of gun or vessel. . . . The best gun and the best vessel should certainly be chosen, but the victory three times out of four depends upon those who fight them.*

—Letter dated November 8, 1864, from Rear Adm. David Farragut, commander of U.S. naval forces during the Civil War, to Secretary of the Navy Gideon Welles

The Navy's role in warfighting is well-known; less well appreciated is its ability to shape the environment in which security, diplomacy, and economics interact. This is a role the Navy has performed throughout its history, and if applied in a deliberate fashion against our competitors, that role affords a more effective approach to protecting and advancing the nation's interests. The Navy's disaster response operations in the 2000s are illustrative of how peacetime naval activities can produce favorable political change ashore. The Navy's 2004 tsunami relief efforts in Indonesia began a rapprochement that greatly improved relations and military engagement. Likewise, the Navy and Marine Corps' response to the 2008 Cyclone Nargis disaster began a chain of events that led to normalized relations with Myanmar.

In comprehensive great power competition with China and Russia, every element of national power must be applied and leveraged. Actualizing this aim requires institutional adjustments: the country-centered approach executed to date along independent military, economic and diplomatic lines has not worked. Maritime contests are by nature regional, requiring that U.S. actions be similarly conceptualized and executed while navigating a mosaic of competing local interests. This necessitates a pragmatic approach blending naval, economic, and diplomatic instruments into a cohesive and adaptable framework. If applied effectively, this form of "naval statecraft" offers a way forward to restore confidence in the rules-based maritime order without escalation to armed conflict. These actions must in turn build on a long-term strategy that evolves with changing global trade, population growth, climate change, and promising new technologies. The goal is to ensure that national interests are protected into the future while being positioned to take advantage of new opportunities—that is, emerging markets, shifting regional geostrategic dynamics. However, the here-and-now cannot be ignored. Analysis conducted in 2020 of disputes short of war from 1991 through 2018 provides several insights into how to integrate the military into broader statecraft:

- Specific demands (e.g., withdrawal from seized territory and cessation of internal violence) have a significantly greater chance of success when military threats are not publicly stated, thereby providing paths to de-escalation.
- Unmistakable increases in military presence geographically proximate to a specific dispute are most effective, but they are undermined if done in conjunction with economic sanctions that signal the unlikelihood of U.S. military action.
- Most important, actions to put at risk the competitor decision-maker's values and goals must be taken early.[1]

Additionally, an "eyes-on" forward naval presence demonstrates unmistakable commitment and provides public narratives contesting Chinese and Russian influence campaigns. This was in fact the case in 2018 when ABC News' Bob Woodruff flew on U.S. maritime patrol aircraft near Chinese garrisons in the disputed South China Sea. Resources such as these can be useful in exposing the ignoble acts of Russian mercenaries (e.g., the Wagner Group) and undermining propaganda from China's energetic new breed of "Wolf Warrior" diplomats.[2] Naval forces acting in concert with economic and diplomatic levers in decisive theaters can hold at risk key goals of Chinese and Russian leaders and shape maritime behaviors while able to respond to or preempt evolving challenges. This is not just an intellectual concept: the U.S. government did just this, unknowingly, in the South China Sea.

Beginning in December 2019, China directed its ire at the Panamanian-flagged *West Capella*, which was exploring for oil in Malaysia's exclusive economic zone (EEZ). The China Coast Guard (CCG) and maritime militia vessels harried the *West Capella* for months as she conducted deepwater surveys for Malaysia's state-owned Petronas oil company. In late April 2020 the large amphibious assault ship *America* and her two escorts steamed toward the scene. In contrast to past behavior, the *America* and her strike group did not merely pass through the area but remained in the vicinity for several days. Following the *America*'s departure, the littoral combat ships (LCS) *Gabrielle Giffords* and *Montgomery* began patrols nearby, thus sustaining the U.S. presence.[3] In mid-May, Seventh Fleet Commander Vice Adm. William Merz asserted, "The U.S. supports the efforts of our allies and partners in the lawful pursuit of their economic interests."[4] Nations in the region took notice of this: upholding economic rights with naval presence was a divergence from the long-standing talking point of "supporting freedom of navigation and overflight." Soon U.S. Air Force bombers overflew the area, culminating in early July with the first sustained dual-aircraft-carrier South China Sea operation since 2012.[5] Amid all this, on July 13, Secretary of State Michael Pompeo issued the first clear statement of U.S. views on China's claims: "They are unlawful."[6] Given the economic nature of the *West Capella*'s survey operations, such statements, adroitly matched with a naval presence, resonated in tangible ways. Soon afterward, Indonesia conducted large naval drills in the South China Sea. After years of pulling its punches, the Philippines began pressing its 2016 maritime arbitration victory against China. In a rare move, Malaysia protested to the United Nations over China's excessive claims.[7] The secretary's July statement was well timed and, given Admiral Merz's earlier statements, poised U.S. involvement in the region as upholding principles and rights welcomed by regional nations. Moreover, public opinion polls conducted by the ASEAN Study Center before and after this incident paint a positive picture for U.S. maritime engagement. Before *West Capella*, the United States led China in confidence and trust by 10 percent, but after the crisis the difference grew to 32 percent in favor of the U.S. Worry about China's economic dominance was also driving unease in the region, resulting in over 70 percent welcoming greater U.S. economic engagement well above

China's 28 percent.[8] The bottom line is that despite China's large economic and military footprint, a U.S. naval presence focused on bolstering a maritime rules-based order, specifically the economic and security interests of regional states, resonated far more than periodic assertions of the U.S. Navy's own rights of freedom of navigation.

Given the way things progressed, one would be forgiven for thinking events were carefully planned ahead of time. In fact, they were not. Rather, a disparate team of policy-makers and military leaders in Washington, Yokosuka, and Hawaii had acted in a complementary fashion. Had the secretary delivered his statement earlier in April, it would have made it appear that the later naval presence was one intended to intimidate, not to uphold shared interests. A common understanding of the strategic environment enabled this team to flip the script on China. The way this crisis played out offers a model for naval statecraft that can be replicated for future successes—but in the future, planning and deliberate action will be needed.

## Economic-Military Nexus of Naval Affairs

Providing a compelling value proposition will be a critical element of sustaining long-term naval statecraft. For example, ASEAN nations do not want to choose between the security offered by the United States and the largesse on offer from trade with China or Beijing's Belt and Road Initiative. A Free and Open Indo-Pacific framework has been well received in Asia in part because it is premised on an understanding that security and economics are intertwined.[9] Building on this understanding requires that the United States better employ economic statecraft, diplomacy, and naval presence. Done right, this approach provides partner nations with a potentially compelling cost proposition compared with that on offer from China or Russia. The U.S. International Development Finance Corporation (DFC), established by the BUILD Act, can direct investments informed by the Navy's need for access to ports and logistics hubs, bolstering a cost-effective forward presence while expanding mutually beneficial trade.[10]

For forward presence to be sustainable it must be strategically effective, economically viable, and politically sustainable. As the *West Capella* case indicates, forward naval presence can be a strategically effective element of such an integrated statecraft. Sustaining such an approach, however, requires providing tangible benefits to the U.S. electorate as well as a host or partner nation. A 2016 RAND Corporation research project provides important insights into the connection of economic activity and military forward presence.

The RAND Corporation, a DC-based think tank, was tasked by the U.S. Air Force in 2014 to investigate the potential implications on trade of U.S. military forward presence being measurably reduced. RAND's team looked at the correlation of trade as a function of number of bilateral agreements and military personnel based in a host country. A strong correlation was found between mutual trade and existence of security agreements that reduced the cost of trade via air and shipping. RAND found that a reduction of 50 percent in overseas security commitments (troops overseas and agreements) would result in a drop in bilateral trade of 18 percent or, according to 2015 trade data, a loss of $490 billion to U.S. gross domestic product (GDP). Moreover, they found that the corollary also indicated a strong correlation; doubling of security agreements saw a 34 percent increase, while a doubling of military personnel in-country saw a 15 percent increase in trade.[11] Stories relayed to me indicate that these findings helped convince a skeptical President Donald Trump. Early in his tenure, President Trump was briefed on the study, which made a strong business case for forward presence in a way a businessman understood— and frankly the same is true for many of our partner nations' leaders. Although RAND had not specifically looked into it, it was noted that there was strong evidence that such troop presence and security agreements had a similar positive effect on international capital flows.

RAND's research advanced the understanding of the correlation between security presence and bilateral trade. While this study looked at troops in-country, there is little reason not to consider a similar relationship exists for naval personnel in-country or with Navy port visits. Such port visits can in fact be very lucrative, injecting a relatively large amount of cash into small waterfront communities. For example, a typical five-day U.S. aircraft carrier port visit, with its approximately five thousand sailors and airmen, can bring local communities $2 million in port services and discretionary spending by the sailors. Depending on the size of the port community, such an infusion of cash can be significant. The Navy is not alone. The Army's Pacific Pathways series of exercises aims to boost forward presence and can likewise impact host country economic development at important maritime nodes. Begun in 2014 and run by U.S. Army Pacific, Indo-Pacific Command's Army component command, Pacific Pathways deploys Army units overseas in extended training missions. These deployments have included upward of eight hundred fully equipped troops to Thailand, Indonesia, Malaysia, and the Philippines. In 2018, Gen. Robert Brooks Brown announced Pacific Pathways 2.0, aiming to extend deployments from four to six months in an effort to provide a persistent Army presence in this key region.[12] When coordinated, port visits and ground force exercises can provide a significant and sustained presence with associated diplomatic and economic benefits. RAND's study did not consider the possibility of translating such benefits into political sustainability, but Alexander Cooley's work on base politics does.

Initially, naval presence serves security goals but can over time become associated with furthering economic prosperity and trade through direct financial inputs supporting forward presence. For the Navy, the maritime security that it provides must be cost-effective and have a strategic impact (e.g., that supports maintaining a forward presence in the South China Sea or Eastern Mediterranean). To be politically sustainable at home, benefits must flow to the U.S. electorate—notably, through two-way beneficial trade with a host country that enjoys the financial inflow of hosting a naval presence (e.g., port visits, refueling). A sample of this dynamic occurred over two decades in Djibouti spurred by the inflow of military forces to combat the terrorist organization Al-Qaeda.

Djibouti as a base for U.S. military operations in Africa and the Middle East grew rapidly after the attacks of September 11, 2001. As the U.S. military presence grew, so did trade with the United States, marking a sixfold increase compared to the average of nine years before September 2001. Despite Djibouti's strategic location astride critical shipping lanes to East Asia and Europe, before September 2001 it had attracted little investment.

The in-country U.S. presence at Camp Lemonnier originally supported operations in Afghanistan and maritime interdiction of fleeing Al-Qaeda across the Arabian Sea. There was scant focus on economic development

# Chart 1. Djibouti GDP, Imports, and Exports

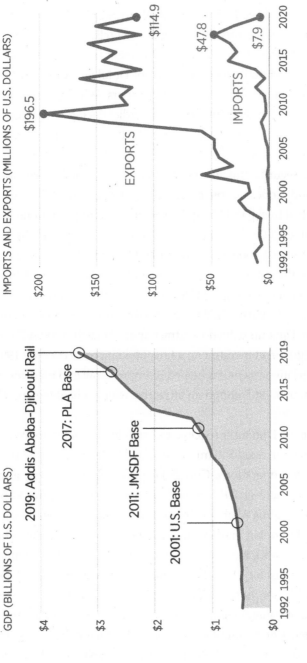

GDP (BILLIONS OF U.S. DOLLARS)

2019: Addis Ababa-Djibouti Rail

2017: PLA Base

2011: JMSDF Base

2001: U.S. Base

$4
$3
$2
$1
$0

1992 1995    2000    2005    2010    2015    2019

IMPORTS AND EXPORTS (MILLIONS OF U.S. DOLLARS)

$196.5

$114.9

$47.8

$7.9

EXPORTS

IMPORTS

$200
$150
$100
$50
$0

1992 1995    2000    2005    2010    2015    2020

**SOURCES:** The World Bank, "GDP (Current US$)," https://data.worldbank.org/indicator/NY.GDP.MKTP.CD (accessed December 12, 2020), and U.S. Census Bureau, "Trade in Goods with Djibouti," https://www.census.gov/foreign-trade/balance/c7770.html (accessed December 12, 2020).

or governance projects. Over time this would change, as the U.S. Agency for International Development (USAID), the U.S. military, and several other U.S. agencies and nations took advantage of the country's strategic location. For example, prepositioning disaster relief supplies reduced delivery time to African destinations by 75 percent from USAID warehouses. Additionally, Djibouti's deepwater port of Doraleh is capable of handling the largest container ships and aircraft carriers. While the presence of the U.S. military was initially intended to interdict fleeing Al-Qaeda, Djibouti gradually grew to support regional multinational antipiracy and counter-terrorism operations.

As the security mission grew, it necessarily had to consider local domestic and economic concerns. Driven by operational necessity, efforts were launched to expand Camp Lemonnier, making sustaining local support critical. In 2006, agreements were completed to expand the U.S. facility from 88 acres to 500 acres; over 1,200 local personnel were employed to complete the construction. Such economic inflows helped to secure a 2014 agreement renewing the U.S. lease for another twenty years. Based on 2011 U.S. State Department data, the presence of several foreign militaries in and near Djibouti helped to attract approximately $200 million annually in foreign direct investment, a fifteenfold increase over the 1995–2005 average. This investment has helped to improve rail and road connections to Ethiopia, making Djibouti an attractive regional banking and shipping hub in East Africa.

Eventually, Djibouti's success and stability attracted more investors. In 2011, Japan invested $40 million to build its first foreign facility to support antipiracy operations. China's People's Liberation Army also established a base there in 2017. Shortly afterward, in 2018, the $4.5 billion Chinese-built Addis Ababa–Djibouti rail line was completed, connecting landlocked Ethiopian markets to seaborne trade.[13] Such activity has been a boon for Djibouti, has provided a modest benefit to U.S. business, and has helped to sustain Camp Lemonnier, an important U.S. military base. One critical lesson here is that successful overseas bases recognize the importance of being integrated with their local communities and economies and hence becoming elements of the host nation's politics. The same dynamic was seen with U.S. bases in postwar Japan and the 2008 arrival of the only overseas homeporting in Yokosuka, Japan, of nuclear aircraft carrier George Washington. As the saying goes, "Politics is local." Base politics is no different.

## Base Politics

Base politics is a nexus of local and national politics of foreign nations regarding U.S. overseas bases. Players include national leaders, security professionals, and business and community groups. As such, base politics does not fit neatly into conventional constructs for executing international relations or defense strategy, but it is a reality that affects overseas military forces. Alexander Cooley, director of Columbia University's Herriman Institute, notes that agreements for military basing among democracies are more sustainable given legal and institutional constraints. Basing agreements negotiated with autocracies, however, are conditioned and reliant on the sanction of the national leader. Further, he notes that managing local politics around bases is critical and that U.S. bases should integrate into the local economy for mutual benefit—a lesson learned from basing in Uzbekistan.[14] Moreover, transactional quid pro quo agreements should be avoided in favor of community or developmental investments proximate to bases—insights from basing rights negotiations in Kyrgyzstan. For instance, basing agreements should include projects such as infrastructure development or transfer of common military equipment.[15]

Looking to the future, in the Philippines the United States has a favorable situation, given the two countries' shared democratic systems. This has contributed to the sustainment of U.S. military access despite several politically charged incidents. This is in part due to a largely depoliticized process of incident resolution decoupled from any single national leader or political party. Despite firebrand President Rodrigo Duterte's 2017 desire to terminate security treaties with the United States, political support and a favorable 2016 Philippine Supreme Court ruling stymied his efforts. Of course, the intensifying shared security interests to fight the terrorist Abu Sayyaf Group or to counter Chinese maritime encroachment helped.

Naval statecraft works here in part because the U.S. and Philippine security interests overlap in the South China Sea, where both nations support a rules-based order that would deter Chinese encroachment. For the Philippines, this is more than a legal construct; it includes the security of fishermen, access to seafloor resources, and territorial integrity. It was one reason that the bilateral Enhanced Defense Cooperation Agreement (EDCA) was agreed to in April 2014. EDCA builds on the 1951 Mutual Defense Treaty (MDT), and both agreements remain in force today despite President Rodrigo Duterte's (2016–22) antagonisms.[16] EDCA enables U.S. access to specific airbases and facilities within Philippine territory, allowing the United States to better support natural disaster response (e.g., Typhoon Goni in November 2020) and Philippine military action during the monthslong 2017 Marawi siege against Islamic State affiliates—the Abu Sayyaf Group.[17] In the Philippines as in other places, great power competition over the Philippines is playing out across the diplomatic, military, information, and economic spheres. Concerted and well-financed Chinese influence campaigns—such as "China TV Theater" broadcasting on state-run Philippine television—may have been working. A 2019 Pew Research Center survey showed that 42 percent of Filipinos have a favorable view of China, versus 26 percent having a favorable view of the United States.[18] Making a compelling case to the Filipino people for a Free and Open Indo-Pacific requires sustaining a comprehensive approach that marries economic development with visible benefits of mutual security obligations ensconced in the MDT.

While China is the Philippines' leading trade partner, at approximately $60 billion in 2019, Manila's trade with four free-market allies (United States, Japan, Singapore, and South Korea) is comparable, at $65 billion.[19] Given China's economic heft in the Philippines and military proximity, it can sometimes seem a lost cause for U.S. strategic investment and diplomatic capital, but this is simply untrue. Sadly, the March 2021 interim national security strategic guidance, despite stressing the importance of allies, failed to mention either the Philippines or the South China Sea, as hundreds of Chinese maritime militia were staked out in an unfolding crisis then called "Scarborough Shoal 2.0."[20] Thankfully the enduring shared security interests prevailed, enabling near-term differences to be resolved such as renegotiation of a Visiting Forces Agreement (VFA).[21] The VFA covers the legal status of U.S. military forces in the Philippines; without it counter-terror operations in the southern Philippines and in-country military exercises would cease.

The case of the Philippines-U.S. VFA provides a few important lessons that apply to other locations the Navy is called on to operate. One is that local incidents can impact national policies and diplomacy. In this case, two high-visibility crimes (a 2006 rape and a 2015 murder) by U.S. service members electrified the Philippine electorate; a similar dynamic was at play in Okinawa following the 1995 rape of a Japanese schoolgirl by several U.S. service members. Such events led to calls for revision or ending of the VFA; in the Okinawa case it amplified calls to relocate U.S. bases out of Okinawa, Japan. Two, basing or military access negotiations often include more than strictly military issues or trades. In the 2020 and 2021 VFA negotiations with the Philippines, it was delivery of millions of COVID-19 vaccines that helped President Duterte relent and accept the VFA; Philippine calls for increased military aid and reciprocity for Filipino services members in the United States were both later dropped. Third, democratic governing systems and established justice practices can depoliticize final decisions regarding bases and access. President Duterte initially threatened to cancel the VFA following a perceived personal insult by the U.S. government when it refused U.S. entry over human rights violations to his close confidant Senator Ronald Dela Rosa, a former police chief. Built into the VFA is a 180-day cooling-off period before an intent to withdraw can be executed. During that time President Duterte relented and entered into prolonged negotiations. This gave local politicians time to campaign on sustaining the alliance. While alliance management is sometimes frustrating, it is a necessary task to sustain the U.S. network of alliances that China and Russia have little chance of replicating.

To mitigate these rocks and shoals, a shared and compelling narrative backed by results is vital. For example, when the South Korean company Hanjin went bankrupt in 2016, the strategically important Subic Bay shipyard in the Philippines was at risk of being taken over by China. Fearing the loss of an important naval port of call, the government-affiliated Overseas Private Investment Corporation—now the Development Finance Corporation—brokered a deal that forestalled a Chinese takeover of the port.[22] That said, the DFC must do more to develop infrastructure guided by the U.S. government's economic interests and military operational needs in order to prevent being pushed out of friendly markets and security partnerships by the CCP. It was partly for this purpose that the DFC garnered bipartisan support when it was created in 2018, but it has since strayed from this intent considerably.[23] In recent years there has been bipartisan convergence supporting foreign policies seeking mutual economic and security benefits.[24] However, without comprehensive engagement (military, economic, diplomatic, and information), it is unlikely Washington will attract and maintain the allies and partners it so desperately needs.

For an archipelagic nation, such as the Philippines, maritime security and economic development tied to the ocean are inherent national interests. An approach acknowledging this element of the U.S.-Philippines alliance in a comprehensive framework makes naval statecraft a great fit. In fact, this is true for many key partners in the U.S. competition with China and Russia. As such, an approach that employs economic statecraft, military presence, and diplomacy can outclass China and Russia in today's great power competition.[25] The same can be said for potential partner nations in the South and Central Pacific, maritime nations along the coast of West Africa, and partners like Malaysia seeking a "blue ocean" strategy that does not directly contest China. In all cases, deterrence remains a critical element of statecraft and important to maintaining the peace. This requires military capacity both of the United States and in concert with allies and partners.

## Building Partner Capacities and Interoperability

Building complementary military capacities with partner nations can complicate a rival's strategic and tactical considerations by raising the cost of conflict on an aggressor as well as by constraining militarily viable options. During the Cold War this played out in a series of proxy wars in Angola, Nicaragua, and Afghanistan, as well as bolstered deterrence through arms transfers notably to NATO countries. Such capacity building for strategic effect relies on getting military equipment into a country as well as developing interoperability with U.S. forces. The impact this can have on an adversary was on display when Ukrainian armed forces employed Western-supplied antitank Javelin and antiair Stinger missiles to stymie Russia's 2022 invasion. This is accomplished through direct military sales approved by the U.S. State Department; foreign military sales (FMS), which come with added U.S. training and oversight; foreign military financing (FMF), when a partner nation is offered favorable financing options to enable the sale; or the transfer of excess defense articles (EDA). U.S. defense equipment is often priced out of the market, however, or comes with too many stipulations or bureaucratic delays to meet a partner nation's security needs—a case in point being Nigeria's preference for cheaper and fewer-strings-attached Chinese military gear.[26] Additionally, U.S. arms trade is not necessarily geared to maritime competition.

Over the period from 2000 to 2020, U.S. arms sales have been dominated by aircraft, followed by missile systems and armored vehicles, according to the Stockholm International Peace Research Institute (SIPRI) database; sales in ships and naval systems accounted for 6.4 percent of the total over this time.[27] Building capacity in ways that are more efficient and more focused on the maritime competition will require a reorientation and retooling of existing processes. Specifically, this means invigorating and targeting military sales to strategically important maritime customers, new leasing mechanisms focused on timely delivery of capability for strategic effect, streamlined EDA transfers of antiquated ships, provisions for supporting third-party military sales where U.S. industry is absent, and new sustained in-country training missions.

Sadly, the focus hasn't been where it's needed. Since the 2012 Rebalance to the Asia Pacific and subsequent Free and Open Indo-Pacific, national strategies have ostensibly prioritized security investments in the Indo-Pacific. However, according to databases maintained by Center for International Policy, from 2012 through 2020, of the $169.94 billion total security assistance, only 1.81 percent went to Asia-Pacific nations, and no maritime Asian nation was included in the top ten recipients.[28] Also needed is a buildup of host nations' capacities for maintenance, coproduction, and distribution to make U.S. military supply chains more resilient.

Another important consideration in enhancing military interoperability with partner nations is shared maintenance facilities and coproduction. Such efforts are not typically considered security cooperation or managed through the above programs (FMF, FMS, etc.); rather, they are realized through agreements made for specific purposes and services. As F-35 fifth-generation fighter production picked up in the United States in 2014, Japan and Australia set up facilities to conduct heavy airframe and engine maintenance.[29] Such regional facilities help distribute workloads and keep aircraft functioning while deployed. Coproduction can increase rate of production and mitigate supply chain disruptions of a common platform. An example of coproduction, in this case with Japan, is the joint development and production of standard missile three (SM-3) block IIA variants, a missile capable of ballistic missile defense.[30] There are numerous examples of coproduction of munitions that can mitigate domestic U.S. production capacity limits, especially when large numbers of these munitions are being expended in a war. Together security cooperation, coproduction, and shared maintenance all contribute to a more resilient forward military presence and enhanced deterrent effect with interoperable allies and partners. The value of such investments has not always been appreciated, especially in the pre–World War II era, where numerous issues conspired against the U.S. Asiatic Fleet in the months following the December 1941 Pearl Harbor attack.

### The Battle of Java Sea: Lessons of Regional Familiarity and Allied Interoperability

Donald M. Kehn Jr.'s book *In the Highest Degree Tragic*, which looks at the American and Japanese navies during World War II, provides perhaps the best historical lesson for forward presence and engagement during peacetime and, failing this, the cost in war. Heavy expenditure of munitions due to limited prewar live-fire practice exposed weaknesses in the Japanese operational plan, and for the United States the inadequate prepositioning of critical munitions took a high toll. As the U.S. Navy looks to concepts such as Expeditionary Advanced Base Operations (EABO) and Distributed Maritime Operations (DMO), it places a premium on resilient logistics and prepositioned munitions. With this in mind, any conflict with China's navy makes the lessons of Java Sea germane. Another historical lesson relevant to the modern maritime peacetime competition is the implication of investing too little in building an ally's maritime capacity.

### Scarborough Shoal, 2012

On April 10, 2012, a series of events began that would overturn decades of internal U.S. government thinking about China and its adoption of Western norms in dispute resolution. On that day, Philippine Navy ship *Gregorio del Pilar* entered Scarborough Shoal to evict a large number of Chinese fishermen poaching coral and giant clams. The *Pilar* was in fact a decommissioned U.S. Coast Guard *Hamilton*-class cutter provided to the Philippines as EDA. Soon afterward, a massive fleet of China Coast Guard (CCG) cutters, maritime militia vessels, and civilian fishing boats arrived, blocking Philippine authorities inside the shoal's lagoon. A monthslong standoff ensued, during which China combined its coercive naval presence with diplomacy and economic muscle to execute a naval statecraft of its own. As negotiations dragged on, China applied economic pressure with a banana embargo that affected 14 percent of Philippine growers and cost $53 million in lost trade. By contrast, the United States relied exclusively on diplomatic tools. Throughout this crisis, the U.S. military role was relatively subdued, despite the large number of Chinese paramilitary and commercial fishing vessels massed around the shoal while the *Pilar* ran short of food and fuel. Aside from diplomatic protests of Chinese cyber-attacks and embargoes, meaningful U.S. economic statecraft in support of the Philippines was not evident.[31] Eventually the United States brokered a deal, with both sides agreeing to withdraw under the pretext of an approaching typhoon.[32] However, the Chinese vessels never fully left, and still retain effective control of the shoal. Subsequently, the Philippines eventually entered into formal arbitration over disputed maritime claims against China (ref. Permanent Court of Arbitration case #2013–19). This is when China began a massive island-building campaign.

That Beijing had reneged on an agreement involving senior U.S. diplomats and policy-makers was sufficiently embarrassing that it forced the United States to reassess its approach to China. Three years later, in October 2015, the United States conducted its first public challenge to China's excessive maritime claims when the destroyer *Lassen* sailed unannounced within twelve miles of Chinese-occupied Subi Reef in the South China Sea. Since then, the United States has continued to conduct such operations.[33] However, freedom of navigation operations (FONOPs) alone have been inadequate.

## A Naval Statecraft

Effective statecraft adapts to changes in geostrategic factors and the natural environment. To do this requires, first, anticipating where the future contested maritime will be, and what emerging forces will alter the nature of naval warfare; and, second, having a deep understanding of rivals and an ability to predict where their interests will take them and how they will challenge our own.

The world of 2050 will be in many ways much as it is in 2022: reliance on maritime trade and those using navies to hold it at risk. While emerging new megacities and changing climate and weather patterns will alter the patterns of life on the sea, key will be the opening of Arctic sea routes and the migration northward and intensification of hurricanes; and as ocean temperatures and currents change, so too will fish stocks and the fishing fleets hunting them. On the other hand, geographic chokepoints (e.g., Panama Canal) remain especially critical for navies responding over the shortest route to crises or enforcing the will of their political masters—a point made clear when the grounding of the *Ever Given* shut the Suez Canal down for a week and snarled global maritime shipping.

Over the next thirty years the world's greatest naval competition will play out between the United States and its allies against the CCP and Russia. In response to CCP and Russian strategic moves, the United States will need to predict and position forces in decisive theaters. Achieving strategic effects and advancing U.S. interests across key maritime regions means executing coordinated efforts across two lines of effort.

*Lines of effort* is a military term that refers to missions linked by a common strategic effect. For naval statecraft these include (1) enhancing the positional advantage and warfighting capability of the military and (2) effectively seizing the initiative in the peacetime maritime competition with the CCP and Russia.

Actualizing naval statecraft requires investments in *posture, presence, partner capacity building, treaties and agreements,* and the *information domain. Posture* is not exclusive to military basing; it also includes economic capital investments. Likewise, *presence* includes the physical existence of military units in a region as well as members of the diplomatic corps and other agencies. *Partner capacity building* includes military sales, training, and exercises, along with efforts that improve institutional and economic resiliency to CCP and Russian influences. *Treaties and agreements* with partner and allied nations is a straightforward concept. *Information* tools include the use of social media, traditional media, and personal networks to inform and shape the political context of great power competition.

Coordinating an effort that encompasses both domestic and international activities will require national-level leadership and frequent engagement of the legislative branch. Legislative support will be critical to sustain the political will and financial resources required. One option is a standing interagency task force with representatives from participating agencies empowered to share information and act on behalf of their parent organization. Joint Interagency Task Forces (JIATF) already exist to perform primarily an information-sharing role, but within a naval statecraft construct, the authority for direct action and economic statecraft would be required. In dealing with the CCP and Russia, however, the implications (political and military) of such actions make it unlikely that this authority would be delegated out from the White House. Rather, the most likely construct would be an enhanced body within the National Security Council (NSC) with representation from agencies with the capacity to contribute in the five domains above. The Navy will also need to be restructured and investment made to optimize it for naval statecraft on a global scale, as will be shown in later chapters.

## Equatorial Guinea as a Naval Statecraft Test Case

To get a better sense of how this new approach comes together in action, consider a potential test case that unfolded over Chinese naval basing in Equatorial Guinea. In December 2021, news reports indicated that for months U.S. intelligence agencies had been aware of attempts by the CCP to acquire naval basing rights in Equatorial Guinea.[34] The CCP's efforts were seemingly eased by the fact the nation is run by a single family. Since 1979, the country has been led by Teodoro Obiang Nguema Mbasogo, with members of his family and close affiliates running the government, the media, and importantly, the nation's oil business, which since 2004 has been the third-largest in sub-Saharan Africa. Important for sustaining the Obiang regime is oil revenue, which accounts for over 90 percent of its exports but is sourced in troubled waters of the Gulf of Guinea, where piracy and maritime crime have been a persistent problem. Nearby oil-producing countries like Nigeria also have had to contend with this threat to their bottom line. In response, Gulf of Guinea nations have come together since 2011 for an annual maritime security exercise called Obangame Express led by the United States. In 2021 there were thirty-two participating nations.[35] Unfortunately for China, this exercise has helped improve regional maritime security against piracy, illegal fishing, and maritime crime.

China too has interests in the region, notably in petroleum and increasingly fishing—sometimes illegally. In 2019 the region supplied 11.4 percent of total Chinese fuel imports. Chinese fishing vessel *Hai Lu Feng*'s 2020 piracy and recapture exposed some uncomfortable truths about Chinese maritime activity in the region. The ordeal exposed a practice of using registration and location data by multiple ships to skirt licensing fees, duties, and limits on fishing.[36] The uncovering of such activities was in many ways enabled by U.S. maritime capacity building and skills practiced at Obangame Express. However, CCP efforts to secure oil by propping up corrupt regimes and protecting its fishing fleet's illegal activities will eventually undermine regional support. A balance must be struck between exposing the corrupting and extractive policies of the CCP and enabling positive economic development. The goal is to welcome beneficial investment and economic engagement—including from China—in a free and open manner at the local level, where the most people can gain, while at the same time preventing threatening developments. As Commander Africa Command Gen. Stephen Townsend testified in April 2021 before the Senate, most threatening would be a Chinese naval base for the arming and repair of warships.

To prevent such an outcome requires an integrated national- and local-level effort synchronizing economic, diplomatic, and military efforts in Equatorial Guinea through several U.S. agencies. The objective would be to deny China a threatening naval base while enhancing the country's resiliency to Chinese coercion. On the local level, USAID and DFC would effect economic development projects that enhance maritime capacities as well as help diversify Equatorial Guinea's trade—something the national government has indicated it wants. For example, microloans to fishermen and training on improving port management can improve local catches, thereby getting more cash into the local economy. Then, to kickstart infrastructure developmental projects, naval port visits and future Obangame Express exercises would be directed to occur at the same port by Africa Command and Navy staff at the Pentagon. Port visits and associated exercise related construction would enable minor pier upgrades and dredging that also allows for an enhanced host nation maritime security presence— that is, patrol vessels, coastal radars, and information centers. According to a 2019 analysis, Equatorial Guinea has limited trained maritime enforcement personnel and no capacity for monitoring fishing in its EEZ.[37] Such capacity building in turn relies on national-level efforts to expand intelligence exchanges. These would expose illicit and corrupting practices by the CCP, while the Navy's presence—like the monthslong deployment of the expeditionary sea-base ship *Hershel Williams* in August 2021, which included counter-piracy drills with the Brazilian navy—would be timed to enhance confidence in the United States as security partner. While local efforts progress, the State Department would engage Equatorial Guinea's national government in pursuit of policies and bilateral agreements to enable larger maritime projects. Success requires providing a compelling option to any Chinese largess—not merely more and faster than China can provide in infrastructure investment. Additionally, to ensure the CCP cannot work between U.S. agencies, enforcing a unity of effort across agencies like Treasury and Commerce with at times conflicting mandates is required. This task would fall on the NSC. As the *West Capella* crisis made clear, timing is important, and the NSC will play a central role in ensuring numerous agencies work in concert. Case in point: not keeping track of events such as the December 2021 announcement by U.S. oil company Chevron to develop an offshore Equatorial Guinea oilfield could imperil diplomatic and economic leverage. Additionally, U.S. interagency coordination allows the focus of U.S. efforts to shift between naval, diplomatic, and economic as conditions dictate in a sustained coherent fashion.

If done well, naval statecraft would bolster Equatorial Guinea's resiliency to Chinese coercion and align interests with the United States for a free and open region. By focusing on the national and local levels, it balances the risk of dealing with the Obiang family with the need to be associated with bettering the local population's prosperity. At the same time, U.S. military needs and economic benefits gained through enhanced infrastructure and maritime security must be better communicated to Congress and the American people to sustain public support. A reminder that China's challenge is global came within a few months of the Equatorial Guinea basing attempt, when China in April 2022 signed a security and basing agreement with the Solomon Islands in the Pacific.

## Conclusion

In summary, conceptualizing naval statecraft draws on several key experiences. Critically, the *West Capella* incident and the Scarborough Shoal standoff underscore the importance of backing diplomacy up with naval presence. Djibouti provides a case study of sustained military presence engendering economic development that in turn politically sustained it, but concurrently revealed the need to manage base politics. All the while, Chinese and Russian influence operations and media such as "China TV Theater" will work to undermine any U.S. effort. This necessitates a new approach, naval statecraft, based on coordinated naval, economic, diplomatic, and information efforts.

Organization is important in actualizing naval statecraft but represents only one part of what is needed. Fielding the right military platforms and developing dynamic leaders for great power competition will be critical. The accelerating pace of technological advance driven by great power competition will have wide-ranging implications on naval warfare. As such, naval statecraft must embrace a future-facing approach that positions the Navy for success in the here-and-now while building an adaptable future fleet. Making sure such investments are effective requires a deeper understanding of the principal competitors—China and Russia.

CHAPTER 2

# Competition to Rule the Seas

——— ∞∞∞ ———

*Command of the sea, therefor, means nothing but the control of*
*maritime communications, whether for commercial or military*
*purposes. The object of naval warfare is the control of communica-*
*tions, and not, as in land warfare, the conquest of territory.*

—Julian Stafford Corbett,
*Some Principles of Maritime Strategy*, 1911

O f the world's maritime nations, two have the wherewithal to
challenge the United States at sea in 2022 and plan to contest
it through 2035—China and Russia. After decades of dogged
determination and investment, both have built (or in Russia's case rebuilt)
a global naval presence to secure their security interests while growing
their global influence. Confronting these nations' maritime forces in a
global competition over the free flow of trade, information, influence, and
security necessitates an understanding of their strategies and the influences
that inform them.

To be clear, great power competition with Russia and China is not new,
and was recognized but weakly addressed in the final years of the Obama
administration, notably during the 2014–16 rapid land reclamation
and garrisoning of military forces by China in the South China Sea and
Russia's annexation of Crimea. The 2012 Defense Strategic Guidance,
otherwise known as the Rebalance to the Asia-Pacific, had mixed results
while beginning an effort to shift institutional and budgetary focus to that
important region. The Rebalance was in part a response to the intensifying
military, economic, and societal pressures that are driving competition
between the United States, China, and Russia. In 2022 this contest is
entering a more dangerous phase, and for the United States the challenge
is compounded by having to confront two great power competitors:

Russia and China. Moreover, simply repeating Cold War approaches is unrealistic, given that China is integrated into the world economy and Russia is unconstrained by ideology.

After a decade of "rebalancing" that has neither deterred nor slowed the steady progress of China and Russia in changing the maritime status quo, a strategic reassessment is required.

## A Dangerous Decade

As China's economic heft and military power has grown, the Chinese Communist Party (CCP) leadership has been less inclined toward accommodation. China's rapidly expanding modern military and Russia's successful 2014 redrawing of borders and 2022 invasion of Ukraine are setting the stage for the 2020s to be an especially fraught time. In this new geostrategic multipolar reality, increased forward naval presence backed by pragmatic diplomacy and economic statecraft can be an asymmetric advantage, but time for acting is short.

China's aging population, unresolved territorial disputes, and a slowing economy are conspiring to challenge the CCP's legitimacy—a legitimacy that since the 1989 Tiananmen uprising has been anchored in delivering prosperity and global recognition. It is also worth noting that in Chinese history, student movements are particularly powerful bellwethers of political change, which made the pro-democracy student protesters in Tiananmen Square a potent threat. After violently suppressing that protest, subsequent CCP leaders have endeavored to prevent a repeat and have suppressed organizations such as Falun Gong and ethnic groups like the Tibetans and Uyghurs.

For the CCP and the Chinese people the simplest measure of prosperity is increasing gross domestic product—and the trends are not favorable. According to the World Trade Organization, China's GDP growth rate has been slowing consistently since 2010, down from 10.64 percent to 5.95 percent in 2019. To sustain its mandate to rule China, the CCP has also stoked nationalism.

The CCP's post-Tiananmen compact with the Chinese people involves provision of ever-improving quality of life on the one hand, while sacrificing personal freedoms on the other. Of course, the CCP leadership understands that to sustain this requires a record of success in overcoming challenges to China—and this is where nationalism comes into play. Since the Tiananmen crisis, the CCP has nurtured and stoked a victim narrative known as the "100 years of humiliation." This period began with China's defeat in the Opium War of 1839 and ended with the CCP's rise to rule mainland China in 1949. This has conditioned the Chinese population to expect sustained improvement in the quality of life while exerting a more forceful presence on the global stage in a return to China's rightful place. Failing either of these imperils the CCP. Yet despite the best efforts of the CCP, GDP growth will invariably ease as China's population ages amid shocks such as reduced industrial activity from 2020 due to the COVID pandemic. As demographic and economic pressures reach a culminating point by 2029, the CCP's military has been growing and modernizing at a remarkable pace. As this situation unfolds, there will be sharpening nationalist calls to resolve the Taiwan dispute—a scenario that could plausibly draw the United States into war.

Important to keeping the peace in Asia has been the "one country, two systems" construct. The CCP has held this up as a way to incorporate Taiwan and Hong Kong into its communist country without altering their free-market and democratic systems. It had worked since Hong Kong's 1997 reversion to China until February 2019 when a new extradition law was proposed. The proposal would subject Hong Kong people to CCP's courts. Ensuing protests and international pressure eventually saw the proposal withdrawn by Hong Kong's chief executive, Carrie Lam, in September 2019. However, the law may have been a formality given the CCP's rendition of Hong Kong publishers for years to the mainland for trial, and arrest of democracy activists by Hong Kong authorities. Such actions on the part of the CCP are a violation of "Joint Declaration on the Question of Hong Kong" that set the conditions on which the United Kingdom would return Hong Kong to the CCP. Enshrined in that agreement was a stipulation that following reversion on July 1, 1997, Hong Kong would retain its unique democratic, legal, and economic systems for fifty years—the "one country, two systems" in action.[1] A consequence of the CCP's actions in Hong Kong since 2019 has been a repudiation of the proposed framework for peaceful resolution of the Chinese civil war with Taiwan.

The absence of a new framework for peacefully resolving the dispute between the CCP and Taiwan, and growing economic pressures, will come to a head by 2029. This is when China begins an unavoidable population decline and the associated shrinking GDP growth rate, down to 3 percent by 2030. Coincidently, the CCP is urgently seeking to field a fully modern military by 2027—a budget priority in the CCP's 2022 five-year plan. To meet this challenge and avert crisis, some in the U.S. Congress, such as Virginia congresswoman Elaine Luria, have called for a "Battleforce 2025" in their push back on plans that do not grow the fleet fast enough to meet the threat this decade. Clearly CCP leadership would prefer to have their ever-growing military be dominant before economic and demographic pressures begin to erode their ability to field it.

For Chairman Xi Jinping, leader of the CCP since 2013, the pressures to deliver are tremendous. In addition to the pressures mentioned already, Xi has taken several actions that overturned decades of CCP party orthodoxy. Notable was the 2018 National People's Congress removal of term limits for China's president, which had been instituted by Deng Xiaoping in 1982 to avoid a repeat of the excesses of Chairman Mao Zedong. Every year Xi retains CCP leadership beyond his second term's end in March 2023, he will be under increasing pressure to live up to the material successes of Deng and the political ruthlessness of Mao to stay in power. Mao is revered for unifying the mainland under communist rule often brutally and at tremendous human cost—40 to 80 million killed during the failures of the Great Leap Forward (1958–62) and Cultural Revolution (1966–76). Deng, on the other hand, is revered for economic reforms that sparked China's meteoric rise to the second-largest economy after the United States and fueled the People's Liberation Army's modernization and growth. So it is no simple task for Xi to have to best both of these iconic CCP leaders to stay on top during this dangerous decade.

All the while, Russia, also active in Asia, remains an opportunistic strategic agitator seeking to weaken a geopolitical order it views as antithetical to its interests. Putin, like Xi, must continue delivering military and economic successes to his people to stay in power (and alive) as he enters his third decade of national leadership.

## Russia

Vladimir Putin unexpectedly came to power when his predecessor Boris Yeltsin resigned as Russia's president on December 31, 1999. At the time, Putin was not expected to last given the chaos of a Russia still transitioning from a Soviet system and dealing with widespread criminality, deteriorating life expectancies, and insurrection in Chechnya. His imperfect leadership has nonetheless delivered a growing economy, domestic stability, and increasing prestige on the world stage that most Russians appreciate. It is his increasingly risky moves abroad, however, that jeopardize the economic progress and international prestige gained since 2000, and inevitably the support of the Russian people.

Putin's initial focus was in strengthening the economy through revenue from oil exports and combating criminal elements and insurrection. His success in this endeavor led to a new emphasis in the "near abroad"— neighboring nations that had been part of the Soviet Union. Most notable in this new focus was the 2008 Russo-Georgian War. While the military's performance in that war was mixed, Putin has since proved adept at leveraging a limited military, economic, and diplomatic hand to great effect. Additional successes include the 2014 annexation of Crimea and the 2015 intervention in Syria in a brash and effective strategy. Even his 2022 invasion of Ukraine follows a familiar pattern.

In 2013, Gen. Valery Gerasimov, then chief of the Russian general staff, penned an article on hybrid warfare that came to be known as the Gerasimov doctrine.[2] The doctrine is an articulation of warfare as the synchronization of hard and soft power transcending peace and war. The implications of Russian hybrid warfare were on grand display during the 2014 Ukraine crisis when "unofficial" Russian military forces—called "little green men" for the color of their uniforms—secured and then ensured Crimea's annexation by Russia.[3] The origin of this particular Russian doctrine originates in forceful Russian foreign policy beginning from 1996 when Yevgeny Primakov became foreign minister.[4] The more appropriately titled Primakov doctrine has since animated Russian strategic activities in Ukraine, Syria, and Libya. There were also ominous indications of Russia's influence in the government's crackdown of opposition protests threatening Russia's ally President Alexander Lukashenko following a flawed August 2020 Belorussian presidential election. In this doctrine, military power is vital, and while most of the action has been from land forces or mercenary groups like the Wagner Group in Libya, the Russian navy too has played a role. The naval element of this doctrine was on display in the Sea of Azov on November 25, 2018, when it captured Ukrainian vessels and sailors, and in a disappointing 2016 deployment of an aircraft carrier strike force in the Eastern Mediterranean to support operations in Syria. Russia's navy has played a traditional role in the 2022 Ukraine war—logistic support, strike, bombardment, and amphibious operations.

The Russian approach articulated by Gerasimov represents "a transition from sequential and concentrated actions to continuous and distributed ones, conducted simultaneously in all spheres of confrontation, and also in distant theaters of military operations."[5] The elevated and sustained operations of the Russian Pacific Fleet in the lead-up to and throughout the invasion of Ukraine offer a good example of this strategy: it is in practice nonlinear and can be confounding to competitors' attempts to discern Russian intent. At the earliest stages of such an operation, the focus is to sow discord among competing interests in a country using economic, information, and diplomatic means while posing a potential military threat. It is important to note that General Gerasimov, when asked, stated that the ratio of nonmilitary to military information operations in the early stages of a crisis was 4:1—an overwhelming emphasis on nonmilitary levers of national power. Then, in a remarkable policy statement of the June 2021 Russia National Security Strategy, in regard to "unfriendly actions by foreign states that pose a threat to the sovereignty and territorial integrity of the Russian Federation, including those related to the use of restrictive measures (sanctions) of a political or economic nature or the use of modern information and communication technologies, the Russian Federation considers it legitimate to take symmetrical and asymmetrical measures necessary to suppress such unfriendly actions, as well as to prevent their recurrence in the future."[6] This suggests a reliance on the military, presuming a requirement for sustaining (or mercenary: e.g., Wagner Group) presence where it matters for Russia, such as the Eastern Mediterranean.

Throughout Russian history, from Catherine the Great to the Soviets, attempts were made to secure lasting footholds in the Eastern and Central Mediterranean as part of a counter-encirclement strategy that endures today. In line with Czarist Russian thinking, since 1964 the Soviets have maintained the Fifth Eskadra (squadron) in the Eastern Mediterranean, ostensibly as a regional bulwark to defend their southern flank in the Black Sea.[7] The principal threat of encirclement of Russia is by NATO and the U.S. military.

The Russian need for defending against strategic encirclement is a strong one. Even during the lean years of the 1990s, Russia sustained a military presence in Syria. Since then Russia has returned to Cuba and added Venezuela, North Korea, and through its mercenary proxies such as the Wagner Group, a substantial presence in Africa. By implementing a counter-encirclement presence in the Mediterranean, Russia can threaten NATO's southern flank as it seeks to solidify its interests in Ukraine, Belorussia, Moldova, and Georgia's breakaway republics of South Ossetia and Abkhazia. With this in mind, Russia made certain that it retained access to and sustained a minimum presence overseas to effect counter-encirclement. It was not until its September 2015 entry into Syria's civil war, however, that there would be a significant, prolonged Russian naval presence overseas. To sustain its renewed regional presence, Russia made a deal in 2017 allowing it to operate up to eleven warships out of its only overseas naval base at Tartus, Syria, until 2066.[8] This base gives the Russian Navy both a springboard for sustained operations further afield and the potential to diminish NATO's relevance in addressing European security concerns such as the flow of refugees from Libya and Syria.[9] Russia has since expanded its posture, with bases straddling the strategic Suez Canal, with an agreement to station up to four naval warships, some of them nuclear powered, at Port Sudan on the Red Sea.[10] With such logistics hubs secured, Russia's ships and submarines with thousand-mile-range Kalibr cruise missiles play an active part in the counter-encirclement strategy burnishing Russia's great power status.

In 2021, the Russian Navy operates out of bases on the Arctic Ocean, Baltic Sea, Black Sea, Caspian Sea, and Pacific Ocean, and in Tartus,

Syria. In 2019 its fleet consisted of 1 aircraft carrier, 4 cruisers, 16 destroy-ers, 14 frigates, 10 ballistic missile submarines, 48 other submarines, and 105 small surface combatants.[11] This force is concentrated in four fleets (the Northern, Baltic, Black Sea, and Pacific Fleets) and one flotilla (the Caspian Flotilla).[12] Despite atrophying to a quarter of its Soviet strength, and despite warships that are twenty to twenty-five years old on average, both training and operations have improved steadily.[13] Even in the darkest days of the post-Soviet Russia in the 1990s, meager resources were devoted to sustaining their advanced nuclear submarine fleet, which for a while in the 1980s rivaled the United States in its quieting ability.

Russia's nuclear submarine fleet remains an active force in counter-encirclement. In December 2017, Rear Adm. Andrew Lennon, com-mander of submarines for NATO, highlighted troubling Russian undersea naval activities in the vicinity of undersea cables used for critical com-munications and $10 trillion in financial transactions.[14] Nuclear-powered submarines also have the endurance and stealth needed for Russia to sneak into striking distance of the U.S. coasts. Moscow has also used long-range strategic aircraft, like the propeller driven Tu-95, in much the same role. Notable examples of this bomber diplomacy include the fol-lowing: (1) On December 5, 2017, a pair of Tu-95s flew from Russia's Far East to Indonesia's Biak Island among resurgent Russian military activity across Southeast Asia.[15] (2) Russia conducted combined bomber opera-tions with China over the Sea of Japan in July 2019 and again in December 2020.[16] Russia has also used larger surface naval formations for strategic communications.

Russian naval operations are routinely conducted in the Barents Sea, Northern Pacific Ocean, Baltic Sea, Black Sea, and (since 2015) Eastern Mediterranean, while long-range deployments occur infrequently in the Indian Ocean, South China Sea, and Caribbean and near the Eastern and Western Seaboards of the United States. A couple of these long-range deployments stand out for their timing and proximity to significant events. In 2014, as national leaders gathered in Brisbane, Australia, for the Asia Pacific Economic Cooperation (APEC) conference, Russia sent a four-ship flotilla led by Russia's Pacific Fleet flagship off Australia's northern coast, while Black Sea flagship *Moskva* conducted live-fire drills in the South

China Sea.[17] Amid Australian naval vessels being sortied in response, the Russian Ministry of Defense stated, "Russian naval vessels have previously been deployed in conjunction with major international summits, such as the APEC meeting in Singapore in 2009. A warship from Russia's Pacific Fleet also accompanied former Russian President [Dmitry] Medvedev's visit to San Francisco in 2010." Then, as the U.S. Navy was ramping up for its first Large-Scale Exercise (LSE21), Russia sent aircraft and naval warships as close as twenty-three miles off Hawaii in June 2021 in its largest show of force in the Pacific since the end of the Cold War—leaving behind a spy ship to monitor LSE21, which began in August.[18] Finally, while less visible, Russia has steadily increased its military presence in the Arctic by reactivating Cold War bases and increasing military deployments.

On October 26, 2020, President Putin signed into law a new Arctic development strategy. It continues an enduring Russian focus on developing its economic and security interests in the Arctic. Past efforts have made progress on several fronts; notably, in the five-year period from 2014 to 2019, the country deployed 18 percent more in modern military equipment to the region.[19] This strategy lays out a development plan from 2020 through 2035 that includes creation of general-purpose Arctic troops, Arctic coast guard, and modernization of aged Arctic military installations.[20] As the Northern Sea Route becomes economically viable for shipping and Russia deploys a modern and significant Arctic maritime presence, it could hold at risk lucrative shipping routes and escalate today's maritime disputes there.

Recent actions indicate Russia's Navy will play a key role in the execution of a counter-encirclement strategy informed by the Gerasimov doctrine. While focus on sustaining a viable and dangerous undersea force will endure into the future, Russia has also invested in a fleet of smaller corvettes and frigates able to deploy long-range missiles. It was from such ships in 2015 operating in the Caspian Sea that several waves of cruise missile attacks were launched against Islamic State in Syria, and against Ukraine in 2022. The effect has been to distribute smaller numbers of these long-range weapons on more ships of the Russian fleet as a means to get firepower forward. Russia's investment in smaller naval warships is not totally by choice but also driven by the limitations of its shipbuilding industry.

Russian naval shipbuilding has suffered since the dissolution of the Soviet Union, which saw it lose not only revenue but also access to key technologies and infrastructure. Russia's current 43,000-ton aircraft carrier *Admiral Kuznetsov* was built in now-independent Ukraine and delivered in 1990; the only other of the class was sold as an unfinished hulk in 1998 by Ukraine to China and eventually entered service with the Chinese navy, where today it serves with an active air wing.[21] Without access to larger dry docks in Ukraine, the Russian navy has had to rely on using a floating dry dock to maintain the *Kuznetsov* at Sevmash Production Association in Severodvinsk. Then in October 2018, the *Kuznetsov* suffered damage during a modernization overhaul when the floating dry dock it was in sank.[22] The Russian Ministry of Defense at the time had stated the *Kuznetsov* would return to service in 2021, but a subsequent major fire on board in 2019 and supply chain delays pushed that return date to 2023.[23] The eventual fate of Russia's largest warship, however, is tied to any replacement of the destroyed floating dry dock, without which the ship will no longer be able to conduct critical maintenance.

Russia's navy has attempted to work around domestic shipbuilding constraints by procuring four 16,500-ton French-built amphibious assault ships of the *Mistral* class. The 2010 deal was eventually canceled following Russia's annexation of Crimea in 2014.[24] In the intervening years, the Russian navy appears to be steadily increasing the size of warships it builds. For example, the *Ivan Gren* class, built in Yantar shipyards in Kaliningrad, began with the first two ships measuring 6,000 tons, then a modified version to be delivered beginning in 2023 at 8,000 tons each.[25] Continuing the trend, on May 22, 2020, a deal was inked that would see Zalyv Shipbuilders in Kerch, Crimea, build two 25,000-ton amphibious ships bearing striking similarities in appearance and capabilities to the French *Mistral* class.[26] While size matters in shipbuilding, access to niche naval technologies has also stymied Russia's naval ambitions. When Ukraine stopped supplying the Russian navy with gas turbines after 2014, it effectively killed its 11356M frigate program after building only three of six ships planned.[27] Russian aircraft engine manufacturer Saturn has been developing a naval gas turbine engine, which may eventually address this gap.

Ambitions to regain Soviet-era naval capacity are misplaced given the dire state of Russia's naval shipbuilding industry. Retired Ukrainian admiral Ihor Kabanenko, who served with the Soviet navy from 1983 to 1990 and the Ukrainian navy from 1993 to 2013, sees obsolescent facilities, financial and management problems, technological flaws, and lack of access to foreign components as impediments to Russia's navy.[28] That said, Russian naval shipbuilding has made incremental progress, and its civilian shipbuilders have unique niche capabilities that will likely sustain it. In a February 2020 interview, the president of Russia's United Shipbuilding Corporation, Alexey Rahkmanov, laid out several observations—modest growth in revenue despite U.S. sanctions that are preventing overseas investments, and steady demand for its niche capability of producing nuclear-powered icebreakers—important to achieving Arctic dominance.[29] In 2020 Russia's naval shipbuilding is concentrated in

- Sevmash Production Association in Severodvinsk, the largest yard, with 100,000 square meters of covered docks
- Four shipyards located in Saint Petersburg on the Baltic
- A small yard located in Tatarstan that produces the Bunyan-M small missile boats and patrol craft
- Yantar shipyard in Kaliningrad on the Baltic
- A small shipyard located at Komsomolsk-on-Amur in Russia's Far East producing missile corvettes
- Zalyv Shipbuilding in annexed Kerch, Crimea, where two 25,000-ton amphibious assault ships are to be built

All of these yards have serious challenges in building ships 8,000 tons or larger for the Russian navy, and the ability to sustain its older and larger vessels like the *Kuznetsov* is questionable. The Washington Institute's Anna Borshchevskaya is not optimistic that Russia's most corrupt and problematic industrial sector can overcome its challenges and expand into a "global blue-water navy."[30] This has led to a reliance on the smaller naval warships that Russia's shipyards have been able to produce, which have less at-sea endurance. It has, in part, driven Russia's pursuit for overseas bases—such as Port Sudan. This fleet, armed with long-range cruise missiles and nuclear submarines, while potent, is by itself inadequate for a counter-encirclement strategy.

The challenge for Russia has been how best to play a weaker hand against the United States and NATO. One increasingly clear choice has been the use of mercenaries closely associated with the Putin government, such as the Wagner Group. At a July 7, 2020, congressional hearing, Kimberly Marten detailed how the malign intersection of Putin's inner circle, Russian special military units of the Main Intelligence Directorate (GRU), and criminal organizations have enabled private military companies (PMC). One such intersection dates to 1990 Saint Petersburg, where Putin was serving as the First Advisor to the Mayor and likely green-lighted Yevgeny Prigozhin's early release from a nine-year organized crime charge and sanctioned his early business efforts.[31] Rising from the ashes of PMC Slavonic Corps' spectacular failure in 2013 in fighting the Islamic State in Syria was the Wagner Group.[32] Owing to patronage by Yevgeny Prigozhin, the Wagner Group—founded by Dmitry Utkin, a onetime GRU special forces officer, and based in Molkino, Russia—began operations in eastern Ukraine in 2014. While PMCs are officially illegal in Russia, there has been mounting evidence that they are not only tolerated but sanctioned and supported by the GRU.

Perhaps by being illegal in Russia, PMCs provide two very tangible benefits for Russian national interests overseas. The most important aspect is the plausible deniability these "off-record" entities provide the Putin government. For one, the anonymity provided as a private organization obscures the cost in human life from the Russian public. Following the annexation of Crimea in 2014, Russian opinion polls since 2018 show that a majority of Russians are uneasy with Putin's active anti-West policies overseas.[33] Second, this anonymity shields the Russian government from direct retaliation; on February 7, 2018, up to eighty Russian Wagner Group mercenaries were killed when attacking U.S. positions at Deir al-Zour, Syria.[34] Despite this fiasco, direct Russian logistic support has intensified—GRU provides security for Wagner's Molkino base and often airlifts Wagner personnel and weapons to Libya, Venezuela, and other destinations. Slavonic Corps' failure in 2013 was attributed in part to a reliance on host nation logistics, which Wagner Group, working with

GRU, seems to be avoiding, albeit with risk to sustaining the farce of plausible deniability.

As of August 2021, Russian PMCs are known to be operating in Syria, Libya, Central African Republic (CAR), Sudan, Mozambique, and Mali. In each of these theaters, Russian PMC actions fall into one of three categories: (1) They play direct military support to a friendly regime, as in Libya and Syria. The operational track record in this role has been mixed, and despite sending over a thousand Wagner operatives to Libya, they failed to secure victory for the Russian proxy rebel Gen. Khalifa Haftar in 2020.[35] (2) In the CAR they play a critical role protecting, advising, and supporting a friendly regime in its fight against insurgents. (3) In conjunction with arms deals, they are providing unofficial training and assistance in Mozambique. This mission was targeted by Islamist insurgents, who killed seven Wagner personnel in the country's northern Cabo Delgado state, and that is rumored to have triggered their departure in April 2021.[36] Despite a mixed operational track record, PMCs remain a valued tool for the Russian government due to a mix of personal connections to the highest levels of leadership, military logistics support, and unofficial sanction.

Russia's strategy of counter-encirclement gives it capacity to exert its limited influence globally. Through covert action it has attempted to develop proxies to prevent its isolation or loss of overseas access (e.g., Syrian intervention) or to create a strategic opportunity (e.g., annexation of Crimea). Nuclear submarines, distant naval deployments, and long-range strategic aircraft provide episodic and visible reminders of Russia's great power relevance, while PCMs and their enablers provide a deniable tool for securing proxies well outside Russia's near-abroad and at little financial or political cost at home. Given this, to execute a counter-encirclement strategy requires Russia's military, notably the GRU, to covertly resupply and transport PCMs.

Undermining the dangerous elements of Russia's counter-encirclement strategy means turning the Gerasimov doctrine on its head. Doing this requires exposing the weakness of Russia's military to sustain distant operations and diminishing the trusted personal and financial networks vital to sustaining PCMs. Tools for achieving this include economic enticements to potential Russian proxies, targeted sanctions on specific

## Map 2. Russian Naval Activity

■ Operating areas — Deployments outside normal operating areas

**GIUK Gap:** Russian activities near undersea cables

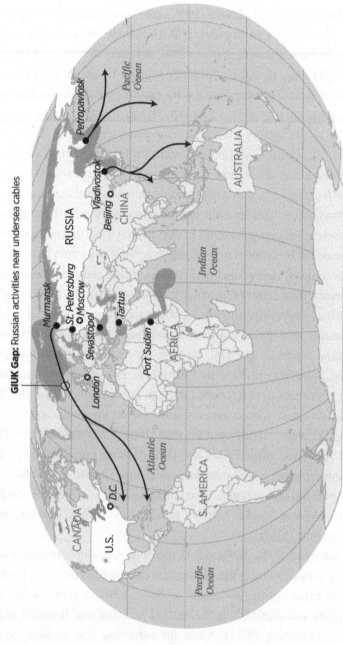

**SOURCE:** Heritage Foundation research

Russian entities, and direct action to undermine reliability and confidence in PCMs. That said, failures by Wagner Group in Libya may already be signaling its eventual demise, but caution is warranted as new patronage networks rise to create a successor PCM. At the same time, exposing the military's logistics support to PCMs erodes a critical benefit—official deniability. Undermining confidence in PCMs and their enablers is not enough, however. Russia's long-range deployments must also be exposed as narrowly focused political efforts—for example, a surface action group near Australia during APEC. Importantly, the effectiveness of such deployments is questionable given their short duration and limited capacity for sustained military operations (e.g., the *Kuznetsov*'s 2016 ill-fated deployment in Syria). While Russia may deploy ships and long-range aircraft off the U.S. coasts that will require being shadowed by U.S. forces, this should not be viewed as equivalent to sizable U.S. deployments sustained for months in waters strategically important to Russia. In short, expose and outclass Russia where it matters in order to diminish its reputation and ability to build proxies. In this role, U.S. and allied maritime forces provide a mobile, unpredictable force able to conduct a range of operations as an asymmetric asset in the competition with Russia.

## China

The Chinese Communist Party officially considers July 1, 1921, its foundation day. Its foundation more accurately occurred on July 23, 1921, at the first National Congress, when a small group gathered in a girl's school classroom vacated for summer holiday in the then–French concession of Shanghai.[37] From this inauspicious beginning, it would take twenty-eight years till October 1, 1949, for the CCP to declare the creation of the People's Republic of China. On that day, Chairman Mao Zedong looked over Tiananmen Square in Beijing and declared, "The Chinese people, comprising one quarter of humanity, have now stood up. . . . Ours will no longer be a nation subject to insult and humiliation."[38]

It was a declaration that made clear the CCP's claim it was responsible for national rejuvenation following a century of humiliation from foreign influences. Left unfinished was the civil war with the Nationalists, who had retreated to Taiwan and outlying islands in what has become a decades-long standoff. As a result, the CCP's main "strategic direction" became unification of Taiwan, by force if need be; this mission informs China's military modernization and expansion.[39] Yet it has been an elusive goal beyond the capabilities of the People's Liberation Army (PLA). The CCP has therefore pursued an indirect and long-term approach to supplant Taiwan's principal supporter, the United States, as the regional economic and military power, thereby setting the conditions for the successful return of Taiwan, preferably without firing a shot.

To execute its preferred course of action, a peaceful takeover, the CCP has sought Taiwan's acquiescence through diplomatic isolation, economic pressures, and the weakening of the island's increasingly separate identity from the mainland. At the same time, should the CCP deem direct action required, the PLA has prepared to execute military operations aimed at forcing Taiwan's capitulation. As the Cold War came to a close, however, China's main threat shifted from being the Soviet Union to the United States, and it became clear that assimilation of Taiwan would be a more distant goal.

Four years into the unipolar post–Cold War era dominated by the U.S. military and economic leadership, the CCP engaged in a showdown with Taiwan. In 1995 and 1996, the PLA conducted a series of provocative and threatening naval exercises and missile tests that disrupted shipping traffic to Taiwan's major ports. The intent was to persuade Taiwan's electorate not to vote for the independence-minded presidential candidate Lee Teng-hui in the island's first free national elections. On the eve of the March 1996 elections, amid increasingly dire PLA activities and threats, the United States sent two carrier strike groups to the area, which checked further escalation. Rather than dissuade voters from choosing Lee, who won the presidency, it demonstrated that any fraternity with their mainland brethren was conditioned on Taiwan's eventual subservience.[40] Since this crisis, Pew Research Center polls have noted an increasing percentage of people in Taiwan identifying only as Taiwanese and not the previous dominant Chinese/Taiwanese mixed identity—by May 2020 the rate was 66 percent identifying only as Taiwanese, the highest proportion being among younger people.[41] This separate identity is not a favorable trend for the CCP's preferred peaceful assimilation scenario and further excites Beijing's sense of urgency.

Since Taiwan lost its seat representing China as the Republic of China at the United Nations in 1971, the CCP has engaged in a diplomatic effort to isolate the island. The United States shifted recognition in 1979, and as of September 2021 there are only fifteen nations recognizing Taiwan—and because the CCP refuses to sanction any shared recognition, those countries do not diplomatically recognize the People's Republic of China (PRC). In the 1990s through 2000s, the CCP and Taiwan engaged in intense checkbook diplomacy to switch diplomatic recognition of a handful of nations. Characteristic of this diplomatic offensive is flip-flopping of recognition enabled by generous aid grants by both CCP and Taiwan. A case in point here is the Pacific island nation Kiribati. The small island nation first recognized the PRC in 1980, then Taiwan in 2003, and back to PRC in 2019 sweetened with generous aid. All told, this global diplomatic contest is estimated to have cost the PRC $1.85 billion and Taiwan several hundred million dollars since 1956.[42] At times, truces have occurred, with both Taiwan and the CCP refraining from actively influencing third-party nations' diplomatic recognition. The most notable was during the tenure of President Ma Ying-jeou (2008–16), who was regarded as favorable by the CCP due to his positive position on cross-strait relations. The diplomatic offensive heated up again with the election of President Tsai Ing-wen in 2016, and the CCP in short order flipped six nations to recognize the PRC.[43] The CCP also sought to keep Taiwan out of multinational organizations such as the World Health Organization—a problematic move during the global COVID-19 pandemic. Moreover, the loss of diplomatic relations by Taiwan precludes it from many military-to-military exchanges such as port visits, exercises, and training.

Diplomatic isolation alone, however, will not deliver favorable policies by foreign governments, access to advanced technologies, or the popular support the CCP seeks to achieve its strategic goals. For this task, the CCP created the United Front (统一战线)—a party-led effort to co-opt or manipulate elites, conduct espionage, and foster subversion domestically and increasingly overseas. As of 2018, both domestic and overseas United Front work has been centralized under the Central United Front Work Department (中央统一战线工作部), which coordinates political activities through twelve bureaus focusing on overseas Chinese affairs, administration of religious affairs, and state ethnic affairs—to include the Taiwan Affairs Office.[44] One example of United Front work is the Thousand Talents, established in 2008 to recruit, sponsor, and direct Chinese students and researchers in the United States to acquire sensitive technical data and report back to the CCP. By 2017, Thousand Talents had recruited over seven thousand "high-end professionals" in the United States.[45] To influence policies and popular views, the CCP has used controversial donations to politicians in Australia and New Zealand, purchase of Western media firms, and a global network of Confucius schools.[46] In Taiwan, the CCP also has a history of using graft, disinformation, and paid media to promote its favored candidates. One example was Kaohsiung mayor Han Kuo-yu, who benefited from PRC-linked media and cyber-actors like the 50-Cent Army; the revelations of these connections led to his early recall in 2020.[47] A description by Zhou Enlai, pioneer of the United Front and first-generation CCP revolutionary, best captures its intent: "using the legal to mask the illegal, deftly integrating the legal and illegal, nestling intelligence within the United Front . . . using the United Front to push forth propaganda."[48]

China's reach today is pervasive and often not realized, such as when CCP leaders pressured Marriot to fire Roy Jones, a social media manager, for using a company Facebook account to "like" a post about Tibet.[49] Rob Joyce, a senior cybersecurity adviser, summarized this environment thus: "Russia is the hurricane: It comes in fast and hard. . . . China is climate change: long, slow, pervasive."[50] China's threat today is real and empowered through social media.[51] Moreover, CCP influence is oftentimes obscured by self-censoring, such as when Hollywood moguls cut unacceptable material (Tom Cruise's fighter pilot jacket with a Nationalist flag on it in *Top Gun 2*) or add it (an expansive CCP map of the South China Sea in the movie *Abominable*) to court CCP censors in order to gain lucrative access to the China market. Another example was a late 2019 kerfuffle involving the National Basketball Association. It started when the general manager of the Houston Rockets, Daryl Morey, on October 4, 2019, tweeted support of Hong Kong democracy protesters, and ended when star-player Lebron James publicly excoriated Morey.[52] Unchecked, such caustic influence on electorates risks becoming conventional thinking that in turn constrains political leaders' options. At worst, this can imperil effective political decision-making at critical moments of a crisis. However, the CCP has not shied from direct action against individuals it deemed troublesome, such as the abductions of Swedish publisher Gui Minhai, Canadian businessman Xiao Jianhua, and Chinese dissident Peng Ming, all abducted outside mainland China.[53]

Another target of the CCP's United Front work has been the U.S. network of alliances that confound PLA planning for potential military operations. Four U.S. Asian alliances are of particular importance and attract the marked attention of the CCP—Australia, Philippines, the Republic of Korea, and Japan. In Australia, the 2017 resignation of parliamentarian Sam Dastyari and subsequent Australian intelligence report detailing CCP connections to Chinese billionaires Chau Chak Wing and Huang Xiangmo, kicked off a political reckoning. Acting on behalf of the CCP, both made large contributions to Australian political candidates and in one case conditioned $300,000 to the Labor Party on it rescinding statements challenging CCP's claims in the South China Sea.[54] Subsequently, Australia's Parliament has taken action to begin curbing undue foreign influence with the Foreign Influence Transparency Scheme Act 2018 and the 2020 Foreign Relations (State and Territory Arrangements) Bill, which together are having some effect.[55] In 2021 the government began a review of a 2015 deal that gave the Chinese multinational Landbridge Group a ninety-nine-year lease to operate the port of Darwin, where U.S. Marine Rotational Forces are based; Landbridge has known connections to the Chinese military.[56] To stop the 2017 deployment of advanced ballistic missile defenses (THAAD) to South Korea, the CCP used economic statecraft (canceled Korean concerts and online gaming access; boycotted Korean cars, resulting in a 52 percent drop in sales; suspended tourism, resulting in a 66 percent reduction); and utilized and cyberattacks.[57] Despite these efforts, the THAAD deployment proceeded in April 2017 amid protest suspected of being in part instigated by CCP sources. Chun Yung-woo, a retired national security adviser to South Korea's president from 2010 to 2013, characterized these events as a wake-up call: "THAAD was an eye-opening event that made us see China for what it is, not the benign version we'd wanted to see. . . . The naive and romantic views we previously held,

China shattered those illusions for us."[58] However, unlike with Australia, this has not resulted in discernible official countermeasures. The CCP's modus operandi of using information operations enabled by social media and economic statecraft seen over THAAD was also used earlier during 2012's Scarborough Shoal dispute with the Philippines.

Overall, the CCP has pursued three lines of effort in the diplomatic realm: (1) isolate Taiwan by getting nations to shift official diplomatic recognition to the PRC through coercion or economic enticements; (2) execute targeted influence campaigns in Taiwan and overseas to sponsor friendly political leaders who will implement sought-after policies; and (3) erode the network of U.S. alliances to diminish its ability to deter and respond to PLA actions against Taiwan. The CCP is not limited to just the diplomatic arena, but in setting conditions for Taiwan's peaceful capitulation, increasingly the PRC's economic heft has been brought to bear.

Beijing's diversification of economic relations through the One Belt, One Road initiative serves a dual purpose. According to the PRC's official State Council website, the aim of this initiative is to "connect Asian, European and African countries more closely and promote mutually beneficial cooperation."[59] On the one hand, it enhances the CCP's resiliency to sanctions and hostile acts against its supply chains; on the other, it creates new dependencies to it. This economic initiative was unveiled by President Xi in a September 2013 speech at Nazarbayev University, Kazakhstan. It was subsequently renamed the Belt and Road Initiative (BRI) amid negative press and detractors who saw the phrase *One Belt, One Road* as implying that the "one" was China. As of late 2021, the initiative comprises six overland economic development corridors in Central and Southeast Asia; the Polar Silk Road, which includes Russia's North Sea Route; and the twenty-first-century Maritime Silk Road, which connects southern China with points in the Indian Ocean region and the Mediterranean. A 2019 World Bank review of BRI concludes its $574 billion in investments has the potential to improve transit times by 3 percent to 12 percent, while enhancing China's centrality to participant countries' economies. However, any trade benefits would be contingent on host countries implementing favorable trade policies and regulatory reforms.[60] For the U.S. Navy, the greater control of ports by Chinese state-owned entities enabled by BRI can be problematic.

The port of Piraeus in Greece is Europe's seventh-largest port and a critical shipping hub. It is also an important port for NATO and U.S. warships. Despite this, Chinese state shipping group COSCO purchased a majority share of the port in 2016 and has since committed hundreds of millions of dollars to, in the words of Kostas Fragogiannis, Greece's deputy minister for foreign affairs, "transform it into the biggest transit hub between Europe and Asia."[61] The port also provides dry dock and repair services with its three floating dry docks (the longest 240 meters) and two graving docks (the longest 140 meters) that can service all but U.S. aircraft carriers and *Wasp*-class and *America*-class amphibious ships.[62] Geoffrey Gresh's book *To Rule Eurasia's Waves* makes the case that through such investments around the world China will have geo-economic leverage over access to other port facilities that could be used to preclude their use by U.S. warships.[63] In July 2017, a port call by three PLA Navy (PLAN) warships portended its potential future naval use, and with COSCO's control of the port, the reality is that U.S. and NATO warships will have to compete with the PLAN for access to limited pier space. This is a concern echoed by the then-commander of Naval Forces Europe, Adm. James Foggo III, who noted this is made more troubling given the Greek court's August 2021 go-ahead for state-owned COSCO's takeover of the port.[64] This competition for port access is of course not limited to Piraeus.

Across the globe, Chinese state-owned enterprises have invested in important ports as well as the Panama and Suez Canals. In the case of the Panama Canal, Chinese firm Hutchinson Ports operates ports at either end of the canal—Balboa and Cristobal. In Egypt, since 2008 China has developed a joint economic zone in Suez, the Tianjin Economic-Technological Development Area or TEDA, that has benefited from ready access to the canal.[65] Then there are the "string of pearls" ports in the Indian Ocean region that China has developed since 2003 in Gwadar, Pakistan; Hambantota, Sri Lanka; Maldives; and, Chittagong, Burma.[66] As of August 2021 the string has added more pearls for a total of seventeen ports in the Indian Ocean region with significant Chinese investment.[67] Ports the CCP controls enable the PLAN to sustain distant operations, while also precluding access to those same ports to the U.S. thereby complicating its forward presence.

Chinese port investments have since 2003 been a perennial concern, partly because of the opaque nature of the deals struck with China. However, for many recipient countries the benefit of easy money and infrastructure development was too good to pass up—until it wasn't. Chief among the concerns at a May 2021 G7 foreign minister and development minister conference was the so-called debt diplomacy—a tactic the CCP is accused of using to create dependencies and exert undue influence over BRI debtors.[68] On this, a watershed event occurred when China acquired a ninety-nine-year lease to the deepwater port and adjacent 15,000 acres of land of Hambantota, Sri Lanka, through a debt-restructuring deal.[69] Many countries' leaders—including those in Southeast Asia at the time, as I can attest—viewed this as a wake-up call to the dangers of uncontrolled debt associated with Chinese infrastructure ventures, leading to many countries reviewing their BRI projects.

There are other objectives at play in BRI beyond gaining control over strategic ports. An early driver was avoiding mass layoffs as the global economy slowed following the 2008 Great Recession by exporting, or dumping, excess domestic production and labor overseas—notably steel. The consequences have often been negative in the host country—failure to meet local hiring goals, elbowing out domestic producers. Additionally, the export of Chinese infrastructure like power grids and high-speed rail lines also establishes Chinese industrial standards in developing markets that will persist well into the future and complicate competitor market entry.[70] To compete with BRI and assure future market access and transparency, a better offer from the United States and its allies is called for. For starters, U.S. overseas investment will have to be more timely, responsive, and infrastructure-focused; in 2020, infrastructure projects accounted for 30 percent of World Bank investments.[71] Whether efforts such as those of the U.S. International Development Finance Corporation can deliver remains far from certain. What is certain is that China has used, and will continue to use, economic statecraft to support its broader geostrategic interests, which include furthering a military strategy.

As the PRC's economy has grown, so too has the need to secure its global interests, always mindful of being ready to prevent Taiwan's independence. To keep up, military doctrine has had to evolve given the shock

# Map 3. Chinese Naval Activity

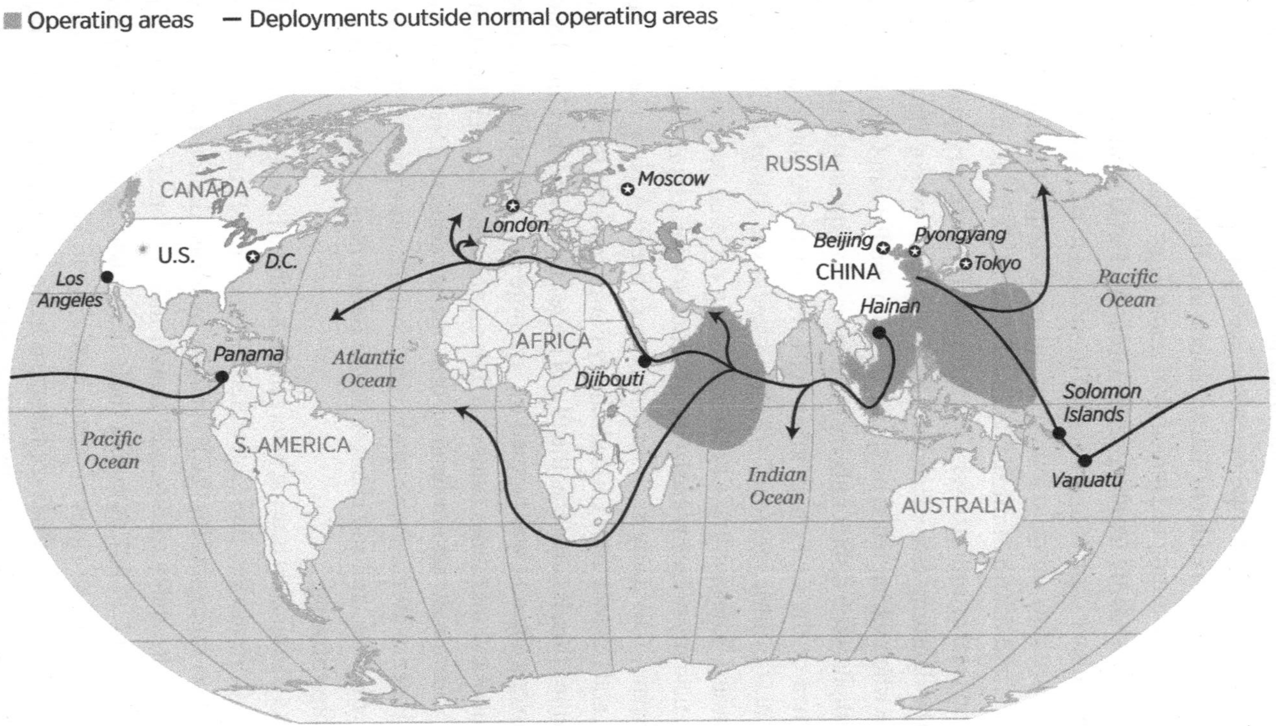

■ Operating areas  — Deployments outside normal operating areas

**SOURCE:** Heritage Foundation research

of U.S. successes in the 1991 Gulf War. The overwhelming success of U.S. high-tech precision weapons and integrated or joint operations in that conflict—and subsequent engagements in Serbia, Bosnia, and Kosovo—hammered home the need for a PLA revolution in military affairs. For the PLA, the goal was winning in *Limited War under High Technology Conditions*. In his 2002 book *Modernizing China's Military*, David Shambaugh detailed twelve military competencies needed to succeed in such a war. By 2021 the list was arguably down to four items, all associated with joint operations, logistics, and dearth of missile defense.[72] The PLA's focus up till 2002 had been on local or regional wars, but that would change very quickly.

The lightning-fast, successful U.S. invasion of Iraq in March 2003, at a time when China relied on crude oil from the Persian Gulf, triggered a new emphasis on distant military missions.[73] Subsequently, at the Sixteenth Congress of the CCP in October 2004, President Hu Jintao articulated four "new historic missions," which marked a sea change in PLA thinking toward "safeguarding China's expanding national interests" overseas. These new missions emphasized expeditionary forces, principally a blue-water navy.[74] To many analysts of the time, the PLA Navy was far from ready, and the May 2004 China Military Power report to the U.S. Congress confirmed this. It noted that the PLAN lagged far behind the United States technologically and was focused on "offshore defense" of China's coastal provinces and maritime claims over Taiwan and the South and East China Seas.[75] Seemingly acknowledging this, the subsequent December 2004 CCP Defense White Paper made clear that the priority would be naval modernization, and the changes in the intervening eighteen years have been breathtaking.

At a March 2009 hearing before the U.S.-China Economic and Security Review Commission, Bud Cole noted that the PLAN's new missions were focused on strengthening CCP interests overseas, demonstrating a confidence in its ability to dissuade Taiwan independence. In fact, the first example of the PLAN executing these new missions was counter-piracy deployments to the Horn of Africa beginning in December 2008, which continue today.[76] The PLA's confidence is in no small part due to the rapid growth of its modern forces. PLAN has added 117 warships to its fleet from 2005 to 2020 (while the U.S. Navy added five), backed by a shipbuilding sector that according to United Nations statistics in 2020 produced 40 percent of the world's commercial ships.[77] In several key sectors the PLA has actually pulled ahead of the United States according to the 2020 annual DoD report to Congress, including shipbuilding, an arsenal of 1,250 advanced ballistic and cruise missiles, and integrated air defense (still limited in missile defenses).[78] This material and technical warfighting capacity with adequate training enables the PLA to execute a counter-intervention strategy intended to deter the United States.

While materially the PLA has made great strides over the past thirty years, its overall progress has not met expectations. President Xi expressed his frustrations in a 2014 speech in which he named the "two insufficiencies," deriding the PLA's slow modernization and command leadership's inability to fight a major war.[79] To address this, military reforms were initiated in 2015 to improve training for real-world events and improve joint warfighting deemed essential in a modern major war. David Finkelstein of the Center for Naval Analyses holds that political control also drives President Xi's reforms in order to reaffirm CCP control of the PLA.[80]

Beginning in the early 1990s, then accelerating after the 1996 Taiwan crisis exposed PLA inadequacies, efforts were made to fight endemic corruption and to professionalize the PLA. Key to the professionalization effort was a July 22, 1998, decree by President Jiang Zemin directing the divestiture of all PLA commercial entities that had served to pad troops' meager salaries and budgets; this did not apply to PLA-run manufacturing in aircraft and telecommunications.[81] Gradually, however, the focus on professionalization was eroding political control, which the CCP deemed had to be checked eventually. While the PLA of the 2020s is much more focused on warfighting, corruption remains an issue, and President Xi Jinping has launched several anticorruption campaigns since 2012—ostensibly to enhance CCP and personal control of the PLA. Additionally, while the 2015 structural reforms are complete, exercising and routinizing the PLA to joint warfighting will be a decades-long endeavor—the U.S. military began its joint reforms with the 1986 Goldwater-Nichols Act and still struggles to overcome interservice parochialism. To get a sense of how PLA reforms are progressing six years later in 2021, the U.S. Naval War College's China Maritime Studies Institute conducted a review of Chinese perceptions of the military balance. It found the PLAN most benefiting from these reforms and getting results from increased investment in naval warfare: more at-sea time for PLAN modern destroyers (two hundred days for 30,000 miles navigated in a year) and realistic naval live-fire drills and unscripted exercises. However, the study found that commentators, policy-makers, and military leaders thought PLA joint warfighting proficiency lagged and was going to have to overcome long-standing military service cultural differences to compete in a major war.[82] While jointness remains a weakness of the PLA, the PLAN is leading in important ways to effect the PLA's Taiwan military campaign.

The counter-intervention strategy, however, is an important aspect of the PLA's military campaign against Taiwan. That campaign, considered by many analysts, consists of four elements: an initial joint strike of the island to attrit island defenses, a blockade against any resupply, attacks against nearby U.S. forces, and finally an invasion. Backed by impressive anti-access and area denial (A2/AD) capabilities, the PLA intends to levy unsustainable costs on the U.S. military.[83] The PLA's capability to effect a successful invasion, however, remains an open question.[84] A critical shortcoming has been sealift to sustain the war effort in Taiwan with supplies and replacement forces; until recently, scant consideration was given to contributions from Chinese commercial ships. In a series of broadcast exercises by the PLA in spring 2021, commercial car ferries and roll-on/roll-off (RO/RO) ships demonstrated the ability to transport and launch at-sea amphibious assault vehicles.[85] Given that China has large numbers of such ships in 2021, this new capability represents a massive addition to the PLA's sealift capacity. Even with this added sealift, there is still significant uncertainty that the PLA would prevail.

Chief among PLA concerns is achieving victory quickly in Taiwan, through either overwhelming force or a fait accompli operation. Accomplishing a lightning victory affords the PLA time to reinforce its position such that the cost to undo its occupation would be too high for the United States and its allies. To avoid this outcome, Elbridge Colby, who led the crafting of the 2018 National Defense Strategy (NDS), advocated for a new warfighting approach: it "involves US forces resisting Chinese or Russian attacks from the very beginning of hostilities, fighting in and through enduringly contested operational environments to first blunt Beijing or Moscow's assault and then defeat it."[86] This requires that U.S. forces be postured forward and in host countries proximate to likely military operations in such a war.

As the PLA develops the capacity to achieve a quick victory in Taiwan, the United States and its allies likewise are in a race to posture forces to confound it. President Xi Jinping has in 2013 and again in 2019 reiterated that peaceful reunification of China cannot be deferred "generation-to-generation" and must be resolved to achieve the "China Dream" of national rejuvenation by 2049.[87] While this has been playing out since 1991, the really interesting and often overlooked action has been in the so-called gray zone of operations below the threshold of conflict.

The first national leader to draw attention to gray-zone operations was Japanese prime minister Shinzo Abe. Like the United Front described earlier, PLA gray-zone operations act in the seams of legality and kinetic military operations—neither considered warfare nor explicitly officially sanctioned. The U.S. Naval War College's China Maritime Studies Institute noted a change in deployment patterns from 2006 into previously unfrequented disputed waters by Chinese maritime forces.[88] Gradually the PLAN, the CCG, and the paramilitary maritime militia have perfected an integrated approach to effectively press China's maritime claims called "echelon defense." Between 2006 and 2010 key lessons were learned, a culminating event being the March 2009 harassment of U.S. surveillance ships like *Impeccable* (T-AGOS-23) in the South China Sea and *Victorious* (T-AGOS-19) in the Yellow Sea—both in international waters.[89] When an incident between the Japanese Coast Guard and a Chinese fishing vessel triggered a nationalistic response in China, Chinese maritime forces were ready.

On September 7, 2010, a Chinese trawler collided with a Japanese Coast Guard vessel near the disputed Senkaku Islands in the East China Sea. After a scuffle, the trawler's captain and crew were arrested by Japanese authorities, triggering a chain of events that fired up Chinese nationalist anti-Japan sentiments and illustrated for the first time a multifaceted gray-zone operation that Japan was ill prepared for. Reflecting on these events, Japan's former chief cabinet secretary Sengoku Yoshito recalled stricter policies against illegal fishing implemented in 2008 and intransigence on the Chinese side regarding Japan's legal inability to release the trawler's captain. Added to this mix, Yoshito noted that nationalist antagonisms on both sides conspired to make what had in the past been fairly common—those caught illegally fishing in Japanese waters being returned to China—into a crisis.[90] On September 21, China halted exports of rare earth elements critical to Japan's high-tech sector,[91] and then, on September 23, Chinese premier Wen Jiabao on the sidelines of his address to the United Nations General Assembly called for the trawler captain's unconditional release—which backchannels indicated was a condition for resuming rare earth shipments.[92] Tensions escalated again when Japan nationalized the previously privately owned Senkaku Islands in September 2012. Ever since, the Chinese have maintained a dramatic maritime presence at times surging and ebbing to reinforce diplomacy.[93] Events in the South and East China Seas in 2012 represented an incremental improvement of "echelon defense," weaving PLAN, CCG, and maritime militia presence with economic statecraft and diplomacy.

However, continued success of "echelon defense" relies on several asymmetries in China's favor in the East and South China Seas—namely overmatch in maritime power, U.S. ambivalence regarding maritime disputes, and low reputational risk to the CCP. To maintain maritime overmatch in areas of maritime dispute, the CCP has greatly expanded the Chinese Coast Guard and reinvigorated the maritime militia—a relic of Mao Zedong's People's War for coastal defense in 1949. Perhaps the least understood is the maritime militia—that is, until Andrew Erickson began researching them in 2015.[94] Prior to his research, U.S. policy-makers generally had not regarded this fishing fleet militia as officially sanctioned, though suspicions peaked during the *Impeccable* incident. Thanks to Erickson's research, a clearer picture emerged. His work showed how the maritime militia acting as a parallel PLAN reserve force was activated as needed to conduct missions that would otherwise risk escalation or tarnish the PLAN's reputation. As such, maritime militia units are afforded training, stipends when activated, and special communications suites outfitted on their boats—most displacing 600 tons and increasingly being outfitted with reinforced hulls and water cannons.[95] The last official Chinese statement on the size of the militia comes from a 2010s Defense White Paper listing 8 million militia members, although it is uncertain how many of these are actually part of the maritime militia. That said, a region of particularly active gray-zone operations is the South China Sea. To advance China's maritime claims, it established on July 24, 2012, Sansha City on Woody Island with administrative control over the South China Sea operating an active and well-financed maritime militia of over a hundred vessels.[96] However, when the maritime militia gets caught, it relies on the CCG.

In March 2016, while Indonesian authorities were towing to port an impounded Chinese trawler illegally fishing in its waters, two CCG vessels intervened. In that incident a CCG cutter rammed the trawler and freed it from Indonesian authorities.[97] Speculation was that the trawler was in fact maritime militia with incriminating communications equipment and weapons, which would explain the extreme measures taken by the Chinese to prevent its capture. When the CCG attempted the same thing two months later, the Indonesian navy intervened and after an exchange of warning shots, the trawler and its crew were safely taken into custody by Indonesian authorities.[98] Media reports are unclear if any maritime militia related equipment was discovered on that impounded trawler—Gui Bei Yu 27088. Such interactions are not uncommon in the South China Sea with Vietnamese, Malaysian, and Philippine maritime forces recording similar incidents. Some of the CCG cutters, however, are as big as a U.S. destroyer, providing greater at-sea endurance and a tonnage advantage in a tactic called "shouldering"—using one ship to push the other.[99] As Chinese fishing fleets increasingly operate in the South Atlantic, Eastern Pacific, and Indian Oceans, these massive Coast Guard vessels may one day protect these distant fishing operations, as they do in the South China Sea. Here is one glimpse of what is to come: in September 2020, 260 Chinese trawlers were often tracked sneaking into Ecuadoran waters off the Galapagos Islands, despite official Chinese assurance to halt it.[100] Should a confrontation become more serious, the PLAN is always ready nearby.

China's maritime "echelon defense" has also been called a "cabbage strategy" for its enveloping layers. The heart of the "cabbage" is where the action is being conducted by the maritime militia—as discussed already, often skirting legal or accepted maritime behaviors. Outside this scrum

is the CCG, providing constabulary protection to the militia and impos-
ing Chinese law into its so-called jurisdictional waters, which really are
foreign or international waters.[101] The outer layer of the "cabbage" is the
PLAN, with its warships typically just over the horizon deterring escalation. To sustain its advantage in gray-zone operations, however, the CCP
has had to invest in larger coast guard vessels and underwrite the maritime
militia. One such investment was a new $6 million maritime militia com-
mand center in the Paracel Islands and acquisition of 750-ton, 193-foot
vessels that will outclass the Philippines' ships, and improve coordinated
operations involving the hundreds of maritime militia vessels, the PLAN,
and the Chinese Coast Guard.[102] While modernizing and expanding the
size of its maritime forces, the CCP also relies on the ambivalence of the
United States and manageable reputational risks—both of which are shifting against the CCP.

Until the Trump administration came into office in 2017, the military's focus regarding military engagement was to prevent unintended
incidents with the Chinese military through various exchanges and crisis hotlines—otherwise known as a red phone. My experiences between
our two navies from 1999 through 2021 was that these engagements were
misguided, premised on a misreading of CCP intentions. The PLA used
such engagements to learn how to improve their own military, while the
United States for many years acted as an apologetic host to events and
exchanges rarely reciprocated in openness or access. A fundamental flaw
was that these engagements often were premised on a rationale explaining
away China's bad behavior due to one hundred years of humiliation and a
fleeting sense of technological and material superiority. The first pumping
of the brakes occurred when Congress laid on restrictions with the pass-
ing of the National Defense Authorization Act of 2000, which required
that annual reports be made to Congress on China's military and began to
place limits on military exchanges with China. The April 1, 2001, collision
of a Chinese Air Force (PLAAF) fighter jet and a U.S. surveillance plane
(EP-3) in the South China Sea, however, shifted the focus for well over
a decade to risk reduction, with military-to-military engagements seen
as a means to this end. A supposed mechanism for risk reduction was
the Military Maritime Consultative Agreement (MMCA), established in

1998 after the 1996 Taiwan crisis. At semiannual meetings, members of the U.S. Navy and PLAN met to exchange views on unsafe encounters at sea, modeled on the 1972 Incidents at Sea (INCSEA) agreement with the Soviet Union. Banking on the higher value given such engagements by the United States, at times the PLA boycotted participation as leverage for concessions.[103] The record on changing Chinese behavior at sea is mixed, especially given the increased use of maritime militia and CCG in gray-zone operations after 2010.

During the waning years of the Obama administration an attempt was made to institutionalize accepted behaviors at sea with the PLAN, but it has fallen short. The vehicle for this effort of risk reduction was an agreement called the Code for Unplanned Encounters at Sea (CUES) that was signed on April 21, 2014, at the Fourteenth Western Pacific Naval Symposium in Qingdao, China.[104] CUES was intended to standardize behavior between navy vessels, especially the PLAN and the U.S. Navy, along accepted customary practices or "rules of the road" and laid out radio communications routines between ships. However, by not including the CCG or the maritime militia in this framework, it has had the unfortunate effect of bolstering "echelon defense" by encouraging navy vessels to interact with the PLAN instead of challenge the misdeeds of the CCG and maritime militia. A partial course correction on this was made in April 2019 when the U.S. Chief of Naval Operations delivered a warning to PLAN commander Adm. Wu Shengli that the U.S. Navy would respond to provocative acts by CCG and maritime militia.[105] On the legal front a decades-long ambivalence on challenging Chinese expansive maritime claims was beginning to change.

To push back on China's expansive rights claims, it is prudent to understand clearly the legal merits of their and other numerous maritime claims, such as in the South China Sea. This is, in fact, the job of the U.S. State Department's "Limits in the Sea" effort, run by the Office of Ocean and Polar Affairs. It is charged with assessing maritime claims against U.S. understandings of international law. In the face of numerous excessive maritime claims by China, few Limits in the Seas reports have been done to attest to their legal merits. One particularly important report is a December 2014 assessment of China's so-called nine-dash line, which declares all waters in the region as Chinese.[106] The report is careful not to make any assertion on the validity of any feature's possession, following long-standing U.S. policy. At the time, arbitration begun in January 2013 was playing out between the Philippines and China at the Permanent Court of Arbitration (PCA) involving these claims.[107] It is unlikely the Limits in the Sea 2014 report had any bearing on the arbitration, which concluded in July 2016, but it did provide added legal basis for invigorated freedom of navigation operations.

Particularly noteworthy is the October 2015 freedom of navigation operation (FONOP) by the destroyer *Lassen* (DDG-82) within twelve miles of China's Subi Reef. After months of high-level interagency deliberations the *Lassen* was given the green light in what was then considered to be highly provocative.[108] Ever since, the U.S. Navy has sustained a fairly routine tempo of such FONOPs. Unfortunately, as of September 2021 additional Limits in the Sea reports have yet to be done assessing Chinese claims or Russia's claims. Of the fifty-one reports conducted between 1990 and 2022, only four were on PRC claims and zero were on Russia's claims. The last report completed in January 2022 was noteworthy in its illustration of what legal precedent would allow South China Sea claimants, most notably those of China. If the United States is serious about entering into a "lawfare" campaign to challenge the CCP's excessive maritime claims, it is not apparent.

Nonetheless, since 2015 there has appeared to be a sustained willingness to conduct FONOPs in disputed Chinese waters, signaling a willingness to engage. While a visible and invigorated "lawfare" campaign remains to be seen, past U.S. ambivalence toward excessive Chinese claims in the South and East China Sea is receding. Regarding ambivalence of the U.S. position regarding disputes in the East China Sea, President Barack Obama's joint press statement with Prime Minister Abe on April 24, 2014, was remarkable: "And let me reiterate that our treaty commitment to Japan's security is absolute, and Article 5 covers all territories under Japan's administration, including the Senkaku Islands."[109] While previous U.S. ambivalence regarding maritime disputes was receding, new efforts would increasingly target the CCP's reputation.

Among sailors the stories of Chinese behavior at sea were no secret, but the general public had little insight into what their maritime forces were confronting on a daily basis. This began to change after China rapidly embarked on its island building and militarization in the South China Sea beginning in September 2013. In what has become widespread practice, the United States began inviting press to ride maritime patrol aircraft to witness Chinese challenges and extensive militarization firsthand.[110] At this time the Pacific Fleet commander, Adm. Harry Harris, famously called this island building China's "Great Wall of Sand," which drew increasing public attention to China's activities.[111] During a spring 2021 standoff at Whitsun Reef, Philippine government and media released video and photos of hundreds of Chinese fishing vessels and maritime militia anchored in Philippine waters. This has encouraged more nations to expose China's bad faith regarding maritime disputes in the region, which the Commandant of the Marine Corps, Gen. David Berger, at a September 2, 2021, Center for Strategic and International Studies speech called "deterrence by detection."[112] This along with sustained FONOPs has changed the previously neutered response to echelon defense, at least in the South and East China Seas, which should not be judged as the geographic limits of the approach—especially as Chinese fishing fleets push into more distant waters and others' exclusive economic zones.

In conjunction with the globalization of China's fishing fleets, there has been a decades-long move to distant seas by the PLAN. In the Western Pacific, PLAN operations include frequent deployments into the Philippine Sea and the Central Pacific, as well as (since 2008) a persistent naval counter-piracy force in the Indian Ocean. In conjunction with counter-piracy operations, the PLAN routinely deploys to the Mediterranean, Atlantic, and Caribbean.[113] Additionally, mirroring U.S. hospital ships in U.S. Pacific Partnership humanitarian missions led by the USNS *Mercy* and USNS *Comfort* in Enduring Promise missions, the PLAN has sent its own hospital ship, the *Peace Ark*, on similar missions in the Central Pacific, Africa, Latin America, and the Caribbean.[114] The PLAN's global reach is enabled by an expanding network of ports made possible in part by China's Maritime Silk Road investments—one component of BRI and a growing fleet of modern logistics ships. PLAN ships, with their long-range strike weapons, have the ability to hold at risk U.S. interests in the Pacific and Indian Oceans.[115] Joining the PLAN and the fishing fleets, which should be assumed include some maritime militia, is the Chinese Coast Guard, which deployed in July 2021 to the Bering Sea near the U.S. exclusive economic zone to enforce Chinese fishing laws.[116] The assumption is that once they begin deploying to distant seas together, the same tactics and operations seen in the East and South China Seas should be expected in the Bering Sea, Gulf of Guinea, and Grand Banks of Newfoundland, among others.

Moreover, the U.S. Navy will have to contend with a large, modern, and global PLAN that today operates over 350 warships in three fleets: North Sea, East Sea, and South Sea. Since then-president Hu Jintao's 2004 "new historic missions" to support China's overseas interests, the PLAN has developed a global naval presence and its first overseas base in Djibouti. China has also joined a small group of nations that produce and deploy their own aircraft carriers. While current carriers are conventionally powered, future carriers are expected to be nuclear powered, providing the PLAN with added endurance and range. For now, the PLAN aircraft carrier fleet includes two conventionally powered ski-jump carriers, and a third (the second to be indigenously built), with the first catapult aircraft launch system, as expected to be operational by 2024.[117] The introduction of catapults into the PLAN aircraft carrier fleet will extend the range of its seaborne air wings.

To pace the globalization of Chinese maritime presence and check its worst transgressions requires a focus and dedication of forces on a similar global scale. It is in fact a challenge the U.S. Navy has not had to contend with since the Cold War, and there is a risk of strategic distraction that must be considered.

## Great Power Multitasking

The U.S. Navy must focus on the global, systematic threats inherent in Russian and Chinese revisionist strategies that have the wherewithal to effect changes that are antithetical to U.S. interests. Iran, North Korea, and violent extremists can cause much harm, but the implications of their capabilities are not necessarily either systemic or existential. For this reason, prioritizing investments to compete with China and Russia will give the Navy the presence and capability it needs to support episodic DoD efforts involving other regional threats. Nonetheless, the Navy will need to multitask and be postured to respond to "black swan" events while maintaining the capacity for great power competition—which brings us back to another complicating factor: the China-Russia nexus.[118]

On June 5, 2019, Chinese president Xi Jinping and Russian president Vladimir Putin issued a joint statement in Moscow committing both countries to an upgraded "comprehensive strategic partnership for a new era."[119] Days later, a Russian destroyer had an unsafe and unprofessional interaction with the U.S. guided missile cruiser *Chancellorsville* in the Philippine Sea. Then, in July 2019, Russian and Chinese long-range bombers, operating together for the first time, circumnavigated Takeshima/Dokdo Island

**Chart 2. United States vs. China and Russia Navies: Fleet Expansion Trends**

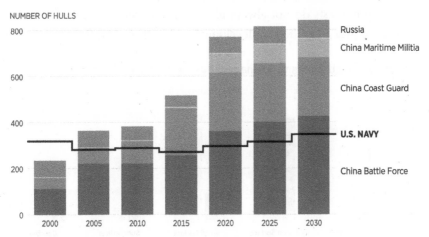

**NOTE:** U.S. figures are actual through 2020. Figures for 2025 and 2030 are from the Navy's December 2020 30-year shipbuilding plan. See U.S. Navy, Office of the Chief of Naval Operations, Deputy Chief of Naval Operations (Warfighting Requirements and Capabilities-OPNAV N9), Report to Congress on the Annual Long-Range Plan for Construction of Naval Vessels, December 9, 2020, https://media.defense.gov/2020/Dec/10/2002549918/-1/-1/1/SHIPBUILDING%20PLAN%20DEC%2020_NAVY_OSD_OMB_FINAL.PDF (accessed September 3, 2021).

**SOURCES:**
- Figure 1, "Growth of China's Maritime Forces Since 2000," in U.S. Department of the Navy, U.S. Marine Corps, and U.S. Coast Guard, *Advantage at Sea: Prevailing with Integrated All-Domain Naval Power*, December 2020, p. 4, https://media.defense.gov/2020/Dec/16/2002553074/-1/-1/0/TRISERVICESTRATEGY.PDF (accessed September 2, 2021).
- Table 2, "Numbers of Chinese and U.S. Navy Battle Force Ships, 2000-2030," in Ronald O'Rourke, "China Naval Modernization: Implications for U.S. Navy Capabilities-Background and Issues for Congress," Congressional Research Service *Report for Members and Committees of Congress* No. RL33153, updated January 27, 2021, p. 32, https://crsreports.congress.gov/product/pdf/RL/RL33153/248 (accessed September 2, 2021).
- U.S. Navy, Office of Naval Intelligence, *The Russian Navy: A Historic Transition*, December 2015, https://nuke.fas.org/guide/russia/historic.pdf (accessed September 2, 2021).
- Michael A. McDevitt, Rear Admiral, U.S. Navy (Ret.), prepared statement in hearing, *Department of Defense's Role in Competing with China*, Committee of Armed Services, U.S. House of Representatives, 116th Cong. 2nd Sess., January 15, 2020, pp. 76-88, https://www.govinfo.gov/content/pkg/CHRG-ll6hhrg40508/pdf/CHRG-116hhrg40508.pdf (accessed September 2, 2021).

in the Sea of Japan. Possession of this island is a subject of dispute between Japan and South Korea, and events led to ensuing recriminations between these two allies. What exposed a seam in U.S. alliances was not the actions of China's and Russia's militaries, but having allies engage in visible diplomatic tussles regarding their armed forces operating in disputed airspace.[120] In other words, if historical and territorial disputes among allies are not addressed, they will be tools for sowing dissension.

With two great power competitors, the Navy will have to balance and synchronize its activities while not becoming distracted by Chinese and Russian efforts to achieve opportunistic gains on opposite ends of the world. This will be difficult because these two revisionist powers appear to be increasingly intent on coordinating maritime operations. At the same time, as evidenced by Russia's military arms sales to Vietnam, Chinese and Russian interests do not always align.[121] Moreover, China is on track to dedicate over $1 trillion to developing its Maritime Silk Road, beginning

## Chart 3. United States vs. China and Russia Navies: Hull Classes

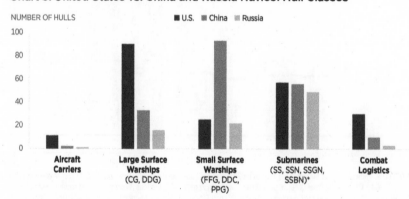

* USN ballistic missile submarines are not included because their mission is strategic deterrence, which makes it unlikely that they will be employed in a combat zone.

SOURCES:
- Michael A. McDevitt, Rear Admiral, U.S. Navy (Ret.), prepared statement in hearing, *Department of Defense's Role in Competing with China*, Committee of Armed Services, U.S. House of Representatives, 116th Cong. 2nd Sess., January 15, 2020, pp. 76–88, https://www.govinfo.gov/content/pkg/CHRG-116hhrg40508/pdf/CHRG-116hhrg40508.pdf (accessed September 2, 2021).
- Graphic, "Major Naval Units," in U.S. Department of Defense, Office of the Secretary of Defense, *Annual Report to Congress: Military and Security Developments Involving the People's Republic of China 2020*, p. 49, https://media.defense.gov/2020/Sep/01/2002488689/-1/-1/1/2020-DOD-CHINA-MILITARY-POWER-REPORT-FINAL.PDF (accessed September 3, 2021).
- International Institute for Strategic Studies, *The Military Balance 2021: The Annual Assessment of Global Military Capabilities and Defence Economics* (London: Routledge, 2021), pp. 196–199, 235–237, and 261–263, https://www.iiss.org/publications/the-military-balance (accessed September 3, 2021).

in southern China and ending in Europe, by 2027.[122] The competition is global and will stress contemporary force structures, but our competitors are not ten feet tall, either. As autocrats, Xi and Putin are externally risk-averse to a prolonged confrontation with a great power, since they must also contend with domestic challenges.

To contest Chinese and Russian theories of victory effectively, the DoD and Navy must compete below the threshold of conflict to confound Xi's and Putin's strategic calculus. To deny them victories without firing a shot, the Navy must build and employ a larger fleet with new competencies to keep Xi and Putin unsure of the correlation of forces, explicitly challenge strategic narratives and influence campaigns, and preempt fait accompli operations through a forward naval presence.

Doing this places a premium on maneuver, positional advantage, and the capacity to assure allies and gain critical insights regarding competitor activities while doing it in an unobtrusive manner. Navies, with their

**Chart 4. United States vs. China and Russia Navies: Missile Density**

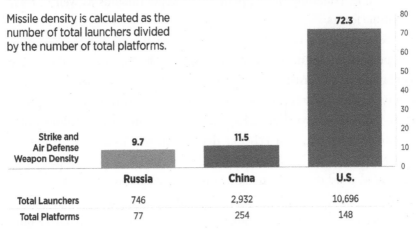

Missile density is calculated as the number of total launchers divided by the number of total platforms.

| | Russia | China | U.S. |
|---|---|---|---|
| Strike and Air Defense Weapon Density | 9.7 | 11.5 | 72.3 |
| Total Launchers | 746 | 2,932 | 10,696 |
| Total Platforms | 77 | 254 | 148 |

**NOTES:** Numbers of launchers do not include reloads. Launchers include torpedo tubes, vertical launch tubes (submarine and surface ships), and mounted canister launchers.
**SOURCES:** U.S. Navy, Office of Information, "Fact Files," https://www.navy.mil/Resources/Fact-Files/ (accessed September 3, 2021), and Naval Sea Systems Command, Naval Vessel Register, "Ship Battle Forces," https://www.nvr.navy.mil/NVRSHIPS/SHIPBATTLEFORCE.HTML (accessed September 3, 2021).

mobility, offshore striking capability, flexibility for a range of missions, and thirst for resources in theater, are ideal for a new statecraft. To accomplish this, the U.S. Navy must field a war-winning fleet while conducting a proactive strategic competition with China and Russia, the goal being to avoid major war by not incrementally ceding interests until war becomes both unavoidable and unwinnable. To this end, the Navy must shift into a new paradigm of naval operations.

## Conclusion

As the United States, China, and Russia vie for influence across the world, it is prudent to prepare for conflict. At the same time, the nation must now deter one opportunistic great power while potentially being in conflict with the other. This makes it important that the Navy be given the tools it needs to constrain future great power confrontations geographically, as well as in duration and scale, so as to husband needed resources. This also requires that the Navy's strategic framework and force design reflect a deep understanding of competitors' strategic calculus as well as their maritime forces.

Neither Russia nor China is a giant that the United States cannot compete with; even together their approaches and capacities have limitations. In the case of Russia, reliance on counter-encirclement and the Gerasimov doctrine is a strategy of weakness and subterfuge. If exposed early, it can be stopped with adequate resolve. China's United Front work, economic statecraft, and echelon defense all rely to a great extent on U.S. and like-minded nations' ambivalence—which is being replaced by newfound resistance. This makes China's development and potential use of advanced anti-access/area denial capabilities in a counter-intervention campaign a pressing risk. Formulating an effective response to both China and Russia requires marshaling forces in decisive theaters in the peacetime competition while solidifying a positional advantage made possible by a network of allies and security partners. This will be a decades-long competition, and we must therefore consider a host of factors impacting activities at sea.

# CHAPTER 3

# Global Maritime 2050

*Each master was dependent wholly on himself for detecting the first symptoms of bad weather, for predicting its seriousness and movement, and for taking the appropriate measures to evade it if possible and to battle through it if it passed near to him. . . . Ceaseless vigilance in watching and interpreting signs, plus a philosophy of taking no risk in which there was little to gain and much to be lost, was what enabled him to survive.*

—Admiral Nimitz, Commander, Pacific Fleet
December 18, 1944

Navies exist to assure access to markets and influence events on land for political ends. Geography and the weather govern maritime activities in patterns that are predictable (albeit evolving due to climate change) and impact naval operations. Relative to these factors, competition with China and Russia is playing out over a rapid time frame, and as will be discussed in later chapters, the most consequential period in this competition will occur from now through 2035. But the tectonic forces shaping the maritime beyond that, out to 2050, are no less strategically important today, as they inform how naval forces are postured, via capability investments that must last fifty years.

Just like the admonition Admiral Nimitz gave his commanders above, the nation's leaders must discern potential dangers. This chapter delves into the trends, bounded by geography, that will inform the future centers of global trade and emerging sea routes shaping the world's political landscape between now and 2050. Factors influencing this future are technological, such as advances in shipbuilding and canal construction, environmental changes leading to the opening of Arctic trade routes and altered weather patterns, demographics and capital flows driving the emergence of new markets, and laws and practices regarding freedom of the seas. This assumes that global trade and maritime commerce remain a necessity for prosperity of the world's nations.

As competition on the maritime grows from state and nonstate actors, nations' reliance on the sea will press their interests far from their shores. The United States provides a historical example of this evolution from the threat of Barbary pirates at the nation's independence to the global naval competition with the Soviet Union during the Cold War. While the United States has been from its inception a maritime nation, it has drifted from that identity to nearly disastrous effect. The first was the absence of a credible naval deterrent to the British Fleet during the War of 1812 and the nearly total dependency on foreign merchants to sustain U.S. trade in the lead-up to World War I. Today the United States is struggling to adapt.

To fulfill its core mission to defend national interest on the seas, the Navy must be able to fight a foe at a place and time of its choosing. This requires the Navy to be present and ready for combat with the right capabilities and appropriate fleet. Getting this right requires considering several long-term forces.

## Emerging and Growing Strategic Sea Routes

The National Oceanic and Atmospheric Administration (NOAA) postulated in 2009 that by 2040 climate change and a shrinking polar ice cap will open new Arctic sea routes.[1] NOAA updated this prediction in 2020, resetting the window of this shift to between 2042 and 2054.[2] Besides the dangers of associated rising sea levels is the positive outcome of new sea routes becoming viable in the high North.

If NOAA's predictive models hold, the Arctic will be ice-free in the summer months around 2050, opening up three potentially lucrative shipping routes connecting the Atlantic and Pacific markets. The first is the Northwest Passage, which follows along the Canadian and U.S. northern coasts; the second, the North Sea Route (NSR), hugs the northern coast of Russia; and the third is a shorter route with no draft constraints transiting directly over the North Pole but requiring the most significant ice melt and shortest annual navigable duration.

## New Ship Designs Needed for Arctic Sea Routes

Arctic shipping routes have become viable due not only to environmental changes but also to technological developments. An example of things to come is Sovcomflot's *Baltika*, a tanker ship of 100,000 tons, which traveled from Murmansk to China via the NSR escorted by two Russian nuclear-powered icebreakers, *Russia* and *50 Years of Victory*, in August 2010.[3] Accomplishing this feat required three thousand miles of ice clearance over three weeks. As a proof of concept, it successfully capped a decades-long Russian effort.

Since then, nations have come together in multinational forums like the International Maritime Organization (IMO) to set minimum standards for ship design, crew training, and safe operation in polar waters. The most notable is the International Code for Ships Operating in Polar Waters (i.e., the Polar Code), which came into force on January 1, 2017. The Polar Code applies to shipping in Arctic and Antarctic waters, sets hull integrity and watertight standards to sustain damage from impact with ice, and specifies propulsion and electrical machinery able to operate in harsh polar conditions.[4] It applies important standards to mitigate the danger of oil spills and conduct of dangerous rescue operations should a ship become stranded in Arctic waters.

Another important organization, the Arctic Council, was established in 1996 to coordinate activities among eight Arctic nations and indigenous peoples.[5] While the council's charter precludes addressing military issues, it has facilitated three legally binding agreements: Cooperation on Aeronautical and Maritime Search and Rescue in the Arctic (2011), Cooperation on Marine Oil Pollution Preparedness and Response in the Arctic (2013), and Enhancing International Arctic Scientific Cooperation (2017). Together these efforts have set important design standards and common operating principles guiding the growing intensity of Arctic maritime activity. Such standards are being incorporated into the design of new icebreakers and container ships optimized for polar operations.

Russian nuclear-powered icebreakers have been deployed to Arctic waters since 1957, when the Soviet Union commissioned the icebreaker *Lenin*. In 2020, following several years of delays, Russia's newest nuclear-powered icebreaker, the *Artika*, arrived at its new homeport in Saint Petersburg as the first in a planned fleet of thirteen such ships capable of clearing ice ten feet thick.[6] Such ships provide a costly but reliable source of power in the harsh and unpredictable conditions of the Arctic. Because of the high cost, Russia is also contemplating developing icebreakers powered by liquified natural gas (LNG), which ostensibly are cheaper and simpler to build and use a readily available fuel extracted in Russia's Arctic.[7]

The United States, on the other hand, has devoted relatively little attention and resources to the Arctic despite abundant resources and territorial disputes. This situation has persisted despite the number of vessels operating in U.S. Arctic waters (U.S. Coast Guard District 17), doubling since 2009 to approximately three hundred annually in 2019.[8] The first alarm was in 2011, when the town of Nome, Alaska, faced a fuel shortage in the winter.

In the 2020 census Nome ranked as Alaska's thirty-first-largest city, with 3,699 people, but it almost didn't survive to be counted. Exceptionally bad weather in the fall of 2011 prompted a crisis that had many fearing its people would freeze to death. Unusually harsh winter storms prevented a routine November visit by fuel barges. Replenishments were needed to ensure that there was enough fuel on hand to last the winter before the port was isolated by annual sea ice. Crisis was averted when Russian tanker *Renda* arrived in January and began transferring needed fuel to the town.[9] The potential of thousands of Americans dying in this way was a national embarrassment, made worse by reliance on Russian shipping. This incident kicked off a decade-long effort to ensure the nation had an adequate security presence and icebreakers in the region. In the intervening years, aside from various polar strategies and impassioned congressional hearings, the U.S. Coast Guard only just began construction of new Polar Security Cutters (PSC) in 2021 to replace its two aging polar icebreakers.[10] But there is more to the security dynamic in the Arctic than ice.

Apart from submarines, the U.S. Navy has no ice-hardened surface warships, and the Coast Guard's aged icebreakers face significant challenges; USCG icebreaker *Polar Star* required $400 million to extend its life to 2025.[11] In 2021, the *Polar Star* and the more modern but less capable icebreaker *Healy* serve as the only Arctic-capable icebreakers in the U.S. Coast Guard.[12] Meanwhile, the commandant of the Coast Guard has determined that a fleet of three heavy icebreakers capable of breaking ice up to eight feet thick operating year-round in the polar region is required. It is uncertain whether the USCG will get what it needs.

As Arctic shipping routes become viable, supporting logistics nodes will become increasingly vital. Anticipating this, the Gulf Agency Company of the United Arab Emirates has established a base on the Svalbard archipelago in the Arctic Ocean, halfway between Norway and the North Pole.[13] The government of Iceland also conducted studies in anticipation of becoming a shipping hub for emerging Arctic trade by specially designed Azipod ships disgorging their cargo in a pendulum pattern between the Atlantic and Pacific Oceans. One optimistic study predicts that as early as 2030 there will be one thousand ships transiting the NSR, putting Russia in a position to challenge Singapore seasonally for East–West trade.[14]

## Operational Impact of Climate Change

Another consideration of climate change is evolving weather patterns, which impact maritime activity such as fishing, resource extraction, and to an extent naval activities. Failure to understand and avoid hazardous weather can be catastrophic. The thirty-three crew members of the container ship *El Faro* were lost at sea when they failed to avoid the category 3 Hurricane Joaquin on October 1, 2015, near the Bahamas.[15] These tropical storms—typhoons, hurricanes, or cyclones—pose the greatest natural threat to maritime activity. Thankfully, these storms have been recorded and tracked for several hundred years, providing a historical database for predicting their formation and progression. With the advent of satellite tracking in the second half of the twentieth century, the prediction of these storms has greatly improved. It began with the launch in April 1960 of NASA's TIROS-1. In climate terms this sixty years represents a statistically small sample of global weather analysis, but it does provide important insights discerning how changing weather patterns will affect maritime activity.

Since 2015 there have been several studies that have provided important insights on the changing patterns of large tropical storms. The first is a migration of tropical storm activity toward the poles at a rate of thirty miles per decade, with the greatest migration northward and southward away from the equator in the Pacific and southern Indian Oceans, but interestingly with no such migration noted in the Atlantic.[16] Based on several years of modeling data and published results since 2015, NOAA has generated these predictions: an increased frequency of category 4 and 5 (the strongest) tropical cyclones; an increase of 10 percent to 15 percent in associated precipitation; and slower cyclone movement, most notably in the mid-Atlantic affecting the U.S. East Coast.[17] This indicates a future of stronger and more persistent adverse weather at sea.

These evolving weather patterns will impact maritime infrastructure critical to sustaining maritime economic activity—ports and intermodal connectors like roads and rail. Slower-moving and larger tropical cyclones will bring greater tidal surges and inundation when they move ashore. To prevent interruptions to maritime activity, onshore infrastructure (e.g., piers and associated hotel services, such as fuel and electrical power) will have to be hardened. For shipping companies this will mean increased costs to repair port infrastructure and more frequent rerouting to avoid these storms both at sea and on landward infrastructure.[18] Should the pace of environmental change quicken, reliability in the models used to predict and avoid dangerous weather at sea will weaken.[19] While such conditions will force changes to shipping routes and maritime activity, the seeking of profit and the need for fish stocks and natural resources will draw human activity to ever-more-dangerous seas.

Already the effects of changing ocean temperatures and currents can be seen in fish migrations and the fishing fleets chasing them. A notable example of a new normal is large Chinese fishing fleets roaming global fishing grounds as far as Argentina, Africa's Gulf of Guinea and in July 2020 in record-setting numbers, the Galapagos Islands.[20] These fleets and others will go where the fish are, risking overfishing and further accelerating the migration of fishing fleets into ungoverned open oceans. A remarkable study conducted in 2009 found that future catch potential through 2055 will be greatest in the North Pacific, the North Atlantic, and the regions south of South Africa, Argentina, and Australia.[21] These are the same waters that will see increased tropical cyclone occurrences. However, as fish stocks diminish by up to 40 percent by 2050 in the tropics, there will be increased pressure for fishing fleets to venture to these polar and other distant waters.[22] The impact of evolving weather patterns and migrating fish stocks will shift maritime activity in general and figure in the disposition of naval forces going into the future.

## Overcoming Geography: Man-Made Canals

Unlike Arctic sea routes, the expansion of the Panama Canal was on a schedule dictated by human effort, not climate change. An eighteen-foot-deeper and seventy-foot-wider parallel canal expansion opened in 2016. Although two years late, it has met expectations, greatly increasing traffic. Throughout the expansion project from 2009 to 2016, however, the canal was operated at maximum capacity.[23] This expansion has allowed 90 percent of the world's ships to transit the canal, obviating the need to transship across the United States from West Coast ports to the East Coast. This expansion also ends the need for longer journeys around the Cape of Good Hope or through the Straits of Magellan, where sea states can be navigationally challenging.

Containerized cargo represents the largest single mode of shipment traveling through the Panama Canal (58.6 of 207 million tons in 2007). In 2006, 75 percent of containerized trade between Asia and the East Coast of the United States went via the overland route, with 12.3 days at sea and 6 days on land; of the remaining trade from Asia, only 19 percent travels via the Panama Canal, at 21.6 days.[24] As such, the canal's expansion has been vital to its continued relevance to global trade, projected to triple from 2010 to 2025.[25]

The expanded canal accommodates post-Panamax container ships—so named as they are too large to pass the original Panama Canal. Yet the trend is for even larger ships taking advantage of economies of scale, though only a limited number of ports can support such vessels. As the canal was being expanded, only Norfolk, Virginia, on the East Coast of the United States, had the depth and pier facilities to allow these larger vessels to dock. Anticipating this, shippers and port managers began exploring potential hubs and spokes of a new maritime distribution system. Such a network allows huge post-Panamax container ships to offload cargo at a hub, which would send it on in smaller ships to its destinations, avoiding limitations of existing port facilities. The hub in this case would be in the Caribbean, the odds-on bet at the time in 2010 being Freetown, Bahamas.[26] What actually happened provides insight into how the shipping industry operates.

On the day before the expanded Panama Canal opened, there was a consensus among shipping companies and maritime security experts that new hub-and-spoke transshipping patterns would evolve. The reasoning was sound, but it was not the only factor driving hub-and-spoke shipping networks. In 2019 there were nine major transshipment hubs in the Caribbean: Freeport, Bahamas; Kingston, Jamaica; Caucedo, Dominican Republic; Cartagena, Colombia; and five located in Panama. The main driver for increased transshipment at these ports was not, it turns out, the larger ships but mergers of shipping companies, most notably the 2017 takeover of Hamburg Süd by Maersk.[27] Such mergers facilitated the forming of shipping alliances with multiple transshipping port operators that offered extra resiliency in routing. Such resiliency, it turns out, is particularly important in delivering time-sensitive perishables such as fruit and seafood.

Unfortunately for longshoremen working in California, the Panama Canal expansion offered an alternative to the expensive and at times unreliable overland route between the West and East Coasts of the United States. West Coast longshoremen and their union have a long history of instigating prolonged port shutdowns; strikes in 1934 shut down all West Coast shipping for three months, and in 2002 caused $15.6 billion in economic losses. The overland west-to-east route delivers approximately 60 percent of Northeast Asian imports bound for East Coast markets in the United States. In the shadow of a history of labor disruptions, the expanded Panama Canal offers the largest container ships that previously relied on this overland route the alternative of bypassing West Coast ports and their longshoremen.[28] For shippers of perishable goods, reliability is especially critical. The lesson of the Hamburg Süd merger and longshoreman labor disputes is that people will matter as much as the actual infrastructure in shaping shipping patterns. Likewise, human error in operating the ships and canals can also have a global impact.

Man-made canals like the Panama Canal, and narrow straits such as the Dardanelles and Bosporus Straits, can be blocked. This happened in March 2021 when container ship *Ever Given* shut down the Suez Canal, causing global shipping disruptions for months after it was reopened. This event gained tremendous attention in part because it occurred amid simmering geopolitical crises and a global economy recovering from the COVID-19 pandemic. The *Ever Given*, however, wasn't the first ship to block the Suez, and the consequences of such a closure shouldn't have been a surprise. An earlier multi-ship pileup in 2018 snarled maritime traffic there for two days.[29] But the massive size of the *Ever Given* proved a much greater challenge—one that took eleven days to clear.

As container ships grow ever more massive, it's becoming increasingly difficult to clear accidents promptly in strategic waterways. This simple reality has troubling economic and military implications. When a strategic maritime chokepoint such as the Suez Canal is closed, global supply chains are thrown into turmoil, and that can delay the movement of Navy forces for weeks.

When the *Ever Given* grounded on March 23, regional tensions had been high for months due to an undeclared tanker war between Iran and Israel.[30] There were also mounting concerns over Russian military forces massing in Crimea and on Ukraine's eastern borders absent any announced exercise.[31] To move forces quickly between the Arabian Gulf and the Mediterranean, the U.S. Navy must have access to the Suez Canal. Without it, naval forces would have to circumnavigate Africa, taking over a week to arrive at a flashpoint but likely much longer. On the day before *Ever Given*'s grounding, the *Eisenhower* carrier strike group (CSG) was in the Eastern Mediterranean conducting operations against ISIS (Islamic State in Syria and Iraq), while the *Makin Island* amphibious ready group was in the Arabian Sea.[32] Had tensions turned to conflict in Ukraine while the canal was blocked, the only other group, *Theodore Roosevelt* CSG,[33] would have had to make a circuitous transit from the Indian Ocean—a danger acknowledged publicly by the Pentagon.[34]

As military planners contemplated their options, a maritime traffic jam ensued. The Suez Canal closure caused a 360-ship backlog, disrupting almost 13 percent of global maritime trade.[35] In addition to adding costs for shippers, the blockage caused downstream backlogs as delayed ships surged into and overwhelmed ports with losses in global trade of up to $10 billion.[36] At the time, the U.S. economy was less reliant on the

## Map 4. The Effect of the Suez Canal Blockage on the U.S. Navy

Suez Canal operations were suspended March 23–29 due to the grounding of a container ship, which created a 360-ship traffic jam. The *Eisenhower* Carrier Strike Group (CSG) transited the canal April 2 and arrived on station in the Arabian Sea 10 days later. If the *Eisenhower* CSG had had to circumnavigate Africa, the trip would have taken about three weeks.

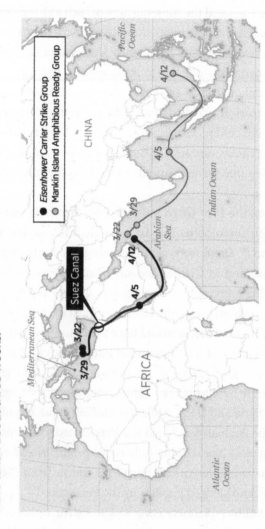

**SOURCE:** U.S. Naval Institute News, "USNI News Fleet and Marine Tracker," https://news.usni.org/category/fleet-tracker (accessed August 19, 2021).

Suez Canal than European and Asian economies were, but had the Panama Canal been similarly blocked, according to a 2010 U.S. government study, the impact to the United States would have been felt immediately and with more severity.[37]

The *Ever Given* episode exposes a weakness of the shipping industry—the inability to clear the ever-more-massive container ships if grounded in a canal and strategic chokepoints. Mitigating this risk requires investment in large modern tugs and salvage ships to clear any blockage quickly. It would take additional weeks for naval vessels to reroute and arrive at a crisis, and global supply chains would need months to readjust after a prolonged disruption of the Panama or Suez Canals. Had this disruption occurred during the early stages of the COVID-19 pandemic, medical supplies would have been delayed, at high human cost. As for the Navy, on April 2 the *Eisenhower* CSG exited the Suez Canal heading south, leaving no naval strike group supporting operations in the Mediterranean.[38] To mitigate such disruptions in the future, navies will be pressured to sustain a distributed forward presence.

However, the priority should be encouraging the shipping industry, with governments adjacent to strategic chokepoints and canal operators to gain the capacity to keep maritime traffic flowing. Such an effort would have natural champions in the world's navies, shipping companies, and merchants who rely on timely delivery of merchandise. After all, keeping traffic moving in the Suez Canal would have been in Cairo's financial interest. The Suez Canal generates annual revenues of $5.6 billion, providing Egypt with critical foreign currency and making up almost 2 percent of its economy. Similarly, the Panama Canal generates $3.4 billion in annual revenues and accounts for 40 percent of that nation's economy.[39] Nonetheless, nations that, like the United States, are dependent on global supply chains must have the capacity to clear blockages of strategic chokepoints should the need arise in a conflict. In the case of *Ever Given*, it required a special suction dredger able to remove two thousand cubic meters of soil an hour and special heavy-capacity salvage tugs, like the Dutch *ALP Guard*, which took five days to arrive.[40]

Grounded ships are not the only way to shut down a strategic chokepoint in peacetime. Third parties with controlling stock of port or canal operations at chokepoints, notably China in the Panama Canal, can likewise impede transit of critical war reserves or naval vessels in crisis.[41] At the time of the *Ever Given* grounding, the U.S. government was seeking a multi-trillion-dollar "infrastructure" bill; sadly, blocked maritime chokepoints haven't led to investments to harden the U.S. economy against future disruption.[42] This is remarkable given that in 2011 the United States relied on maritime shipping to receive 53 percent of its imports and send 38 percent of its exports, and these figures remain much the same today.[43]

*Ever Given*'s grounding came at a time when more and more U.S. political leaders and naval thinkers were turning to the precepts of America's revered maritime visionary Alfred Thayer Mahan to answer the core question: "What is a navy for?" The sight of hundreds of ships backed up around the Suez Canal as tensions rose from the Taiwan Strait to the Black Sea should be instructive.

## Connecting Markets: The Role of Undersea Cables

Shipping carries commerce to markets, but without telecommunications and submerged fiber-optic cables carrying financial and marketing data, global trade would slow to a glacial pace. E-commerce, or business conducted over the Internet, is a significant enabler of global trade both in terms of business-to-business (B2B) transactions and with consumers. When the communications connecting customer with supplier are severed or degraded, the effects are felt immediately.

In 2008, Asia lost 79 percent of its Internet capacity when a ship's anchor in Alexandria, Egypt, severed a key fiber-optic cable. That unfortunate incident severed Internet services for 80 million users and cost tens of millions of dollars in lost trade over the course of twelve days. It then isn't too much of a stretch to imagine what a determined attack to this global network would do to trade. Although that event occurred over ten years before the writing of this book, these communications remain fragile and just as vital to commerce. The potential business loss is huge: for example, in 2009 $33.3 billion of U.S. consumer retail sales were conducted over the Internet, and almost 26 percent of B2B trade, valued at $2.7 trillion, was conducted as e-commerce.[44] By 2019 the digital economy in the United States represented 9.6 percent of GDP, averaging a 6.5 percent annual growth from 2005 to

2019, which consistently outpaced overall U.S. economic growth.[45] Of the three hundred undersea communications cables operating as of 2019, only sixty were licensed by the United States, carrying $10 trillion in transactions daily.[46] At this scale, there is motivation by many state and nonstate players to protect, eavesdrop on, or cut these cables.

Awareness was raised in 2012 when a hurricane damaged cable landings concentrated in New York and New Jersey, severing U.S. connectivity with Europe. A similar problem affected communications in Asia when a 2006 earthquake in Taiwan severed seven undersea cables. Dispersing where cables come ashore has mitigated the interruption of service in some cases, but it still occurs. Annually there are two hundred interruptions to communications via undersea cables, with two-thirds due to human error.[47] While diversification has progressed apace—the United Kingdom, for example, has almost fifty cables connecting it to the world—the danger remains, especially against a determined adversary wishing to cripple a nation's communications and economy.

One such adversary who has demonstrated the wherewithal to execute a concerted attack against a country's undersea cables in peacetime is Russia. In 2015 the alarm was first raised publicly when the *New York Times* ran a story detailing apparent Defense Department concerns over a Russian spy ship lingering around key undersea cables in the Caribbean Ocean.[48] A 2017 report by United Kingdom parliamentarian Rishi Sunak and Adm. James Stavridis, USN (Ret.), drew further attention to the danger. They specifically called attention to Russia's 2014 severing of all communications in Crimea and its predilection for hybrid and economic warfare.[49] The visible part of Russia's seabed warfare is the Yantar naval spy ship, with its deployable deep submersibles. In 2016 this ship operated for ten days over Syrian undersea cables during a time when the Syrian government announced a ten-day internet outage for "submarine cable repairs"—a demonstration of Russia's capabilities in support of an ally.[50] While severing an undersea cable would be effective in at least slowing a nation's communications, undersea cable eavesdropping poses another risk.

The U.S. Navy's submarine fleet is known to have tapped Soviet undersea cables during the Cold War. In a now-well-known but extremely sensitive mission, the Navy tapped undersea cables in the Soviet Far East in an operation called Ivy Bells that provided vital insights into Soviet military thinking and possibly avoided nuclear war.[51] Less certain is the capability of China to tap or sever specific cables on the seafloor. Nadia Schadlow, a veteran of the White House's National Security Council, argues that China poses such a threat in a conflict over Taiwan, and its telecommunication company Huawei Marine would likely target these cables.[52] By September 2019 Huawei Marine had laid one hundred undersea cables globally, providing the Chinese with military access to and potentially control of the data flowing over them.[53] Given such warnings and the importance of these cables to the Chinese economy and their danger to adversaries, the assumption should be that China has this capability and is using it.

Of course, nonstate actors too have been accused of severing undersea cables intending to harm a hostile government; during a 2008 incident there were rumors that Al-Qaeda might have been involved. Since that time, the increased number of undersea cables and improved ability to detect and localize damages has enabled rapid repair, diminishing the effect a terrorist or criminal syndicate attacks would have. This is not to say that it won't happen, only that the effect would be narrowly focused and over a relatively short duration.

Looking out to 2050, there is no reason to believe these undersea cables will not continue to play a critical part in the global economy, carrying not only economic information but also sensitive military data. The bandwidth limitations of satellites to transmit data rapidly cannot compete with the speeds of undersea cables, and for this reason the latter will remain relevant to the global economy. Not surprisingly, these cables are densest beneath the sea routes connecting major markets and thinnest when connecting remote military sites; a map of these cables is maintained by TeleGeography.[54] Because of all this, undersea cables will remain of keen interest to adversaries and will be targeted early in any conflict.

## Emerging Maritime Metropoles

Driven by supply and demand, maritime trade and undersea cables will go where there are the most people with the most money. As in real estate, waterfront property in this global economy will come with a premium, not for beach access or the views but for the access to world-class ports and the associated trade. This can be seen in the trends of the world's largest cities—so-called megacities. Access to ports enables these cities both to grow their economies and to sustain their people with internet access, food, fuel, and water. Megacities rely on overseas connections to survive a modern update to the bygone imperial city-state metropoles that relied on overseas colonies. Three factors are at play in the emergence of these new maritime metropoles: location, population, and capital.

### Location

Of the world's thirty-seven megacities identified in a 2018 United Nations study, twenty-five were colocated with a major port. The ratio of inland versus maritime metropolises in the same study among projected megacities in 2030 holds, at roughly two-thirds being maritime.[55] In yet another study, by 2050 thirty of the fifty projected megacities will be maritime metropolises roughly equal to the ratio found in the United Nations study.[56] Of the third that are inland megacities, the majority are connected with large navigable rivers or overland rail for moving large amounts of freight to a port. Rather than dive into the many reasons megacities rise where they do, the main takeaway here is that most will be adjacent to major ports.

### Population and Capital

The next two factors—population and capital—must be considered together. Population for our purposes here is a measure of labor but also impacts the scale of consumer demand for resources and trade. Capital here is considered a measure of industrial capacity and discretionary monies available by a population for investment or consumption on the higher end of production. A 2018 study approached this similarly, classifying megacities as developed and developing as it relates to social health and security.[57] What this study found was that the vast majority of megacities in 2017 were developing (twenty-six of thirty-three) and will remain so through 2030, with 80 percent of megacities being categorized as developing. If China's recent meteoric economic rise is any indication, these developing megacities will be sources of production and consumption, to include increasingly high-end products for the nouveau middle class and rich. China and India also provide a lesson on the movement of production to cheaper sources of labor living in developing megacities.

Labor and population movements will shift future economic centers of gravity, likewise becoming new sources of income or remittances from evolving diasporas. Well-known cases include the growth of Bangalore in southern India as the overseas diaspora returned, fostering the city's rise in the technology sector. Western Europe has also attracted a large Middle Eastern population for menial jobs, much as immigration from Latin America into the United States. Some countries such as the Philippines rely on overseas remittances for their economy; 2020 World Bank data showed that remittances were 9.7 percent of Philippine GDP. Key to this movement of labor is the ability to move remittances around the world quickly and reliably.

Increasing labor costs, however, generate a push for offshoring production, while growth in disposable income exerts a pull for trade. This idea is based on economist and Nobel laureate Milton Friedman's permanent income hypothesis, which postulates that permanent income composed of human capital (or labor), property, and assets is the driver of a market's consumption, which can enable investment in a rapidly developing national economy—or a megacity.[58] In the case of postwar Japan, short-term gains in income above the permanent income level (or long-term expected level) were consciously funneled into state-directed investment in an export economy. It is expected that as a population's permanent income levels stabilize through either demographic trends (i.e., aging population) or economic growth, saving rates will subside and consumption will increase. The case of Bangalore, however, points out that populations move—and in the case of China, both the workers and factories move. The constant in all these cases was trade-led economic growth and development.

Deng Xiaoping's Open Door policies took off in the 1980s, ushering in an era of breakneck economic growth for China. A consequence of this decades-long economic miracle has been two labor migration movements: the domestic move of labor from the poor interior to the coastal manufacturing cities, and the recent shift of multinational investors and their factories relocating outside China. This trend is driven not only by the search for cheaper labor but also, since 2018, by the desire to avoid an increasingly politically obstructive China market.

For Western businesses in China the environment has taken a turn for the worse, and it isn't limited to the mainland; it also affects the once-sacrosanct freewheeling business environment of Hong Kong. The political and economic system of Hong Kong was to remain untouched by the CCP till 2047 given the terms of the 1997 handover from United Kingdom to China. But cracks in this arrangement became impossible to obscure in 2016, with the increasing frequency of publishers and media voices the CCP deemed harmful being abducted from Hong Kong and taken to China for trial. A notable early case was the abduction of Lee Bo of Causeway Books, whose crime was publishing a book unflattering to CCP chairman Xi Jinping's love life. Others would follow, such as the August 2020 high-profile arrest of Hong Kong pro-democracy media figure Jimmy Lai and his associates. Then, in December 2019, in what has become too familiar, the CCP arrested two Canadian businessmen in retaliation for the arrest of Huawei's Meng Wanzhou for violating sanctions on Iran and fraud by Canadian authorities. Conditions in Hong Kong have degraded to a point that on July 1, 2021, the White House issued a rare business advisory, reminding U.S. businesses of the dangers of doing business in China and the need to comply with sanctions.[59] The effect has been a chilling of Western business in China, made worse since 2020 given the impacts of the COVID-19 pandemic.

Amid this eroding business climate in China and Hong Kong, the CCP has been attempting to mitigate its ebbing labor advantages. Since at least 2010 workers seeking higher wages have increasingly protested for them. An early example was a Chinese protest against Honda—exacerbated by anti-Japanese feelings—that saw workers get a 24 percent to 32 percent pay increase.[60] Such labor strife is stressing the self-proclaimed "factory of the world" and forcing changes that will alter global trade patterns. The example of Ben Fan's Taiwanese lighting company, Neo-Neon Holdings, is a good example of how this has been playing out since 2010. In the 1990s Fan moved his company's manufacturing to mainland China, but he recently moved his factory to Vietnam in the search for cheaper labor.[61] Similar moves are being made by major retailers like Walmart, Home Depot, and Target, which has been a boon for producers in Vietnam, Bangladesh, Indonesia, and Sri Lanka.

Not willing to relinquish its global manufacturing leadership, the CCP has at the same time returned to a Chairman Mao–era strategy. This "third front strategy" was an effort by Chairman Mao during the Cold War to move industry into the hinterland away from potential attack from Western powers. For the CCP today the One Belt, One Road initiative (renamed the Belt and Road Initiative in 2017) shares the goal to develop its underdeveloped western provinces, the source of much of the cheap internal migrant labor in the coastal provinces. If done right, it can flatten national prosperity differentials between the rich coastal provinces and poorer western districts. It is an effort greatly aided by Yangtze and Pearl River developments that push navigable waters farther inland. This "Go West" initiative also expands the cheap labor base, at least until wage pressures catch up in the interior provinces. Thanks largely to the Three Gorges Dam, the Yangtze River is an artery for shipping stretching hundreds of miles inland to Chongqing. This development is aiding the movement of factories to the western provinces, from which many of the nation's 131 million internal migrant workers largely come. While much of this new internal industry caters to a domestic market, it is not expected to diminish overseas trade and will go a long way in diversifying China's overland trade with Central Asia and the Middle East.

That said, internal migration in China has bedeviled the CCP and its attempts to update its welfare system, *hukou*, which encompasses social services such as education, medical care, and pensions that are firmly fixed to an approved place of residence not easily transferred to other locations. The effect is a disenfranchisement of 131 million internal migrants and their families from basic services.[62] This modern third front alleviates the CCP of the need to reform *hukou* but has also encouraged the worst of Han Chinese behavior, notably against the Uyghur people, which the United States has called genocide.[63]

Regardless of how the *hukou* system is reformed, the westward movement of China's industry will continue. The move will likely enhance domestic consumption by fostering development in the interior that will further spur a growing moneyed class. This demand will in turn shift emphasis from export production to domestic consumption. As manufacturing migrates up the Yangtze and Pearl River systems opening new labor markets, the pressure for increased wages is not likely to abate as some firms move production to outside China. One beneficiary is Mexico, which enjoys a combination of low labor costs and proximity and access to U.S. markets thanks to the North American Free Trade Agreement, updated in July 2020 to the U.S.-Mexico-Canada Agreement. In 2011 labor costs were higher in China than in Indonesia, Philippines, India, and Thailand. In all these locations, manufacturing increased as industry moved out of China during the 2010s. By 2020 comparative labor costs in China were double those in Vietnam and 135 percent of those in Mexico.[64] Given the diminishing comparative advantage of Chinese manufacturing, Mexico may have another chance to cash in on a competitive labor market that was sidelined after China joined the World Trade Organization in December 2001.

While geography is important in the rise of a maritime metropole, people and policies are critical. The case of the CCP in China is a cautionary one where rapid economic growth fueled by global trade could just as easily be cashiered by communist policies that undermine the business environment—as has happened in recent years in Hong Kong and in the mainland under "COVID zero" policies. However, manufacturers in search of skilled, affordable labor will continue to drive the movement of production while megacities act as an anchor of capital and demand. At the same time there will be those seeking to profit in illegal trade or piracy, which left unchecked can undermine the rules-based economic discourse among nations on which such megacities' survival will depend.

## Erosion of the Maritime Rules–Based Order

Left unchecked, illicit trade on the seas and piracy can cow empires, as was true for the Roman Empire and is still true for today's modern nation-states. Following successful campaigns against Carthage ending in 146 BC, the Romans reduced their fleets, but they were compelled to reverse course when piracy got so bad that it cut off critical Mediterranean trade. Pompeius the Great recapitalized the Roman fleet and in a series of naval campaigns in 67 BC freed the Mediterranean of pirates, leaving behind a constabulary naval force that kept the seas open until Rome's fall five hundred years later. China's Qing dynasty, as well as the Spanish and Dutch, had the pirate king Koxinga to contend with, who terrorized the China coast, conquered most of Taiwan, and threatened Luzon until his death in 1662. Then as today, illicit trade and piracy can corrode the rules-based order on which maritime trade rests and can weaken security to a point at which trade ceases.

At the same time, there is big money in illicit trade, and criminal syndicates have the ability today to commission submarine construction to ferry narcotics or overturn governments. Illicit trade involves anything illegal and in which a ready profit can be turned—from human trafficking and illegal fishing to deals involving exotic animals, narcotics, and sanctions violations (e.g., oil sales to North Korea).[65] A case in point: in 2008 the head of the navy in Guinea-Bissau, Bubo Na Tchuto, who had connections to narcotics trafficking, staged a coup that in part aimed to expand his illicit moneymaking.[66]

Complicating efforts to interdict this trade is the fact that the identity of the owners for a large number of vessels remains unknown and is easily obscured in the registration process.[67] As one of those tasked with countering drug trafficking and narco-terrorism, Gen. Douglas Fraser, commander of the U.S. Southern Command, was well aware of the cat-and-mouse game played between interdiction and the countermeasures of the traffickers.[68] As maritime interdiction in Central America improved in recent years, the traffickers have increasingly used semisubmersibles and submarines to evade detection, deploying them from the jungles of Colombia.[69] Colombia's improving stability and governance, however, has pushed traffickers into Venezuela in search of safe operating bases.[70] Circuitous trafficking patterns to Europe from Brazil for cocaine via Western Africa have emerged, with Guinea-Bissau and the Bight of Benin as major nodes. Interestingly, arrest records indicate that this growing narcotics trade is run mostly by Nigerian crime syndicates aided by corrupt local officials.[71] The phenomenon of traffickers shifting production, modes of transportation, and transit routes, as seen in West Africa and Venezuela, is called the "balloon effect" because when this illicit trade is squeezed by police and coast guards, it expands out into less governed spaces.[72]

From 2004, European and Latin American governments had been reducing narcotics trafficking. Then in 2009 traffickers once again adjusted their modus operandi and the narcotics trade rebounded. There is plenty of motivation for the criminal syndicates to persist in this trade. The trade in cocaine alone was estimated by the United Nations to total $88 billion in 2008—and this hasn't subsided since.[73] Human trafficking includes on average 1.4 million souls in a business estimated to earn $31.6 billion a year.[74] The attraction for organized crime to create a network of illegal shipping and marketing is immense and fosters other forms of illicit trade. The trafficking in prohibited exotic animals, according to a World Wildlife Fund study, is controlled by organized crime.[75] The unregulated transport of wild, exotic animals across many regions poses a health risk and ecological damage due to infestation or importation of diseased animals.[76] This danger is very real given the recent COVID-19 pandemic, which some believe resulted from trade in exotic animals.

Piracy has also experienced a resurgence off the Horn of Africa and Straits of Malacca in the post–Cold War era. At the annual Sea Air Space naval conference in National Harbor, Maryland, in 2021, speakers detailed the threats to the merchant fleet—electronic spoofing of navigation and communications, armed drone attacks, and piracy.[77] For years the threat of modern piracy didn't gain much attention, despite considerable losses, until there were several brazen attacks off the horn of Africa in the Indian Ocean, the most notable of which was the 2009 capture by Somali pirates of the MV *Maersk Alabama* and its captain, Richard Phillips, an event made famous in *Captain Phillips*, a 2013 movie about his abduction and rescue.

Modern high sea piracy saw its resurgence in the early 1990s chaos following the fall of the Soviet Union and the implosions of governments dependent on Soviet support. Between 2000 and 2004 pirate attacks peaked at an average 350 to 450 a year, then gradually declined except in the waters off Somalia.[78] The problem had grown so dire that in May 2008 Lloyds of London's maritime insurance underwriter declared the waters off the Somali coast a "war risk," subjecting merchant shipping to special insurance premiums. Eventually, international actions through the United Nations were taken, and Combined Task Force 151 was established in January 2009 to deter, disrupt, and suppress piracy off the Horn of Africa.

By the late 1990s piracy was also threatening the strategically important Straits of Malacca, through which a quarter of the world's trade passes. In fact, when I arrived for my first assignment on a submarine in 1995, senior officers recounted being attacked in these same waters; luckily no damage or harm was done, but it left an impression when I returned to these waters a year later. Beginning in 1999 a multinational effort called the Regional Cooperation Agreement on Combating Piracy (ReCAAP) was gaining momentum. ReCAAP's Information Security Center (ISC) was established in November 2006 in Singapore and enabled better-coordinated maritime policing through timely information sharing. Since 2007 there have been an average of fourteen incidents of piracy covered by the ISC in the Straits of Malacca, with no more than four incidents occurring annually from 2018 through 2020.[79] While the danger has subsided in the waters off Somalia and in the Straits of Malacca, it is far from gone.

According to the International Maritime Bureau (IMB), in 2020 there were 195 worldwide incidents of piracy and armed robbery of anchored ships. Since 1992 IMB has been monitoring and advising mariners of dangerous waters. As of this writing, in August 2021, three regions have piracy and armed robbery at-sea warnings: Southeast Asia (Malacca Straits, Sulu Sea, Bay of Bengal), West Africa's Gulf of Guinea, and the Caribbean.[80]

Illicit trade in all its forms offers huge profits, making complete eradication impossible—there will always be those willing to risk it all for a quick score. The scale of illicit trade, however, approximating 1 percent of global trade, can cause immense harm if not constantly addressed.[81] For this reason, navies and coast guards today and well into the future will be engaged in interdicting illicit trade and piracy on the high seas. Likewise, combating this scourge has been and will likely again galvanize multinational maritime efforts.

## Strategic Supply

Supply of petroleum is and will likely remain strategically important well into the future, and it is and will be a fundamental force of modern economies. The vulnerability of petroleum resources was the topic of a 2011 study by William Komiss and LaVar Huntzinger at the Center for Naval Analyses (CNA) titled "An Economic Impact Assessment of Maritime Oil

Chokepoints."[82] They found that the impact of closing several chokepoints would be catastrophic to the global economy, stressing the need for the U.S. Navy to patrol these areas. The study did not make recommendations regarding expanding or adapting to new sources of fuel in the future, which would also mitigate the danger. Petroleum, however, is only one critical resource and strategic product of concern.

The National Research Council's (NRC) 2008 study, "Managing Materials for a Twenty-First Century Military," concluded that the DoD had inadequate means of identifying key material needs and vulnerabilities. Going on to point out that lack of certain rare earth elements alone could bring an economy to a standstill—with security implications.[83] Due largely to cost-benefit decisions, a lack of domestic production had by 2010 resulted in the United States being 100 percent dependent on imports to meet its rare earth element (REE) needs. China has consistently conducted over 90 percent of global REE production for years.[84] Since 2002 no new domestic U.S. mining of REE has occurred due to costs and environmental concerns. Some demand is met using stockpiled raw sources at the sole REE domestic source at California's Mountain Pass mine.[85] Once those reserves run out, U.S. domestic production will require ten years to restart and expand to a level meeting domestic demand.[86] Until domestic mining and refining of REE is expanded, the United States will need access to Chinese or other overseas REE markets. REEs are important to the U.S. defense industry for producing permanent magnets and to provide raw materials for a growing domestic solar panel and wind power industry.[87]

The U.S. REE vulnerability was brought to public attention in 2010 by events in the East China Sea (ECS). That summer a dispute between China and Japan regarding the Senkaku/Diaoyu Islands resulted in the detention of a Chinese fisherman. In the ensuing tit-for-tat, Japan accused the Chinese government of withholding REEs exports as an economic weapon in response to the ensuing acrimonious exchange between the two governments. Whether this was China's intention or not is immaterial; what is important is that the episode exposed the weakness of U.S. and allied economies to Chinese REEs coercion.

In view of U.S. dependence on China as a source of REEs, members of Congress have introduced several bills to identify resource vulnerabilities and enlarge domestic production. House Bill 4866, "The Rare Earths Supply-Chain Technology and Resources Transformation Act of 2010," sought to reestablish a competitive domestic REE production industry. The aim was to rebuild domestic mining capacity to meet the majority of the nation's needs by 2020, but in reality not much has changed.[88] To mitigate supply shocks during crisis, the Defense Logistics Agency is charged with maintaining stocks of critical materials. The current National Defense Stockpile of rare earths, some 14,000 tons, is not assessed against the demands of sustaining a prolonged conflict, which would be the likely scenario in a war with China. This is likely true of other critical materials stockpiles on which the United States is also import dependent: manganese (100 percent dependent), bauxite (100 percent), platinum (94 percent), and uranium (90 percent).[89] As is the case with petroleum and REEs, access to vital materials underlines the importance of maritime routes connecting sources to the United States.

During the 1980s Iran-Iraq War, the belligerents attacked neutral shipping in the Persian Gulf, putting the free world's oil supply at risk. The Cold War was still very cold, and the United States and its allies were reliant on Persian Gulf oil to drive their economies and militaries. To safeguard supply of this strategic resource, Washington initiated Operation Earnest Will on July 24, 1987. It was, and remains, the largest maritime convoy operation since World War II. The cost to the Navy was thirty-seven sailors killed, more than thirty injured, and two warships severely damaged.

Today the United States relies on several foreign-sourced strategic materials that will have to be secured in times of crisis or conflict. It is a risk that has been acknowledged by both political parties and reaffirmed by presidential executive order (Executive Order on America's Supply Chains) on the thirty-sixth day of President Joe Biden's administration.[90] As such, the Navy can be expected to execute one of its traditional roles—safeguarding the nation's maritime trade. The question is, What essential materials will need to be secured, and where will the Navy be required to operate in order to secure them?

Alfred Thayer Mahan's seminal 1890 work *The Influence of Sea Power upon History* remains relevant in today's age of global supply chains, distributed manufacturing, and instantaneous global communications via undesea cables. A central lesson of this book comes from Mahan's account of the Dutch war with England in 1653–54. Blockaded by the British, the Dutch Republic's maritime commerce was choked off. Its navy was unable to acquire the timber needed to build and sustain it, leaving the country powerless to break the blockade. Driven by such historical lessons, the British initiated the Suez Crisis in 1956 in an attempt to secure access to oil supplies in the Persian Gulf, and the United States fought the 1990–91 Gulf War at a time it was importing over half its oil from the region.[91] Until fairly recently, the United States has not had to worry about its overseas trade being held at risk, save from Somali pirates, Al-Qaeda terrorists, or renegade Houthis. Needless to say, such threats posed no real threat to the viability of our international trade.

As serious threats to trade have emerged, however, so has national awareness. Since 2019 Iran has engaged in an undeclared assault on shipping in the Persian Gulf.[92] China, meanwhile, has embarked on a yearslong effort building military installations and fortifying garrisons astride critical shipping lanes in the disputed South China Sea. Adm. Philip Davidson, commander of Indo-Pacific Command, reiterated that the danger is real in 2019 while at the Halifax International Security Forum. Noting that trillions of dollars in trade and critical natural resources flow through the South China Sea, he concluded, "Freedom and support of the international order is worth defending."[93]

The U.S. government has since produced several reports reflecting a growing awareness of the nation's susceptibility to coercion through the suppression of trade in strategic materials—including, notably, the 2013 creation of the Industrial Base Analysis and Sustainment (IBAS) program, intended to ensure adequate defense supplies. Later, Executive Order 13806 (July 2017), a 2018 interagency task force report, and a January 2021 Defense Department's Industrial Policy Report to Congress further raised awareness.[94] From these reports a short list of strategic materials becomes clear, and a picture forms of important trade relationships and vulnerabilities.

A sample of five strategic materials impacting the Navy's supply chain and difficult to onshore production include microprocessors (i.e., micro-electronic logic circuits), precision machine tools, tungsten (i.e., electron tubes), titanium, and high-performance aluminum.[95] This is not an exhaustive list, to be sure, and consideration was given to LCD and OLED displays used across naval platforms and aircraft, as well as rare earth elements (e.g., neodymium-iron-boron permanent magnets). In both later cases, however, a combination of domestic onshoring production and sourcing matched with congressional attention mitigated some of the risk. Despite this, Maiya Clark at Heritage Foundation has spent several years looking into the state of defense industrial capacity and strategic reserves, and what she has found is not reassuring.[96] A bright spot is that at least since 2016 the Navy and Air Force have been working together to improve critical nodes of the defense industry supply chain, partly through the establishment of the Office of Commercial and Economic Analysis (OCEA). Through its strategic research efforts, the small team at OCEA has brought to light critical dependencies on microelectronics and intellectual property important to the military.[97] However, awareness of the challenge is only the first step.

The first strategic material is microelectronics, which are pervasive in many finished products of the modern global marketplace. They make our daily routines possible, they keep the economy humming, and they allow our military to operate in the field. Failure to manage the supply of these critical components can bring an entire industry to a standstill—as has played out in the auto industry. Beginning in early 2020, COVID-19 had slowed production of microelectronics by their regular suppliers, leaving Volkswagen and Ford scrambling to find new sources for these indispensable components as demand returned in late 2020.[98] It did not go well. Production of popular vehicles like the Ford F-150 slowed dramatically. Overall, 672,000 fewer vehicles were produced globally in the first quarter of 2021. To meet U.S. domestic demand for microelectronics would cost $10 to $30 billion to expand or onshore production—and it would take years to accomplish. Obviously, that is too expensive and slow to enable a prompt post-COVID-19 economic recovery and is certainly not adequate during wartime. In the meantime, the nation and the Navy overwhelmingly (more than 80 percent) source microelectronics from East Asia—Korea, Taiwan, China, and Japan, in descending order.[99] A compounding and growing issue identified by the Navy is counterfeit microelectronics, which must also be screened from defense use. On this, action is overdue, but the Federal Acquisition Regulatory Council's November 2019 requirement that defense vendors report cases of counterfeit microelectronics is hopeful.

The second strategic material is precision machine tools, which are necessary to fabricate and meet stringent military requirements. Shipyards in particular rely on precision machine tools, a cross-cutting impact to numerous production lines. Here again, the United States relies on foreign sourcing. According to 2019 market data, the world's top machine tool producers include China ($19.42 billion), Germany ($14.00 billion), Japan ($12.99 billion), Italy ($6.51 billion), the United States ($6.00 billion), South Korea ($4.47 billion), and Taiwan ($3.95 billion).[100] As additive manufacturing, or 3D printing, matures, there is the potential that it can mitigate some reliance on precision machine tools in the defense sector. However, this eventuality is uncertain and years in the future.

The third is tungsten, which the Navy uses as a critical component in its communications and radar systems. According to a 2021 U.S. Geological Survey report, China dominates the global trade and tungsten production, controlling over 80 percent of the market. Although the United States does have significant tungsten deposits, it has not mined the mineral commercially since 2015. Instead it relies on six domestic companies to reprocess scrap and use chemical processes to convert concentrates.[101] This does not produce nearly enough to meet needs. Aside from China, current imports are sourced from Bolivia, Germany, and Spain.

The fourth, titanium, is an important element in aircraft construction and marine hardware due to its corrosion resistance and strength. In 2019 the United States sourced 86 percent of its titanium needs overseas, principally from Japan, Kazakhstan, and Ukraine.[102] Domestic production is limited today to a mine in Utah that is producing 500 tons a year for electronics. Total U.S. consumption of titanium was 24,100 tons in 2020. Two additional titanium mines in Nevada and Utah have been idled due to market conditions, but could produce more than 23,500 tons in a year if reactivated.

Finally, the fifth, aluminum, figures significantly in the fabrication of several modern naval ships such as the *Independence* variant of the littoral combat ship, the *Spearhead*-class expeditionary fast transport, and various exhaust components and superstructure of the Navy's fleet. Aluminum is imported as scrap, as refined material, or as raw bauxite that is then refined domestically. In 2020, the United States imported over 75 percent of its bauxite and 49 percent of its alumina—precursors for aluminum.[103] Primary sources for these imports are Brazil, Australia, Jamaica, and Canada.

Today there are actions the U.S. government has taken to secure strategic materials. These can be categorized as protections from foreign predatory practices, expansion of domestic production, and strategic stockpiling. In 2018 President Donald Trump, in order to protect U.S. industry from predatory practices, and exercising authorities granted by the Trade Expansion Act of 1962, imposed duties on aluminum imports from China. That decision was based on findings of the Commerce Department that China had been dumping imports, causing harm to the nation's security. The Trump administration subsequently expanded those antidumping duties to an additional eighteen countries.[104] Sadly, this alone has been inadequate in addressing the need to improve the nation's resilience to strategic material blackmail. There is promise that progress can be made in bolstering the nation's access to strategic materials. Notable has been the growth of domestic production in rare earths. As I mentioned earlier, China's 2010 rare earth export shock stimulated a host of congressional actions to shore up domestic production that continue today—notably, grants and tax incentives to encourage domestic production.[105] The Defense Production Act (Title III) has been used to sustain a range of critical industrial resources and has aided in the production of rare earths. The act was last reviewed in 2018, but domestic production of rare earth still lags, leaving much to be done in securing the nation's economy from economic coercion.

Finally, since the oil shocks of the 1970s the nation has maintained the Strategic Petroleum Reserve, but today the military stockpiles a range of materials needed in a crisis. For example, the National Defense Stockpile and the Defense Logistic Agency's Warstopper Program are conceived to ensure that the DoD has war reserves adequate to see it through the initial phases of a crisis.[106] Less clear is how long these stockpiles would last in a prolonged war or how much time the nation would have to find alternate sources.

In recent years the U.S. government has come to realize the danger posed to the defense supply chain, but more is needed. On January 25, 2021, the Commerce Department established the Aluminum Import Monitoring and Analysis system, modeled on a similar program established for steel. Similar programs should be established for strategic imports such as microelectronics, tungsten, and titanium to ensure fullest knowledge of market trends that could jeopardize needed access to these materials. In certain cases, a strategic product or natural resource cannot feasibly be onshored or domestically sourced within the time frames of a conflict. An awareness of such cases should both guide where the Navy operates and inform its wider engagement plans to ensure the nation's access to these resources and markets.

## Return to Mercantilism

The challenges of emerging markets and maritime security concern a traditional principle of U.S. power harking back to the days of the nation's founding. In fact, the first article of the U.S. Constitution includes pro-trade provisions: it explicitly prohibits the taxing of exports, while charging Congress with combating high sea crimes such as piracy. Trade has been an enduring part of the nation's way of life and governance and predates the Constitution. In a 2011 essay, Bryan Clark and Dan Whiteneck make a compelling case for the need of a new naval strategy and the strengths a navy offers in protecting U.S. interests in a dynamic and changing world.[107] Building on their conclusion for a new naval strategy, designing the future fleet and its operations must adjust to emerging markets impacting maritime trade and changing conditions at sea.

Of the several long-term influences shaping the design of a future fleet, maritime commerce is foremost in defining where a nation's interest lie. For the United States, foreign trade is expected to grow and constitute almost half of GDP by 2037, making especially vital the guarantee of access to markets and freedom of movement traditionally provided by the U.S. Navy. While command of all the world's seas by a single navy is not achievable, localized command of the sea is. Because of this fact, the United States must prepare for the rise of states intent on closing the sea to trade or transit, and at the same time foster the norms that underlie global trade and freedom of the seas. Doing this, the United States can safeguard access to vital resources and trade, which are key to the nation's prosperity in a future that will be crowded with maritime challengers and economic competitors.

Even localized sea control requires knowledge of the capabilities and interrelationships of competitor maritime states. This task is complicated by the greatly expanding number of blue-water naval powers fostered by emerging markets: economies that have prospered through open markets and security for commerce at sea. Since the end of the Cold War, the trend has been toward diffused prosperity. This is perhaps best represented by the diminished influence of the G7 to the G20 grouping of largest economies. The G20 in 2020 represented over 80 percent of world GDP, 75 percent of global trade, and 60 percent of the world's population.[108] Despite this development, given the rise of China's naval power, global economic heft, and increasingly revisionist aims, optimism that the G20 can be an effective body to foster consensus is misplaced. What is occurring instead is regionalization and competition, the chief example being China's One Belt, One Road (aka Belt and Road) Initiative, which is tied closely to the interests of the Chinese Communist Party. With the emergence of a cacophony of more militarily and economically impacting regional powers such as Turkey, Brazil, India, and South Africa, there will be more impetus to compete instead of seek global consensus. This situation is what China's Communist Party is banking on as it grows its influence in preferred bilateral security and economic agreements globally in a hub-and-spoke network in which all roads lead to Beijing. Standing in the CCP's way are poor demographics, systemic corruption, and an increasingly inhospitable business environment at home.[109] Nonetheless, China's need for overseas fuel and critical raw material for its industry make it an inevitable global competitor with the United States for market access through 2050.

What is underappreciated in China's case, as with the BRICS, is the potential to generally agree with the United States on the importance of freedom of the seas.[110] Such nations have common interests in freedom of the seas and promotion of trade as they seek to meet resource needs for continued prosperity and economic growth—growth that in China is vital to the Communist Party's survival. On this, the United States is in a very favorable position for the future.

The United States fronts two major oceans and has easy access to large and prosperous markets on five continents. Because of its geography and its large domestic markets, the nation is well positioned. Perhaps the geographic determinism of Sir Halford John Mackinder, an early exponent of geopolitics, a topic revisited by Robert Kagan in his 2009 article "The Revenge of Geography," needs an update.[111] Past conventional wisdom regarding the centrality of the Eurasian landmass must reconsider the global role the United States plays located at the oceanic hub of the Atlantic and the Pacific Oceans. Geography merely underlines the need to invest in a maritime force that can ensure a global network of commerce when only localized control or security of the seas can be assured. One response has been to establish the norms by which states conduct and protect trade—envisioned within the United Nations Convention on the Law of the Sea (UNCLOS). Compounding this challenge is international discord over maritime rights and perceived threats to vital trade. This discord is exciting naval rivalries contrary to the interests of all trading states, and failure to judge and respond in a timely manner to such challenges will exacerbate the threats. The question then becomes, How are we to compete in this environment and sustain the Navy needed while advancing the nation's interests?

"No bucks, no Buck Rogers"—or, said another way, without a strong economy building and sustaining the Navy needed to secure trade becomes impossible.[112] This is a play on Robert Lucas and Paul Romer's economic theory of endogenous growth, which stipulates that domestic factors enabling economic growth are vital to continued U.S. prosperity.[113] Key to this effort is the fostering of trade, which in turn requires furthering global trends in improving security for stable, emerging markets.[114] In short, growing and connecting new and emerging markets to the United States in effect enlarges the home market and creates more wealth. Increasingly, these markets will be the locus of great power competition playing out with China.

To begin with, several conclusions can be made by drawing heavily from models based on New Trade Theory (NTT), the Home Market Effect (HME), and Hub Effect among member states of the G20. NTT indicates that large and centrally located markets will dominate production as international transportation costs drop. Niepmann and Felbermayr conclude from their research that in a globalizing world, industrial production will move toward locations with large domestic markets and where global trade is easier, with geography being the increasingly determinate factor.[115] This bodes well for the United States' continued economic dominance of global trade and supports a more prominent future role for South Africa, Brazil, India, and Northeast Asia (especially China) as primary nodes of global production. This also would indicate Western Europe being a persistent node of production as well.

Extensive studies have also been conducted regarding the manner in which the shipping industries will most cost-effectively service new nodes of production. Judging two very basic approaches, hub-and-spoke (H&S) and Multi-port Call (MPC), regarding rapidly growing container shipping, it appears that MPC serviced by smaller container ships is most efficient in North American and European trade lanes.[116] Similar results are being found regarding overland transport in studies in the European Union (EU) and the United States. Such studies help identify a connection between shipping and overland transit, with well-positioned and connected ports acting as conduits to internal markets. While the EU study did not consider the connection to maritime shipping, researchers Limbourg and Jourquin interestingly show that an optimal seven-city-node overland transport network in Europe would include the port cities of Barcelona (globally ranked eightieth in trade volume) and London (globally ranked seventy-sixth in trade volume).[117]

Studies regarding the United States point to the vital importance that West Coast ports Los Angeles/Long Beach, Oakland, and Seattle-Tacoma have in connecting the East Coast markets to global trade. Underlining the importance of this overland connection, Levine, Nozick, and Jones found in 2008 that of the 600,000 Twenty-Foot Equivalent Units destined for New York City from China, only 35 percent entered the United States through the port of New York, with the remainder entering through Los Angeles/Long Beach.[118] Their study also illustrates the significance that disruptions in earthquake-prone ports in California can have on the U.S. market and global trade. This weakness and the expense of overland transshipment makes the potential for shipping from Northeast Asia to/from

East Coast United States and Western Europe via Arctic shipping routes potentially worthwhile.

As supply chains take on ever-greater national security implications, control of both the means of delivery (shipping, ports) as well as production (mining, fabrication) will be contested by more than economic means. This will inevitably take on a military aspect, as seen in the naval buildup in the South China Sea and the use of REE for diplomatic leverage in 2010. In this new environment of great power competition, there will be impetus to secure supply chains while excluding a rival. This has been a fear of the CCP's often-opaque One Belt, One Road initiatives, which are carefully watched, as once-lucrative deals end up turning over national infrastructure to Chinese entities. Such debt diplomacy harks back to nineteenth-century Shanghai, divided among foreign extraterritorial concessions that excluded the benefactor's competitors. It is increasingly evident, but not preordained, that the world is drifting into a new era of mercantilism and neocolonialism.

## Navy's Role in the Maritime System

Overall, a free market connected globally provides the best environment for widespread prosperity, but reliance on overseas markets comes with security risks that must be weighed carefully. Driven by favorable market trends so far, China has become the principal source of too many vital products and materials. This creates a serious strategic imbalance, one that may be ameliorated only by market diversification and at least some degree of onshoring by the United States. The forces shaping our world make clear that there are decisive theaters the United States must secure in order to safeguard its prosperity and liberty.

For the Navy, the mission is to minimize susceptibility to coercion, deter conflict, and maximize sustainment of forces if conflict becomes necessary. Sadly, not since the Cold War has there been a sustained and comprehensive attempt to mitigate overreliance on overseas sources of strategic resources, information, and associated means of conveying them. How the Navy is postured into the future will be shaped by these trends setting the demand signal for naval forces out to 2050.

# Map 5. Other Key Areas of Naval Activity

- ▨ Areas of significant pirate activity
- ▨ Areas of significant seismic activity
- — Coastlines vulnerable to tidal surge from cyclones
- ▨ Exclusive economic zones
- — Major energy transportation routes
- O Major chokepoints
- --- Major undersea cables

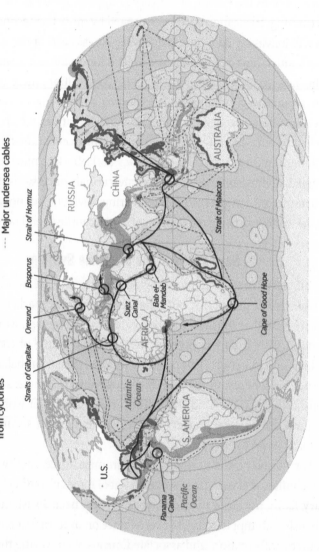

NOTES: Locations are approximate.
SOURCE: Heritage Foundation research.

# CHAPTER 4

# Decisive Theaters

*Ensure that both plan and dispositions are flexible, adaptable to circumstances. Your plan should foresee and provide for a next step in case of success or failure.*

—B. H. Liddell Hart, *Strategy*

C onfronted with a changing geostrategic environment, in 1986 the CCP began shifting its military focus from coastal defense to "off-shore defense," beginning a decades-long process of the People's Liberation Army Navy (PLAN) becoming a blue-water navy. Leading this evolution in Chinese naval operations was PLAN Commander Adm. Liu Huaqing, who famously laid out the first, second, and third island chains construct to guide this modernization. Beginning his career as a PLA Army officer, Admiral Liu geographically explained the goalposts for the PLAN's development. The first goal was to defend CCP interests extended out to the first island chain by the year 2000, centered on the Yellow Sea and the East and South China Seas; then, by 2020, to extend the ability to "command the seas" out to the second island chain, centered on the Philippine Sea; and finally, at the centennial of the PRC's establishment in 2049, to have developed into a force able to project power globally.[1] Initially this was called "active defense, near seas operations" and its first test came in 1988 during a violent confrontation with Vietnam over Johnson South Reef, resulting in dozens of Vietnamese casualties.[2] That test demonstrated the scheme's potential for success, and once the Soviet Union collapsed, the push to modernize the PLAN went into over-drive, with Admiral Liu's framework guiding its rise. Such a construct would be instructive as the U.S. Navy itself confronted a changed geostra-tegic environment.

The U.S. Navy has been a global fleet since the conclusion of World War II, and since the end of the Cold War it has taken on the role of defender of the global maritime rules-based order. This is not unlike what the British Navy's role had been since Lord Nelson's 1805 victory over the combined fleets of Napoleon's France and ally Spain at Trafalgar, lasting until World War II. Yet the U.S. Navy resisted the system defender role until *A Cooperative Strategy for 21st Century Seapower* was released in 2007 and reaffirmed in subsequent naval strategies. In his book *Toward a New Maritime Strategy* Peter D. Haynes details how the Navy came to connect its mission to securing the international economic and political system on which U.S. power rests. Key to this evolution were the failures to prevent insurgencies in Afghanistan (2001) and Iraq (2003), which overturned post–Cold War assumptions that technological military overmatch would organically lead to political goals and stability.[3] These experiences shifted conventional wisdom, which held that achieving political goals would require more than sheer military might. While Admiral Liu's island chains worked for the PLAN, such geographic stepping stones are not what the U.S. Navy needs. Rather, the Navy's endeavor to defend the maritime rules–based order requires deploying limited resources prudently, prioritized globally according to risk and opportunity.

Building on the last chapter and through the lens of risk and opportunity, several maritime regions of the world take on new strategic importance. For the U.S. military the allocation of forces is governed by the Global Force Management process. Outside the DoD, there are few processes informing the allocating of national resources to strategic ends. One area of shared responsibility with the Department of State (DoS), however, is security assistance. To coordinate security assistance resources, DoD and DoS come together annually at what is called the "security cooperation roundtable" and formulate a plan for the next budget. But a whole-of-government framework and associated mechanism for prioritizing and managing comprehensive national power and resources in a sustained and strategic manner is lacking.

Employing national power to the greatest strategic effect requires quantifying by region the risk to and opportunity for advancing favorable legal and diplomatic norms, expanding economic interests, bolstering military alliances, and securing operational military necessities for war-fighting. These four measures then inform the prioritization and composition of national resources allocated to one of eight maritime regions key to sustained U.S. prosperity and security. These eight maritime theaters of activity are the Arctic, North Atlantic, Caribbean–Gulf of Guinea, South and Central Pacific, Indian Ocean, Eastern Mediterranean, South China Sea, and Northeast Asia. Using Admiral Liu's island chains as a guide, the United States must likewise employ a regionally tailored, time-phased approach that holds, builds, and advances its interests.

Given the imperatives in Moscow and Beijing discussed previously, the really interesting time frame for action is now through 2035. Within this window, it will be necessary to *build* the economic connections underpinning a regional military presence and U.S. influence where they are thinnest. In areas where the U.S. maritime presence is strongest relative to threats, and where manageable economic and diplomatic challenges exist, the focus is to *hold* or pace the risk. Finally, where the maritime order is under extreme threat and military operational needs are greatest, action to *advance* interests while seizing strategic opportunities quickly is taken. So let's see what the "hold, build, or advance" scheme would look like for each area.

## Hold (and Respond)

Conditions in the North Atlantic, the Arctic, the Indian Ocean, and Northeast Asia–Northwest Pacific (stretching from Taiwan to Kamchatka Peninsula) have moderate risk and offer measured opportunity due in part to more fixed political and military parity.

### Indian Ocean

The Indian Ocean connects the world's largest economies with vital energy resources in the Persian Gulf. Moreover, the region represents an enduring economic opportunity for trade and will contain a third of the world's megacities by 2050.[4] Key allies' dependence on Persian Gulf oil will be a persistent concern, however.

Despite U.S. oil independence (primarily due to shale oil production), through 2050 key Asian allies will continue to rely on Gulf oil producers.[5] In 2019, Gulf nations supplied large proportions of the oil needs of U.S. treaty allies Japan (82 percent), South Korea (50 percent), and the Philippines (73 percent).[6] Until U.S. exports of liquefied natural gas and shale oil supplant Russian and Middle East energy producers, the danger to allies and the global economy necessitates U.S. military presence and ability to secure key shipping lanes at the Straits of Hormuz and Bab al-Mandab.[7] The threat to this vital supply includes Iran, pirates, terrorists, and increasingly the PLAN. Driven by the need to meet its growing energy demands, China has grown its presence in the region aided by the One Belt, One Road initiative, its first overseas military base in Djibouti, and its increasingly frequent naval deployments.[8] Despite efforts to diversify its energy imports via overland pipelines in Central Asia and Siberia, in 2019 China imported over 43 percent of its crude oil from this region.[9] While this increased Chinese presence poses a risk, its reliance on the movement of shipping here is also a vulnerability.

In its decades-long quest to secure its energy needs, China has alien-ated a key regional power in India. Most troubling to India has been China's efforts to secure trade routes by investing in a "string of pearls" of ports, a ramped-up naval presence, and close relations with India's archenemy, Pakistan. To be clear, India and China have not been on good terms since a 1962 border war along the Himalayan Mountains, which flared up again in 2021 with casualties on both sides.[10] This has created an opening that is the greatest strategic opportunity for the United States in its competition with China. Importantly, this relationship is founded on more than secu-rity concerns driven by China. As of July 2021, India ranks as the tenth-largest overall trade partner with the United States.[11] That trade includes cooperation on sensitive civilian nuclear power, which began after the United States lifted a thirty-year moratorium on nuclear trade with India on July 18, 2005.[12] And the people-to-people bonds are strong, with a large, successful, and influential Indian diaspora in the United States, which in 2014 numbered 2.6 million people, concentrated in the Silicon Valley, New York City, and Chicago.[13] Finally, as the world's most populous democratic nation, India shares legal and institutional views with the United States that are more likely than not to sustain the relationship in hard times. One example is the 2014 settlement of the maritime border with Bangladesh by the Permanent Court of Arbitration, which comported with U.S. under-standings of UNCLOS.[14] The gradual evolution in the U.S.-India rela-tionship has been overshadowed, however, by the wars in Afghanistan (2001–21) and Iraq (2003–11).

After two decades of war, the U.S. military presence in this region became accustomed to counterinsurgency operations and deterring Iran—not Chinese encroachment or Russian military activities. That leg-acy military posture includes the U.S. Fifth Fleet based in Bahrain, Camp Lemonnier in Djibouti, and Diego Garcia in the center of the Indian Ocean. The challenge will be refocusing to keep pace with China's increas-ing military presence in the region, while encouraging the U.S.-India stra-tegic alignment. India's "Act East" initiative is one indication of common cause with the United States.[15] The decades-long drift to alignment finally culminated with the first summit of the "Quad"—India, Japan, Australia, and the United States—on March 12, 2021, bearing a common interest in promoting a free and open rules-based order and prosperity.[16] The genesis of the partnership with India and the rest of the Quad was a naval exercise called Malabar that began in 1992.

Begun as a bilateral naval exercise, Malabar gave senior policy-mak-ers in Washington, DC, a vehicle for communicating a desire to enhance the relationship by the late 1990s. As the flag lieutenant for the Seventh Fleet, I witnessed this effort unfold firsthand while attending India's first International Fleet Review in Mumbai in January 2001. This event began a yearslong courtship that made possible expanded naval exercises, technol-ogy transfer, and increased military arms sales; by 2018 the United States had become India's second-largest supplier of its armed forces.[17] This is important not only to ensure that our militaries can operate together easily but also because it is a lucrative market: in 2020 India had the third-largest military budget, after the United States and China.[18]

Pacing the threats in the Indian Ocean region will require sustaining a maritime presence able to deter Iran, responding to episodic terror threats emanating from the region, and rebalancing maritime forces able to moni-tor Chinese and Russian activities and, if need be, hold at risk their sea-lanes. Managing U.S. security interests in this region are three geographic combatant commands: Central, Africa, and Indo-Pacific Commands. In the event of war with China, the region has added value as a vector for launching long-range strikes.

## *North Atlantic*

The North Atlantic is the thoroughfare over which the greatest volume of the world's trade (digital and shipping) travels, and it connects the United States with NATO allies. The outcomes of two world wars were determined by submarine battles over these waterways, and if the Cold War had become a hot war, it would have hinged on a submarine battle here. A key event in ending the Cold War was a newly devised annual naval exercise called Ocean Venture, which began in 1981. These operations, as intelligence would indicate later, impressed upon the Soviet Union the vulnerability of their northern naval bastions and land-based European supply lines.[19] With this exercise, then–Secretary of the Navy John Lehman had demonstrably shifted the Navy from a convoy service in a European ground war, into an offensive arm centered on the long-range striking power of its naval carrier air wings and Tomahawk cruise missiles. For a while after the Soviet Union collapsed and the Russian navy withdrew from these waters, the U.S. Navy too withdrew maritime patrol forces based at Keflavik, Iceland, in 2008 and retired its Second Fleet in 2011, and the United Kingdom operated its last maritime patrol aircraft in 2010.[20] Then things changed dramatically in 2014 when Russia annexed Crimea, and the previous few years of Russian naval activity in the Baltic and North Atlantic took on ominous new meaning.

Vice Adm. James Foggo III, at that time the commander of the U.S. Sixth Fleet based in Naples, Italy, in 2016 called the situation "The Fourth Battle of the Atlantic." In a new world of gray-zone operations and Gerasimov doctrines, the admiral was not speaking in hyperbole. The U.K. Royal Navy's Clive Johnstone, a vice admiral and the commander of NATO's maritime forces, noted then that his forces reported "more activity from Russian submarines than we've seen since the days of the Cold War."[21] And the head of the Russian navy, Adm. Viktor Chirkov, admitted on Russian news in 2015 that their submarine activity had indeed doubled since 2013.[22] Finally, as already mentioned in previous chapters, Russian naval activity in the vicinity of undersea cables also increased.

China's presence, while episodic, is increasing in frequency in the wake of its growing European economic investments and ongoing Russian strategic partnership. In response, NATO and the United States have begun recapitalizing their naval capacity in the region. On December 31, 2019, a reestablished Second Fleet, based in Norfolk, Virginia, and dedicated to naval operations in the North Atlantic, reached full operational capability.[23] Then, on September 21, 2021, the United Kingdom received its sixth P-8A Poseidon maritime patrol aircraft—thus reestablishing Squadron 201.[24] Also in 2021 a four-year upswing in Paris' defense budgets continued on track for a 4 percent increase in 2022 to US$49 billion, representing 10 percent of the total French budget.[25] Another key ally in the North Atlantic naval competition is Norway, whose defense budget will also sustain increases through 2028 and fund a new class of submarine by 2030.[26] Importantly, after Russia's 2022 invasion of Ukraine, some previously neutral nations are reconsidering joining NATO (Finland and Sweden, for example, have applied and are awaiting ratification as of August 2022), and Germany has indicated it is reversing a decades-long trend and increasing defense spending to above the agreed target of 2 percent of GDP.[27] Rather than divide and slow NATO's moves eastward, Putin's invasion has seemingly accelerated and unified NATO; should longtime defense laggards like Germany deliver on their promises, it will be a remarkable and long-overdue strengthening of NATO.

The principal naval effort will be protecting the homeland from asymmetric threats and monitoring Russian out-of-area military deployments and operations. Doing this will necessitate recapitalizing closeted bases and revitalizing maritime patrols in this onetime Cold War hotspot. To achieve this, Iceland, Greenland, and Portugal's Lajes airbase in the Azores are once again hosting U.S. and NATO forces and supporting an enhanced maritime presence.[28] Such posture and growth in military capacity will be needed to pace rising Russian activities in the region and Chinese fleets increasingly operating there.

Likewise, the challenge of illegal fishing, terrorism, and pandemic spread via the maritime have been acknowledged for over a decade. In this regard, a key effort is the Maritime Operational Threat Response (MOTR), established in 2010 to facilitate prompt information sharing and operational coordination against these maritime threats in the Global MOTR Coordination Center (GMCC).[29] This interagency effort consists of the Departments of Homeland Security (DHS), Defense (DoD), State (DoS), Commerce, Transportation, and Justice. While GMCC is principally focused on U.S. homeland threats, it complements wider U.S. maritime security efforts instigated after the terror attacks of September 11, 2001—an intelligence and operational failure that resulted in several thousand American deaths in New York City, in Washington, and on United Airlines Flight 93 that day. To counter the proliferation of weapons of mass destruction, the State Department led the creation of the Proliferation Security Initiative (PSI) on May 31, 2003, which as of September 2021 consists of 107 participating countries.[30] To screen containerized maritime cargo as a means of delivering a weapon to the United States, the Container Security Initiative (CSI) was launched in January 2002, and as of May 2019 it screens 80 percent of all inbound container cargo—most of this before it even arrives in the United States.[31] Given the persistent nature of these unconventional threats, CSI and PSI will play an important role in enabling active defensive measures well into the future and beyond the North Atlantic where they were first implemented. For all these reasons the United States will need to remain engaged in this region in order to sustain successful programs like PSI, CSI, MOTR, and the NATO alliance.

## Arctic

In framing the military and security challenges in the Arctic, a useful geographic construct is needed. For this purpose, the Arctic Council's Arctic Monitoring Assessment Program is most helpful, based on environmental and geographic features that are more commonsensical than a simple latitude demarcation.[32] This framing includes the Bering Sea and portions of the extreme North Atlantic, encompassing Cold War Soviet ballistic missile submarine bastions used by Russia's fleet today.

Over half of U.S. commercial fishing is done in Alaskan waters. Fishing employs over 60,000 people in a trade worth $5.6 billion in 2018, conducted by over nine thousand vessels; Dutch Harbor is the largest base of this fishing fleet.[33] As one of the world's richest fishing grounds, these waters are becoming a lucrative area for Chinese fishing fleets, and in a rare move in summer 2021, China's navy and coast guard made deployments to the region.[34] Also, the Russian military operates nearby and has on occasion intruded into U.S. waters and airspace, though rarely interfering unexpectedly with U.S. fishermen. That changed during the summer of 2020 when Russian warships and aircraft conducted live-fire drills and a major exercise, Ocean Shield, inside the U.S. exclusive economic zone (EEZ).[35] On September 22, 2020, before Congress, Stephanie Madsen, executive director for At-Sea Processors Association, testified how several dangerous encounters in the Bering Sea resulted in the loss of hundreds of thousands of dollars' worth of catches and made great power competition very real for U.S. fishermen.[36] If not adequately addressed, these activities can undermine the rules on which freedom of the seas rests.

Strictly speaking, the 2020 Russian naval exercise and its intrusion into the U.S. EEZ was not a violation of UNCLOS. Nevertheless, UNCLOS part 5 articles 56 and 57 stipulate that coastal states enjoy rights to the economic exploitation of natural resources within two hundred nautical miles from their coastal baseline—the EEZ.[37] These economic rights, however, do not impinge on the rights of other parties to the freedom of navigation afforded on the high seas, which includes the EEZ.[38] In exercising its freedom of navigation, Russia interfered with U.S. economic rights in its EEZ, violating two premises of UNCLOS: namely, prohibitions of using the sea for nonpeaceful purposes, and interfering in the reasonable use of the seas by others.[39] Based on this, freedom of navigation in an EEZ cannot impinge on the reasonable execution of a coastal state's economic rights in its EEZ.[40] With increasingly aggressive Russian naval activities and a growing Chinese maritime presence, vigilance will be needed to safeguard U.S. economic interests here.

Aside from fish and crabs, the waters around Alaska include significant reserves of oil and natural gas. Within Alaska's outer continental shelf (OCS) in the Chukchi and Beaufort Seas there are predicted to be 26 billion barrels of oil and 132 trillion cubic feet of natural gas.[41] To get a sense of scale, according to the U.S. Energy Information Administration, in 2020 the United States consumed 18.12 million barrels of oil and 0.084 trillion cubic feet of natural gas an average day; these Alaskan reserves would be enough to power the United States for four years.[42] Access to these reserves, however, is dependent on how the U.S. OCS is defined. In the simplest terms, the OCS effectively extends an EEZ beyond the nominal 200-mile limit to a maximum of 350 miles based on continuity of seabed features.[43] To adjudicate claims to the OCS, in 1997 the Commission on the Limits of the Continental Shelf was established. UNCLOS aside, the United States has already negotiated its maritime claims bilaterally, specifically in a 1990 pact with the Soviet Union known as the "Baker-Shevardnadze line," which is still respected today.[44] While the boundaries may be settled for the United States, unrestricted execution of its exclusive economic rights is not assured, as Russia's Ocean Shield exercise demonstrated.

Discussed in earlier chapters, maritime presence in the Arctic is increasing to include many non-Arctic nations. This new reality elevates the importance of the Arctic Council as a standards setter. As international interest has grown, so has the roster of the council's observer states, which as of September 2021 number thirty-five, including China. Aside from Russia's militarization of its Arctic territories, however, the military threat remains limited. That said, there are several military and safety missions that will endure.

The Navy will need to retain the ability to operate its submarines in the Arctic and under sea ice for extended periods of time to, if necessary, hold at-risk ballistic missile submarines operating here. Another Cold War mission persisting today is strategic defense from Russian nuclear forces (ballistic missile and bombers) and, in recent decades, Chinese intercontinental missiles. Importantly, in 2006 the U.S. and Canada Aerospace Defense Agreement was expanded to include a maritime warning system. It was originally established in 1958 to provide a mechanism for monitoring and defending shared airspace headquartered at the North American Defense Command (NORAD). To accomplish this mission, the North Warning System includes eleven long-range and thirty-six short-range radars arrayed across Alaska, Canada, and Greenland.[45] U.S. secretary of defense Lloyd Austin and Canada's minister of national defense, however, acknowledged in an August 2021 joint statement the need to modernize these radars and command and control for today's threats—hopefully to include enhancements for maritime domain awareness.[46] While these strategic missions persist and will have to be modernized to pace the threat, the really interesting mission growth will be in maritime security and EEZ rights enforcement.

As more and more maritime traffic enters the Arctic, a complicated mosaic of fishing fleets, seabed resource extraction, and military operations is evolving. Amid this, the greatest day-to-day challenge will be ensuring U.S. economic rights in its EEZ and OCS. The U.S. Coast Guard is uniquely suited to this mission but will need to enhance its Arctic capabilities and posture in order to execute this mission while performing traditional life-saving missions (e.g., search and rescue).

### Northeast Asia / Northwest Pacific

Northeast Asia has been a cauldron of strategic tension and warfare, beginning in modern times with the 1894 Sino-Japanese War. That war set in motion a chain of events culminating in World War II and today's multifaceted standoff on the Korean Peninsula and Taiwan Strait. Peace has held due to a relative balance of military power among the principal belligerents—the United States, China, Japan, Russia, Taiwan, and North and South Korea. At the same time the region is host to the world's largest economies and sources of critical materials, like microelectronics, making the region an enduring U.S. national interest. Sustaining the peace and maintaining key alliances and access to markets will require vigilance.

A crisis in the region would imperil tens of thousands of American lives directly, shutter industry, and easily become a global conflict. According to data tracked by the U.S. State Department, and immigration statistics provided by the Republic of China, there are between 13,000 and 38,000 U.S. citizens living in Taiwan.[47] If you add the citizens in Japan, PRC, and South Korea, the total climbs to over 150,000 U.S. citizens residing in the region.[48] Any conflict there would likely result in American civilian casualties and a rapid exodus.

For the United States, the region is a critical center of economic activity, comprising a quarter of its overall trade. This includes irreplaceable imports such as microelectronics.[49] This point was hammered home in 2021, during the COVID pandemic, when car manufacturers had to dial back production as supply lagged microchip production. The last regional economic crisis was in 1997, but its impacts were largely contained and small because the countries involved then (South Korea, Thailand, Malaysia, and Indonesia) represented a small portion of U.S. trade.[50] Things are clearly different in 2020; based on World Bank data in 1997 South Korea's economy was only 6.6 percent of that of the United States, while in 2020 it had grown to a quarter of the States'.[51] A rerun of the 1997 crisis emanating from this region, however, would not be limited or small in its impact on the United States. Moreover, a sizable diaspora and significant economic connections mean that when a market there shakes, it can roil the United States. And the stability of the region is not guaranteed.

Even under the best of diplomatic relations, the region is host to simmering territorial disputes, always one drunk fisherman away from an international crisis. In fact, every country here has a beef with a neighbor —China with Japan and South Korea, South Korea with Japan, Russia with Japan. In each case a seemingly small incident can rapidly inflame nationalisms. This occurred during a 2010 incident between China and Japan over the Senkaku Islands (in Chinese, the Diaoyu Islands) in the East China Sea. There has been loss of life at most of these flashpoints: Senkaku/Diaoyu (1996), Northern Territories/Southern Kuril Islands (2006), Socotra Rock (2012). The only exception to maritime dispute-related deaths was between Japan and South Korea over Takeshima (in Korean, Dokdo Island). Keeping a lid on these disputes will require persistent diplomatic engagement, for sure, but this all rests on a military presence geared to deterring two flashpoints—conflict on the Korean Peninsula and a battle over Taiwan.

On July 27, 1953, the three-year Korean War was frozen, and the armistice has held for decades despite periodic hostilities. The last significant test of the armistice occurred over eight months in 2010. The crisis began when a North Korean mini-submarine launched a torpedo that sank the South Korean Navy's corvette *Cheonan*, killing forty-six sailors in disputed waters of the Yellow Sea.[52] Crisis culminated with a November North Korean artillery attack that killed two Marines and two civilians on the Yellow Sea island of Yeonpyeong.[53] Despite these provocations, the armistice held and a wider war was averted. Had it not, most experts expect the South to have prevailed eventually in what is often characterized as a suicidal attack by the North. The cost would be high, however. According to a 2020 RAND Corporation study, over 200,000 in Seoul would be casualties within the first few days from 5,700 North Korean long-range artillery systems within range of the city.[54] This has quite literally placed the South under the gun, resulting in marked defense spending. Gen. Robert Abrams recognized this significant contribution to peace on the peninsula by South Korea before Congress in March 2021. In testimony before Congress, the general highlighted South Korea's significant increases in defense spending: a 7.4 percent rise from 2020 to 2021, representing 2.8 percent of gross domestic product, and in previous testimony $2.16 billion in purchases of military hardware from the United States that included P-8A maritime patrol aircraft.[55] Since the sinking of the *Cheonan*, South Korea's defense budget has more than doubled, and since 2016 it has sustained an average 5.75 percent year-on-year increase.

These enhanced defense allocations contribute directly to the military balance on the peninsula, but they also sustain a U.S. military presence in a country with region-wide deterrent value. The South Korean government provides host nation support under a Special Measures Agreement (SMA) that funds some of the overhead costs of U.S. military forces based in South Korea. Negotiations in March 2021 reached consensus on a 13 percent increase over time reaching $1.2 billion in annual contributions, but not before lapses caused U.S. Force Korea (USFK) to furlough 9,000 local hires.[56] This lapse was unusual and likely a one-time event in the history of an alliance with a country that is home to over 28,000 U.S. service members. Some of these local hires work for the naval component of USFK at two annexes on Korean naval bases. Commander Naval Forces Korea operates a headquarters in Busan and an operational support staff in Jinhae, both on the southern coast of South Korea. There has not been a permanent homeporting of U.S. warships in Korea, unlike in Japan.

While the correlation of forces has kept a violent peace in Korea, the sizable naval presence in Japan is poised to deter the most dangerous contingency—a war with the CCP over Taiwan. In a remarkable move in July 2021, former prime minister Shinzo Abe joined a growing number of sitting Japanese parliamentarians to assert publicly that Japan would have to work with the United States to defend Taiwan in case of a war.[57] This would potentially add Japan's fleet of over 155 warships and auxiliaries to the 50 to 70 warships of the U.S. Seventh Fleet. Like South Korea,

Japan also provides host nation support, which was $1.84 billion in 2021, partly funding the maintenance of 21 Japan-based U.S. warships.[58] Adding in Taiwan's 86 warships, the day-one total armada arrayed against China's 348 warships would be an allied fleet of 311 warships.[59] These numbers do not account for coast guards, which in war would be expected to support naval operations. In this regard, China Coast Guard's 255 ships provide the PLAN with additional capacity but limited warfighting effectiveness. The balance gets tenuous when we consider that China's air force (PLAAF) has 1,500 jet fighters and rocket forces comprising 700 short, intermediate-range ballistic and cruise missile launchers.

Nonetheless, the combined military balance in Northeast Asia and North Pacific has remained stable. Ensuring this stability into the future will require sustained forward presence of U.S. naval forces and alliance engagement to maintain a united front before any Chinese aggression. At the same time, there will be upward pressure on these forces to match the consistent growth of China's military and Russia's renewed Pacific naval activity. Underscoring this point, Russia has signaled its intent to deploy more modern assets to its Pacific Fleet. Already they have based 15 smaller warships and auxiliaries in 2020 alone, and by all accounts to eventually be joined by its newest *Belgorod*-class submarine with Poseidon nuclear-powered drones.[60] The addition of such advanced nuclear submarines and weapons to Russia's existing ballistic missile armed submarines from Petropavlovsk in the Bering Sea necessitate an enduring U.S. strategic deterrence and maritime patrol mission in the region.

U.S. military presence in the Indo-Pacific is anchored in Northeast Asia despite past efforts to rebalance it to Southeast Asia. This was notable during the Obama administration's 2012 Defense Strategic Guidance—otherwise known as the Rebalance to the Asia-Pacific. Given the threat, this has been appropriate, but any rebalancing of U.S. forces across the Indo-Pacific must come from additional forces, as moves from this region could upset the above-described balance. While the threats have evolved, the U.S. military posture here remains a legacy of World War II and the Korean War. The alliances with Japan and South Korea have evolved too, however, and their militaries have grown, mitigating somewhat the need for additional U.S. forces in the region. That said, U.S. forces here are

# Chart 5. China's Rapidly Growing Naval Fleet

China's navy is projected to grow to more than 760 ships by 2030, a daunting force compared to the 70 ships in the U.S. 7th Fleet and deployed warships that operate in the South China Sea region.

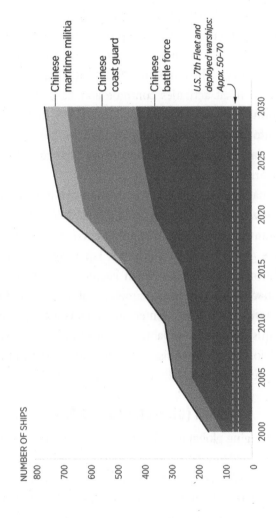

**SOURCES:** U.S. Department of Defense, "Advantage at Sea," December 2020, p. 4, https://media.defense.gov/2020/Dec/16/2002553074/-1/-1/0/TRISERVICESTRATEGY.PDF (accessed April 22, 2021); Congressional Research Service, "China Naval Modernization: Implications for U.S. Navy Capabilities—Background and Issues for Congress," CRS *Report* RL33153, p. 32, https://crsreports.congress.gov/product/pdf/RL/RL33153/248 (accessed April 21, 2021); and Commander of the U.S. 7th Fleet, https://www.c7f.navy.mil/ (accessed May 10, 2021).

proximate flashpoints in Taiwan and Korea, which puts the balance of U.S. Pacific naval forces within range of thousands of Chinese ballistic and cruise missiles. Sustaining these key alliances is a vital part of the deterrence of Chinese adventurism, and U.S. in-country presence is critical to doing this despite Chinese rocket forces.[61] At the same time, these forward naval forces must conduct day-to-day operations such as sanctions enforcement and counter-proliferation, expressly against the North Korean regime. Most notorious was the regime's use of ship-to-ship fuel transfers at sea in the East China Sea to skirt sanctions implemented in 2017. These illicit activities continue and have drawn international condemnation, and the United Kingdom's HMS *Richmond* conducted sanctions enforcement during a deployment to East Asia in September 2021.[62] Such day-to-day activities validate the alliances, while an enduring presence deters major wars.

In the final analysis, the Navy with allies can together pace the rap- idly metastasizing military threat from China, North Korea, and Russia. At a minimum this will mean sustaining current forces centered on the carrier strike group based in Yokosuka, Japan, while increasing capac- ity for maritime patrols in the North Pacific. These new patrols will be needed to shadow Russian ballistic missile submarines and Chinese out- of-area deployments and to counter sanctions violations. Finally, the use of ballistic-missile-defense-capable warships in the Sea of Japan as senti- nel against North Korean ballistic missiles will persist until shore-based alternatives are found (e.g., AEGIS ashore and THAAD).

## Build (Strengthen and Bolster)

Given the changing global geostrategic environment, two regions merit a fresh look and invigorated national attention. These regions offer oppor- tunity in fluid political and economic dynamics, and they are areas with a limited military threat, but they are also areas where influence is increas- ingly contested. Both have strategic value, especially given a globalized Chinese maritime presence in the Central and South Pacific and in the tropical Atlantic (Caribbean to Gulf of Guinea). Limited persistent mili- tary presence in these theaters makes it important to build new security partnerships and enhance naval access to ports there as well as, where needed, to build critical infrastructure in support of efforts to secure the sea- and air-lanes.

## Caribbean–Gulf of Guinea

Stretching across the tropical latitudes of the Atlantic is a band of ocean connecting the Americas with Africa and Europe. Today shared colonial histories tie Caribbean nations, notably Brazil, with countries of Africa. Brazil's Portuguese ancestry ties it to Angola, Guinea, and Sao Tome and Principe. Seventeenth-century Jesuit missionary Frei Antonio Vieira described Brazil as "the body of America and the soul of Africa." The maritime geography of this band of ocean has made it a thoroughfare for infamous cargo—until the mid-1800s slaves, and in modern times narcotics. China and Russia too have taken an interest in the region.

A notable example of Russian and Chinese interests in the region is Venezuela and its remarkable 2019 descent into political chaos. Crisis was sparked in January 2019 when president of the National Assembly Juan Guaido claimed to be the rightful president of Venezuela and was subsequently recognized by fifty democratic nations. Amid street violence in the capital, Caracas, two Russian military aircraft and one hundred troops arrived in March.[63] Russia's interest is apparently based on military arms and energy development, with $10 billion in back-due payments as of July 2019, but it also serves as a diplomatic jab at Washington, especially bomber diplomacy; two strategic bombers (TU-160 Backfire) visited the country in December 2018.[64] Like Russia, China's engagement in Venezuela took off with the rise of socialist President Hugo Chavez (1999–2013), with investment worth $62.2 billion over 2007–19.[65] China has not limited its activities to Venezuela: it has significant investments and infrastructure projects across the Caribbean and Gulf of Guinea, totaling over $222 billion from 2005 to 2021.[66]

Already discussed is the importance of the Panama Canal and the evolution of new shipping hubs. In the Caribbean, key transshipment hubs include the Bahamas' Freeport, Jamaica's Kingston, and Trinidad's Point Lisas. In the Gulf of Guinea, key container ports include Togo's Lomé, Nigeria's Lagos, Ghana's Tema, and Ivory Coast's Abidjan, in descending order of volume of containers handled in 2017. The area is also home to significant gas and oil fields, utilized principally by Brazil, Mexico, Nigeria, Angola, Venezuela, and Colombia. Chinese investment in these countries constituted 80 percent of its overall commitments in the Caribbean and Gulf of Guinea. Underlying a targeted strategy of access to energy sources and control of key ports is also a military aspect that has in recent years come to light. In a familiar Chinese pattern, in October 2021 news reports indicated that Equatorial Guinea was offering China a naval base, which would have given ready access to a sensitive U.S. missile range at Ascension Island.[67] Chinese investments and military basing are a challenge to be addressed, as is piracy in the Gulf of Guinea and narcotics trafficking in the Caribbean.

Incidents of piracy in the Gulf of Guinea have ebbed and flowed. The pattern of piracy follows the monsoon season (June to September), and a 40 percent spike of incidents in 2020 saw shippers in the area hiring armed guards and escort vessels.[68] In September 2020, Secretary of State Mike Pompeo announced that the Navy would homeport expeditionary sea base *Hershel "Woody" Williams* (ESB 4) in Souda Bay, Greece, as a permanent assigned warship to the Africa Command.[69] Delivered to the Navy and commissioned in 2020, this ship provides a platform for rotary aircraft and special operations well suited to the interdiction of pirates. In August 2021, the ship conducted maritime security exercise Obangame Express in the Gulf of Guinea.[70] As a floating command center, an ESB provides a base for operations and sensors, enhancing maritime domain awareness of potential illicit activities at sea.

The Caribbean basin has seen illicit trade routes morph over time to take advantage of gaps in law enforcement, from overland routes to use of submersibles to circuitous routes via Africa. As already mentioned, the 2008 Guinea-Bissau coup is illustrative of the shoreside corrupting effect of illicit trade. The United Nations Office on Drugs and Crimes has been monitoring these trends since 1997 and have consistently shown sea and air routes in this region, including the Gulf of Panama, as critical paths in the global flow of cocaine and heroin.[71] Narcotics trafficking is a massive illegal enterprise that in 2017 was estimated to be worth $426 to $652 billion by the think tank Global Financial Integrity.[72] According to the DHS's annual report to Congress, in 2019 the U.S. Coast Guard interdicted 33 metric tons of cocaine in the Caribbean basin and 175 metric tons in the

Eastern Pacific (i.e., Gulf of Panama). Key to these interdictions has been cueing by intelligence sources, then getting a ship at sea positioned for the takedown. The key to making this happen has been the Joint Interagency Task Force South (JIATF-South) established in 1989 and based in Key West, Florida.[73] JIATF-South brings together intelligence agencies like the CIA and Defense Intelligence Agency with operators in the Navy and Coast Guard and regional liaison officials from twelve countries; none among these twelve is African, and the continent's nations' inclusion is long overdue.

Great power competition is real in the region. Most notable in this regard has been China's significant investments and associated influence of local governments. The operational challenge, however, will remain battling illicit trade and suppressing piracy. Success in counter-influence and counter–illicit trade campaigns place a premium on intelligence collection and maritime domain awareness. And when called on, there must be forces on hand able to interdict smugglers or respond to episodic Russian and Chinese military presence in the region. The hallmark of U.S. efforts in this region, however, will be security cooperation efforts: specifically, building the regional capacity for maritime domain awareness, maritime security, and hardening partner nations to nefarious influence campaigns. More than perhaps any other region studied, the illicit trade emanating from and across this region directly harms the most Americans.

### South and Central Pacific

After World War II, the resounding defeat of Japan and the decimation of colonial powers in the region left the Pacific Ocean an American lake. With China's rise this has begun to change, ushering in a return to the geopolitical intrigue of the late 1800s, when Germany, Russia, Japan, the United Kingdom, France, and the United States all vied for Pacific spheres of influence; Spain was already diminished by this time and would be ejected after its defeat in the 1898 Spanish-American War. Germany would follow after its defeat in World War I, losing its possessions in the region. An early example of Pacific intrigue was Russia's ham-handed attempted Hawaiian coup in 1815, which left only the ruins of Russia's Fort Elizabeth on the island of Kauai. The most famous was the slow progression of American dominance in Hawaii, and its eventual annexation in 1898. Trading rights, the whaling industry, and the need for coaling stations in the late 1800s drove the Great Powers' Pacific island grabs.

Echoes of that time can be seen in China's economic statecraft and interest in Pacific islands possessing diplomatic and strategic value. One example is Kiribati, a target in the CCP's diplomatic offensive against Taiwan, which places Chinese space-tracking stations close to sensitive missile testing sites at Kwajalein, Marshall Islands. Additionally, the lucrative Pacific whaling trade of the 1800s has its modern corollary in tuna fishing. More recently, in April 2022 China signed a security agreement with the Solomon Islands undermining decades-long pacts with Australia and posing a potential military risk to the United States. For China, a presence across the Pacific contests assumptions of U.S. suzerainty across the region and threatens militarily important air- and sea-lanes, transpacific routes that U.S. forces would have to cross on the way to any Asian war.

The legacy of World War II largely frames U.S. relations in the region and its obligations. These include territories, compact of free association (COFA) states, and unassociated Pacific island nations—notably Kiribati. U.S. Pacific territories in the South and Central Pacific include Guam, the Commonwealth of Northern Marianas, and American Samoa, with expansive EEZs. Next, the COFA states include the Federated States of Micronesia (FSM), the Republic of the Marshall Islands (RMI), and the Republic of Palau. COFA agreements oblige the United States to provide certain services and economic assistance that the Department of the Interior manages. In return, the United States is granted access for its military and also has the right to foreclose access to any third party's military.[74] Independent Kiribati has a long legacy of close association with the United States, with a military presence on Canton Island until 1976, when U.S. missile-tracking facilities were closed.

All of these islands have legacy military infrastructure, most left over from World War II, that could in short order be useful in a new era of Pacific intrigues. Amid war ruins on Palau's island of Peleliu—site of one of the U.S. Marine Corps' most vicious battles, Bloody Nose Ridge—is an airfield and port. After renovations to the airfield, in September 2019 an Air Force C-130 cargo plane delivered Army soldiers, validating its viability.[75]

Likewise, Canton Island's 6,230-foot runway could also once again become useful for modern maritime patrol aircraft like the P-8A. The range of legacy facilities in places like Yap, Pohnpei, and Chuuk Lagoon include outdated but perhaps once again useful ammunition bunkers, airfields, and ports that could be reconstituted.

Recapitalizing many legacy facilities rapidly is a heavy lift, but the Navy could turn to another World War II legacy of the Pacific for the task—the Seabees. Made famous by John Wayne in a 1944 movie of the same name, the Seabees are a military construction unit that would follow combat units and begin repairs and construction of airfields and ports, occasionally pausing to pick up arms and fight. These construction units' heroism and importance to the Pacific campaign is one reason Admiral Nimitz famously kept on his desk a miniature of their mascot—a fighting bee. Marking a return to its historic roots, on July 1, 2018, the Thirtieth Naval Construction Regiment relocated from Port Hueneme, California, to Guam. Ever since, the Seabees have increased their operations across the Pacific, including renovations in 2020 on the island of Tinian, where on August 5, 1945, the B-29 bomber Enola Gay launched the nuclear attack on Hiroshima, Japan. Renovating legacy infrastructure will keep the Seabees busy, but Chinese pressures are adding even more demands.

Refusing to recognize the PRC, Palau began to feel the sting of CCP displeasure. In 2017, Palau lost significant tourism business when Chinese authorities refused to honor package tour deals. The effect was to energize efforts by Palau to bring U.S. military forces to the nation permanently. In a similar offer, the president of Papua New Guinea, on the sidelines of the 2018 Asia-Pacific Economic Cooperation meeting, offered the United States access to a port on the strategically important Manus Island. Subsequently, the plan was expanded to a partnership with Australia to develop the naval base, and could in time include the colocated commercial airport.[76] Partnership with Australia also has wider benefits in building Pacific island nations' maritime security capacities.

Beginning in August 1984, the Australian government has helped Pacific island nations build up their maritime patrol capacities. For island nations reliant on the sea, Australia's provision of patrol boats and associated support has proven successful in Papua New Guinea, Fiji, FSM, Tonga,

Solomon Islands, Cook Islands, Kiribati, RMI, Palau, Western Samoa, Tuvalu, and Vanuatu. An important aspect of this Pacific Patrol Boat Program was the detailing of officers and enlisted staff with each patrol boat to provide training and logistical support.[77] In 2016, twenty-one replacement 39.5-meter patrol boats were ordered by the Australian government at $242 million; the last Austal-built boat is to be delivered in 2023.[78] This capability in particular has been welcome in fighting illegal fishing.

Illegal fishing, however, is also an increasing issue for the U.S. Coast Guard (USCG), charged with safeguarding the nation's economic rights across its expansive Pacific EEZs. In September 2020, the commandant of the USCG announced the "Illegal, Unreported, and Unregulated Fishing Strategic Outlook." It asserts that 20 percent of catches are in fact illegal, impacting a global trade worth $401 billion and a U.S. commercial fisheries market worth $5.6 billion.[79] The announcement was timely, coming in the wake of a large Chinese fishing fleet operating off the Galapagos Islands in July and the first time in eight years foreign vessels had been intercepted poaching in U.S. Central and Western Pacific EEZs.[80] In the South and Central Pacific waters, tuna is the principal catch, and in 2016 the value of illegal Pacific catches was estimated at $616 million out of a total catch worth $5.3 billion.[81]

An example of how some island economies are reliant on fishing, tuna particularly, is American Samoa, which has been hit economically by several events in the recent past. After the closing of tuna canneries in 2009 and 2016, only Starkist's cannery continues operations on the island, employing 2,439 people (14 percent of the local population), down 45 percent from 2007 to 2018. Most of these downward pressures are due to price competitiveness, but there have also been pressures on supply. Chinese government subsidies have redirected tuna supply away from Samoan canners, and the designation of national marine sanctuaries has reduced the traditional supply to the island.[82] Acknowledging the potential for poaching in U.S. Pacific EEZs, the USCG has been studying the basing of fast-response cutters (FRCs) in American Samoa.

Since 2019 the USCG has been working to build up its presence in the Pacific, partly in response to the threat of poaching in U.S. EEZs. The urgency was underscored in October 2020 when National Security Advisor

Robert O'Brien reiterated the threat from Chinese illegal fishing and the need to enhance our maritime security in the region.[83] The following year, the USCG commissioned three new FRCs to join a large buoy tender in Guam.[84] Building on experience gained from thirty-day extended deployments to the region in 2019, the USCG is looking to use large buoy tenders as mother ships for even longer deployments by FRCs. Building up the capacity to detect poachers and patrol expansive EEZs secures needed resources of island economies dependent on the sea. They thereby establish an environment conducive to deeper regional security partnerships that can mitigate against Chinese encroachment in the region.

Once again the Central and South Pacific is entering the geostrategic stage as great power competition plays out between the United States and China. Tightening common interests with partners in the region will be key, and one way to work toward this goal is to build partners' capacity to secure the fish stocks in their EEZs. Diplomatically, the Pacific Island Forum can be useful in this regard, though it must overcome a split over a dispute in the selection of the group's secretary general in February 2021. It is composed of eighteen island nations in three groupings—Micronesia, Melanesia, and Polynesia. The six closely U.S.-aligned Micronesian nations departed when they were denied the leadership role due them per a rotation plan. The split also cuts across those nations that still recognize Taiwan; the new secretary general, Cook Islands' Henry Puna, who campaigned on friendly relations with Beijing, stated, "China is very present in the Pacific. Unfortunately for a long time, America has not been." The United States will have to address the sense that it is absent in the region and build new bridges there.

For the Navy and the USCG, it is time to recapitalize antiquated wartime infrastructure and update it for modern use. By renewing its access rights among the COFA states, the Navy and USCG can build back a backbone of airfields and ports important to secure critical air and sea corridors to Asia in a conflict. A return to the region also means building networks of partner nations and enhancing their capacity to enforce their EEZ rights. To this end, Australia's Pacific Patrol Boat program is one example worth emulating, in conjunction with improved capacity to patrol the U.S. EEZs.

## Advance (Seize the Initiative)

In order to reset the status quo and push back against the Communist Party of China and the Russian oligarchy, two decisive theaters stand out: the Eastern Mediterranean and the South China Sea. Peacetime U.S. naval action taken in decisive theaters, like pressure points in the martial art Aikido, can enable an economy of force to cause a competitor to change behavior. This requires that the Navy's presence be rebalanced to enable specific targeting of Chinese and Russian national leadership's strategic calculus while attracting new security partners and bolstering alliances.

### Eastern Mediterranean

In the case of Russia, most of the crises since 2008 have occurred in the Eastern Mediterranean region, including the Black Sea. U.S. programs such as the Black Sea Maritime Initiative and enhanced Baltic Integrated Air and Missile Defense have been employed to boost theater posture. In the North Atlantic, predictable Carrier Strike Group and amphibious presence has been coupled with reactivation of the U.S. Second Fleet. This all helps provide necessary maritime command and control capability in the Atlantic.

To affect Russia's strategic calculus, however, a naval presence must put at risk Russian "counter-encirclement efforts" and undermine naval operations that are intended to sow discord among U.S. partner nations. A dedicated U.S. naval force in the Eastern Mediterranean would complicate Russian military adventurism, contribute to mitigating Russian malign influence, and bolster security commitments to NATO and Israel. Such a force would support current NATO standing naval forces, such as Group Two operating in the Mediterranean.[85] Due to differences within NATO over executing great power competition regarding China, however, such a task force would have to be independent from NATO. Its proximity to the Suez Canal and the Black Sea would make such a force a strong guarantor of access to critical ports (e.g., Greece's port of Piraeus) that are increasingly operated by Chinese state-owned entities.

An Eastern Mediterranean task force would have to be structured and postured to affect several key elements of Russia's strategic efforts. In this region, it principally focuses on undermining confidence in Russia as a security partner and weakening its illicit networks by (1) undermining confidence of regional customers in Russian arms; (2) bolstering NATO unity, especially in confronting irregular migration from Africa and the Middle East; (3) confounding and, when necessary, interdicting illicit financial flows and sanctions violations, especially those in place on Syria, Iran, and Libya; and (4) outclassing any naval demonstration by Russia and China in the region. The intent is to undermine Russia (and China) as a reliable security partner, and doing this will require an enhanced naval presence in the region.

Undermining confidence in Russia as a reliable arms supplier will require demonstrating the ineffectiveness of their military hardware, as well as unreliability in sustaining it. Russian-supplied air defense system Pantsir S1 performed poorly against Turkish-supplied drones in Libya in 2020. The flow of Turkish weapons to Libya stopped an offensive by Russian ally warlord Khalifa Haftar to take the capital, and subsequently led to an October 2020 ceasefire with the internationally recognized government in Tripoli.[86] At about the same time a forty-four-day war erupted in September between Russian-supplied and -trained Armenia and Azerbaijan, whose war effort relied heavily on Turkish drones and loitering Israeli munitions to dominate the battlefield.[87] During a meeting with researchers at the Heritage Foundation's Center for National Defense in early 2021, Army analysts detailed how Azerbaijani drones destroyed 1,020 Armenian vehicles in what was the first war determined by unmanned platforms. Col. Scott Shaw, the outgoing head of the Army's Asymmetric Warfare Group, credited Azerbaijan's drones with destroying over $1 billion in Russian hardware, including four S-300 air defense batteries and 250 tanks.[88] In Syria and Libya at least, analysts in part attribute the poor performance to inadequate training before weapon systems were turned over to a customer. To counter this poor performance, Russia would be forced to conduct longer, risky, costly training with customer nations' militaries or proxies with significant diplomatic risks. This wouldn't address technical limitations demonstrated by Azerbaijan's success, however, or the maintenance of sensitive weapon systems.

The goal is not to stanch sales of Russian arms—which are too cheap to cut off completely—but to demonstrate to any competitor Russian arms' inferiority against a U.S. ally or supplied military, and the unreliability of Russia as a security partner. Regarding the effectiveness of the Pantsir S1, much discrediting of that system and Russian support has occurred. Still, Russia has sold S-400 advanced air defense systems to Turkey and operated them in Libya and Syria, and is marketing its Su-57E fifth-generation fighter jets to Turkey and Algeria.[89] Demonstrating their weakness against a Western-supplied and trained military would be needed as well. In the case of Turkey, the consequences are higher, making prevention of a repeat of its S-400 purchase critical. Subsequent to that purchase, Turkey was ejected from the advanced F-35 fighter project, raising questions about its continued interoperability with U.S. platforms as a NATO member.[90] Given the poor performance of Russia's military during its 2022 war with Ukraine, this effort may not be as challenging as it seemed before Russia's invasion.

The second effort focuses on bolstering NATO unity by strengthening its effectiveness. A recent test of this effort has been the humane control of illegal migrant flows at sea. As 2011 protests during the Arab Spring turned to full-blown civil war, conditions deteriorated and Syrian refugees flooded into Europe, peaking in 2015–16. The increased inflow of people foreign to Europe's progressive and Christian culture was a shock to the system that threatened several governments—notably Hungary under Prime Minister Viktor Orbán. Migrant flows are not limited to Syrian refugees, however. Refugees come via three main routes: the western route via Algeria and Morocco into Spain, the central route via Libya into Italy, and the eastern route via Turkey into Greece.[91] Common to all these routes is a final leg that involves movement over water. The summer months see the highest frequency of crossings; in April 2015, deaths peaked at 3,770 in the central route.[92]

Critically, the flow of Syrian refugees exacerbated an already simmering difference within the EU on how to confront irregular migration into Europe. Opinion polls in Poland, Hungary, Greece, and Italy all saw a strong majority viewing migrants as a major threat. Less than a plurality saw it this way in France, Spain, and Germany; nonetheless, overwhelming majorities across Europe were unhappy with the way the crisis had been addressed.[93] This divide often pitted its newest Eastern European members—notably Hungary and Poland—against the more liberal and larger nations of the EU. This had a spillover effect on confidence in NATO, with polls showing a measurable drop across European member states from 2015 to 2019.[94] In fact, this has provided Russia and its proxies an opening to sow discord among NATO members.

NATO secretary general Jens Stoltenberg has called the one million irregular immigrants that entered Europe in 2015 "the greatest migrant and refugee crisis since the Second World War."[95] In response, NATO agreed on February 11, 2016, to send NATO Maritime Group Two to support Greek, Turkish, and EU border agency Frontex to stem the flow in the Aegean Sea.[96] According to the International Organization for Migration of the United Nations, the total migrant flow from 2014 through 2018 (the peak of the crisis) was 1.9 million, with almost 18,000 deaths at sea.[97] Images of drowning children, capsizing overcrowded boats, and masses of immigrants trekking across Europe did much to undermine confidence of Europeans in existing security structures, to Moscow's benefit.

In the summer of 2021, Belorussia was accused by neighbors Poland and Lithuania of using immigrants from Iraq, Syria, and Afghanistan as a political weapon in retaliation for sanctions. Tensions ramped up following the May interdiction of Ryanair flight FR4978 and subsequent arrest of Belorussian dissident Roman Protasevich, who had been outspoken against the flawed presidential elections in the country in 2020.[98] Shocked by this action, the EU enacted sanctions on the Alexander Lukashenko regime in Belorussia in August.[99] Poland and Lithuania have both stated that they see Russia enabling this movement, encouraging and facilitating refugees with promises of entry into Europe.

The third Eastern Mediterranean effort focuses on complicating or interdicting Russia's illicit activities, notably financial flows. Dark money is useful for a range of nefarious purposes—sanctions avoidance, arms trade, political influence, and tax evasion for personal enrichment. All of these purposes have been used by Russian entities—the mafia, government, and otherwise innocent individuals. In 2017 it was estimated that Russian sources control the largest share of dark money, at $1 trillion—off-the-grid money to buy influence and conduct covert operations.

In 2005, gigabytes of files on financial dealings by Mossack Fonseca—an offshore financial provider—were leaked to the press, uncovering the inner workings of dark money. These files, the "Panama Papers," uncovered a network of shell companies, offshore finance entities, and mirror trading schemes that facilitated the movement of billions of dollars across national borders without scrutiny. They also began to link close Putin associates to dark money networks: for example, Sergei Roldugin, a professional cellist and friend of Putin's since the 1970s, was found to control hundreds of millions of dollars.[100] Unsurprisingly, Russian intelligence services have utilized organized criminal syndicates, cyber-hackers, and shadow finance networks not only for personal enrichment but also, importantly, for state activities.

The rise of these nefarious finance networks and their connections to the very top of Russia's political leadership was the focus of Catherine Belton's 2020 book *Putin's People*.[101] The danger is that these financial tools are enabling state-sanctioned assassinations, influence-peddling, and covert movement of military arms and mercenaries.[102] Examples include the poisoning of defector Alexander Litvinenko in London (2006) and contracted operations with the Wagner Group, a private military organization, in Africa and the Middle East. Key hubs for obscuring the origin of Russian dark money flows through the Mediterranean including places like Malta and Cyprus. These networks rely on trusted personal connections to function, as the "Pandora Papers" leaked in October 2021 are showing; notable dark money transactions detailed include those of close Putin associates Oleg Deripaska, Gennady Timchenko, and Peter Kolbin.[103] Exposing these connections can be dangerous. Maltese investigative reporter Daphne Caruana Galizia was assassinated in March 2017 for exposing dark money networks in Malta.[104] Common to operating these networks is a reliance on trusted actors, providing a human link in the dark money chain that can be targeted for interdiction or weakening.

In many cases, domestic laws don't forbid much of the dark money movement. In one notorious case known as "Laundromat," the Moldovan government provided legal schemes to shield regulators while moving $20 billion in dark money into the EU between 2010 and 2014.[105] This provides a second contact point in dark money—compliant governments. Cyprus in particular has played an important role even after a 2013 financial crisis resulted in numerous reforms. Those reforms included a scheme that transferred debt into stock holdings that gave the sizable Russian diaspora holding them greater influence on the island's banking sector and politics. Reflecting the growing size of the Russian diaspora and its political interests, in 2017 the "I the Citizen" political party was established by Russian expats.[106] While doing this is perfectly normal in democratic systems, the specific function of Cyprus in dark money and its connection to the livelihood of the Russian diaspora does raise concerns.

The movement of dark money, however, can rapidly adjust to sanctions and around noncomplicit governments, making the physical nodes in the network more vulnerable. As such, U.S. sanctions will be only partially effective, such as in the cases of those against the agencies and individuals associated with the 2018 poisoning of defector Sergey Skripal in the United Kingdom and the 2020 attempted assassination of political activist Aleksey Navalny.[107] A maritime presence incorporating special forces can add pressure on these networks by interdicting what the dark money enables—the movement of arms, illicit trade, and support for mercenaries such as Wagner Group. It would have to be able to prevent repeats of the October 2020 shipment of oil to Syria from Iran escorted by two Russian naval ships in violation of EU sanctions.[108] The oil supplied from Iran is critical for the survival of the Assad regime in Syria, a Russian proxy. By escorting this Syria-bound oil, Russia's government further exposed itself to sanctions and economic isolation. Sanctions and attacks on the dark money networks alone, however, have not worked in stopping such illicit activities.

The final effort in this region is to enhance naval presence so as to demonstrate the shortcomings of any competitor's military and enable the above actions. Specifically, a sustained naval presence can best monitor, confound, and deter Russian, and increasingly Chinese, maritime activities in the region. Such a naval force would have to be equipped and authorized to conduct a range of operations. These operations would degrade trust in the network of illicit financiers by interdicting physical transactions (i.e., suitcases of cash) and confounding the physical movement of enablers. This will place a heavy reliance on special forces and boarding teams, as well as experts in identifying and tracking key players in the dark finance network. The intent is to establish a maritime network that can take on Russian illicit networks. The commander of joint special forces and commander of U.S. and NATO forces in Afghanistan, Gen. Stanley McChrystal, describes this lesson thus: "It takes a network to defeat a network." At the same time, this naval force would have to be sized to match any Russian or Chinese naval deployments to assure deterrence and provide a visible reminder of the more capable force. At the high end would be the episodic deployment of a Russian carrier strike group, and Chinese surface action groups like the three warships that visited Greece in 2017. While both China and Russia are increasing their presence here, if CCP military interests remain fixed elsewhere, the Russian navy will be of greater military concern through 2035.

### South China Sea

China's southern coast is dominated by Guangdong province, which has long been a doorway to the Chinese mainland as a conduit for global trade and ideas. This has not always endeared the region to its overlords in Beijing, especially the province's freewheeling economic proclivities. The last imperial dynasty—the Qing—eventually succumbed in 1911 to foreign ideas and a leader from the region—Sun Yat-sen. After severe repression following the June 1989 Tiananmen Square massacre of student protesters seeking democratic reforms, Deng Xiaoping went on his 1992 "southern tour" and electrified the country to open up and reform its economy.[109] Hong Kong and Guangdong together are the engine of the modern Chinese economic miracle, and strategically important as a springboard for military operations against Taiwan.

So it is really no surprise that China's provocations in the South China Sea have increased markedly in the years since the departure of U.S. forces from their Philippine bases in 1991. This began with China's occupation of and construction of facilities on the Philippines' Mischief Reef in 1994, which were further expanded in 1999, and it culminated in the 2015 massive island-building campaign.[110] Such activities contribute to China's "counter-intervention" strategy in two key ways: they bolster the isolation of Taiwan both diplomatically and militarily, and they enhance the PLAN's posture in case of war over Taiwan. These man-made island garrisons also enhance a sustained CCP maritime presence that undermines U.S. security partnerships. Despite promises to the contrary made by Chairman Xi

Jinping to President Barack Obama in 2015, China now has an archipelago of man-made islands with naval and air bases backing what Secretary of State Michael Pompeo has called China's illegal maritime claims.[111]

Regaining control of Taiwan is a stated CCP core national interest and principal strategic direction. It was also a major inspiration for wide-ranging PLA military reforms.[112] In recent years, the danger of conflict has taken on added urgency as the People's Liberation Army (PLA) has out-paced the capacity of U.S. and allied conventional deterrence. However, success in such a conflict is far from certain, and an apparently incremental strategy is being pursued at minimum risk to the survival of the CCP.[113] Control of the South China Sea plays a key role in this approach and is driving the PLA's effort to build a modern military by 2035.[114] Rather than taking on China's sizable maritime forces, a smarter approach would lever-age the region's political, economic, and security dynamics.

For the United States to remain a relevant player in the region and be able to safeguard its interests, greater presence and engagement are neces-sary. Key will be regaining a military balance favorable to the United States and its partners in the region, one of which—the Philippines—is a treaty ally. This is especially important in the peacetime competition playing out over clusters of atolls and rocks that is dividing the Association of Southeast Asian Nations (ASEAN). Effectively engaging the region requires balanc-ing Chinese economic heft in the region with a new bargain attractive to security partners—especially those with maritime disputes with China, like Malaysia, Indonesia, Brunei, the Philippines, and Vietnam. According to World Trade Organization 2020 data, all five claimant states rely heavily on trade with China despite geostrategic differences, and will likely remain this way. The United States will have to balance partners' economic inter-ests with the need to secure a favorable military posture that complicates any effort by the CCP against Taiwan.

The stakes are very high for the United States. CCP dominion over the South China Sea and its critical sea-lanes could make China the hegemon of the Indo-Pacific.[115] Should the United States continue its past reactive or relatively passive approach in this peacetime contest, it risks miscommuni-cating its interests, and in turn could lead to miscalculation on China's part and potentially a long and costly war. To avoid this, the United States must pursue a three-pronged approach: (1) improve maritime security capacity of partner nations through a range of initiatives in concert with allies such as Japan; (2) enhance the deterrent value of the current U.S. military presence by enhancing existing security partnerships and increasing deployed forces and frequency of exercises with partner nations; and (3) develop an attractive economic alternative to Chinese debt diplomacy and its corrupting influence. Unlike the other regions discussed, proximity to China necessarily makes economics an inescapable element of any effective engagement in this region.

China's growing military presence in the region has been enabled by its economic growth. The pursuit of greater growth has led the CCP to seek significant and expanding economic inroads in Southeast Asia. Spearheaded by the BRI's Maritime Silk Road and Silk Road Economic Belt, the balance of CCP economic investment has been here. Under this initiative, 24 percent ($147 billion) of all BRI investment and construction contracts through 2018 have gone to Southeast Asia, led by Singapore (as a financial hub), Malaysia, Indonesia, and Laos.[116] How such events play out with ASEAN is of utmost economic importance. For one thing, ASEAN is the United States' fourth-largest trading partner after Canada, Mexico, and China, as well as China's second-largest trading partner after the United States. With ASEAN's unity uncertain and with regional partners questioning U.S. commitments in the face of increasingly aggressive Chinese maritime activities, the South China Sea is clearly a critical maritime arena for great power competition. In the most notable example, Beijing attempted to use codevelopment and infrastructure investments to lure Manila into relinquishing its legal rights in its economic exclusive zone.[117] Failing this, the PLAN has backed more coercive approaches to expanding its military footprint in the region at the added expense of U.S. regional credibility.

Perhaps because of China's overwhelming mass economically and militarily, Malaysian prime minister Najib Razak saw potential utility of a so-called Blue Ocean strategy.[118] According to the 2004 book with that title, a Blue Ocean strategy seeks to develop new markets to unlock new demand in place of competing over market share.[119] This would seemingly solve two issues for Najib, allowing him to avoid confrontation with China while securing Malaysian prosperity. Critically, Malaysian domestic politics are

# Map 6. Major Developments in Chinese Naval Expansion

China has been expanding and reinforcing its naval bases, both close to home and deep into the South China Sea.

**1** **Zhanjiang South Sea Fleet HQ.** Significant pier expansion for additional ships and shore support facilities.

**2** **Yulin Naval Base.** Pier expansion to accommodate a carrier battle group and dry dock to accommodate next-generation Chinese super carriers.

**2** **Yulin Submarine Base.** Pier expansion and shore facilities to accommodate additional submarines and ships of additional carrier battle groups.

**3** **Fiery Cross.** Construction of 10,252-foot runway and port with 4,350-foot pier space; logistic support facilities added with fixed-weapon positions.

**4** **Subi Reef.** Construction of 9,800-foot runway and port with 3,650-foot pier space; logistic support facilities added with fixed-weapon positions.

**5** **Mischief Reef.** Construction of 8,900-foot runway and port with 6,370-foot pier space; logistic support facilities added with fixed-weapon positions.

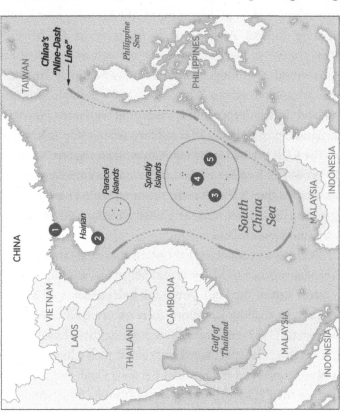

SOURCE: Author's research

shaped by a large electorate in Eastern Malaysia deriving significant monies from offshore resources in the South China Sea. And Malaysia has not been able to develop a new market outside Chinese competition. As a consequence, Malaysia will invariably have to contest Chinese encroachment in its South China Sea waters. Aside from Malaysia, other countries have yet to pursue a Blue Ocean strategy, and attempts will likely prove illusory against a behemoth like China already competing across many sectors. Absent a viable Blue Ocean option, the claimants have various security structures at their disposal.

Similar to Russia's aversion to NATO, China has attempted to weaken U.S. alliances, notably with the Philippines. To this end, past U.S. ambivalence regarding maritime disputes has facilitated the weakening of its security partnerships, and an undermining of ASEAN unity over South China Sea maritime disputes. And the cracks are growing: ASEAN's so-called ten-nation consensus has split into claimant and nonclaimant camps,[120] Philippine president Rodrigo Duterte has walked away from a win in maritime arbitration against China to curry economic enticements,[121] and Thailand drifted deeper into China's orbit with arms purchases since the downgrading of the U.S.-Thai military relationship following a 2014 coup.[122] The CCP is aided in its effort to weaken regional security structures by economic leverage backed by military intimidation. One structure has avoided the CCP's ire so far, however—the Five Powers Defense Arrangement (FPDA) between the United Kingdom, Australia, Malaysia, Singapore, and New Zealand.

The FPDA is a product of two historical events—an undeclared war over the independence of Malaysia and Singapore, and the withdrawal of British forces east of the Suez. Amid the independence of Malaysia and the eventual split creating Singapore, there occurred an undeclared war—the Konfrontasi (1963–66)—over incorporating these Malay lands into a greater Indonesia. The effort failed and in part fuels a lingering distrust in Jakarta of Australia, and the biennial Bersama Gold exercises conducted in support of the FPDA.[123] Looking ahead from its fiftieth anniversary in 2021, three questions have lingered regarding FPDA's future role in the region.[124] These include concerns over low public awareness in each of the five capitals, weakening interoperability given that only three of the partners operate F-35 jet fighters, and debates over the arrangement's enlargement to add the United States. This last issue is perhaps the more contentious, as Malaysia and Singapore have feared abandonment, while Australia jealously guards its role and access to bases in Malaysia—such as Butterworth Airfield. As a claimant state, defense of Malaysian claims in the South China Sea against China could conceivably trigger FPDA consultations and potential concerted action. As it is today, the FPDA is not a mutual defense treaty but does pose an eventual challenge to Chinese encroachment into Malaysian waters.

With or without mutual defense obligations, arrangements like the FPDA provide a mechanism for enhancing limited regional maritime security capacity without a direct U.S. presence. It does this by enabling information exchanges that enhance the operational effectiveness of limited maritime forces. Without adequate maritime security forces, however—Navy and Coast Guard—the information sharing is meaningless and unable to deter Chinese encroachment. Capacity among the claimants will have to be built up, and the United States and its allies like Japan have a role.

Security cooperation improves partner nations' capacity for maritime security and is a tool that can level the playing field against the Chinese Coast Guard and maritime militia. Security cooperation includes favorable financing of military arms sales, training, and exercises that together enhance a partner nation's security capacity, as well as interoperability. The Defense Security Cooperation Agency (DSCA) within the DoD is charged with advancing U.S. defense and foreign policy interests by building the capacity of foreign partners in order to encourage and enable allies and partners to respond to shared challenges.[125] Increasingly, the five claimant states with China over maritime rights in the South China Sea have turned to the United States while increasing their defense budgets, despite overwhelming economic ties to China. Over the years 2008–17, claimant states have increased both their military inventories and defense budgets: Indonesia (+99.5 percent budget, +57 percent inventory), Vietnam (+75.5 percent budget, +15 percent inventory), the Philippines (+50.3 percent budget, +38 percent inventory), Malaysia (–18.5 percent budget, +19 percent inventory), and Brunei (–7.9 percent budget, +108 percent inventory). The principal arms suppliers to Southeast Asia from 1999 to 2018 include Russia, at 26 percent overall, mostly to Vietnam; the United States, at 20 percent; and China, at 6.3 percent.[126] Despite its small scale, Chinese arms exports are targeted to neighbor countries, with Pakistan making up over half of these sales from 2010 to 2020.[127] The DSCA is only one arm of security cooperation; another is the State Department's Bureau of Political-Military (PM) Affairs, a critical partner overseeing the sale and transfer of armaments overseas.

Amid Chinese island building in 2015, the Maritime Security Initiative (MSI) was announced by the secretary of defense at the Shangri-La Dialogue in Singapore, which has become an annual premier event for senior world defense leaders to launch regional security policies. MSI was established specifically to help claimant states secure their maritime rights by facilitating transfer of capabilities that enhance maritime domain awareness and police their waters.[128] In the president's fiscal year 2021 budget, MSI was aligned to the National Defense Strategy Implementation accounts, signaling its continued importance to this strategy.[129] MSI was controversial at its inception because it focused security cooperation resources on the maritime claimant states, but it has endured due to support from the claimant states themselves while remaining strategically relevant. Since its inception, Vietnam has benefited from the transfer of two decommissioned U.S. Coast Guard cutters worth $58 million, Malaysia received 12 ScanEagle drones worth $19.3 million, and the Philippines has built a network of coastal surveillance sites and a national maritime information fusion center in Manila with U.S. assistance. Japan too has joined the effort and transferred patrol boats to Indonesia worth $20.2 million. Such assistance from the United States and its allies is helping claimant states better police their own waters. As successful as these programs have been, however, they have not kept pace with the Chinese maritime capacities. More is needed that enhances existing military presence.

The South China Sea is open for competition, with its wide-open maritime space and deep waters surrounded by nations with various allegiances. Such a key strategic theater provides the potential for incremental Chinese peacetime successes in undermining U.S. partnerships and credibility while being a favorable setting for a major naval showdown. Like the Fulda Gap in the Cold War era, peacetime and wartime operations conducted on the South China Sea will be a key factor in determining the fate of Taiwan. The PLA Navy (PLAN) and CCP have invested tremendous resources in this key strategic maritime theater. The most advanced Chinese naval platforms are based there, leading-edge joint operations are practiced there, and PLAN senior leaders have served there. In fact, both of the last two PLAN commanders, stretching back to 2006, served previously as commanders of the South Seas Fleet based in Zhanjiang on the China mainland's southern coast.

In a prolonged battle over Taiwan, PLA control of the surrounding waters and airspace would be needed to secure the landings and win the subsequent land campaign. This makes controlling the East and South China Seas critical to Chinese military planners. Without logistical support, PLA forces fighting in Taiwan would eventually succumb. The shallow waters and proximity of key U.S. ally Japan's military forces in the nearby Ryukyu Islands mitigate the opportunity value of the East China Sea in an arena for incremental peacetime contests. Given this, the East China Sea theater affords little opportunity given a relatively fixed tactical and strategic dynamic.

In peacetime confrontations, a tactic often used by the CCG is shouldering, which requires using one's own ship to physically move another's. In such cases, the size of the ship matters, and the CCG has some of the largest cutters in the world. At the same time, the CCG has a huge lead over any other coast guard or maritime police force in Southeast Asia.[130] In an unusual move, as maritime militia massed at Whitsun Reef to the South, two PLAN *Houbei*-class missile boats relieved CCG cutters as they drove off a commercial vessel carrying reporters in waters off Palawan in the Philippines.[131] The use of PLAN vessels in this way could be unremarkable. If, however, it represents a change in Chinese tactics it could be more of a concern. Such a change could be caused by the increased U.S. maritime presence in the region and partner nations emboldened by the successful 2020 completion of survey operations conducted by the chartered ship *West Capella* in Malaysia's EEZ. It is important to note that tactics evolve constantly.

A substantial buildup of maritime capacity has unfolded in China's south, including commercial shipping as well as military infrastructure ashore. Most notable has been the growth of commercial piers and increased numbers of ferries on Hainan Island. Thomas Shugart, an adjunct senior fellow at the Center for a New American Security, has noted the buildup of "large roll-on/roll-off ferries" that can be activated by the PLAN for military sealift.[132] Open-source satellite images clearly show a remarkable expansion of port facilities and numbers of large roll-on/roll-off ferries operating out of Hainan Island and other southern ports that could just as easily support military operations in Taiwan if called into service.

The growth of the CCG and maritime militia has also been remarkable. Andrew Erickson has exposed the extent to which the Chinese maritime militia has matured operationally and grown in size, with eighty-four of the most modern ships based at Sansha City on Woody Island 175 miles southeast of Hainan Island.[133] The bottom line: to compete in peacetime, it is necessary for the United States and its allies to neutralize the effectiveness of coordinated PLAN, CCG, and maritime militia operations.

Most troubling, however, have been the PLAN's annual naval and maritime joint warfare exercises in the South China Sea. In these exercises, the PLAN has increasingly worked with the PLA Air Force (PLAAF) and the PLA Rocket Force to practice coordinated strikes on allied warships.[134] This includes the operational testing in August 2020 of antiship ballistic missiles against a moving naval target south of Hainan Island.[135] Such coordinated operations, which were also attempted by the Soviets in the 1980s, have the potential to overwhelm a ship or even a battlegroup's defenses and greatly increase the chance of a kill. They also have the advantage of enhancing the lethality of shore-based Chinese assets in a naval battle.

The South Sea Fleet has seen appreciable modernization and growth in numbers. As of August 2020, this fleet included the PLAN's first operational aircraft carrier, its only four nuclear ballistic submarines, its two most modern nuclear attack submarines, its four largest and most capable amphibious transport warships, and some of the most modern escorts for a total of 118 warships.[136] This force is likely to grow with the addition of an anticipated new dry dock at the Yulin naval base on Hainan Island that will be capable of servicing the next-generation PLAN aircraft carrier, the Type 003.[137]

In addition, the completion of massive dredging operations and construction of port and airfield facilities at Fiery Cross, Mischief Reef, and Subi Reef in early 2018 enabled the PLAN and CCG to sustain a greatly enlarged presence along the so-called nine-dash line marking CCP claims to the entirety of the South China Sea.[138] The sizable nuclear submarine presence at Yulin also indicates a strong emphasis on undersea operations in the region. There is a strong likelihood that the PLAN is developing the South China Sea into a bastion for its strategic missile submarines. This would be similar to what the Soviets did to defend their strategic missile submarines in the Arctic and adds strategic importance to this theater of operations, as it would allow the Chinese to secure their second strike capacity and nuclear deterrent forces.[139] From such a bastion, the PLAN's Type 96 ballistic missile submarines armed with the newest JL-3 missiles could reach Alaska and the U.S. West Coast.[140] Assuming that the PLAN continues to advance the range of its submarine-launched ballistic missiles, the entirety of the United States could soon be reached from a South China Sea bastion.

Although the PLAN has demonstrably improved logistics, readiness, and command and control, it continues to manage all such deployments from PLAN headquarters in Beijing. While this enables coordination with the Ministry of Foreign Affairs and state-owned shipping company COSCO, among others, command and control that is so distant from the operational units and their support units can be problematic in a crisis.[141] Recent PLA reforms have given rise to theater commands that approximate U.S. combatant commands, as the PLAN continues to refine its distant sea operations or out-of-area deployments that began in earnest in 2008. How such a command structure performs in multiple overseas crises or in a conflict remains to be seen, and it could evolve into theater commands outside China. One possibility would be a new theater command in the Indian Ocean centered on the naval base at Djibouti.

This maritime region is important to the CCP as a strategic theater in realizing its ambitions over Taiwan while undermining U.S.-Asian alliances, and as a springboard for wider maritime ambitions in the Pacific and Indian Oceans. To respond, an action plan is needed that leverages partner nations' concerns over Chinese encroachment while not forcing an explicit choice that diminishes economic benefits for China. That said, a Blue Ocean strategy alone will not work against a China encroaching in every domain, and which market claimant states could enter or create. Backed by effective diplomacy for a rules-based order supporting free and open markets, an expanded naval presence can slow Chinese encroachment and mitigate its worse influences.

A persistent naval presence is needed in the South China Sea to monitor, anticipate Chinese challenges, and preempt with shows of force. During peak exercise and fishing season (February through October), the force would swell in numbers of surface combatants (guided missile frigates [FFGs] and littoral combat ships [LCSs]) to include an aircraft carrier strike group. During the lighter operational season, the aircraft carrier could be replaced by an amphibious ship optimized for air operations (e.g., landing helicopter assault ships [LPDs]). While the actual composition would unavoidably change, it would have to include an air element (sea-based and shore-based) that is strong enough to outclass any immediate air challenge to its operations and a submarine component. This would likely mean sustaining an aircraft carrier strike group in the Western Pacific not unlike the carrier presence maintained in the Persian Gulf until the mid-2010s. Eventually, extra-large unmanned submarines (XLUUVs) and a task-specific scout platform employing mostly unmanned platforms would be operated in this theater to pace the large number of maritime militia, Chinese Coast Guard, and PLAN. At a minimum, the task force would have to be resourced on any given day to ensure its ability to monitor and make an adequate display at one of three disputed features (e.g., Scarborough Shoal, Second Thomas Shoal, and South Luconia Shoals). Such a minimum force would likely include three FFGs/LCSs with a lead destroyer or cruiser, maritime patrol aircraft, LPD, or like ship with embarked special forces to conduct vessel boarding and limited small island resupply, and two submarines.

## Conclusion

To compete against two global maritime great powers, the United States will have to act to hold, build, or advance its interests according to risk and opportunity. To best judge these factors and match appropriate actions, the United States needs a narrow geographic focus. This consists of eight key maritime theaters where the maritime competition with China and Russia is playing out. To sustain military advantage and economic interests, the United States must pace the threat in the Arctic, North Atlantic, Indian Ocean, and Northeast Asia. At the same time, there is the opportunity to secure interests and build an advantageous military posture in two oceanic regions—the Caribbean to the Gulf of Guinea, and across the Central and South Pacific. The greatest urgency, however, is for decisive action in the Eastern Mediterranean and South China Sea due to these regions' centrality to Russian and Chinese strategies and rising risks. The challenge now turns to matching forces to these regions appropriate for the missions expected to be executed.

# CHAPTER 5

# Posture, Presence, and Platforms

⊶⊷⊶

*We sleep peaceably in our beds at night only because rough men stand ready to do violence on our behalf.*

—Attributed to George Orwell

By contesting the United States below the level of armed conflict, both great power competitors avoid U.S. military strengths by operating in a Navy blind spot. Peacetime U.S. naval action taken in decisive theaters, like pressure points in the martial art Aikido, can enable an economy of force to cause a competitor to change behavior. This requires that the Navy's presence be rebalanced to enable specific targeting of Chinese and Russian national leadership's strategic calculus while attracting new security partners and bolstering alliances.

Ever since promulgation of the 2018 National Defense Strategy, a concept called Dynamic Force Employment has ostensibly provided a framework for the execution of such missions. To be effective, however, such operations must have a lasting impact on the strategic calculus of leadership in Moscow and Beijing. Preventing a repeat of Russia's interventions in Syria and Ukraine, as well as China's South China Sea island-building campaign, requires a presence both significant and sustained. With respect to China, the size of China's maritime forces precludes a force-on-force response; a better option is required.

The last chapter provided a global maritime framework for accomplishing the above tasks. In it, three categories of maritime theaters were identified, with priority given to the South China Sea and Eastern Mediterranean. In these two decisive theaters, dedicated U.S. naval task forces would draw on lessons learned from experiences of the Combined Joint Task Force–Horn of Africa and Central Command's Naval Task

Forces in the Persian Gulf. To ensure mission focus while not alienating some partners that are wary of participating in great power competition, these task forces would initially be limited to U.S. participation. Only after registering measurable successes should options to include allies be entertained, and at the request of partner nations. In short, act first, earn credibility through results, then grow the effort.

While prioritizing presence in decisive theaters, the Navy obviously will have to be present in other places and respond to crises there. When responding elsewhere, however, it must not detract from maintaining a persistent presence in these two decisive theaters. The DoD mechanism for ensuring this is called Global Force Management (GFM).[1] Today, however, the GFM process is driven by risk calculations of the geographic combatant commands, such as Central Command, which is responsible for the Middle East. Each geographic command is responsible for ensuring adequate forces for potential war and near-term military objectives in its particular corner of the world. To put it another way, GFM prejudices force assignments to the detriment of effecting a long-term global competitive strategy. To fix this, the DoD has to reform the GFM process.

Before GFM reforms can be contemplated, the structure on which military presence is conceived must be addressed. The GFM process is aligned to the six existing geographic combatant commands that in turn are defined by the Unified Command Plan (UCP), which is approved by the president. As of December 2021, these geographic commands include North Command at Peterson Air Force Base, Colorado; South Command in Miami, Florida; European Command at Patch Barracks in Stuttgart, Germany; Africa Command at Kelley Barracks, also in Stuttgart, Germany; Central Command at MacDill Air Force Base, Florida; and Indo-Pacific Command at Camp H. M. Smith, Hawaii. South Central, and Africa Command are unique in that the headquarters are not located in the area of responsibilities. This is due to fiscal constraints as well as political considerations in finding a host country while not alienating U.S. presence across its region of responsibility. For regional political reasons, Israel was considered within European Command until January 2021. But as Arab relations began to normalize with Israel through the successful Abraham Accords, this was changed to align Israel to Central Command's

# Map 7. U.S. Navy Operating Areas: Current and Future

● Current major operational bases
● Proposed future operational bases
■ Fleet concentration areas since 2001
■ Decisive theaters for sustained increased naval presence
— Large-scale exercises and dynamic force employment

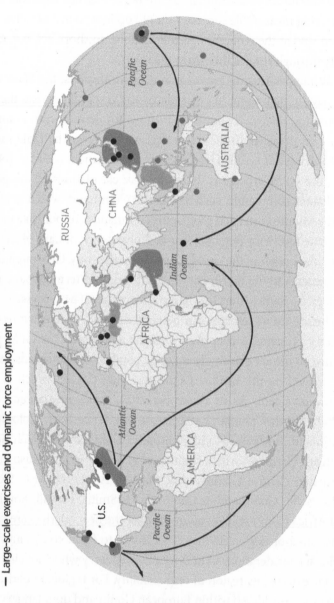

**SOURCE:** Heritage Foundation research.

area of responsibilities.[2] As the names imply, the geographic commands are focused on dividing responsibilities principally according to terrestrial national boundaries. The UCP also covers a second category of joint commands—functional commands.

Functional commands, such as Transportation Command, provide unique capabilities to the geographic commands on a global scale. As of December 2021, the functional commands include Transportation Command, Special Forces Command, and Strategic Command, which oversees nuclear deterrent operations. Since 2010, two domain-oriented vice capability or geographically focused joint commands have been established—Cyber Command and Space Command. The funding of each joint command's operations is from the respective services (Navy, Air Force, etc.) to execute joint exercises, contingencies, training, and specific operations.[3] The Navy has since aligned its maritime operations and structured its fleets according to the geographic commands. This may not be the most effective construct for executing a sustained global maritime strategy.

Based on current geographic command structures, there are several geostrategic and maritime oddities the Navy has to work around. For one, the Indian Ocean is shared by Africa, Central, and Indo-Pacific Command. Again due to political concerns, India and Pakistan remain in different geographic commands even though India has a regional presence spanning all three commands. In a similar way, Arctic operations necessarily cross the European, Indo-Pacific, and North Commands. The maritime connections between South America, notably Brazil, and Western Africa are shared between Africa and Southern commands. This occurs because the lines drawn on a map do not consider the maritime domain an interconnected domain. Had this been the case, as seen earlier, the Navy's numbered fleets' areas of responsibilities would look different.

There is recent precedent for the Navy changing its current numbered fleet structure. The Navy's numbered fleets are commanded by three-star vice admirals, who are supported by logistic and operational subordinate commands. Importantly, fleet commanders sometimes operate from a flagship; today only the aging Seventh Fleet's *Blueridge* (LCC-19) and Sixth Fleet's *Mount Whitney* (LCC-20) serve as afloat fleet commands. Change is nothing new, the most recent being the 2018 reestablishment of the Second

# Map 8. Key U.S. Naval Installations

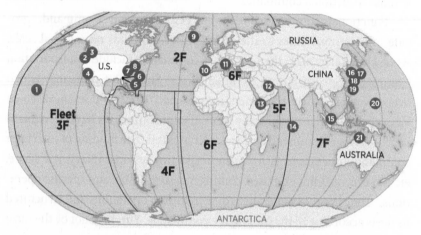

1. **Joint Base Pearl Harbor-Hickham, HI**
   U.S. Pacific Fleet headquarters
2. **Naval Base Kitsap, WA**
3. **Naval Station Everett, WA**
4. **Naval Base San Diego and Naval Base Coronado, CA**
   U.S. Third Fleet headquarters
5. **Naval Station Mayport, FL**
   U.S. Fourth Fleet headquarters
6. **Naval Submarine Base King's Bay, GA**
7. **Naval Base Norfolk and Joint Expeditionary Base Little Creek, VA**
   U.S. Fleet Forces Command and U.S. Second Fleet headquarters
8. **Naval Submarine Base New London, CT**
9. **Keflavik, Iceland—Expeditionary Maritime Operations Center**
10. **Naval Station Rota, Spain**
11. **Naval Support Activity Gaeta, Italy**
    U.S. Sixth Fleet headquarters
12. **Naval Support Activity, Bahrain**
    U.S. Fifth Fleet headquarters
13. **Lemonnier, Djibouti—Camp Lemonnier**
14. **Diego Garcia—Navy Support Facility Diego Garcia**
15. **Singapore—Commander Logistics Group Western Pacific**
16. **Buson, South Korea—Fleet Activities Chinhae Navy Base**
17. **U.S. Fleet Activity Yokosuka, Japan**
    U.S. Seventh Fleet headquarters
18. **U.S. Fleet Activity Sasebo, Japan**
19. **Okinawa, Japan—Naval Base White Beach**
20. **Naval Base Guam—Navy Expeditionary Force Command Pacific headquarters**
21. **Darwin, Australia—Marine Rotational Force Darwin**

**NOTE:** Fleet boundaries are approximate.
**SOURCE:** Heritage Foundation research.

Fleet to address resurgent Russian naval activities in the North Atlantic.[4] Before this, in 2008, the Fourth Fleet responsible for maritime South America was reestablished. Conditions warrant that the Navy consider a new numbered fleet structure that considers long-term trends out to 2050 and the regional prioritization for great power competition. With this in mind, the Navy's current six numbered fleets would be reassigned to each of eight maritime regions laid out in chapter 4. This would see the Second Fleet covering the North Atlantic, Arctic, and Baltic, while the Sixth Fleet would be constrained to the Mediterranean, the Black Sea, and portions of the Red Sea proximate to the Suez Canal. The Fourth Fleet would see its area of responsibility cover the seam between South and Africa Commands across the Caribbean to Gulf Guinea. The Fifth Fleet would expand from the Persian Gulf and Arabian Sea to cover all of the Indian Ocean, while the Seventh Fleet would focus on operations in Northeast Asia and North Pacific. The Third Fleet would relinquish its responsibilities in the North Pacific while expanding into the South and Central Pacific. Finally, to keep pace with the rapidly growing Chinese naval presence and the strategic importance of maritime Southeast Asia the First Fleet would be reestablished to cover this important region and Australia.

As the Navy ponders how it might best compete with China in maritime Southeast Asia, the lessons of the Battle of Java Sea are especially relevant. A reconstituted First Fleet initially operating from an at-sea flagship would focus on expanding port access, developing regional supply and maintenance networks, improving regional familiarity, and growing operational relationships with partners. For a region roughly approximating the continental United States, a dedicated fleet would be better positioned to set the theater for success in peacetime competition and potential combat operations against the PLAN. The Seventh Fleet, based two thousand miles away in Yokosuka, Japan, could then focus on geographically proximate flashpoints and set the theater for potential Taiwan, Korean Peninsula, or Russian contingencies.

Pursuing a new maritime paradigm can focus limited naval forces most effectively for global naval operations. This would see the proposed numbered fleet structure used for allocating forces in a reformed GFM process rather than regional combatant commands. In turn, naval forces would be allocated annually to one of eight maritime regions led by a numbered fleet supporting specific geographic commander requests—not unlike the functional commands. As such, should the Department of Defense treat the maritime as a domain, then the Navy too should become a global operational command, not unlike Space or Cyber Commands, providing unique, domain-centered capabilities. Of course this will come with added costs to adjust and grow current force structures, but it would be less costly and disruptive than wholesale review of the joint force structure as governed by the 1986 Goldwater-Nichols Act.

## Great Power Competition Requires an Improved Naval Force Posture

The U.S. way of war depends on secure air- and sea-lanes to move men and matériel to a fight. The tyranny of distances involved requires a significant investment and recapitalization of Cold War (and even some World War II) bases that were once considered irrelevant. The focus of today's logistic network and posture must change from focusing on efficiencies to enhancing the resilience of military basing or posture. Specifically, DoD and Navy internal processes must become more responsive to new basing opportunities, must better leverage other agencies to enhance forward posture, and must increase the Navy's organic capacity to recapitalize antiquated infrastructure in order to build a dispersed basing posture more resilient to attack. As laid out in chapter 4, the maritime theaters in most need of investment include the Caribbean to Gulf of Guinea maritime corridor, and the South and Central Pacific—the *build* regions.

Despite the advent of great power competition and the 2012 Rebalance to the Asia-Pacific, the intervening years have seen little growth in or diversification of the Navy's basing network. There are signs things are changing, however. At his change of command, outgoing Naval Forces Europe-Africa Commander Adm. James Foggo III called the increased competition in his area of responsibility "the Fourth Battle of the Atlantic."[5] This increased competition has led to improvements at a Cold War airbase at Keflavik, Iceland, to support renewed maritime patrols in the North Atlantic.[6]

While the challenge in Europe is largely to deter a land war with naval operations playing a supporting role, the maritime environment is very different in Asia. Since withdrawing from bases in the Philippines in 1991, the center of gravity for U.S. forces in the Pacific has been in Northeast Asia. This posture is vulnerable to Chinese ballistic and cruise missile saturation attack. Additionally, it engenders long supply lines that will be stressed to ensure prompt response to crises and natural disasters across a massive area of responsibility. The need to find new basing and posture options to mitigate these threats is palpable. However, despite recent offers by Papua New Guinea for a base on Manus Island and by the Republic of Palau for permanent basing of U.S. forces, the only significant growth in basing has been the Marine Rotational Forces in Darwin, Australia, which is as far away from the South China Sea as U.S. bases in Guam. Indo-Pacific Command has attempted to address this posture challenge.

Several recent commanders of U.S. Indo-Pacific Command (INDOPACOM), notably Adm. Philip Davidson, have made clear that a new posture construct is required to meet the challenges from China and Russia in the Indo-Pacific.[7] Admiral Davidson has stressed that what is needed is a more distributed posture of forces sustained by resilient logistics, capable of interconnected shore and naval long-range fires, and highly mobile for survivability.[8] As Chinese and Russian naval activity moves farther into the Pacific, they jeopardize critical lines of communication, creating a need to recapitalize bases in the Central Pacific. To this end, INDOPACOM has proposed a package of initiatives called Regain the Advantage to secure logistic routes, bolster allies in East Asia, and improve military effectiveness by enhancing integrated air defense capability in Guam, increasing the arsenal of long-range precision munitions, and developing infrastructure west of the dateline.[9] Davidson's five-year, $20 billion proposal is modeled on the European Deterrence Initiative, which has invested $22 billion in Europe since Russia's 2014 annexation of Crimea. While remarkable in its detail and scope, Regain the Advantage represents a request that would have to be executed on INDOPACOM's behalf by the various services (e.g., the Navy).

Combatant Command budgets, such as INDOPACOM, are facilitated through its Service Component Commands, such as the Pacific Fleet.

Those service component commands request the allocation of requested funds via their parent service headquarters in the Pentagon, where the personnel with expertise required for budget management and accounting reside. So in the case of Regain the Advantage, items such as maritime strike Tomahawk clearly aligned to the Navy would come from the Navy's budget. Things get murkier and more contested among the service branches in funding large-ticket, multiyear posture initiatives such as those included in the Guam proposals, or whether the DoD should take Palau's offer and base forces there.

Changes to the U.S. military's overseas posture are managed by the DoD's Global Posture Executive Council (GPEC). This executive decision body and associated posture management are governed by DoD instruction—Management of U.S. Global Defense Posture (ref. DoDI 3000.12).[10] The GPEC meets typically once a year to resolve issues and deliberate requests of the combatant commands, but more frequent routine posture issues are managed on a daily basis by the Office of the Secretary of Defense. When decisions involve bases in allied countries, senior-level meetings such as the "2 plus 2" involve Ministers of Foreign Affairs and Defense deliberating with their U.S. cohorts. A frequent issue is the level of host nation support, such as the November 2019 negotiations with South Korea, which saw an 8 percent increase (to over $960 million) of Korean monies to support the basing of 28,000 U.S. personnel at several bases.[11] Ally Japan provided $1.6 billion annually in host nation support via a Special Measure Agreement and Facilities Improvement Program, compared with the $2.7 billion the United States spends annually for forces based in Japan.[12] Special Measures Agreements (SMAs) govern host nation support, while Acquisition and Cross-Service Agreements (ACSA) more broadly govern logistic support among signatory countries—as of February 2020 there are 120 nations that are signatory to an ACSA.[13] A lesser-known and smaller resource supports construction in conjunction with military exercises—Exercise Related Construction (ERC). ERC budgets are small and typically involve building or refurbishing barracks and helicopter landing pads and upgrading communications for command posts involved in exercises with U.S. forces.

As long as construction costs such as ERC are less than $6 million, they do not require congressional authorization. Title 10 U.S. Code 2805 governs these projects, termed "minor," and requires the secretary of defense to notify Congress only when they cost more than $2 million. Congress has allowed the secretary of defense to use appropriated military construction funds, or operations and maintenance funds when construction costs less than $2 million; anything larger than $6 million requires an act of Congress.[14] The greater need is for larger projects like port dredging and airfield expansion, which can take more than five years to plan, approve, and execute. As mentioned in chapter 4, the Navy has relocated Naval Mobile Construction Battalions (NMCB), otherwise known as Seabees, to Guam to better execute such construction. Three battalions (NMCB-3, -4, and -5) under the Thirtieth Naval Construction Regiment rotate on deployments to the Indo-Pacific, conducting missions such as airfield damage repair and establishing expeditionary advanced bases.[15] A core capability of the NMCBs, exercised by deployed units, is providing an air detachment of eighty-nine people within forty-eight hours for rapid response projects.[16] On July 1, 2018, the Thirtieth Naval Construction Regiment was relocated from Port Hueneme, California, to Guam to enhance the operational effectiveness of NMCBs deployed to the Western Pacific.[17] NMCB will play a key enabling role in rapidly establishing expeditionary bases under threat to support mobile expeditionary forces under current concepts of operations—Distributed Maritime Operations (DMO) and Expeditionary Advanced Base Operations (EABO). Basing and infrastructure, however, are half of the equation; sustaining a fleet forward requires access to consumables (i.e., fuel, food) and trusted, expert technicians to conduct deployed repairs.

To sustain a crew and deployed warship requires contracting a variety of services, often with little local knowledge of those providing the services, let alone the language. Timely contracting of services during port visits is the shared responsibility of the ship's supply officer, regional fleet logistic center (FLC), and type commander (TYCOM). TYCOMs provide platform-specific (i.e., submarines, surface warship) logistics policies and plans for repairs. Operational planning for which ports and when to be visited is the responsibility of the numbered fleet commander—for example, the Seventh Fleet. Before a ship arrives in a foreign port a logistics request is transmitted by the ship's supply officer, and the FLC begins contracting for requested services. Meanwhile, the associated U.S. embassy's naval attaché secures diplomatic clearance for the visit. Due to the limited on-scene contracting capacity of the FLC, the Navy has relied on husbanding support providers (HSB) like the infamous Glenn Defense Marine Asia (GDMA) led by Leonard Glenn Francis, better known as "Fat Leonard." Over time, the Navy had grown overreliant on HSBs, which enabled unscrupulous contractors such as GDMA to fleece the Navy. A scandal of corruption spanning the 1990s through 2014 resulted in thirty-three federal indictments and twenty-two guilty pleas over corruption, costing the Navy $35 million.[18] As news of the scandal broke, it had a chilling effect on Navy port visits in Southeast Asia, with FLC and the Seventh Fleet preferring to avoid port calls in the region. Driven by competition with China and Russia, the Navy is once again returning to the region in more frequent port visits. Sadly, the corrupting risk remains evident by the arrest of Frank Rafaraci, who defrauded the Navy of $50 million between 2011 and 2018 by inflating port services.[19] Operating a forward-deployed Navy means such contracting is unavoidable, and better processes with trained in-country contractors are needed. Stopping corruption is part of the challenge; the other is overcoming nefarious efforts to complicate the Navy's ability to sustain forward operations.

The purchase and delivery of needed fuel requires contracted services and a logistics vessel or warship that can moor in a port where the fuel is available. Critical repair parts are often shipped via commercial air cargo to a port for pickup by the ship in need or transshipped to the ship by military aircraft. The fact "that China has access to 10% of the points of entry into and out of Europe" has drawn attention to vulnerabilities in this type of naval logistic network.[20] In a crisis—and certainly in war—deliveries that in peacetime often rely on commercial carriers could be interdicted or delayed with operational consequences. The challenge is especially stark in the Western Pacific and Indian Ocean regions far from U.S. suppliers and with limited choices for transshipment to cover the great distances involved. The bottom line is that the Navy will need multiple suppliers and ports of convenience to operate and sustain itself against Chinese and

Russian attacks and other activities—a logistics resiliency it has lacked due to a pursuit of cost efficiencies.

Where port facilities or local technical expertise is limited, the Navy will have to leverage resources across the government to support a more resilient overseas posture. Specifically, the U.S. International Development Finance Corporation (DFC) was created by the BUILD Act in 2018 and is in effect a U.S. government development bank. The DFC provides several services that can enable investments helpful to the Navy: investment funds, debt financing, political risk insurance, and technical assistance.[21] Had the Navy realized this, it would have embedded staff experienced in security cooperation and naval operations at the DFC. When I looked into this possibility for the Navy in 2019, there were already ten staff from USAID embedded at the DFC. However, USAID institutional culture and focus is very different from the Navy's, and to date, little development investments beneficial to the military have been pursued by the DFC. This is unlikely to change without greater involvement by the Navy. Likewise, to ensure DFC efforts to support great power competition, Congress should require that the DFC include in its annual report, as required under Section 403 of the BUILD Act, information on the efficiency of specific projects with respect to military access and forward sustainment with an initial focus on Southeast Asia.

Executing naval statecraft to better compete in the peacetime with China and Russia will require several changes to how posture is done. First, the Navy will have to pursue a more distributed basing construct with new near-term basing in the Pacific. Second, the chilling effect of scandals on overseas contracting for port visits must be overcome, as the frequency and scope of such activity unavoidably increases with increased forward presence. Third, new partners like the DFC will be needed to grow infrastructure and technical expertise in key locations to sustain the Navy's forward operations. Likewise, the U.S. Coast Guard is having to address both limited shoreside technical support in places like American Samoa and inadequate port and airfield access as it expands its presence to enforce U.S. EEZ rights in the South and Central Pacific. Like the Navy, the U.S. Coast Guard could partner with the DFC to improve shoreside support in austere locations.

## A Fleet Design for Contested Operations

For the first time since World War II, the Navy's movement across the Pacific Ocean is being contested. Driven by the rapid modernization and expanding operational presence of the PLAN, this includes Chinese efforts to gain control of strategically located ports in Fiji, Kiribati, the Solomon Islands, and Vanuatu. Unlike the Cold War contest in the Pacific, in order to deter—let alone prevent—China from achieving its objectives, the Navy must operate under a pervasive and dangerous anti-access and area denial (A2/AD) umbrella of cruise and ballistic missiles that stretches out into the Philippine Sea over one thousand miles from the China coast.

The Navy will sustain damage operating in this theater of operations, and with limited numbers and capacity to replace lost ships, the ability to repair and keep today's fleet in the fight will be an imperative. In peacetime, the ability to return a damaged warship to duty expeditiously (e.g., the 2017 *McCain* after a collision) also signals the Navy's resilience and staying power, even against Chinese efforts to push it out of the region. The dynamic is less disruptive in the Atlantic, where trends point to a limited return to Cold War antisubmarine and maritime patrol missions.

The platforms and weapons used by the Navy since the end of the Cold War to project power reflect an assumption of freedom to maneuver. The proliferation of cruise missiles with creative means of targeting by drones, however, has necessitated a longer standoff range for power projection into littorals. Notable examples of this trend were the September 14, 2019, Houthi rebel cruise missile attacks on Saudi oil facilities using drones for targeting and the September 30, 2016, attack on a United Arab Emirates ship, the former U.S. HSV-2 *Swift*. Over time, the effect on U.S. carrier operations has been to shift emphasis from sortie rates to longer range of carrier-launched precision strikes. This is especially true for scenarios involving an adversary with capable air defenses. In response, carrier-launched F-35Cs with long-range strike munitions are an attempt to address the operational imperative to out-range Chinese weapons. To extend the range of carrier-based strikes, new refueling options provided by the Navy's unmanned MQ-25 tanker aircraft, and new standoff munitions with longer operational ranges and new operational concepts are being pursued to better contest Chinese and Russian forces.

What's more, in sustaining forward crisis operations, the availability of necessary sealift to move critical matériel and personnel is in doubt. In September 2019, the DoD conducted its largest no-notice sealift activation exercise, Turbo Activation 19-Plus, with sixty-one ships. Results were troubling but not surprising. The commander of Transportation Command (TRANSCOM) had testified that there were problems in March 2019,[22] and a December 2019 exercise after-action report stated that only thirty-nine of the sixty-one vessels in the Ready Reserve Fleet, which provides sealift for the military, were ready for tasking.[23] An additional concern is the Navy's admission in late 2018 that it lacks capacity to escort sealift during combat—and this as the Russian and Chinese navies increasingly hold previously secure sea-lanes at risk. It is important to note that Chinese military strategists have made it clear that the Navy's logistics and communications networks will be the first targets in a "paralysis and destruction warfare" campaign.[24]

Today's fleet reflects the missions of the past thirty years and the threats with which it has had to contend. As such, it remains centered on the carrier strike group, amphibious ready group, and small mission purpose task forces (e.g., theater antisubmarine warfare) or single ships on independent tasking (e.g., exercises and engagement with partner navies). Driven by Russian and Chinese capabilities and the geography of the battle space, naval forces have been adapting their operational concepts, such as EABO and DMO. As these concepts progress to ever more complex field testing, lessons are being learned. These point to the inevitable conclusion that the future fleet will have to incorporate new designs as it adapts to the China-Russia challenge.

For a fleet in transition, assumptions that have informed past force structure and force design will be challenged as new platforms come online leveraging, then replacing existing legacy platforms. Adapting the fleet to contested naval operations will require addressing six insights:

*First,* the Navy has only limited assets available for convoy escort duty. The Navy does not intend to use battle force ships for convoy duty; there are simply not enough ships. The MQ-4C unmanned patrol aircraft, which reached initial operating capability as of May 2020, is supposed to replace the Navy's aging EP-3 intelligence aircraft, but development of sensors needed for an antisubmarine role will require significant work. Another potential unmanned platform, the MQ-9, could operate more easily at lower altitudes and be modified for antisubmarine warfare (ASW).[25] It also has a potential role in convoy protection, using radar and sensors optimized for ASW such as miniature sonobuoys being developed to localize hostile submarines. An MQ-4C and MQ-9B with submarine-detecting sensors working with existing maritime patrol aircraft such as the Navy's P-8 can hold hostile submarines at risk. It may be just as easy to avoid the threat, however, if hostile submarines can be detected at adequate range. Once threats are localized by the MQ-4C or rotary-wing MQ-9, convoys could be redirected while manned P-8 aircraft engage threats with air-dropped torpedoes. To accomplish such an air patrol cordon in the Pacific in a cost-effective way will require an archipelago of supporting bases.

*Second*, the Navy has no screen or escort vessel, logistics, or amphibious platforms optimized for sustained operations in a hotly contested first island chain. Dispersal is a method of defense against the large number of Chinese cruise and ballistic missiles targeting the Western Pacific. It is one tactic ostensibly to be employed by the large numbers of small amphibious vessels and associated logistics support ships, proposed by former secretary of defense Mark Esper. Preventing the large numbers of Chinese aircraft, submarines, warships, and maritime militia from intercepting such dispersed U.S. expeditionary forces requires an escort or screen. This takes into account the protection afforded by expeditionary Marine Corps and Army land-based, long-range antiship weapons as well as air and missile defenses. Without a platform capable of limited but sustained air and maritime control within the first island chain, however, it is doubtful that such effect could be provided with manageable risk by existing aircraft carriers operating outside the first island chain.

On October 6, 2020, Secretary Esper hinted at what the screen force could be during a "fireside chat" hosted by the Center for Strategic and Budgetary Assessments (CSBA).[26] Given past congressional mandates requiring the Navy to field a fleet of no fewer than eleven aircraft carriers, the secretary's call for as many as six light aircraft carriers to augment a smaller fleet of *Nimitz*-class and *Ford*-class nuclear aircraft carriers was unexpected. A light aircraft carrier (CVNE) designed to operate in this highly contested maritime environment in the East and South China Seas is appropriate and necessary. In order to mitigate the need for the additional logistic support (i.e., fuel tankers) associated with added escort ships and to maintain a nimble force in this hotly contested theater of operations, the CVNE should be nuclear powered and employ robust active defenses against cruise and ballistic missile attack. The design should be such that construction takes place at alternate yards, mitigating any impact to ongoing *Ford*-class aircraft carrier construction. It's worth pointing out that while submarines will play a vital role in the first island chain, control of the sea and defense of expeditionary forces require robust communications that vitiate the stealth that is critical for a submarine's survival. Moreover, as demonstrated during the Pacific campaigns of World War II, submarines have a mixed track record when it comes to sea control—important when replenishing and moving expeditionary forces in the first island chain in wartime. A new light aircraft carrier could be cost-effective if designed using existing propulsion systems, hull forms, and support systems. Outside the first island chain, a second smaller light aircraft carrier (CVS) could be designed for antisubmarine operations utilizing existing LPD-17 hull and propulsion designs already under construction, which could also be built sooner, bolstering the Navy's near-term needs. Both these platforms also necessitate a long-overdue effort to grow the shipbuilding capacity of the nation—more on this in later chapters.

With this in mind, CVNE and CVS could prove invaluable to the success of the National Defense Strategy in protecting sea-lanes as well as covering the movement of expeditionary forces in the first island chain. To be clear, developing a CVNE will be expensive and initially take eight or more years to construct, while a CVS could be fielded in five years. The Navy has considered such ships before, however, and that experience should inform new designs moving forward. For example, a 2017 RAND study found that a 70,000-ton (smaller than today's 100,000-ton Ford-class) light nuclear carrier (RAND's CVN LX) could be a viable adjunct to the CVN.[27] While the RAND study did not evaluate a light carrier in a screen role, it should inform the design of a future light aircraft carrier optimized for sea control in the first island chain. A CVNE designed for first island chain operations should have resilient defenses (i.e., laser and rail gun for cruise and ballistic missile defense); drafts less than 35 feet for access to a wider array of ports and waterways; speed over thirty knots; and the ability to deploy rapidly from forty to sixty unmanned and ten to fifteen manned aircraft for local air and sea control. To be clear, the CVNE and CVS are not a cost-benefit proposition for a cheaper CVN replacement but a means to execute the fight expected in the next major war. As such, these ships should be considered to augment CVNs, expanding the Navy's depth of at-sea airpower capacity and fulfilling new missions. That said, if the program is not managed well there is risk that the added demand on existing supply chains could cause unexpected costs and delays and could thus strain existing shipbuilding programs—capacities that must grow anyway.

*Third*, current logistics ships and amphibious warships are too large, crewed by civilians, or of questionable survivability for combat operations in the first island chain. As the Marine Corps and the Army develop new maritime weapons and ship-to-shore vehicles, the Navy will have to develop the ships to move and sustain dispersed small but lethal expeditionary units. The Navy's amphibious fleet currently consists of 33 large warships, which are suited to moving hundreds of Marines largely uncontested, and a logistic fleet operated by the Military Sealift Command (MSC). MSC operates 110 ships around the world, and right now all but the expeditionary fast transports (EPFs) are large ships with drafts of more than 25 feet and displacements of over 33,000 tons. This makes the majority of these ships ill suited for operations at austere ports and shallow waters in and among atolls, rocks, and small islands where expeditionary forces would need to maneuver and be resupplied in order to execute their missions effectively. Only the EPF, with a 15-foot draft and top speed of forty knots, is well suited to the type of maritime maneuver warfare envisioned. Although the October 2016 loss of the ex-USNS *Swift* to a Houthi rebel cruise missile off the coast of Yemen does raise questions about this class of vessel's survivability, retaining the EPF's shallow draft, small crew, helicopter deck, six-hundred-ton cargo capacity, and ability to transport more than three hundred personnel while sacrificing some speed to enhanced survivability could offer a future viable platform for these operations. The fact that these vessels are manned by civilian crews, however, raises multiple legal and operational questions. Either these questions must be resolved, these ships must be given a new mission, or the crews must be shifted to military personnel.

*Fourth,* American submarine design is not optimized for sustained shallow-water operations in a contested area. The Navy's fleet of submarines, all nuclear powered, consists of ballistic missile, attack, and guided missile boats. All of these subs are optimized for stealth and extended operations underwater to monitor an adversary, attack shipping, destroy enemy submarines, and launch land attacks with long-range cruise and ballistic missiles. In a fight against China, particularly within the first island chain, operations in very shallow waters would be highly likely. Submarines longer than the water is deep (377 feet for a *Virginia*-class sub) require cool and steady commanding officers and highly experienced crews to sustain days and weeks of such high-stress operations. The dangers of entanglement with masses of fishing vessels and their nets, being run over by a high-speed deep-draft merchant ship, or running into an uncharted sea mountain are always present and are made worse when an enemy is searching for you or when dodging mines without the luxury of being able to hide in deep waters. For shallow-water operations, unmanned, smaller submersibles like the 51-foot Orca extra-large unmanned undersea vehicle (XLUUV) are a better choice. And at a cost of $3.4 billion per unit and with construction spanning upward of five years, the manned submarines available to the Navy if war does come will likely be all it will have, and their employment must therefore be judicious.

As future *Virginia*-class attack submarines are being built with an 84-foot payload module for vertical launch weapons, the design indicates that the Navy intends to focus these boats on strike missions and deepwater operations. Lessons from the last Pacific War, however, illustrate the importance of shallow-water operations. As new platforms like XLUUV join the fleet, its smaller size and quicker, cheaper replacement provide a better-adapted shallow-water submarine option. That said, development of a manned nuclear submarine optimized for shallow waters, less than six hundred feet deep, should be considered to operate in support of very-shallow-water operations conducted by XLUUV.

*Fifth*, the Navy has only limited forward repair capacity. The Navy currently operates two submarine tenders and no similarly tasked ships for the repair of surface warships at sea. Because frontline ports and repair yards are within range of Chinese cruise and ballistic missiles, a mobile repair capability is necessary. World War II demonstrated the importance of forward repair ships and Service Squadron 10 at Ulithi Atoll. Tenders providing "good enough" repair utilizing underwater cofferdams, temporary bows, and jury-rigged steering systems, among many other creative battlefield repairs, ensured that ships could return to the fight promptly or, if more extensive repairs were needed, make the journey home safely.

Today the Navy operates its only submarine tenders, *Frank Cable* (AS-40) and *Emory S. Land* (AS-39), in the Indian and Pacific Oceans, supporting up to twelve submarines at any given time. When these two tenders reach the end of their service lives in the mid-2020s, unless a replacement is built, the Navy will be left with no dedicated at-sea repair capacity and will have to rely instead on in-port repairs far from the theater of operations. Complicating things further, the Navy now lacks any large floating dry docks, which proved critical in repairing the submarine *San Francisco* following a fatal grounding in 2005.

The repair of new unmanned systems will also create an unmet demand, and the expertise and capacity to sustain these platforms at sea will be needed on new task-designed repair platforms. Float-on, float-off (FLO-FLO) ships like the MV *Treasure*, which lifted the *McCain* out of the water and transported it after a 2017 collision, have potential for use in a forward repair role.[28] Having adequate repair ships operating with the fleet is a lesson that the Japanese Imperial Navy, British Royal Navy, and U.S. Navy all learned during World War II's Pacific campaigns, and it should not have to be relearned in a present-day conflict. Unglamorous for sure, deployable floating dry docks, FLO-FLO ships, and tenders will remain critical for sustaining a fighting fleet.

*Sixth*, the U.S. fleet is not optimized for sustained contested strike operations. The Navy's long-range strike capacity against land and naval targets is deployed by launch systems from ship, submarine, or aircraft. These platforms would in turn be reloaded on aircraft carriers or airfields, and submarines would conduct reloads in port with a submarine tender.

Surface ships with a vertical launch system (VLS) can be reloaded only at select bases with task-specific cranes and proximate arsenals. Together, this concept of operations results in limited time on station for combat missions and fixed logistic bases an adversary can attack. A CSBA study found that a vertical launch reload-at-sea capability could provide the equivalent of an additional eighteen destroyers or cruisers in a Pacific war scenario.[29]

In another novel approach to sustaining forward strike capacity, researchers Bryan Clark and Timothy Walton have recommended six unmanned or optionally manned corvettes (DDC) joined with two larger manned destroyers (DDG) in a strike surface action group.[30] The six DDC would then rotate from firing points to rear locations for reload. Disaggregating VLS-capable warships in this way could provide a 133 percent increase in VLS cells available for missiles while allowing for deployment of more air defense or long-range hypersonic weapons from larger manned ships. Still another possibility would be to use the known design of the large amphibious ship (the *San Antonio*–class LPD-17) and modify it to act as a support ship to reload and maintain the DDCs. It could also carry vertical launch cells for hypersonic long-range strike missiles and have high-power radars installed for a command cruiser (CLC) role. Such a ship could also become a replacement for the existing fleet command ships (LCCs). A future command ship will have tremendous importance in a future fleet where effective command and control will be critical in employing unmanned platforms.

It is assumed that in a future conflict, shoreside or global communications will be denied at least for prolonged, critical periods of time. A command ship will therefore become a critical node providing local command and control and battle space awareness to ships associated with its battle group. The sharing of battle space information and interoperability in communication systems will be critical across all service branches—capabilities the Chief of Naval Operations (CNO) and the Air Force have partnered to develop in the Joint All-Domain Command and Control (JADC2). Such local at-sea networking of manned and unmanned joint forces will be a key element of the evolving American way of war, with successors to today's LCCs providing a critical node in a JADC2 communications architecture.

*Seventh*, the fleet has limited options for operations below the level of armed conflict. The Defense Science Board has found that the DoD is underperforming and ill equipped for great power competition in a "gray zone," below armed conflict. The board recommended that the military build new capabilities to force countries like China and Russia to suffer consequences for their nefarious gray-zone activities.[31] Experience of Russian activities in the Sea of Azov and Chinese coercive tactics in the East and South China Seas are instructive. To compete more effectively in the gray zone, commanding officers must have more options for the employment of nonlethal force. To counter aggressive and unprofessional seamanship, U.S. ships with reinforced hulls can enable the shouldering of hostile ships without outright use of weapons. An added benefit that enjoys Congress' attention is that such ships could also operate longer in the Arctic because the reinforced hulls could be designed to double as ice protection.

Aside from fire hoses and lasers intended to disable small watercraft and drones, the Navy has yet to invest in and repurpose promising riot-control technologies for use in maritime situations. Such capabilities could have had a positive impact during several maritime incidents. In March 2009, for example, while in international waters in the South China Sea, five Chinese fishing vessels surrounded and harassed the *Impeccable*, causing it to come to a full stop on several occasions and use its fire hoses at least once against the harassers. Similar incidents have since occurred, and the potential remains that future freedom of navigation operation could be confronted in much the same way by a swarm of maritime militia.

A common lesson from such incidents is the importance of having methods to keep harassers at a distance from the ship's track and, failing this, the ability to shoulder other vessels safely. As the U.S. Coast Guard looks to expand its presence in these waters, it too will benefit from additional nonlethal options to compel harassing vessels to remain clear. While promising technologies are coming, the Navy's deployed ships' best option for gray-zone confrontations remains a blast of water from a fire hose and, when available, speed to get away.

Rival doctrine as laid out in China's *The Science of Military Strategy* and by Russia's General Gerasimov is in both cases leveraging the U.S. military's weaknesses in the gray zone.[32] By addressing these weaknesses, the Navy can become a more resilient and unpredictable opponent in great power competition.

# CHAPTER 6

# A New Model Navy

*It is change, continuing change, inevitable change, that is the domi-
nant factor in society today. No sensible decision can be made any
longer without taking into account not only the world as it is, but
the world as it will be. . . . This, in turn, means that our statesmen,
our businessmen, our everyman must take on a science fictional
way of thinking.*

—Isaac Asimov, *Asimov on Science Fiction*

In 1993, Andrew Marshall, director of the DoD's Net Assessment, stated, "I project a day when our adversaries will have guided munitions parity with us and it will change the game."[1] On December 14, 2015, Deputy Secretary of Defense Robert Work announced that day's arrival when arguing for a Third Offset during comments at the Center for a New American Security. A military offset strategy seeks to leverage emerging and disruptive technologies in innovative ways in order to prevail in great power competition. The First Offset strategy in the 1950s relied on tactical nuclear superiority to counter Soviet numerical conventional superiority. As the Soviets gained nuclear parity in the 1960s, a Second Offset in the 1970s centered on precision-guided munitions and stealth technologies to sustain technical overmatch, conventional deterrence, and containment for another quarter century. The Third Offset, like previous ones, seeks to change an unattractive great power competition, this time with China and Russia, to one more advantageous.

Since the 2015 announcement that the DoD would pursue a Third Offset, the Navy has grappled with the implications. The advent of a fourth industrial revolution, in which an increasingly digitized world teams smart, learning machines with manned platforms, is making this new offset possible. Yet when a few exquisite technologies become viable in the near future, notably quantum computing, a fifth industrial revolution enabled by advances in material and genetic sciences will accelerate the trends of today while introducing living, bioengineered machines to a future Navy. The only constant will be the Navy's mission to safeguard national interests on and from the seas. Driven by ever-faster targeting cycles and debilitating manpower costs, militaries will continue to invest in and embrace fleets of autonomous vessels operated by artificial intelligence, greatly increasing the range, omnipresence, and speed at which maritime forces respond. Such a future demands a New Model Navy, featuring profound new capabilities and relationships made possible by exciting advances in nanotechnology and bioengineering. Like Cromwell's 1645 New Model Army, the future Navy of, say, 2045 must be revolutionary in order to remain relevant. The genesis for this will be in the Navy of today, which will soon be tomorrow's legacy platforms.[2]

## Lightning Bolts and Power Points: In Pursuit of Modern Command and Control

The Navy's establishment of Fleet Cyber Command at Tenth Fleet in 2010 marked the beginning of a new chapter of the Fleet's embrace of cyberwarfare. This will be an important aspect of how the Navy will fight a war with China, and one aspect has been consistent throughout—the need for a common operational picture and resilient communications. Countless PowerPoint briefings ensued with a consistent picture that any staff officer can attest to having seen at least half a dozen times: ships, aircraft, soldiers, and tanks, all connected by nondescript lightning bolts. These images are meant to convey a systems approach to warfare that relies on the connections; but investments have overwhelmingly been in the nodes—in platforms like ships, aircraft, and tanks. As the Navy contemplates a family of unmanned platforms joining its fleet as part of its operational design or DMO, the importance of how these lightning bolts are actualized becomes vital. This is what the Navy's Project Overmatch and investment in Joint All-Domain Command and Control (JADC2) are intended to address.

The Navy's communications dependent systems approach originates from Adm. William Owens' system of systems concept and Vice Adm. Arthur Cebrowski's "network-centric warfare," first espoused from 1996 to 1998. They saw that computer processing power, greater precision and range of weapons, and digital communication were quickening the speed of warfare. Networking a large number of sensors to a family of armed platforms would likewise enable distributed operations with a speed and scope that overwhelm an adversary. Their predictions were timely, as China's rapid naval modernization and expansion, along with large numbers of antiship ballistic and cruise missiles, meant the U.S. Navy would have to disperse to survive. Dispersing while retaining a lethal striking power requires timely targeting information while having a fleet-wide common operational picture. Today this also includes command and control of an increasing number of unmanned platforms. To achieve this situational awareness and effective command and control over a geographically dispersed naval force, the Navy initiated Project Overmatch.

On October 1, 2020, the CNO, Adm. Michael Gilday, signed two memos establishing Project Overmatch. In these memos, the CNO directed that investments be made to deliver network architectures, unmanned capabilities, and data analytics to ensure that the Navy can operate and dominate in a contested environment.[3] The two memos directed the Navy to leverage related Air Force efforts with JADC2. Remarkably, despite the significance of the effort, little has been released publicly on Project Overmatch; what's known is that it involves three classified funding lines, with initial deployment slated in 2023.[4] That said, public statements indicate its objective is to connect all platform data flows, analyzing them for classification and predictive targeting, and making recommendations for how best to engage targets. If successful, artificial intelligence paired with resilient communications and big data analytics can enable a key element of DMO—decision-centric warfare.

In a nutshell, decision-centric warfare aims to enable effective and faster decisions by operational commanders, while degrading the same of an adversary. Although not stated, Project Overmatch is likely also developing the ability to degrade an adversary's decision-making through traditional electronic warfare and cyber-operations. To this end, the Defense

Advanced Research Projects Agency (DARPA) has formulated an approach and tested it in a series of simulations and war games called *mosaic warfare*. What they have found is that disaggregated decision-making enabled by artificial intelligence can generate greater simultaneous operations at greater complexity than traditional command and control, greatly degrading an adversary's ability to orient its forces in response.[5] Central to realizing this is commitment to mission command, the delegation of authority to act in accordance with general mission orders emphasizing unit-level initiative. This approach confounds the rigid Russian and Chinese operational hierarchies while also mitigating attacks against U.S. networks—or, in Chinese operational terms, system destruction warfare.[6] To actualize this, however, requires sensors, communications, data analytics, electronic warfare capacity, and training not yet in the fleet.

To effectuate mosaic warfare, the Navy needs platforms that are able to communicate across multiple frequencies and data rates seamlessly, detect and degrade adversary sensors, and process massive amounts of data. Communications have traditionally included satellites, shore-based transmitters (e.g., high frequency and extremely low frequency), and line of sight—all these remain unchanged in a mosaic warfare context. But platforms will have to be able to send and receive in a wide array of frequencies and data rates to enable resiliency in connectivity against an adversary actively degrading those networks. A constraining factor is that lower-frequency systems will operate at lower data rates and require long antenna arrays, limiting their utility on smaller platforms or those unable to tow a long antenna. More interesting is the next generation of shipboard electronic warfare suites, the Surface Electronic Warfare Improvement Program (SEWIP), which will provide the Navy's large warships with electronic jamming to prevent detection and defeat enemy attacks.[7] Efforts are progressing to develop a "lite" version of SEWIP for the littoral combat ship (LCS) and a new frigate, the *Constellation* class, as well as a new block III *Arleigh Burke*–class destroyer that will include advanced electronic attack capabilities utilizing active electronically scanned arrays technologies and artificial intelligence to more rapidly discern enemy signals and combat them.[8] Finally, assuming periods of limited communications, platforms will require organic massive parallel processing power to store, process, and analyze using artificial intelligence algorithms. The reliance on information passed over networks and its processing opens another consideration—cyber.

The ability to network information digitally, then process and act on that same information in a meaningful way while denying an adversary the same, is the essence of cyber-warfare. But the Navy's fleet must be able to do more if it is to dominate the naval domain in a conflict: it must execute information maneuver warfare. To do this, Brian Kerg and Gary Lehmann argue, warships and their crews must be able to attack the enemy's cognitive decision cycle and entice him into actions that lead to his loss.[9] This means employing capabilities that disrupt as well as condition an enemy's sensors and analytical systems—not the same thing as jamming or decoying. As artificial intelligence is more widely employed, this type of information maneuver warfare will become dominant, with electronic warfare, cyber-warfare, and kinetic attacks all linked.

There are several historical cases that illustrate what this entails. In one, automated systems reliant on provided data can, if not complete, give dangerously erroneous outputs. This was the case of the Soviet strategic warning systems in 1983 when Lieutenant Colonel Stanislav Petrov intervened, confirming no such attack was under way from independent satellite launch sensors—likely averting an erroneous nuclear retaliation by the Soviets.[10] In a second, too much data fed to human operators can overwhelm and create a false sense of urgency to act without confidence in intelligent machine discrimination. Investigators found that the crew of the cruiser *Vincennes* in 1988 became overwhelmed by data amid running engagements with Iranian naval forces, and for this reason they shot down an Iranian passenger airliner.[11] In a third case, assurance of digital data is critical to ensure that systems operate as expected and present accurate operational pictures and assessments. This third case involves an errant spy drone (RQ-170) that in 2011 apparently directed itself to land in Iran; while unconfirmed, there has been speculation that Iranian forces managed to hack into the control systems or disrupt the drone's sensors to cause the landing.[12] U.S. Naval Academy professor Gavin Taylor calls this "data poisoning," and it can likewise materialize in corrupting the training or historical data on which autonomous machines rely.[13] For the Navy to engage in information maneuver warfare, its ships must be equipped and manned to operate in concert across domains and great distances.

In the future, the Navy's ships must be the nodes in the network as well as the lightning bolts connecting them. This mitigates the danger from an adversary by disaggregating the Fleet's ability to sense the battle space, discriminate valid targets, transfer machine learning, and monitor the network for nefarious actors. This also means sharing and disaggregating large amounts of historical data critical in assessing and making accurate machine recommendations from immense digital data streams from an array of sensors. Think of it this way: each ship and its crew (manned or unmanned) benefits instantly from the operational experience of any one unit, which adds to the historical knowledge of an enemy's behavior, perhaps down to specific ships or even an enemy ship captain's predilection. Unfortunately the Navy is not currently organized to take advantage of this.

According to a recent Government Accountability Office analysis, the Navy's divided approach to unmanned platforms along subsurface, surface, and air units will not deliver the integrated interdomain and interplatform class architecture required.[14] Unless this situation is addressed, the Navy is at risk of developing unmanned platforms without the required digital architecture. Worse still, the Department of the Navy has not had a dedicated office responsible for developing this needed architecture since the 2018 disbanding of a dedicated unmanned systems office (i.e., Navy's N99 unmanned office and Deputy Assistant Secretary of the Navy for Unmanned Systems). Workarounds to this lack of leadership involved congressionally mandated portfolio management and formalization of processes between the Office of Naval Research and the Naval Sea Systems Command.

When the Navy's Project Overmatch does deliver the needed digital architecture, it will be important to judge success using four metrics: (1) adequate security of and reliability in the programming and associated databases on which machine learning and big data analytics rely; (2) assurances that zero-day attacks cannot be built into systems or their programming during the fabrication process, necessitating a level of supply chain security not yet demonstrated; (3) the ability of the Navy's fleet to implement dynamic, effective network defense from cyber, electronic warfare, "data poisoning," and other vectors of attack; and (4) the ability to conduct effective offensive information maneuver warfare. To achieve this requires that the Navy embrace a systems approach where lightning bolts and platforms are integrated coequals, or in the CNO's words, "swarm the sea . . . every axis, and every domain."[15] There is little doubt, however, that mosaic warfare and information maneuver warfare will be parts of future naval operations and fleet design.

## The Mighty Trio

Today's trends point to a future fleet composed of large numbers of autonomous and likely even bioengineered platforms. Making this possible are tremendous gains anticipated in the near future in genetic engineering, artificial intelligence (AI), and quantum computing. These society-impacting technologies are what Lars Jaeger calls "the Mighty Trio" in his book *The Second Quantum Revolution*.[16] Predicting the arc of technological advance precisely, however, is impossible, but the trajectory toward greater degrees of machine autonomy is clear.

On this technological trajectory, a critical moment will be when quantum computing achieves the capacity to manage materials, innate and organic, at the molecular level, as well as to drive revolutionary advances in intelligent learning machines. How the Navy chooses to incorporate such advances will dictate fleet structure and manning, and will likely predetermine operational success. Such was the case when the Spanish king failed to arm the Grand Armada in 1588 with long-range guns to match the British and thus suffered the destruction of half his fleet. The motivation for incorporating new technologies remains unchanged. Since our Navy's birth, there has been tension to balance the need for sustained distant operations in the Pacific with effective firepower and defense.[17] To balance this tension, history can be a guide in embracing this brave new naval world.

Navies of the late 1800s began a piecemeal transition from sail to coal to long-range cannon and use of wireless communications. Only once these capabilities were brought together in 1906's HMS *Dreadnought*, however, was naval warfare truly revolutionized, as demonstrated at the 1916 Battle of Jutland. Likewise, for the Navy to realize and remain a maritime leader it must consolidate multiple technological advances into an operationally effective platform. But as I will discuss in later chapters, packaging too many novel and unproven technologies into a single hull comes with risk.

With so many unknowns under an ever-accelerating pace of technological advance, field testing is imperative to speed the Navy's operational learning and inform future investments. Yet doing this alone will not guarantee technological dominance; rivals China and Russia already invest heavily in these fields and will influence the developmental arc. Moreover, given the organic and AI nature of this future, traditional first mover advantage may not apply until a fleet is able to be built, trained, and operated incorporating the "Mighty Trio" advances.[18] Historical examples of revolutionary capabilities adopted too late and in too few numbers in World War II include Germany's development of the snorkel on its submarines to avoid detection and Japan's use of suicide rocket planes. For autonomous fleets of the future, numbers and speed of machine learning or transfer learning among autonomous platforms will be key.

Looking to 2045, the development and adoption of revolutionary technologies alone are inadequate, since dominance in future naval warfare with such capabilities will likely rely on differentiation in machine learning, and that learning's dissemination across autonomous platforms, akin to the training and readiness of manned fleets today. This, of course, assumes that various engineering challenges to operationalize advances in genetic engineering, artificial intelligence, and quantum computing can be overcome.

## Engineering a Revolution in Military Operations

In a particularly prescient paper, Michael J. Mazarr wrote in 1994 that a new revolution in military affairs was unfolding—and in 2021 it is still unfolding. He described this revolution as emphasizing non-nuclear warfare, as highly decentralized yet interdependent economically, and as blurring distinctions between the military and the civilian.[19] The arrival of the revolution he described, however, is conditioned today on the technologies of the Mighty Trio. To deploy these revolutionary technologies, the U.S. military must overcome various engineering challenges within five key fields: AI and big data analytics, robotics, nanotechnology, genetic engineering, and quantum computing and sensing. Doing this will speed the transformation of maritime operations.

## AI and Big Data Analytics

Progress in this field will enable the ability to produce learning machines and rapidly share learning between them enabled by 5G communications. Key to unlocking these potentials for the Navy will be the massive digitization of sensed information: shipboard, biomedical, and external sensor data, and rapid access of historical databases.[20] Such digitization or "informatization" will lead to exponential technological advances, including the potentiality of merging biological and nonbiological intelligence, following Ray Kurzweil's Law of Accelerating Returns.[21] That is, as more sensed data is digitized, the more it can be processed at machine speed, further accelerating machine learning.

## Robotics

AI may be the brains, but a fully autonomous machine without robotic muscle, energy, ears, and eyes is just a data processor. A critical challenge is development of fine motor skills in robotic systems. This commonsense ability of humans has proven challenging for robots but, once overcome, promises roles for robots in performing delicate processes: for example, surgery and battle damage repair.[22] Additionally, advances in high-density energy sources (i.e., batteries) to drive robotic systems is critical to battlefield effectiveness. Likewise, learning machines rely on sensory input to complete tasks as well as to learn, so just as critical will be developing consistent and high-fidelity sensors.

## Nanotechnology

New materials and their control at the molecular level are becoming possible with the successful creation of microscopic machines and new materials such as graphene. Today DNA (deoxyribonucleic acid in cells) can be used in what is called "smart glue" for precise molecular-level pairing and self-assembling of nano-layers that promise enhanced energy generation and storage.[23] Extrapolating such developments out to 2045, the potential exists for self-healing metals and systems, as well as the production of lightweight, exotic new metals that can be fabricated from the molecular level up. Applied in shipbuilding, radical new designs with revolutionary resilience become possible: for example, pipes that reseal if ruptured, or skin on a warship's hull that can sense when a saboteur attempts to place mines and prevent natural hull fouling.

### Genetic Engineering

The ability to engineer living machines is already upon us. Using frog cells, a team in 2020 designed a simple living system at the cellular level based on those frog cells, with the ability to move in a selected direction using pumping actions.[24] A year later, the same DARPA lab reported that engineered frog cells were found to be able to replicate, promising the ability to sustain or repair themselves. In the future, living robotic systems could augment humans, as well as act as fully autonomous task-designed systems: for example, fish bioengineered to foul a warship's prop. The challenge is to scale up the size and complexity of such living machines while retaining cognitive control of them.

### Quantum Computing and Sensing

Perhaps the most critical advances will be in quantum computing. Its promise of rapid parallel processing of tremendous amounts of data is required to unlock the potential of nanotechnology and genetic engineering. Closer at hand are advances in hard-to-decrypt quantum communications. In 2017, a Chinese team conducted a video teleconference using quantum key encryption over a satellite connection.[25] For the Navy, however, the truly remarkable advances will come once quantum teleportation becomes viable; teleportation of photons allows communications across the globe without satellites or into otherwise impenetrable locations like submarines deep undersea.[26] On top of this, quantum sensing offers the potential to detect perturbations in gravity to see through the ocean and detect submarines and seabed mines, as well as to detect stealth aircraft.[27] Needless to say, there is a lot of engineering to do before any of this comes to pass, but when it does the changes to naval warfare will be dramatic and fast.

## 2045 Naval Operations

No matter what future technological or societal changes come, navies are built to operate at sea and will remain so dedicated. In the 2015 "Cooperative Strategy for 21st Century Seapower," missions included and remaining relevant in 2022 were forward presence, deterrence, sea control, power projection, maritime security, and humanitarian assistance and disaster relief (HA/DR). Arguably only two missions rely on direct human interactions to succeed—forward presence and HA/DR. In all of these missions, the interplay between man, machine, and living systems will be profound and will open up some interesting considerations.

1. *Return of the draft—just not what you expect.* Already the Navy is in a contest over the speed to innovate and field new capabilities and associated concepts of operation. The outcome of this race can not only determine wartime success but also, more consequentially, win the peacetime strategic competition. The DoD has even now embraced industry concepts of agile product development to field new capabilities rapidly, in "sprints" built around task-specific teams. For the Navy, this could see the draft being brought back, not to fight a major war but, rather, to access exquisite technical skills required during intense technological competition. Even more novel, as autonomous learning machines become prevalent we could witness the "drafting" of intelligent machines into naval service, where they would be repurposed or retrained for naval utility.

2. *AI fog of war.* The nineteenth-century Prussian general and military theorist Carl von Clausewitz is credited with coining the term *fog of war*, referring to the uncertainty battlefield commanders must confront during the chaos of battle, due to gunsmoke literally obscuring a commander's view of the battlefield.[28] As autonomous systems increasingly team with humans, the potential for a new *fog of war* will emerge, emanating from the interaction between man and machines on the battlefield—in place of gunsmoke, the speed of machine decision-making will be the cause of obscurity. This will necessitate new considerations in developing rules of engagement, and establishing accountability when operations do not go as planned. These considerations will necessarily inform new quality standards in the programming and manufacture of learning machines.

3. *Smaller human crews.* Robotics offers the potential for keeping sailors from dangerous settings and obviating the need for a human maintainer

in otherwise inaccessibly tight spaces. As robots become viable on board ship, they will potentially take on the role of damage control teams, performing maintenance in confined or dangerous spaces (e.g., nuclear reactor compartment), which will allow for radically different ship designs. One effect will be reduced cost to maintain, man, and operate each ship, thus enabling a larger, globally distributed fleet.

4. *Globally networked (on-demand) fleets.* The ability to operate with greater degrees of autonomy by unmanned platforms allows for a greatly distributed and persistent forward presence. At the same time, the ability to rapidly share lessons learned among robotic systems greatly accelerates learning and adjusting concepts of operations against a dynamic adversary. This involves a combination of federated and transfer learning among autonomous platforms. At the same time, quantum communications offer the potential for greatly enhanced secure communications, may reduce the long-term reliance on satellites, and may provide new means of communicating with undersea platforms, thereby relieving undersea platforms of the necessity to come shallow to conduct communications.

5. *Energy weapons will become the standard armament of Navy ships.* The cost effectiveness of shipboard lasers and rail guns for air and missile defense has progressed but has not yet been fielded in an operationally effective way. Should rail guns become viable for long-range strike and hypersonic missile defenses, they, together with lasers, could become the main armament of future warships. Yet power demands for such systems will constrain them to large, manned vessels able to reliably provide needed power and the capacity to replace rail gun barrels degraded under the intense magnetic stresses involved. As such, there is a potential secondary effect—the need for power may even drive a renaissance of naval nuclear power.

6. *Distributed production and autonomous repair.* New materials developed in nanotechnology as well as living materials from genetic engineering could usher in new shipbuilding processes and exotic new methods of sustaining hull life or repairing damage. As robotic advances are made and future ship designs incorporate them, there is

a high potential for them to become integral to how future warships operate and fight. Robot designs already exist to fight shipboard fires (e.g., SAFFiR) and conduct dangerous inspections (e.g., Recon Scout, MINOAS).[29] To truly achieve the full potential of robotic systems on board warships, both are needed—technological advances and alterations to ship design. In the nearer term, additive manufacturing, or 3D printing, of replacement parts as well as for medical use (e.g., prosthetics, artificial organs) can enable distributed logistics and medical services.

Additive manufacturing, utilizing one of seven techniques, is unique in that a "printer" using downloaded blueprints builds layer-by-layer complex components. It does this with less waste and has enabled producing lightweight parts not possible by traditional milling or casting. Distributed production will be enabled by additive manufacturing, mitigating the need for large centralized logistic hubs, and by long-distance transport networks servicing the fleet. The Navy first installed an additive manufactured metallic critical flight part in one of its aircraft in July 2016 in a successful proof of concept. Grasping this technology's potential to greatly improve the Fleet's material readiness, the Department of the Navy since May 2017 has focused on certifying additive manufacturing in operational (i.e., at-sea) settings.[30]

In January 2021, the Defense Department doubled down and committed all services to adopting additive manufacturing, and identified eight U.S. firms as additive manufacturing innovation institutes to help bring this technology to the military.[31] As additive manufacturing proliferates commercially, it will shift the bulk of on-hand inventories to just those products that cannot be fabricated on-site—like microchips. As these processes mature and new materials are developed to enable fabrication of higher-stress metal parts, having on hand the requisite bulk feeder materials will be important. This will necessitate having available bulk storage spaces on board ship and having methods for replenishing the raw feeder materials.

7. *New class of ships.* With new technologies come new logistical and technical demands, which will influence future classes of warships. Large logistics vessels with extensive additive manufacturing capacity

will see their mission merge with those of ships providing medical support and repair functions at sea—a "nurse ship." New materials will likely also enable new platforms that can operate across domains, complicating detection and enhancing defense; inspired by the flying fish, a future corvette may one day operate over, on, and under the sea, evading detection and attack. A third new class of ship would be purpose-built to provide a platform for sustaining and deploying a fleet of autonomous systems. Its mission: to provide region-wide sustained maritime domain awareness and to augment carrier strike groups for sea control—an updated escort carrier.

8. *Ships stay at sea while crew elements rotate.* Today manned naval warships plan, train, and then deploy for overseas operations and return after six to ten months. During this time they conduct numerous port visits and a mid-deployment maintenance period. With priority given to sustaining forward operations, keeping fleets at sea forward-deployed will become greatly enabled by autonomous systems. When deployed with a manned mothership to sustain unmanned or lightly crewed ships, a small task force could stay on station much longer. Instead of ships and crews returning together at the end of a deployment, personnel needed to operate and sustain the unmanned ships would be rotated as needed via a mothership with a flight deck. This would allow ships and associated autonomous platforms to remain at sea for prolonged periods of time. That said, presence operations to signal strategic intent, foster maritime partnerships, and exercise interoperability with allies will persist. These missions rely on human relationships and would remain for traditionally manned warships to conduct. When these are operated with a fleet of unmanned vessels, however, each manned warship's combat effectiveness and its regional strategic influence will be greatly enhanced.

## Conclusion

In order to ensure that the Navy is prepared for the future, lessons learned from the interwar period of the 1920s and 1930s are illuminating. One lesson was to implement career and bureaucratic encouragements while investing in experimental platforms to advance technologies as well as develop associated concepts of operations.[32] This was the track, certainly not a smooth one, taken for naval aviation and submarines early in the twentieth century. Likewise, just as the *Langley* was used to experiment and develop aircraft carrier operations, a similar experimental ship is needed to refine unmanned operations. The practical at-sea experience gained from the interplay between man, learning machine, and bioengineered systems will be invaluable in informing future resource decisions.

With this in mind the Navy may consider reestablishing a directorate at Navy staff dedicated to advancing a coherent approach to fielding maritime autonomous systems, including bioengineered systems. In 2015, the U.S. Navy established N99 within the Navy Staff of the Pentagon to guide unmanned efforts in the air and on and under the sea.[33] It was shuttered barely a year later. A resurrected unmanned directorate should include experts in artificial intelligence and robotic systems. Given the long-term potential of bioengineered systems, medical and genetic experts should also be included, the goal being to drive effective coordination and coherence among the various arms of the Office of Naval Research, National Institute of Health, Joint Artificial Intelligence Center, and Congress.

As learning machines become prevalent, new demands on human operators and mariners will grow. The expertise required will be unique and require specialized training. In short order, the Navy will find itself in a competition for such experts and will have to train and retain them. This will require establishing a dedicated cadre of officers and enlisted specialists in the operation, maintenance, and training of thinking machines and bioengineered systems and integrating them into the fleet. Not unlike the Navy's nuclear submarine force led by an active-duty four-star admiral at Naval Reactors, creating a Naval Autonomy directorate led by a similarly senior officer provides young officers with a viable promotion path and offers critical bureaucratic support to a young service community—a community that will blur distinctions among warfighting competencies, medical expertise, robotics, and AI.

The changes about to unfold as the fourth turns into the fifth industrial revolution will profoundly change operations at sea. But more than a mechanical, technological era, the next era in naval warfare will see the blending and teaming of manned systems with learning machines as well as bioengineered systems. Naval competition then turns on the speed and scale at which data is collected, digitized, analyzed, and acted on for effect. The Navy can take some comfort in that many of the technologies mentioned remain in their infancy. But failure to position the Navy today to take rapid advantage of capabilities unleashed once quantum computing at scale becomes feasible will leave the Navy outclassed and irrelevant.

Previous chapters described the locus of maritime power and a framework for competition. The next task is to determine what forces are needed and how to build the Navy required. The stresses of great power competition and the demands of executing naval statecraft make it imperative that a new model navy be designed with missions described in this chapter in mind. A strategy for future force design must address both contemporary and enduring demands, while building a fleet able to incorporate future capabilities incrementally into a fleet that can compete in peace and win in conflict.

# CHAPTER 7

# Fleet Design 2035

――――∞∞∞――――

*A good Navy is not a provocation to war. It is the surest guarantee of peace.*

—President Theodore Roosevelt, December 2, 1902,
second annual message to Congress

To execute an effective competitive strategy against China and Russia using naval statecraft requires the appropriate navy. Building such a navy requires marrying strategy to execution in an effective force design. An approach used in the electronics industry to do this, and it has utility for building a new model navy. System design focuses on the interaction of parts in a larger system for desired output and ease of fabrication. Applying this approach to execute naval statecraft requires defining the fleet architecture, interfacing with other agencies on individual ship designs, and determining what resources are required to build and operate this new model navy. Moreover, with the right fleet design supporting good strategy, smart resourcing decisions are more likely to be made.

These resourcing decisions include not only research and development but also, critically, human capital, shipyard infrastructure, and shipbuilding. Perhaps the biggest question for many is, How many ships are needed and by what time? A key element in deciding this number is also arming for the most dangerous war scenario: coincident wars with Russia and China; or a very dangerous but more likely wartime scenario, a war over Taiwan with Russia conducting opportunistic aggression. The DoD does operational planning for these types of wartime scenarios, but at a highly classified level not open to the public. That being the case, what is publicly available is adequate to make an informed recommendation of forces needed to address the two scenarios given above. All things considered, the final analysis must strike a balance in force design with the capacities needed in peacetime competition and to prevail in conflict—the fleet force structure.

Fleet design and force structure set objectives for the Navy, for the maritime industry, and for Congress to work toward in providing the Navy the nation needs. A critical third element is applying a rational and informed roadmap to building this fleet while balancing shipyard capacity and training of crews with a dose of budgetary reality. But simply staying within current means is inadequate; getting the needed fleet will require growing the Navy and the maritime industry and boosting the associated budgets as warranted by the threat. This will be important in delivering the needed force structure, growing maritime capacities to sustain it, and assuring that it operates properly, all the while sustaining public and political support.

## Fleet Design

At a CSBA virtual event on October 6, 2020, then–secretary of defense Mark Esper unveiled Battle Force 2045. This was a plan to operate a fleet of more than five hundred warships by 2045.

It was doomed. First of all, it came at the end of an administration. Second, it was not clearly tied to a strategy. What the secretary should have stressed is that this fleet be designed to accomplish two strategic goals:

- Compete effectively against China and Russia in the peacetime day-to-day contests over the principles of a maritime rules-based order, while securing national economic and security interests.
- Develop, build, and sustain a fleet that can win wars and be reconstituted quickly both in war and between wars.

Battle Force 2045's greatest weakness, however, was that it failed to pace the buildup with the challenges coming from China and Russia, a shortcoming some in Congress were quick to point out—especially given the March 2021 testimony from the commander of Indo-Pacific Command, Adm. Philip Davidson, that China was preparing for conflict over Taiwan by 2027. To many at the time, the goal of a five-hundred-ship battle force in 2045 seemed divorced from the threat. One of the more outspoken on this has been Rep. Elaine Luria, a retired naval officer, who instead called for urgency and a battle force 2025. Such a time frame is smart, given that intelligence projections on future threat forces and budgets beyond five years into the future become increasingly meaningless. Also, China too will respond, execute course corrections, and depending on the U.S. countermove, either exacerbate or defer the danger of 2027. All this uncertainty leads to a biasing of efforts before 2027, while sustaining the fleet expansion and delivering new classes of warships out to 2035—the key being that fleet design cannot be undertaken in a vacuum, failing to consider the political as well as military-threat environment in which it will be operating.

Part of understanding the environment is predicting where and when maritime activity of concern is most likely to occur. Treating the world's oceans as a probability map with weather, naval activity, and economic activity as variables, it is possible to discern where limited naval forces will have to be positioned for day-to-day operations and for the unexpected natural disaster. The consequence of not being postured appropriately is twofold: (1) We run the danger of not being present where a competitor is acting against the United States. (2) An unexpected crisis requiring forces could derail the main effort to compete with Russia and China. Regarding the potential for operational distraction, consider the political imperative for a quick military response when the U.S.-flagged *Maersk Alabama* was hijacked in April 2009. The Navy was nearby, and within four days the crisis ended. Having a ship close by and able to respond to such events minimizes the chance that ships in a decisive theater (e.g., the South China Sea) will have to be withdrawn. In fact, the Somali pirates, like fishing fleets and smugglers the world over, follow seasonal patterns dictated by the weather, sea state, and yearly societal patterns—for example, the Vinta Festival in the Sulu Sea. Knowing what influences maritime activities and the associated patterns is important to inform what, when, and where naval vessels are operated.

The weather has an impact on naval operations, for sure, but less so on submarines and larger naval vessels. Still, even large naval vessels have constraints, as relearned during the Cold War exercise Ocean Venture '81. Those operations in the extreme North Atlantic saw the Navy rediscover the challenges of severe icing and damage from rough seas. Training regimens and national holidays even factor into the level of naval activity. It is a well-known doctrine of the Chinese and Russians to use military exercises as a pretext for offensive operations, as Russia did in the lead-up to its 2022 invasion of Ukraine. In recent years, both the Russian and Chinese navies have conducted naval exercises throughout the year, some without much warning, such as Russia's limited snap exercises. Nonetheless, larger vessel operations, especially submarines, are not so constrained by the elements and require persistent U.S. vigilance in case they should be a pretext to a larger operation.

With this in mind, a probability map of the world's oceans, tracking maritime activity of interest, serves as a guide to forward naval presence requirements. This indicates where naval forces should be at various times of year, as conditions warrant. The following sections offer insight into how this was done for several key operating areas: the Taiwan Straits and East China Sea; the South China Sea; the North Atlantic; the Eastern Mediterranean; the Indian Ocean Region; the Persian Gulf; and the Central Atlantic and Caribbean.

### Taiwan Straits and East China Sea

An untoward incident involving fishing fleets and illegal landings on the Japan-administered Senkaku Islands is most likely to occur during annual Chinese fishing bans from May through August. Summer months generally have calmer seas, with monsoon storms most frequent between May and December, and April being ideal navigationally.[1] Nonetheless, Chinese government (Coast Guard and Navy) vessels have become a persistent presence in these waters since 2012 at least.[2] Called the "Black Ditch" by 1700s merchants, the Taiwan Strait has notoriously strong winds and rough seas, driven by South China Sea and Kuroshio Branch currents, with the winter months the roughest.

### South China Sea

As in the East China Sea, the Chinese government implements a four-month summer fishing ban here, typically running from May to September. Wind-driven seas are strongest from November to March, with the threat of typhoons greatest in July and August in the northern approaches to Hong Kong.[3] Peak fishing activity in the region is March to

April, and in August.[4] Since 2014, thanks to a massive building program, the Chinese maritime militia, coast guard, and navy are able to sustain a persistent presence.[5]

With regard to Chinese conscription and naval exercise season, conscript basic training since 2013 has shifted earlier, to September, to support large-scale exercises early in the new year, usually after a two-week Chinese New Year holiday in January or February according to the lunar calendar.[6] But the Chinese navy continues to conduct major exercises and, increasingly, joint operations with other branches of their armed services in the summer months, notably the South Seas Fleet.[7]

### North Atlantic

Winter months here have challenging seas; gale winds, rough seas, and unpredictable storms often make surface operations challenging. Typically the months of May to early July are the calmest and most navigable.[8] Unlike in the South China Sea and East China Sea, here military activities are not tied to fishing. Russian naval activity is year-round, especially undersea, with surface exercises and operations nominally occurring from May through August.

### Eastern Mediterranean

Overall, the Mediterranean is unaffected by tropical storms and is calm most of the time. Winter months do see occasionally rougher seas and gales that are historically common enough to be given names: the Gregale (February) around Malta and the Meltemi (July and August strongest) in the South and Southwest Aegean Sea. Storms that are hard to predict and are sometimes dangerous to small boats are common from November to February.[9] Overall, commercial and government maritime activity is nearly constant throughout the year.

### Indian Ocean Region

The seas in the Indian Ocean are driven by the northeast and southwest monsoon cycles. Piracy, once a scourge of this region, is also a seasonal activity tied to the monsoon cycle—most successful attacks occurred in seas of less than seven feet, with the majority of attacks occurring in

October through May.[10] Cyclones occur between July and September, but the strongest occur in May–June and October–November, with a ratio of 4:1 occurring in the Bay of Bengal compared with the Arabian Sea.[11] Diego Garcia, a major U.S. military base, is located between these two monsoon systems and the South Indian Ocean, where the cyclone season runs from January to February.

### Persian Gulf

A wind heavily laden with dust, called a shamal, can hazard navigation due to the reduced visibility it causes—strongest in April. The fine dust can also be a problem if it clogs ventilation and mechanical systems. Toward the southern parts of the gulf, two dangerous weather patterns occur: a winter wind called the *suhaimi*, and the more dangerous *laheimar*, which occurs between mid-October through early November and which local mariners will go to anchorage to avoid.[12]

### Central Atlantic and Caribbean

The area of interest here is the roughly rectangular area comprising the Caribbean and the Gulf Guinea in West Africa. Hurricanes (August to October) affect the Caribbean, but an area beginning with coastal Venezuela and its offshore islands and heading eastward to the Gulf of Guinea is generally free of tropical storms.[13] As a route for illicit narcotics, the Caribbean has somewhat diminished, as new routes have emerged via West Africa to Western Europe.[14] In recent years, Chinese fishing fleets have become more common in West African waters, threatening overfishing in these underpatrolled seas.[15]

The next step was to apply the above probability map to the earlier-discussed maritime theaters. From this, general mission sets and the beginnings of a force disposition became clear—the system architecture. Geographically this architecture aligns with the eight maritime regions mentioned, with one exception. A north–south lateral area from Japan through Borneo Island (i.e., First Island Chain) was added to address unique operational demands in an area tactically significant in a Taiwan contingency. The following list provides a listing of proposed mission focus for the various numbered fleets of the U.S. Navy:

- *South China Sea:* A newly established First Fleet (C1F) would be tasked with engaging in proactive great power competition activities and effective counter-gray-zone operations.
- *North Pacific and Northeast Asia:* The Seventh Fleet (C7F) would conduct maritime and submarine patrol, missile defense operations, and episodic shows of force.
- *First Island Chain:* A Seventh Fleet Task Force would execute key operational concepts (e.g., EABO, MDO, and Littoral Operations in a Contested Environment [LOCE]).
- *Central and South Pacific:* The Third Fleet (C3F) would be charged with reconstituting and, if need be, expanding and updating antiquated basing facilities to support extended maritime patrol and secure sea- and air-lanes.
- *Eastern Mediterranean:* The Sixth Fleet (C6F), with a reduced theater of operations, would be tasked with undertaking proactive great power competition activities and patrol posture for contingencies in the Black Sea, Suez Canal, and Mediterranean.
- *Northern Atlantic and Arctic:* The Second Fleet (C2F) would take over responsibility for the Atlantic from C6F, and focus on conducting maritime and submarine patrol, as well as episodic shows of force into the extreme North Atlantic and Baltic Sea.
- *Caribbean and Gulf of Guinea Operating Area:* The Fourth Fleet (C4F) would expand to take responsibility for all South Atlantic naval operations focusing on a naval corridor from the Caribbean to the Gulf of Guinea. Its primary mission would be to conduct maritime patrol and counter illicit activities.
- *Indian Ocean Region:* The Fifth Fleet (C5F) would expand its area of responsibility from the Persian Gulf to include the entirety of the Indian Ocean. Its principal mission would be to conduct maritime and submarine patrol, conduct strike operations, and act against violent extremists.

Such an architecture emphasizes the role of numbered fleets in executing a global maritime strategy. The fleets are subordinate to four-star admirals leading a naval component command who report to an associated joint geographic combatant command: Pacific Fleet, Fleet Forces Command (until 2006 the Atlantic Fleet), Naval Forces Europe/ Africa, Naval Forces Central Command, or Naval Forces Southern Command. In some cases the numbered fleet commander and the joint component commander are one and the same, such being the case with C4F and C5F. The component commands (e.g., the Pacific Fleet) coordinate with the joint geographic command to meet operational and planning requirements, while type commands—for example, submarine forces in the Pacific or naval surface forces in the Atlantic—are responsible for the manning, matériel readiness, and training of specific types of platforms. Importantly for naval statecraft, the type command sets standards and procedures for contracting and coordinating deployed replenishment and repairs. A type command is responsible for administrative support

**Chart 6. Maritime Activity around the World, by Month**

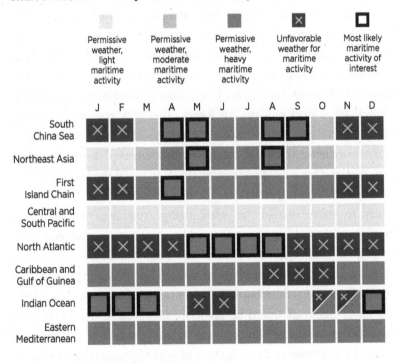

SOURCE: Author's analysis, based on his article "Rebuilding America's Military Project: United States Navy," p. 22–50.

for a specific class of platform, such as aircraft, submarines, and surface warships. A good overview of how the Navy's operational and administrative control of its forces is structured today can be found on the DoD website.[16] This existing architecture, however, emphasizes individual geographic commands' requirements to the detriment of a coherent global maritime strategy. Prior to the 1986 Goldwater-Nichols Act, the CNO at the Pentagon had significantly more operational control over his forces. This situation contributed to the success of Secretary of the Navy John Lehman's Ocean Venture '81 and subsequent large-scale naval exercises. Absent a wholesale revocation of the Goldwater-Nichols Act, a change would do the Navy good in a few small ways.

As mentioned in the last chapter, the Navy will always be pressed for forces and so it is imperative that persistent operations in decisive theaters be emphasized. Doing this most effectively would require adjustments to how naval forces are allocated through the joint force Global Force Management process—namely, by moving away from assignment based on geographic command areas of responsibility and shifting to the eight maritime regions described in chapter 4. This would emphasize the numbered fleets as they are associated with each of these maritime regions, while the naval component commands (i.e., Pacific Fleet) translate joint force requirements into naval operational requests for forces. This only goes so far, and to better enable a coherent global maritime strategy, the Navy will have to be given more operational control, not unlike that executed during President Reagan's tenure. One way of addressing this is to recast the Navy as a joint functional command responsible for all maritime forces.

Such a move would be challenging, requiring congressional notification, and would not be welcomed by some senior naval leadership and the Joint Staff. The consequence for them would be a loosening of the Joint Staff's control over naval operations. But, emphasizing the numbered fleets and resourcing them better in their execution of a globally scoped naval statecraft would be far more manageable. To do this, the numbered fleets would need more support from the type commands and component commands as the frequency of port visits, exercises, and scale of deployed repairs increases to support a long-term posture plan. That plan would develop more forward training ranges, repair facilities, storage of ammunition, and access to fuel. At the same time, these efforts must be sustainable, requiring collaboration with the State Department, the Commerce Department, and developmental organizations such as USAID and the DFC. To do this, the Navy will have to devote more personnel with operational experience to serve as liaisons and embedded staff at these organizations, with the objective of enhancing forward naval presence. The small cost of embedding a staff officer at the DFC, for example, could help flag promising projects that open inaccessible ports and modernize maritime facilities overseas at little cost to the Navy. To sustain access to such infrastructure overseas, however, means the Navy will have to use it, adding another requirement that emphasizes the role of numbered fleets.

To sustain a forward-deployed fleet, it is critical to have access to logistics hubs for repairs, replenishment, and regionally tailored training. As the lessons of the Battle of Java Sea illustrate, regional operational familiarity and available prepositioned resources will be critical in a fast-paced conflict. Port visits and exercises with partner navies are important to this end, and the coordination with a host country to plan and execute is manpower intensive. The burden for this often comes to the naval attaché based in the host nation's capital—sometimes very distant from where the naval activity or port call will occur. This I can personally attest to, having served as an attaché in Malaysia, where most port calls were an ocean away, in Eastern Malaysia. Conducting local contracting and building up relationships with local port authorities and the host military will be important to sustaining and safeguarding a growing naval presence. Other navies use port liaison officers to coordinate waterfront operations in commercial ports, or to support foreign ship visits; the Malaysian Navy has such an officer in Penang on the Bay of Bengal. Fleet liaison officers working out of the U.S. embassy but stationed at key ports of call would be tasked with supporting naval activities in-country while growing the infrastructure and technical expertise needed to better sustain naval forces. This is a task beyond the capacity of the naval attaché, who is in the capital most of the time focused on discerning the host nation's naval policies; the fleet liaison officer would be assigned to the waterfront.

Opening ports and sustainment facilities to the Navy can enable a more enduring forward naval presence, but just as important is how the Navy manages its fleet for operations. In 2014, the Navy rolled out its Optimized Fleet Response Plan (OFRP), intended to increase stability in maintenance and deployments. As conceived and detailed in Navy instructions, the notional OFRP thirty-six-month framework includes a maintenance phase consisting of a six-month shipyard repair (up to sixteen months for aircraft carriers in dry dock) and a one-month shakedown; an eight-month period of training culminating in certification of a ship for deployment; a seven-month deployment (traditionally capped by a month of in-port reduced activity for crew rest); and a thirteen-month sustainment phase during which the ship may be tasked for short-duration operations such as Dynamic Force Employment (DFE).[17] DFE operations are conducted for a specific strategic message or effect in accordance with the National Defense Strategy to increase operational unpredictability against an adversary.

Two years into the OFRP's implementation, then–Fleet Forces Commander Adm. Philip Davidson expressed optimism that the predictability it offered the Navy would lead to improved retention of sailors and the clearing of backlogged maintenance.[18] Six years later, results have been mixed: deployments of CSGs have not averaged the targeted seven months, and maintenance delays continue.[19] Acknowledging challenges in executing the OFRP, CNO Adm. Michael Gilday indicated that there is probably no room for changes in the training and maintenance phases, but that he was looking at the sustain phase following deployment, when readiness is highest. Then in January 2020, it was announced that DoD and the Navy were conducting reviews of the OFRP, acknowledging that the number one factor in its success was dependence on the clearing of maintenance backlogs.[20] Without any viable alternatives proposed by the Navy, it appears that the OFRP will continue into the foreseeable future, amid excessive wear on warships, higher frequency of deferred maintenance, and exhaustion of crews; deployments must be held to historical standards of no more than six months without CNO-specific permission. Under these restrictions, the current OFRP construct on a by-warship basis generates roughly one-quarter of forward-deployed presence a year. At the same time, forward-based warships remain in the theater of operations continuously, conducting operations roughly six months of the year, the other six in maintenance or training. This provides a starting point for

## Chart 7. Keeping Pace with Chinese, Russian Naval Growth

Shown below are the number of ships the U.S. must have in its fleet in order to keep pace with both the Russian and Chinese navies while maintaining a 30 percent operational tempo.*

NUMBER OF SHIPS

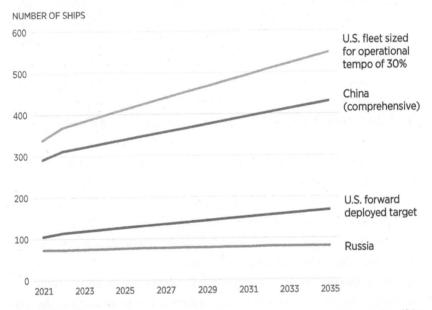

* A 30 percent operational tempo ensures adequate time for ship maintenance and crew training without sacrificing day-to-day operations.

**SOURCES:**
- Defense Intelligence Agency, "Russia Military Power: Building a Military to Support Great Power Aspirations," 2017, p. 66, https://www.dia.mil/Portals/27/Documents/News/Military%20Power%20Publications/Russia%20Military%20Power%20Report%202017.pdf (accessed January 13, 2021).
- Office of Naval Intelligence, "UPDATED China: Naval Construction Trends vis-a-vis U.S. Navy Shipbuilding Plans, 2020-2030," unclassified paper prepared for Senate Armed Services Committee, February 2020, p. 4.
- John Grady, "Analyst: China Exceeded Expectations in Speed of Naval Growth," USN/ News, September 10, 2020, https://news.usni.org/2020/09/10/analyst-china-exceeded-expectations-in-speed-of-naval-growth (accessed September 10, 2020).
- Michael A. McDevitt, "China's Navy Will Be the World's Largest in 2035," Proceedings, February 2020, https://www.usni.org/magazines/proceedings/2020/february/chinas-navy-will-be-worlds-largest-2035 (accessed October 20, 2020).
- Michael Kofman, "A Year of Challenging Growth For Russia's Navy," Proceedings, March 2020, https://www.usni.org/magazines/proceedings/2020/march/year-challenging-growth-russias-navy (accessed October 20, 2020).

determining the number of vessels necessary to sustain the forward presence to execute the above missions by maritime region.

As new unmanned or optionally manned platforms begin to enter the fleet in the coming years, the hope is that they will reduce operational stress on the manned ships and provide much-needed capacity. It is promising that Pacific Fleet's Surface Development Squadron One has recommitted to conducting fleet battle problems; its focus has been to refine the Navy's unmanned fleet design and the roles for the large unmanned surface vehicle (LUSV) and the extra-large unmanned underwater vehicle (XLUUV). Previous experience with carrier-borne MQ-25 unmanned tanker aircraft, the K-MAX optionally manned logistics helicopters used in Afghanistan, the MQ-4C drone deployed to Guam in 2019 for maritime patrol, and the Sea Hunter (now MUSV) that sailed unmanned in a 2018 round trip from San Diego to Hawaii indicate that current conceptualizations are focusing on narrow benefits. But as the test launch of an SM-6 antiship missile from an unmanned vessel in spring 2021 proved, this can change quickly. Congress has been right to be skeptical, having previously placed limits on future procurement of unmanned platforms pending certification of critical subsystems, and prohibiting the installation of offensive systems on unmanned platforms, pending legal reviews.

Such concerns aside, it appears that the development and deployment of unmanned systems in the Navy are an irreversible trend and that the task will be to determine how missions are shared among unmanned, manned, and mixed formations of ships and aircraft. Until reliability is proved with sea-time experience, unmanned platforms will likely perform missions in the near term that enhance the operational effectiveness of the manned ships, or they will operate as unmanned support ships.

Additionally, evolving deployment patterns and maritime capabilities of the Army, Air Force, Marine Corps, and Coast Guard should inform the Navy's own deployments. As the Army and the Marine Corps begin fielding new antishipping capabilities and implementing their warfighting concepts, it will be critical to coordinate and exercise their deployed forces with the Navy. Likewise, the Air Force's forward deployment of B-1 and B-52 bombers in Continuous Bomber Presence and forward deployment of fighter aircraft in Theater Security Packages will be coordinated with naval operations, as was done in June 2020 in the South China Sea. While these ground-based maritime capabilities and units should be active elements of naval statecraft, they are not a replacement for naval power at sea. Nevertheless, when it comes to wartime planning these forces will impact subsequent correlation of force calculations in Beijing and Moscow, given the manner in which U.S. forces plan to fight.

Finally, the successful Western Pacific deployment of the Coast Guard Cutter *Bertholf* (WMSL 750) in 2019 made a compelling case for continuing such deployments.[21] That deployment impressed upon many the unique role the Coast Guard plays in engaging with partner nation maritime security forces for training, building capacity, and exercising to bring about greater interoperability. How the Navy and the Coast Guard choose to employ such cutters in the future will be an important factor in enabling better interoperability with the region's coast guards and maritime police. For naval statecraft the Coast Guard will be a critical partner and is considered in the force design with its cutters playing a key role in forward presence in the Central and South Pacific, Caribbean–Gulf of Guinea corridor, and South China Sea.

Focus has been on a force designed for peacetime competition using naval statecraft. This is incomplete without considering wartime needs, which are in some cases additive, especially for strategic deterrent forces like nuclear ballistic missile submarines. Since 2015, the think tank the Heritage Foundation has conducted an annual review of current U.S. military forces' ability to prevail in conflict—the "Index of US Military Strength." Having been a part of these assessments, I have used a similar approach. In sizing the wartime fleet several factors must be considered: the available forces of threatening militaries, the historical record of past U.S. military wartime operations, and importantly, an on-the-record assessment of force requirements for two major regional contingencies fought simultaneously.[22] In 2019, an expert bipartisan National Defense Strategy Commission cochaired by former CNO Adm. Gary Roughead recommended retaining the two-MRC construct. Moreover, given the uncertainty inherent in how the U.S. military would manage multiple simultaneous crises across the five challenges of the National Defense Strategy, a more specific construct was recommended by this commission.[23] Building on those recommendations, the future fleet design must include adequate disposition of forces during war to enable "deterrence by punishment" against any unengaged rival (e.g., North Korea or Iran). It must also be postured to conduct targeted operations of short duration such as suppression of violent extremists planning attacks against U.S. interests. While the "two major regional contingencies" construct has fallen out of favor in military circles, it remains an instructive starting point for building the needed fleet. For the Navy in 2018, such a warfighting force would comprise no less than 12 ballistic missile submarines, 13 aircraft carriers, 105 large surface combatants, 65 attack submarines, 45 amphibious warships, and 89 logistics and support ships.[24] Such forces do not, however, lend themselves to the way the military will fight the next war or to the peacetime competition with China and Russia. Still, this force design serves a well-informed starting point.

Wartime planning requires that the Navy, with the Coast Guard, fight in concert with the other services to prevail in the most dangerous and likely scenario—a war with China over Taiwan, while denying opportunistic adventurism on the part of Russia as well as Moscow's efforts to prolong a U.S.-China conflict. Guiding how the U.S. military will fight in such a conflict are several concepts of operations—or CONOPs. They include the Army's Multi-domain Operations (MDO); the Marine Corps' Littoral Operations in a Contested Environment (LOCE) and Expeditionary Advanced Base Operations; and the Navy's Distributed Maritime Operations. All of these CONOPs aim to complicate Chinese targeting by dispersing strike capabilities both at sea and, increasingly, from shore as new ground-based antiship and long-range antiair capabilities mature.

To increase the survivability of forces executing EABO and MDO operations within dense Chinese offensive capabilities, numbers and stealth will be important. The numbers of units the Chinese would have to target is intended to overwhelm their systems and accelerate the depletion of their long-range weapons, notably midrange and long-range ballistic missiles and cruise missiles. Stealth, including decoys, is also important to ensure that small, dispersed forces can execute their own offensive operations against Chinese maritime forces.

As Bryan Clark and Timothy Walton have argued, these forces will need the ability to conduct targeting passively, so as to not give away their location. One technique is multistatic electromagnetic sensing, in which radar transmitter and receiver are geographically separate.[25] Another force design recommendation is the use of unmanned ships with vertical launch systems (VLS) to provide more strike capacity while freeing space on manned ships for defensive weapons (i.e., air and missile defenses). As envisioned by Clark and Walton, replacing one destroyer in a three-ship surface action group (SAG) with six VLS-equipped unmanned corvettes (DDC at approximately 2,000 tons) can increase strike capacity by 133 percent while increasing a defender's targeting problem by 267 percent.[26] These recommendations are currently conceptual, but clearly they will have a part to play in the realization of EABO and DMO concepts.

The Navy in 2021 is structured for a different era and will need to be updated for the demands of naval statecraft and future warfighting. Today the Navy employs a fleet in several formations appropriate to the mission. These formations include SAGs; the Carrier Strike Group (CSG); the Expeditionary Strike Group (ESG); the Amphibious Ready Group (ARG); and independent operations. The CSG and ESG are the largest groupings and are intended to execute contested operations: CSG for strike operations and ESG for amphibious operations.[27] As the Navy looks to incorporate several new capabilities and concepts of operations (e.g., DMO), new formations will need to be considered along with new missions.

Peacetime success requires a naval force that is tailored to the specific challenges of its theater of operations while able to reposition rapidly, execute combat missions, and respond to an unexpected crisis. Grouping ships with differing capabilities into a coherent task-focused force is long-standing Navy practice, but today's CSG, ESG, and ARG do not address the full range of this era's peacetime missions, let alone take advantage of new capabilities. Naval statecraft and new technologies will necessitate further additions to how the Navy is organized in operational force groupings to best execute naval missions and fight and win in war. A summary of these future groupings include

1. *Task Force South China Sea.* This task force would provide a persistent presence in the South China Sea to monitor, anticipate Chinese challenges, and preempt with shows of force. During peak exercise and fishing season (February through October), the force would swell in

numbers of surface combatants (FFGs and LCSs) to include a carrier strike group. During the lighter operational season, the aircraft carrier could be supplemented by an amphibious ship optimized for air operations (e.g., landing helicopter assault ships [LHAs]).

While the actual composition would, unavoidably, change, it would have to include an air element (sea-based and shore-based) that is strong enough to outclass any immediate air challenge to its operations and a submarine component. This would likely mean sustaining an aircraft carrier strike group in the Western Pacific not unlike the carrier presence maintained in the Persian Gulf until the mid-2010s. Eventually, XLUUV submarines and a task-specific scout platform employing mostly unmanned platforms would be operated in this theater to pace the large number of maritime militia, Chinese Coast Guard, and Chinese PLAN.

At a minimum, the task force would have to be resourced on any given day to ensure its ability to monitor and make an adequate display at one of three disputed features (e.g., Scarborough Shoal, Second Thomas Shoal, and South Luconia Shoals). Such a minimum force would likely include three FFGs/LCSs with a lead DDG or CG; maritime patrol aircraft, LPD, or like ship with embarked special forces to conduct vessel boarding and limited small island resupply; and two submarines.

2.  *Task Force Eastern Mediterranean.* This task force would provide a persistent presence in the Eastern Mediterranean to monitor, complicate, or challenge Russian naval operations like those in Syria and Libya today. Russia has agreements in place to base as many as eleven ships in Tartus, Syria, and potentially Port Sudan on the Red Sea for as many as four warships. A U.S. naval presence should be sized to pace regional Russian naval presence, as well as episodic Chinese deployments, and be able to conduct limited strike operations. At a minimum, such a force would include two large surface warships (i.e., destroyer) armed with a balance of antiair, antiship, and land-attack weapons; one submarine; and a large amphibious ship like an LPD with embarked special forces for vessel boarding and counterterrorism operations. Maritime patrol and air

support could be provided from land-based aircraft operating out of NATO bases and (if offered) Britain's Akrotiri airbase on Cyprus. As with the South China Sea task force, the mission is to effect proactive great power competition activities.

3. *Carrier Strike Group.* A CSG is designed to provide airpower for strike operations, principally land strikes, and localized air dominance. These groups as traditionally constituted are large (a CVN and air wing, mix of four to six destroyers and cruisers, two logistic ships, and a submarine) and are intended to project power into contested waters. The geostrategic statement that a CSG makes when it arrives in a region is unmistakable, and backed by decades of historical precedent. These forces are constituted for projecting power forward and should be used judiciously.

4. *Fast Carrier Screening Force.* As concepts for contested operations in the first island chain (i.e., EABO, LOCE, MDO) mature, there will be a need for a covering or screen force. Such a grouping would be centered on a carrier designed for air dominance and secondarily antisubmarine and antisurface warfare. It would be assumed that this group would operate in and among the many islands and shallow waters often encountered among the Visayas in the Philippines, the Sulu Sea, and the South China Sea.

    Development of such a new platform would take more than eight years, but when fielded it would be composed of a CVNE (displacing approximately 60,000–70,000 tons) with a primarily unmanned air wing and two or three large surface warships (i.e., destroyer). Logistic support is mitigated by the CVNE being nuclear-powered, which allows it to carry more aviation fuel, with replenishment forces composed of an oiler and tender (munitions replenishment and repairs) that would rendezvous at secure sites following screening operations in conjunction with Marine and Army movements along the first island chain.

5. *Surface Strike Group (with DDC).* As originally proposed by Bryan Clark and Timothy Walton, this concept envisions a surface action group designed to conduct land strikes using long-range cruise missiles and forthcoming intermediate-range conventional prompt-strike

hypersonic missiles. The group would include six LUSV (DDCs) with VLS carrying strike weapons, two DDGs for air and missile defense, and a munitions logistic ship for VLS reload (T-AKM).

To support the unmanned LUSVs, either a purpose-built support ship would be needed for repair and maintenance (i.e., AR) or an associated T-AKM would have to be designed to provide these services with trained maintainers. One solution that would accomplish the repair and maintenance, and T-AKM roles could be a modified LPD-17 hull. A single hull would incorporate improved radars and VLS systems for long-range hypersonic strike weapons, and with its larger size would conduct VLS reloads at sea with the LUSVs. A repurposed LDP-17 in this fashion would approximate a command cruiser or CLC.

6. *First Island Chain ARG (Fast and Traditional Versions).* An Amphibious Ready Group is typically a group of three large amphibious vessels (LHD or LHA, LSD, and LPD) used to move Marines in an uncontested environment. This grouping would be used in peacetime or in areas where a maritime threat is low. A modified ARG would be designed for the movement of Marines among the first island chain during contested operations or conflict. Ideally, the modified ARG would operate in conjunction with a Carrier Screening Force and consist of fast-moving (sustained speeds of twenty knots for five days unrefueled), shallow-draft (less than 22 feet) vessels: a frigate, two Light Amphibious Warships (LAWs), and two to four MUSV optimized for deception operations and limited defenses.[28] In addition to the Marines carried, Navy combat engineers (SeaBees) would deploy for airfield and port repairs to enable follow-on forces as needed. Finally, these forces should be able to acquire fuel without access to modern port facilities or an oiler for at-sea replenishment—in other words, they must be able to live off the land.

7. *Expeditionary Strike Group and Lightning Strike Group.* In essence, an Expeditionary Strike Group is an ARG with a naval force in escort designed for forcible entry in contested littorals. Proposals for a repurposed LHA for air operations would employ F-35 aircraft in place of amphibious assault aircraft (helicopters). This so-called Lightning

Strike Group would be intended for air defense and maritime presence operations in areas with a limited threat. A second iteration of the Lightning Strike Group would see an air wing designed for antisubmarine warfare using helicopters and unmanned XLUUV and MUSV deployed from flight-one LHA variants with a well deck. Such a variant of the Lightning Strike Group for ASW would be a transition to the next force grouping.

8. *Theater Reconnaissance and Antisubmarine Patrol Force (Opposed and Unopposed).* Such a group would be centered on a conventionally powered scout carrier deploying future fixed wing unmanned air, sea, and subsurface platforms to conduct and sustain wide-area patrol and reconnaissance. In an opposed configuration, deployed MUSV or LUSV could be configured for air defense with a DDG or FFG attached, depending on the surface or subsurface threat expected. Cost and delivery timelines for such a ship could be minimized by using the existing LPD-17 hull design. This allows for keeping propulsion and the majority of ships' systems unchanged. Some adjustments could be made for increased fuel capacity and an improved flight deck that supports F-35B vertical takeoff and landing and unmanned flight operations. F-35B capacity would be for air defense and as an at-sea forward arming and refueling point (FARP) for Marine Corps units ashore.

9. *Contested Logistic Support Force.* Amphibious and land forces operating within the first island chain during a crisis will require urgent, at-sea battle damage repair and logistic support necessitating a new Contested Logistic Support Force. This grouping would be centered on a multirole logistic ship to provide urgent repairs, enabling a damaged ship to retire to a shipyard for critical repairs, and replenishment of munitions and refueling. Today this mission would be conducted by large Combat Logistic Forces (CLF), like 50,000-ton oilers and 40,000-ton dry cargo ships. To service a geographically dispersed, large number of smaller units (First Island Chain ARGs), more numerous logistic vessels would be needed that could operate in the shallow waters and under threat in the first island chain.

While most often operating with an escort (an FFG or a DDG), these logistics ships (i.e., AR-L) would require limited defenses to enable independent and dispersed operations while under threat of attack. Ideally, these units would operate within the anti-access capabilities employed ashore by the Marines and the Army to protect against attack from air or surface ships. The submarine threat would have to be considered in the ship's hull design to allow for deployable sensors (i.e., torpedo detection) and limited defensive weapons (e.g., torpedo decoys and point missile defenses).

10. *Basing and Heavy Logistics Support Force.* Sustaining the fleet in battle will require repairs and advanced bases. This force, operating away from immediate threat, would focus on establishing bases for operations, much as Ulithi Atoll was during World War II in the Pacific. In peacetime, such a grouping would be focused on reconstituting antiquated bases or upgrading existing infrastructure for U.S. forces (Chuuk Lagoon, Pohnpei, etc.) and would consist of large CLF ships, construction battalions for port and airfield work, and a new large repair-and-manufacturing ship (AR).

A new class of surface tenders or repair-and-manufacturing vessels would provide substantial battle damage repairs, utilize additive manufacturing to supply needed replacement parts quickly, and employ a team of naval architects and craftsmen. In the immediate peacetime future, expeditionary fast transports with embarked construction teams would be deployed to the Central and South Pacific to conduct infrastructure upgrades for follow-on forces, ideally in conjunction with military exercises utilizing ERC funds to improve port and airfield infrastructure at key locations.

11. *Maritime Escort Force.* As noted earlier, the Navy today will not be able to provide convoy escorts to military sealift. This predicament can be addressed in several novel ways centered on a Maritime Escort Force construct composed of unmanned vessels, land-based manned and unmanned maritime patrol aircraft, traditional escort warships when available, or deployable defensive systems installed on merchant vessels and operated by Navy sailors.

The first layer of defense would be provided by a maritime patrol force of P-8 manned aircraft and unmanned MQ-4Cs and

MQ-9s operating from land for sustained maritime surveillance. For unmanned aircraft, it will be important to develop sensors that are optimized for ASW; notably miniature sonobuoys being developed by ERAPSCO and Spartan Corporation will be needed to localize hostile submarines.[29] A second layer of defense would be deployable sensors, decoys, and defensive armaments installed on select merchant vessels operated by deployed naval teams and, when available, a traditional escort (an FFG or LCS, potentially augmented with MUSV).

12. *New Naval Air Wings.* The evolving missions for the Navy within the first island chain and broad-area antisubmarine patrol in the Central Pacific and North Atlantic will see the evolution of three classes of aircraft carriers: the well-known CVN of the *Nimitz* class and *Ford* class, a CVNE designed for screening operations of expeditionary forces within the first island chain, and a CVS designed for large-area maritime patrol and antisubmarine operations. Each class of carrier with its specific role requires an air wing appropriate to the mission. For CVNs of the future, the air wing will retain a strike mission focus likely consisting of forty-four strike fighters (28 F/A-18E/F and 16 F-35C); five to seven EA-18G electronic warfare aircraft; five E-2D for air command and control; six to ten SH-60 helicopters; three CMV-22 Osprey tilt-rotor aircraft for logistics support; and five to nine MQ-25 unmanned tanker aircraft.[30] While the CVN air wing is optimized for strike operations, the CVNE and CVS air wings would be optimized for their role and incorporate more unmanned platforms to allow more aircraft to be carried and allow more flight hours supported on a smaller hull.

In the future, partnering unmanned air platform designers with shipbuilders should be pursued to inform ship designs optimized for unmanned naval air operations. Beginning with the 2021 establishment of an Unmanned Carrier-Launched Multi-Role Squadron (VUK-10), the MQ-25 is first in line among unmanned platforms to be incorporated into the air wing in an air-refueling or tanker role.[31] Future developments will likely see the MQ-25 take on new roles utilizing electronic warfare and sensor underwing pods for sea control and air dominance.

The Navy has also been investing in unmanned helicopters, such as the MQ-8C Fire Scout, with a twelve-hour endurance carrying a 300-pound payload.[32] Future developments could enable the MQ-8 to participate in sea-control and antisubmarine operations. Assuming the Navy is able to continue recent years' advances in existing unmanned aircraft, it is reasonable to project that by 2030, they could be incorporated into future aircraft carrier air wings optimized for unmanned systems.

The role and area of operations expected of a CVNE deemphasizes the need for long-range strike operations while emphasizing sustained air defenses. The concept would center on teaming one manned F-35 with two MQ-25s (one tanker, one armed) for sustained air defense operations. SH-60 and MQ-8 helicopters would conduct ASW and intercept hostile small-surface vessels; it is also expected that an SH-60 would be available for rescue and recovery operations in a long-standing role on CVNs. The embarkation of the tilt-rotor CMV-22 is intended for logistic support and can also support remote Marine or Army advance operating bases in a limited capacity. To support rapid sortieing of air defense aircraft in the face of a threat, the CVNE would likely incorporate three catapult systems: the Ford-class Electromagnetic Aircraft Launch Systems.

The CVS would be intended to fill a peacetime presence and maritime patrol mission while filling in gaps in shore-based air cover of key sea- and air-lanes in wartime. It would not employ a catapult system but would rely instead on vertical takeoff and landing aircraft for air defense and helicopters to execute its patrol and antisubmarine mission. A future CVS design would build on lessons of the 1964 *Master Stroke* exercise and the 1960 *Wasp*-CVS design that proved the value of CVS bow-mounted sonar and close-in antisubmarine weapons and defenses; today, in place of bow-mounted sonar, a towed variable-depth array is more appropriate. Or, an escort with a towed variable-depth sonar array could be paired with the CVS to bolster submarine detection and close-in defense.[33] An option to consider is repurposing the *San Antonio* class (LPD-17) or *America* class (LHA-6) for a CVS role by reinforcing its large flight deck for F-35s and converting its well deck for extra fuel storage and aircraft. Repurposing the LPD-17 hull for this role must address stability concerns caused by the greater topside weight.

# Chart 8. Comparing Three Potential Air Wings of the Future

SOURCE: Richard R. Burgess, "Navy's Future Carrier Air Wing Configuration Coming into Focus," Seapower Magazine, September 14, 2020, https://seapowermagazine.org/navys-future-carrier-air-wing-configuration-coming-into-focus/ (accessed November 23, 2020).

**SHIP TYPE**

| Aircraft | | CVN — Strike/Sea Control | CVNE — Air Dominance/Sea Control | CVS — Maritime Patrol/Anti-Submarine Operations |
|---|---|---|---|---|
| F-35C | Carrier version | 16 | 12 | |
| F-35B | Short takeoff and vertical landing | | | 4 |
| F-18E/F | Strike fighter | 28 | | |
| EA-18G | Electronic warfare | 5–7 | | |
| E-2D | Air command and control | 5 | | |
| SH-60 | Helicopter rescue and anti-submarine operations | 6–10 | 4 | 4 |
| CMV-22 | Tilt-rotor for logistics, i.e., carrier on-board delivery | 3 | 2 | |
| MQ-25 | Unmanned tanker | 5–9 | 5 | |
| MQ-25 | Unmanned electronic warfare, tanker | | 12 | |
| MQ-25 | Unmanned air dominance, anti-surface vessel operations | | 12 | |
| MQ-8 | Unmanned helicopter anti-submarine, anti-surface vessel operations | | 4 | 12 |

The addition of two new classes of aircraft carriers provides the Navy several benefits in the long run. First, it disperses its high-end fighter-strike aircraft among more platforms, mitigating the loss of any single CVN. Second, by increasingly leveraging unmanned aircraft, the CVS and CVNE can deliver significant airpower, ostensibly from smaller hulls and fewer pilots, thereby mitigating some construction and operation costs and broadening the shipyards where they could be built and repaired. Third, the addition of a CVNE and CVS to the fleet provides more flexibility in peacetime presence operations, alleviating the demand on CVNs, and during wartime augments the CVN for deterrence operations against opportunistic foes.

## Getting Down to Numbers . . .

Several factors were weighed in order to determine a recommended force structure, starting with the current size, capacity, and operating patterns of the threat (in this case, China's and Russia's navies) and then using the current U.S. fleet size and disposition to determine where and with what capabilities to prioritize presence. Allowance was then made for the growth of the threat navies and likely deployments out to 2035 (much beyond which projections become very fluid). These projections draw on several sources, but notably the work done by the Office of Naval Intelligence and Rear Adm. Michael McDevitt of the Center for Naval Analyses in predicting the size of China's and Russia's blue-water fleets out to 2035. The CNA's analysis anticipates that China's blue-water (or distant seas) navy will grow from today's 131 ships to 270 large modern warships with a larger proportion of nuclear submarines, not counting another 160 near-seas vessels.[34] The overall number grows to over 600 Chinese maritime vessels of concern when CCG and maritime militia are factored in. Russia's blue-water navy will likely remain relatively flat at 73 blue-water ships with perhaps modest growth in the numbers of submarines and frigates or destroyers. The rationale is based on several factors, notably that shipbuilding is considered Russia's worst-performing defense sector and faces a host of challenges in overcoming obsolescent infrastructure and flat budgets.[35] For the United States, the most recent at the time thirty-year shipbuilding plan (FY 2020) was used as a benchmark for fleet growth, with typical design-to-fabrication of a lead ship taking from three to eight years. This will depend on how much the new designs utilize existing systems, hull forms, propulsion plants, and shipyard capacity. In rare cases, such as the *Victorious*-class ocean surveillance vessel, timelines can be expedited further with effective early design collaboration and adherence to as many existing systems and designs as possible. Importantly, in the following list of new classes of warships that are needed, all the technology included in them already exists in 2022:

The new classes of ships recommended include

- a nuclear-powered aircraft carrier (CVNE) optimized for Western Pacific operations;
- a scout carrier (CVS) using the hull and propulsion system of the *San Antonio* class (LPD);
- a command cruiser and strike-support ship for Strike Surface Action Groups and fleet command ships (CLC) based on the *San Antonio* class (LPD);
- a small "nurse" repair and replenishment ship (AR-L) supporting first island chain littoral operations; and
- a factory and repair ship (AR) to repair damaged vessels nearer the conflict and minimize the time during which a vessel has to operate in extremis.

Additionally, others (notably Bryan Clark and Timothy Walton) have recommended the following new classes of ship, with some already in prototyping:

- A 2,000-ton unmanned or optionally manned corvette (DDC or LUSV) with VLS cells[36]
- A missile reload ship (T-AKM) operating in conjunction with the DDC[37]
- A Light Amphibious Warship (LAW) of 1,000–8,000 tons[38]
- A large unmanned submersible (XLUUV in prototyping)[39]
- A medium unmanned surface vehicle (MUSV in prototyping)[40]

Implementation of a new force design will be a long-term process and, considering that the strategic environment is driving the Navy to consider several new platforms, is likely to be a generational program. Initial adjustments to deployment plans, assignment of forces such as home port changes, and validation of concepts of operation like EABO and DMO can take one to three years from approval to execution. These time frames drive a three-phase approach to building this future fleet.

The first phase, would focus on minor adjustments to force allocations occurring in the first few years and acceleration of currently planned shipbuilding—for example, more than four SSNs being built a year. This would include a surge of as many as three reactivated reserve ships to bolster the Fleet's homeland defense, validate reserve fleet reactivation assumptions, and establish a reserve force plus platforms dedicated to fleet experimentation and training. Following this would be a *buildup* phase consisting of five years for focused development of new classes of ships and their joining the fleet (MUSV, LAW, etc.). Also, during this time fleet experimentation and lessons learned from large-scale exercises will refine concepts of operation while also working out any problems with new platform designs. During the third phase, which extends to 2035, increasing numbers of unmanned vessels would enter the fleet as first-in-class CVNE, CVS, AR, and AR-L are delivered. Spacing these developments out is important not only to consider the engineering involved, and limitations on shipyard capacities, but also to budget, which is the next topic.

## The Cost of Building a Strategy-Driven, Threat-Based Fleet

The final number of ships required, and what types are built, is based on the most likely and dangerous scenario, with capacity for peacetime competition across eight regions. In each region the likely at-sea forces and potential challenges from China and Russia were used to baseline the peacetime force structure. This was done only for the peacetime competition informed by force disposition, while ensuring total fleet size met threat versus total Chinese and Russian fleet capacity. Additionally, weather and seasonal maritime activity (maritime militia, Coast Guard, border police, fishing fleets, etc.) were weighed to determine the times of the year when incidents or challenges are most likely to be encountered. Considering such factors mitigated the total required fleet size, as ships could be shifted across regions depending on seasonal threats. Not surprisingly, the greatest threat is in the South China Sea, peaking in

April–May and August–September for the foreseeable future, and that is where the greatest investment in presence is recommended. Each of the maritime operational regions went through the same analysis. In a mathematical format, the Force-Structure Equation looks like this:

$$BF(t) = BF_0 + OFRP \sum_{r=1}^{8} (W(r) * (PLAN_r(t) * OPTEMPO_{PLAN} + RN_r(t)$$

$$* OPTEMPO_{RN})) - Losses(t)$$

---

$BF(t)$ = Battle Force U.S. Navy by year

$t$ = time in years

$OFRP$ = factor accounting for per ship average time forward deployed normalized on a per-year basis

$OPTEMPO$ = a historical rate of Chinese and Russian blue-water navy operational tempo

$r$ = region: there were eight subregions analyzed (e.g., South China Sea, East China Sea, North Atlantic, Eastern Mediterranean)

$W(r)$ = a factor to account for weather impact on maritime activity in each region analyzed

$RN(t)$ = Russian Navy battle force as a function of operating areas or region and by year

$PLAN(t)$ = People's Liberation Army Navy battle force as a function of operating areas or region and by year

$Losses(t)$ = decommissioning, battle, or accidental loss

---

The next step was to assess the cost of designing, building, and operating such a new fleet. Building on analysis conducted by Bryan Clark and Timothy Walton for Navy's 2020 FNFS and utilizing the Congressional Budget Office's Interactive Force Structure Tool, an informed estimate was made.[41] The largest margin of error pertained to estimates for operation and support costs of the future unmanned fleet. During the process of analyzing the resourcing and employment of the future fleet, one question that arose was how best to manage two spikes in the shipbuilding estimate arising from the design and procurement of two variants of new aircraft carriers.

**Table 2. Naval Shipbuilding Proposal**

| | 2020 | 2021 | 2022 | 2023 | 2024 | 2025 | 2026 | 2027 | 2028 | 2029 | 2030 | 2031 | 2032 | 2033 | 2034 | 2035 |
|---|---|---|---|---|---|---|---|---|---|---|---|---|---|---|---|---|
| CVN | 11 | 11 | 11 | 11 | 12 | 12 | 11 | 11 | 10 | 10 | 10 | 10 | 10 | 10 | 10 | 10 |
| CVNE | | | | | | | | | 1 | 1 | 1 | 1 | 1 | 2 | 2 | 2 |
| CVS | | | | | | | | 1 | 1 | 1 | 2 | 2 | 2 | 3 | 3 | 3 |
| DDG-1000 | 3 | 3 | 3 | 3 | 3 | 3 | 3 | 3 | 3 | 3 | 3 | 3 | 3 | 3 | 3 | 3 |
| CG-47 | 22 | 18 | 16 | 16 | 14 | 12 | 10 | 10 | 8 | 3 | 1 | 0 | 0 | 0 | 0 | 0 |
| DDG-51 | 72 | 76 | 81 | 84 | 87 | 90 | 94 | 97 | 100 | 100 | 96 | 92 | 88 | 82 | 82 | 79 |
| DDG(X) | | | | | | | | | | | 1 | 3 | 5 | 7 | 9 | 12 |
| LCS | 22 | 25 | 27 | 31 | 35 | 35 | 35 | 35 | 35 | 35 | 35 | 35 | 35 | 34 | 34 | 33 |
| FFG | | | | | | | 1 | 2 | 3 | 5 | 7 | 9 | 11 | 13 | 15 | 17 |
| FFG(X) | | | | | | | | | | | | 1 | 2 | 3 | 4 | 6 |
| MCM | 8 | 8 | 5 | 1 | | | | | | | | | | | | |
| SSN | 51 | 52 | 53 | 53 | 50 | 50 | 50 | 47 | 46 | 45 | 45 | 44 | 43 | 43 | 42 | 42 |
| SSN(VPM) | 2 | 3 | 5 | 7 | 9 | 11 | 13 | 15 | 17 | 19 | 21 | 23 | 25 | 27 | 27 | 27 |
| SSN(X) | | | | | | | | | | | 1 | 1 | 2 | 2 | 3 | 3 |
| SSGN | 4 | 4 | 4 | 4 | 4 | 4 | 4 | 2 | 1 | | | | | | | |
| SSBN 726 | 14 | 14 | 14 | 14 | 14 | 14 | 14 | 13 | 12 | 11 | 10 | 9 | 9 | 8 | 7 | 6 |
| SSBN 826 | | | | | | | | | 1 | 1 | 1 | 1 | 2 | 2 | 3 | 4 |
| LHD/LHA | 10 | 10 | 10 | 10 | 11 | 11 | 11 | 11 | 11 | 12 | 12 | 12 | 12 | 12 | 13 | 12 |
| LSD/LPD/LPD(X) | 23 | 24 | 24 | 24 | 25 | 26 | 25 | 26 | 25 | 26 | 25 | 24 | 24 | 24 | 25 | 25 |
| LAW | | | | | | 1 | 2 | 4 | 6 | 8 | 10 | 12 | 14 | 16 | 18 | 20 |

| | | | | | | | | | | | | | | | | |
|---|---|---|---|---|---|---|---|---|---|---|---|---|---|---|---|---|
| LUSV/DDC | | 1 | 2 | 4 | 4 | 6 | 8 | 10 | 12 | 16 | 22 | 28 | 34 | 36 | 38 | 40 |
| MUSV | | 2 | 2 | 4 | 6 | 9 | 12 | 15 | 21 | 27 | 35 | 43 | 51 | 57 | 61 | 63 |
| XLUUV | | | | 1 | 2 | 4 | 7 | 11 | 15 | 19 | 23 | 25 | 27 | 29 | 31 | 33 |
| AS | 2 | 2 | 2 | 2 | 2 | 2 | | | | | | | | | | |
| AS(X) | | | | | | | | 1 | 1 | 2 | 2 | 3 | 3 | 3 | 3 | 3 |
| AR | | | | | | | 1 | 1 | 1 | 1 | 2 | 2 | 2 | 3 | 3 | 3 |
| AR-L | | | | | 1 | 2 | 3 | 4 | 5 | 6 | 7 | 8 | 9 | 10 | 11 | 12 |
| LCC | 2 | 2 | 2 | 2 | 2 | 2 | 1 | 1 | 1 | 1 | 1 | | | | | |
| LCC(X) | | | | | | | | | 1 | 1 | 1 | 2 | 2 | 2 | 3 | 3 |
| T-AKM | | | | | 1 | 1 | 2 | 2 | 2 | 3 | 4 | 5 | 6 | 7 | 8 | 9 |
| T-AOL | | | | | 1 | 2 | 4 | 4 | 6 | 8 | 10 | 13 | 14 | 16 | 18 | 20 |
| Command & Support | 25 | 27 | 30 | 34 | 37 | 40 | 41 | 43 | 47 | 46 | 46 | 49 | 51 | 52 | 52 | 51 |
| Logistics | 31 | 32 | 32 | 32 | 32 | 31 | 31 | 31 | 32 | 32 | 33 | 31 | 32 | 33 | 33 | 34 |
| **Total** | **302** | **314** | **323** | **338** | **352** | **369** | **385** | **403** | **426** | **444** | **470** | **493** | **521** | **541** | **563** | **575** |
| 2016 Navy FSA | 301 | 305 | 311 | 314 | 314 | 313 | 314 | 316 | 322 | 325 | 331 | 337 | 343 | 351 | 355 | 355 |

**SOURCE:** Author's proposal. Data for 2016 Navy Force Structure Assessment (FSA) comes from Office of the Chief of Naval Operations, "Report to Congress on the Annual Long-Range Plan for Construction of Naval Vessels for Fiscal Year 2020," March 2019, p. 13, https://media.defense.gov/2020/May/18/2002302045/-1/-1/1/PB20_SHIPBUILDING_PLAN.PDF (accessed December 6, 2020).

Given that the Navy has too few ships in its current reserve fleet and that a third of its fleet will age out by 2035, there is urgency required in shipbuilding. Service life extensions of older *Los Angeles*-class submarines and *Avenger*-class mine warfare ships can at best defer the inevitable decommissioning of large numbers of ships by 2035. In the case of the *Avenger* class, the potential exists that the Navy may lose an entire capability —mine sweeping—without proven alternatives and new purpose-built platforms. The rapidly aging fleet raises several concerns that underscore the need for a near-term bias in shipbuilding.

## Chart 9. Restructuring the Navy Fleet

The Navy fleet of the future will have a diminished reliance on large surface combat ships and an increased reliance on unmanned vessels.

SHARE OF TOTAL VESSELS IN U.S. NAVY FLEET

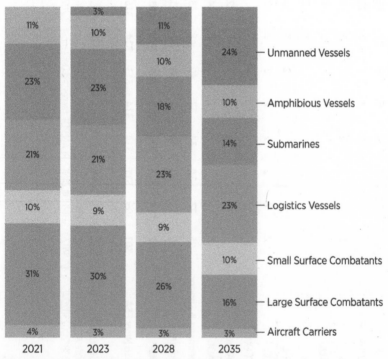

| | 2021 | 2023 | 2028 | 2035 | |
|---|---|---|---|---|---|
| Unmanned Vessels | 11% | 3% | 11% | 24% | |
| Amphibious Vessels | | 10% | 10% | 10% | |
| Submarines | 23% | 23% | 18% | 14% | |
| Logistics Vessels | 21% | 21% | 23% | 23% | |
| Small Surface Combatants | 10% | 9% | 9% | 10% | |
| Large Surface Combatants | 31% | 30% | 26% | 16% | |
| Aircraft Carriers | 4% | 3% | 3% | 3% | |

**NOTES:** Aircraft Carriers-CVN, CVNE, CVS; Large Surface Combatant-CVN, CVNE, CVS, CG, DDG; Small Surface Combatant-FFG, LCS; Unmanned-XLUUV, LUSV, MUSC; Amphibious Vessels-LHA, LHD, LPD, LSD, LAW; Submarines-SSN, SSGN, SSBN; Logistics Vessels-AO, T-AKE, AS, AR, AR-L, T-AKM, LCC.
**SOURCE:** Author's analysis based on U.S. Navy's 2016 Integrated Naval Force Structure Assessment and the Office of Naval Intelligence.

*First*, a new submarine tender is urgently needed to replace the aging *Emory S. Land* and *Frank Cable*, both of which were commissioned in 1979 and both of which survived attempts at decommissioning in 1996. These tenders have been important for sustaining the nuclear Navy while forward deployed, and their value will increase markedly as larger numbers of submarines and unmanned submersibles are expected to be put into operation overseas.

*Second*, when the last guided missile submarines (the four repurposed *Ohio*-class SSGNs) are retired from service in 2027, the proposed force design plans their immense capacity to launch land-attack strikes with conventional cruise missiles to be replaced by large surface ships and a future DDC. To replace one of four SSGNs' firepower of up to 154 Tomahawk land-attack cruise missiles equates to one new DDG (96 available missile cells) and four new DDCs (estimated 32 missile cells) while allowing some capacity for self-defense weapons. Additionally, if the command cruiser concept is pursued, it too could mitigate this lost capacity for long-range strike.

## Chart 10. Navy Combat Ships Nearing End of Service Life

| Combat Class | Ships | Average Years Until Class End of Service Life |
|---|---|---|
| *Avenger* MCM | 8 | 1.1 |
| *Los Angeles* SSN | 28 | 3.2 |
| *Ticonderoga* CG | 22 | 9.0 |
| *Ohio* SSGN and SSBN | 18 | 9.6 |
| *Seawolf* SSN | 3 | 11.9 |
| *Whidbey Island* LSD | 7 | 12.7 |
| *Harpers Ferry* LSD | 4 | 14.8 |
| *Wasp* LHD | 7 | 15.6 |
| *Independence/Freedom* LCS | 23 | 20.9 |
| *Nimitz* and *Ford* CVN | 11 | 22.0 |
| *Virginia* SSN | 19 | 24.9 |
| *Arleigh Burke* DDG | 67 | 26.2 |
| *Zumwalt* DDG | 2 | 26.3 |
| *San Antonio* LPD | 11 | 30.0 |
| *America* LHA | 2 | 36.1 |

**NOTE:** Figures are based on calculations for August 2021.
**SOURCE:** Naval Sea Systems Command, Naval Vessel Register, "Fleet Size," http://www.nvr.navy.mil/NVRSHIPS/FLEETSIZE.HTML (accessed August 2, 2021).

*Third,* the *Avenger*-class mine countermeasures (MCM) ship represents the only dedicated vessels countering the mine threat. On August 20, 2020, the Navy decommissioned three of its aging *Avenger*-class MCM ships, leaving eight in service overseas in Sasebo, Japan, and Manama, Bahrain. The last of these ships will be retired by 2024, leaving a capability gap. The Navy is relying on the development of mine countermeasure mission packages for its LCSs to provide this capability. China and Russia possess a significant mine threat that the Navy cannot ignore and must retain the capacity to defend against.

When all is said and done, this represents a best estimate of the cost of an optimum fleet design, assuming an inherent but manageable margin of error. Additionally, to build such a fleet requires tandem investment to increase shipyard maintenance capacities that conservatively, per the Shipyard Infrastructure Optimization Program (SIOP), will cost an additional $1–2 billion annually to implement—and most likely significantly more once shipyard optimization modeling is complete and more informed requirements are defined. Additional monies will be needed to recruit the mariners and skilled workers to man and maintain a larger merchant fleet through an expanded Maritime Security Program (MSP) and attract bright and imaginative naval architects to help the Navy become a smarter ship-buying customer. It is reasonable to assume that this would equate to an additional $1 billion per year. I discuss this further in the next chapter.

Taken together with a 10 percent margin of error, the cost of a national maritime program would range from $150 billion to $160 billion over thirteen years (2022–35) above a 2020 naval budget with inflation-only growth. Biased to the higher estimate, the average annual cost would be $12.3 billion in additional funds over inflation for shipbuilding and conversion (SCN) and operation and support, as well as additional funds to support shipyard capacity expansion and initiatives to address shortfalls in the merchant marine. In the context of historical and current budgets, such an increase (approximately 1.8 percent of the 2020 defense budget) should be achievable without poaching funds from other DoD accounts or services. Even such modest increases, however, must come with commitments and safeguards to ensure that the money is used wisely and that each dollar has maximum strategic impact on our competitors—the real measure of success.

## Chart 11. Costs for Navy Procurement, Operations, and Support

 ----- Actual FY 2021 figure, then adjusted for inflation
 ——— Author's revised plan

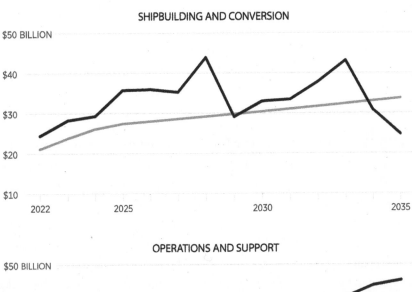

SHIPBUILDING AND CONVERSION

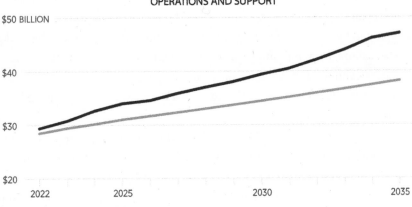

OPERATIONS AND SUPPORT

**NOTE:** Figures are by fiscal year.
**SOURCES:** Congressional Budget Office, "CBO's Interactive Force Structure Tool," https://www.cbo.gov/publication/54351 (accessed December 2, 2020), and Bryan Clark, Timothy A. Walton, and Seth Cropsey, "American Sea Power at a Crossroads: A Plan to Restore the US Navy's Maritime Advantage," Hudson Institute, October 2020, https://s3.amazonaws.com/media.hudson.org/Clark%20Cropsey%20Walton_American%20Sea%20Power%20at%20a%20Crossroads.pdf (accessed December 3, 2020).

# CHAPTER 8

# A National Maritime Program

―――― ⚬⚭⚬ ――――

*Whoever said the pen is mightier than the sword obviously never encountered automatic weapons.*

—attributed to Gen. Douglas MacArthur

T he Navy's demonstrated inability to return ships to service in a timely manner is unacceptable. After their collisions with commercial ships in 2017, it took the *Fitzgerald* over a year to depart its dry dock and almost two years to return to sea,[1] and the *McCain* spent nine months in dry dock.[2] With a fleet that is small relative to its responsibilities and with limited shipbuilding capacity, quick turnaround on battle damage repairs is vital in war, and the lack of this capability in peacetime can be exploited by adversaries. Despite the Navy's best effort, often on the backs of its sailors, its public shipyards charged with sustaining the nuclear submarines and aircraft carriers completed 75 percent of maintenance more than thirty days late during the years 2015–19.[3] Such delays have operational implications.

Moreover, the post–Cold War record on shipbuilding is not a reassuring one. A culture of organizational efficiency and cost savings has led to an institutional predilection for reducing fleet size, the atrophy of supporting infrastructure, and the near-elimination of in-house naval engineering design support. The Navy's fiscal year (FY) 2021 shipbuilding budget, for example, was $3.6 billion less than the amount projected in its own thirty-year shipbuilding plan.[4] Then, in the first long-range shipbuilding plan of the Biden administration, the Navy would shrink further, to a new low of 280, in 2027—the very year China is preparing for a showdown with Taiwan and the United States. At the same time, the cost to implement long-delayed infrastructure investment in the SIOP will likely grow beyond the initially projected $21 billion over twenty years just to support today's fleet. Additionally, in order to ensure a continued undersea nuclear second-strike capability, the Navy must dedicate a substantial portion of its shipbuilding budget (an average of approximately 20 percent annually for FY 2021 to FY 2025) to ensure that the *Columbia*-class ballistic missile submarines arrive on schedule to replace the aging *Ohio*-class subs.[5]

The Navy's shipyard predicament is the result of decades of near-term operational requirements being given priority. On the day after the Iron Curtain came down, the Navy had eight public shipyards to service its nuclear fleet: four on each coast. Amid the euphoria created by the successful 1990–91 war in Iraq and the collapse of the Soviet Union, the Base Realignment and Closure (BRAC) Act of 1988 began to deliver on the post–Cold War "peace dividend" by closing half of the Navy's public shipyards.[6] To insulate post–Cold War base closure from domestic politics, Congress created a process whereby Congress had forty-five days to reject recommendations of the president; otherwise, they would be approved pursuant to BRAC. This represented a continuation of efforts to rationalize base infrastructure begun under President John Kennedy in 1961 and culminated with the final round of BRAC recommendations in 2005.[7] Since 2017, Congress has included language in the annual National Defense Authorization Act precluding any new BRAC rounds. Therefore, to disperse basing and increase shipyard capacity, a new process modeled on the BRAC is needed. To this end, DoD would need an interagency body to review and recommend specific new domestic basing options and foreign posture projects. An early goal should be to recommend the addition of one new shipyard on the West Coast with a dry dock suitable for a *Ford*-class aircraft carrier and the longer *Virginia*-class submarines with installed payload modules. This added capacity will be urgently needed as these ships join the fleet, especially given the larger proportion of naval assets in the Pacific and earthquake structural integrity concerns at Puget Sound Naval Shipyard's Dry Dock No. 6 in Washington State. The challenge, however, isn't merely getting more dry docks or public shipyards for nuclear ship work.

Not only is today's workforce overworked but it also must make do with antiquated equipment, such as sheet metal rollers, plasma cutters, and cranes that are on average twenty-four years old, compared with private shipyards' capital equipment that averages just seven to ten years in age. The Navy has recently begun to address some of the shortfall in maintenance capacity with its SIOP submitted to Congress in September 2018.[8] Unaddressed, however, are the Navy's four overseas shipyards (one in Spain, one in Bahrain, and two in Japan), in which about 70 percent of all maintenance is completed late.

In the United States, the Navy also uses twenty-six private shipyards, located mostly near naval bases, for over 240 conventionally powered ships. Reflecting a Cold War European theater focus, dry-dock capacities are disproportionately located on the East Coast despite a larger number of ships on the West Coast.[9] This has also placed tremendous hardship on families who must relocate in the middle of an assignment from a homeport to a shipyard across the country.

Although fully funding the Navy's SIOP is necessary, it will not address the shortfall in the servicing of today's fleet, let alone a larger one that the nation will need for great power competition. Some of the near-term shortfall can be mitigated by shifting workload from the four public shipyards to private shipyards, but that will not address the shortfall in nuclear maintenance capacity unless a fifth modern public shipyard is established, preferably on the West Coast. Another urgent need will be to increase the shipyard workforce through invigorated training and retention incentives.

Finally (and surprisingly), no comprehensive root-cause analysis of maintenance delays at all shipyards servicing the Navy has been conducted. To ensure that monies are spent wisely and the correct remedies are put in place, a comprehensive root-cause analysis will be needed with periodic progress reports accompanied by SIOP updates submitted to Congress. Real-world events would highlight the importance of making real changes.

On November 30, 2020, the CNO decided to forgo replacement or repair of the severely damaged *Bonhomme Richard* following a days-long fire during the previous summer. The obvious rationale seemed plausible: $3 billion for a new ship was too much compared with $30 million over a year's time to decommission the ship.[10] Easily missed in the Navy's press statements, though, was the compounding rationale of shipyard capacity too limited even to consider repair or replacement. The Navy's decision to decommission the ship based on costs and expected impact on limited repair facilities raises serious doubts about the Navy's ability to sustain the fleet in war. These doubts were amplified following a subsequent incident.

On October 2, 2021, the nuclear submarine *Connecticut* hit a seamount in the South China Sea, causing damage to its ballast tanks. Because of this damage it was unable to submerge for an exposed five-day journey to Guam for emergency repairs. If this had occurred during heightened tensions, or a war, the boat, lacking the ability to submerge safely, would have been an easy target. Shipyard capacity quickly became an issue again when acting Assistant Secretary of the Navy Jay Stefany testified to the House Armed Service Committee that repairs to the nuclear submarine *Connecticut* would cause "perturbations" to the workload at the Navy's shipyards. Stefany's comments reveal that the Navy has so little shipyard capacity on hand that it is pressed to deal with unexpected damage, let alone manage maintenance without delay as countless Government Accountability Office reports have found.

Complicating things, the Navy now lacks any large floating dry docks; this proved important in repairing (just barely) the submarine *San Francisco*, which limped to Guam following a fatal grounding in 2005. Floating dry docks were critical throughout the Pacific campaign of World War II, with their ability to be close to the fighting and provide timely battle damage repairs, saving many ships and lives. All that remains now of that war-winning legacy is a small floating dry dock in Norfolk, Virginia. Definitely unglamorous, deployable floating dry docks are critical for sustaining a fighting fleet—a point also made clear when Al-Qaeda suicide bombers attacked the destroyer *Cole* in Aden, Yemen, in August 2000, killing seventeen sailors and causing extensive damage. To save the ship, the Navy chartered the heavy-lift ship *Blue Marlin* to return the *Cole* to Pascagoula, Mississippi. In a modern war, a combination of such heavy-lift ships and floating dry docks may once again prove decisive in the Pacific.

Sadly, a post–Cold War culture of organizational efficiency and cost savings has instilled an institutional predilection for atrophy. Despite a presidential policy requiring a 355-ship fleet by 2034[11]—a policy codified in law since 2017[12]—shipbuilding has been limited and budget requests

Morotai naval anchorage under Japanese aerial attack, July 18, 1945. *Photo by Ens. William C. Sadler, USN*

Destroyer escort USS *Manning* in a floating dry dock, 1945. Exact date unknown. *Photo by Ens. William C. Sadler, USN*

have been reduced. The Navy's "Annual Long-Range Plan for Construction of Naval Vessels" (December 9, 2020), intended to bend this curve and sustain increased shipbuilding rates over the next five years, funds eighty-two new ships at a cost of slightly more than $147 billion.[13] Addressing these constraints effectively and building the Navy the nation needs is not impossible, but it will require becoming a smarter shipbuilding customer and heeding important lessons of the recent past.

The U.S. Navy's December 2020 "Annual Long-Range Plan for Construction of Naval Vessels," focusing on great power competition and covering FY 2022 to FY 2051, is a useful statement but inadequate by itself. As was true during President Ronald Reagan's naval buildup, the greater budgets required to enlarge the Navy as envisioned by the most recent ship-building plan must be accompanied by commitments to greater diligence

Mine warfare vessel YMS47 damaged by a mine off Balik Papan on July 19, 1945. *Photo by Ens. William C. Sadler, USN*

and effectiveness in the use of these funds. Specifically, naval shipbuilding must improve on its 2008–18 track record of $8 billion more than planned in cost overruns for eleven lead ships produced, half of those more than two years late.[14] While things have improved, the ultimate metric for judging the commitment to this promise is, first and foremost, delivering warships on time and in the numbers needed to keep pace with China's and Russia's maritime threats. At the same time, partnership with Congress will be vital to ensuring predictability in shipbuilding plans with long-term budgeting, stability in design, and adequate interval in series production to take advantage of economies of scale and fabrication experience.

## Construction of Navy Ships

Navy shipbuilding is guided by instructions promulgated by the Secretary of the Navy,[15] under federal law (i.e., Title 10 U.S. Code section 254),[16] and by customary precedent. Although little discussed, how these elements come together to guide or constrain the Navy's shipbuilding program is important. The overarching "Two-Pass, Seven-Gate Process" includes one pass for senior leadership to decide on design requirements, a second to ascertain acquisition planning, and seven decision gates along the way. The key decision-makers in design progression from conceptualization to construction are the CNO and the Assistant Secretary of the Navy for Research, Development and Acquisition.[17]

Weighing heavily on these decision-makers and a key element throughout the design and construction of the Navy's warships is the setting of engineering requirements. The successful development of durable warships depends on setting the right requirements to address specific and enduring tactical and operational challenges, but the Navy does not identify or develop capabilities to address these challenges in a vacuum. It must first validate and define future capabilities through the Joint Capability Integration and Development System. A process run by the Joint Staff intended to ensure that all the military forces are addressing capability gaps in a comprehensive and effective manner. As appropriate, this considers how new operational concepts (CONOPs) using existing and future systems can mitigate capability gaps before new platforms are developed.

## The Need for Resourcing Predictability

In recent times, the Navy has tended to underestimate the costs of bringing new classes of warships to the fleet. This has been due in part to the changing nature of the naval threat from China and Russia, and wartime lessons informing military specifications to ensure survivability. It has also been due to a resourcing environment that encourages the underestimation of costs.

While congressional appropriations committees and the Navy have utilized several financing mechanisms effectively in recent years, pressures to expand the fleet are likely to strain existing methods of shipbuilding budgeting. For one thing, a larger portion of the shipbuilding plan must fund the *Columbia*-class submarine fleet while also increasing the size of the fleet and beginning the production of large numbers of unmanned vessels. To manage this, the Navy and Congress must do several things:

- avoid cost overruns by better enabling good engineering decisions in design and fabrication;
- avoid delays by requiring better up-front cost estimates to obviate the need for costly in-process redesign;
- adhere more closely to the thirty-year shipbuilding plan to reduce costs and enhance industry stability; and
- provide mechanisms for capturing savings and flexible budgeting to meet planned ship delivery intervals.

Fabrication of highly complex warships takes from three to five years (and longer for lead ships in a new class), including more than three years in design, giving ample opportunity for unexpected or tardy new requirements to be levied. Overall, providing greater predictability and stability in shipbuilding can provide cost savings and better ensure on-time delivery. To this end, the Navy has used several ship-purchasing methods over the years, and depending on the circumstances, each is more appropriate than a one-size-fits-all approach. Since 1950, the principal method used has been full funding of a ship in the year when it is procured. At times, however, the Navy has also used multiyear procurement, advance payments, and incremental funding. All four methods have utility. For example:

- Multiyear procurement is used when design changes are no longer expected and there is high certainty that several ships will be purchased, in which case the Navy contracts for a set number of ships at a set price. If the Navy or Congress reneges, the shipbuilder still gets paid, which assumes a degree of risk to the Navy budget.
- Advance procurement has been used to purchase materials with long lead times (e.g., ship reduction gears can take three years to produce) that otherwise would have delayed ship delivery and caused cost overruns.
- Incremental funding divides the total cost of procurement over several payments and allows for year-to-year budget flexibility.[18]

A final method, advance appropriations, has not yet been used for shipbuilding. In the president's budget for FY 2018, nondefense advance appropriations accounted for more than $339 billion.[19] This is a legislatively locked-in appropriation of monies in future years and would count in those future-year budgets. The Navy tried to use this in 2001 but was rebuked by congressional appropriations committees and has not attempted to use it since then.[20] To enable purchasing flexibility, a novel method was approved several years ago and is available today. Established with the FY 2015 budget, the National Sea-Based Deterrence Fund provides the Navy with an account to hold appropriated funds for up to five years and grants several authorities within one budgetary package. These authorities include the above-described methods and add advance construction and cross-class common component purchasing. These two new authorities allow:

- advance construction funds infrastructure and workforce stability needed in the fabrication of a ship; and
- common component purchasing—that is, the transfer of funds between accounts for the same parts.[21]

On at least two occasions, funds have been transferred from the Navy's shipbuilding account to the National Sea-Based Deterrence Fund, some $630 million was transferred in 2017,[22] and $209 million was transferred in 2020.[23] Although there could be wider utility, as currently authorized the fund is being used only for the *Columbia* class.

Another way of looking at the National Sea-Based Deterrence (NSBD) Fund is as a capital account. A new (or replacement of the NSBD Fund) account would be structured similarly and use previously approved congressional authorities, but would expand to fund all shipbuilding. Such a mechanism offers flexible budgeting that can enable appropriation of multi-year monies where there's utility. Doing this would encourage department-wide savings while funding an approved thirty-year shipbuilding plan. Such a mechanism would also avoid delays of budget reprogramming, which is required when moving appropriated monies between accounts. As Heritage Foundation defense budget expert Frederico Bartels has observed, reprogramming is cumbersome, involves multiple offices with veto power, and can take four to six months to approve, which likely runs into a new budget, further compounding delays.[24] The use of a multiyear shipbuilding capital account also mitigates the year-on-year shocks caused by unpredictable continuing resolutions or budgets frozen at the previous year's level by program lines, widely viewed as deleterious to Navy shipbuilding.[25]

The Navy's FY 2020 budget request included a two-ship aircraft carrier procurement, saving an estimated $3.9 billion compared with buying the ships separately.[26] With a capital account, such savings, when realized, could be rolled over to mitigate unexpected engineering challenges and cost growth while delivering on the shipbuilding plan. In 2004, for example, the Navy delayed the *Ford*-class aircraft carrier and *Zumwalt*-class destroyer for a year to meet immediate fiscal constraints; with a shipbuilding capital account, things might have been different. In addition, until the establishment of the National Sea-Based Deterrence Fund in 2015, the *Columbia*-class ballistic missile submarine program was two years behind schedule; it has since remained on track but with no margin for additional delays. The success of NSDB gives tangible insights that a shipbuilding capital account would be beneficial for fiscal responsibility and on-time ship delivery. That said, it's worth pointing out the nature of defense budgets relative to the broader federal budget.

Defense budgets are discretionary spending, and because of this they are subject to annual congressional authorization and appropriation. This is different from Social Security, Medicaid, and other entitlement programs making up half of the federal budget with mandatory funding.[27]

Since defense spending requires annual appropriation, budgets are rarely passed on time, and continuing resolutions are often used as stopgap funding mechanisms.[28] This has led to fiscal inefficiencies, hiring delays that exacerbate manning shortages, and delays in contracting for needed work.[29] In a unique session before the Senate Armed Service Committee in November 2013, the service chiefs detailed the impacts of budget uncertainty. For the Navy, there were immediate implications for shipbuilding and maintenance that included (among others listed) cancellation of five deployments, a six-month delay in deployment of a carrier strike group, a 30 percent reduction in facilities restoration, and a 20 percent reduction in base operations.[30] Getting the money right is important, but it also assumes the Navy is being a smart customer.

## Rebuilding the Naval Architect Design Factory

In a 2018 report, the Government Accountability Office made a key assessment: the greatest root cause of cost overruns and delays since 2008 has been concurrency. The term *concurrency* refers to the overlap in technology development, design, and construction of a ship. For example, in the case of the *Ford* class there was prolonged technology development concurrence as thirteen key novel technologies matured. The resulting redesign caused the eventual cost of construction to be $2 billion over estimate and delivery to be delayed by two years. As we will see, doing better will require recapitalizing the Navy's in-house engineering capacity, which is critical in early design and program success. It will also mean adjusting ship acquisition processes and revitalizing the partnership between the Naval Sea Systems Command (NAVSEA) charged with engaging the shipbuilding industry to construct and maintain its warships.

Seeking cost savings, the Navy reduced its in-house NAVSEA naval engineer staff some 75 percent by the late 1990s. The effect was to outsource new warship design to industry. Consequently, it has drawn out processes that took an average of forty-eight months to reach preliminary design and contract design milestones, compared with twenty-four months in the case of in-house design.[31] The British Royal Navy noted a similar effect when it downsized its Royal Corps of Naval Constructors. Having outsourced its design competencies, the Navy relied on industry to design the littoral combat ship and the *Zumwalt* DDG 1000. Series production for both ships was less than originally planned: only thirty-two of fifty-two for the LCS and three of thirty-two for the DDG 1000. In addition, cost overruns were 173 percent for the LCS and 47.9 percent for the DDG 1000, plus it took two years for both ships to reach initial operational capability.[32]

In the final analysis, the lack of in-house naval architecture expertise in developing specifications useful for industry has made the Navy a less than fully informed customer, and this has led, in turn, to costly decisions. An effective remedy for concurrency is better design and requirement development, which is more likely with greater in-house expertise in ship design. Best business practices indicate that unexpected engineering problems and fabrication issues (availability of dry dock, special machined tools, etc.) can be minimized by using Integrated Product Teams (IPTs) led by NAVSEA with industry subject-matter experts. IPTs can devise manufacturing strategies for each class of ship to be built, including long-term supplier agreements. These strategies should be developed both to plan delivery of critical parts and subsystems and to inform the thirty-year shipbuilding plan for better budget planning. In addition, a life-of-project (design through lead ship delivery) flag-level officer or Senior Executive Service civilian should be assigned to oversee a review board made up of members from the Navy and industry who can use good engineering sense to address changes in the operating and policy environment. This way, leaders can execute a sustainable long-range building plan while making judicious decisions when weighing the risks involved in incorporating new technologies.

Several key lessons can be derived from the history of Navy shipbuilding:

- *Do not change too much in a new class of ship.* Evolutionary change is cost effective. One success story is the use of a common hull design from the *Spruance* class in the *Ticonderoga* class, and common systems from the *Ticonderoga* class in the *Arleigh Burke* class. Adequate built-in excess capacity is important for future enhancements (e.g., modifications for *Ticonderoga* class to employ the Aegis radar and for flight IIA *Arleigh Burke* class to include space for two helicopter hangars).[33] Spurred by Secretary of Defense Donald Rumsfeld's push in the early 2000s to include revolutionary capabilities, the *Ford*-class aircraft carrier attempted to incorporate too many novel technologies—the Electromagnetic Aircraft Launch System (EMALS); a new aircraft arresting system, the Advanced Arresting Gear; the ship's primary radar, the Dual Band Radar; and the advanced weapons elevators to facilitate rapid arming of aircraft—and this led to significant delays in delivery. Delays in the *Ford* class and the Navy's emphasis on unmanned systems spurred Senators Jim Inhofe (R-OK) and Jack Reed (D-RI) to argue that critical subsystems must be successfully prototyped before being integrated into a ship's design, as was done with the SPY-1 advanced radar system before its initial integration into the *Ticonderoga* class.[34] In ship design, three components generally make the ship: the hull, propulsion, and installed systems. Changing any one or two is manageable, but changing all three in a new design comes with elevated risk of cost overruns and production delays, as was seen with the *Ford* class in the early 2000s. A good sign that the Navy appreciates this lesson is that the next-generation radar (SPY-6) being installed on *Arleigh Burke*–class destroyers will also be included on the next-generation destroyer, or DDG(X).[35] That the enemy also has a vote is shown by the fact that rapid Soviet undersea acoustic advances caused the Navy to design a technological leap-ahead with the *Seawolf*-class attack submarine. As the Cold War came to an end, the Navy could not validate the increased costs associated with improved acoustic stealth, a complex weapons handling system, and new hull materials and design.[36] Eventually, what was envisioned as the successor to the *Los Angeles*–class nuclear attack submarines resulted in only three boats built.

- *Build ships with room to grow.* Allowances for excess tonnage for future growth have actually resulted in designs that are cheaper to build, easier to operate, and easier to maintain. For their *Kongo*-class destroyer, for example, which resembles a U.S. *Arleigh Burke*–class destroyer, the Japanese allowed tonnage requirements to grow by one thousand tons, providing the space needed for future upgrades, simplified maintenance, and eased fabrication.[37] The added space allowed by increased tonnage enabled cost-effective fabrication and eased lifetime maintenance. The South Korean navy also incorporated this lesson into its *Sejong*-class (KDX) destroyers. Amplifying this is a good rule of thumb used by shipyards regarding the ratio of time to manufacture a ship—a factor of one when built in an enclosed shop in modules, three times longer when fabricating unprotected from the environments, and eight times longer when conducting fabrication in a hull that is completed. The bottom line: a little extra space in a surface ship can provide long-term cost savings. As new classes of ships field high-energy weapons, rail guns, electric drive propulsion, and a battery of new power-hungry sensors and radars, adequate power generation is critical. For the same reasons already given for excess tonnage, excess power generation capacity facilitates future upgrades and modifications of power-intense defenses and sensors. The *Ford* class is a power-hungry ship, and its design had to triple electrical power generation over the preceding *Nimitz* class to drive its radar, EMALS, and potential future high-energy defenses.[38] Whether the *Ford* (CVN-78) and other future classes of warship become obsolete prematurely will be, in part, a function of designed excess power generation.

- *Enforce strict mission design requirements.* For the *Oliver Hazard Perry*–class frigates of the Reagan buildup, strict displacement and manning constraints ensured that cost stayed within limits for large series production. This assumed a degree of mission design discipline lacking in the design of the littoral combat ship and contributed to a twenty-ship reduction in series construction.[39] A similar mission creep occurred with design of the *Zumwalt* class, which began as a naval gunfire support ship and then migrated to a ballistic missile defense platform, only to run into significant cost and design limitations in the employment of needed radar and spiraling costs for the advanced gun system. Moreover, lessons from the Navy's 2001 Optimum Manning experiments and the *Fitzgerald* and *McCain* collisions in 2017 indicate that ship designs must strike a balance between reducing manning with managed shipboard workloads. Specifically:

1. A February 2010 review found that the net effect of Optimum Manning was a lack of shipboard-experienced technicians compounded

by a smaller crew. Specifically, "Limitation to our legacy manning and distribution processes are [*sic*] resulting in low attained values of Navy Enlisted Classification (NEC) fit (rank, rating and NECs) with a 2009 manning average of 61% for at-sea surface units."[40]

2. An August 2020 National Transportation Safety Board report reaffirmed a conclusion reached as a result of a December 2017 internal investigation led by Adm. Philip Davidson, then-commander of U.S. Fleet Forces Command, that an overworked and underexperienced watch team was a significant contributor to the 2017 collisions.[41]

3. In setting manning constraints for ship design, it is imperative that crew size and experience levels be matched to the complexity of shipboard systems in order to execute its primary mission. If costs dictate a smaller crew, then design must likewise incorporate automation, simplified maintenance, and narrowly focused missions in order to ensure that crews can operate the ship safely. A legacy of Optimum Manning is the realization that retroactively reducing manning on a ship designed for larger crews will have disastrous effects.

- *Early industry-Navy collaboration:* Beginning with design, industry collaboration can ease the challenges involved in manufacturing a new class of ship. Given only fifteen months from mid-1985, the Navy succeeded in designing and procuring the first Small Waterplane Area Twin Hull (SWATH) ocean surveillance ship, the *Victorious* class. Thanks to its Continuing Concept Formulation program, which gave the Navy leadership in SWATH technologies, NAVSEA was able to convince the Secretary of the Navy that its engineers should have an active role in the design, which was granted, but only with significant industry involvement. Because existing ocean surveillance ships were mission incapable in rough winter seas at a time of heightened Cold War tensions, the program was given urgent priority. Based on their extensive experience in leading high-stress design projects and specific experience with SWATH, a hand-selected ship design manager and a design integration manager proved critical in making design decisions on technical issues for which either only incomplete or no validated modeling was available.[42] Partnering with industry early in the design phase contributed to delivering a design that could be built on a greatly compressed timeline, and with desired winter months' capability (95 percent versus the monohull predecessor's 57 percent).

## Adequate Interval

Setting the interval during which a class of warship is built determines whether the shipbuilding infrastructure increases, maintains, or shrinks capacity. Shipbuilding that is too fast can outpace supply chains, overtax the workforce and infrastructure, and lead to costly delays in delivery. Too little demand, driven by overhead costs, leads shipbuilders and suppliers to reduce workforce and curtail capital investments such as modernization of precision equipment, cranes, and docks. The ideal is demand within existing shipbuilders' capacities that leads to modernization and growth in capacity, or at least precludes a loss of capacity. In the early 2000s, the nuclear submarine force struggled to achieve this balance during a time of reduced budgets and faced the prospect of losing the capacity to build future nuclear submarines. Recovery was exacerbated as critical skilled workers such as submarine hull and nuclear power plant welders were laid off or retired without replacements.

The problem confronting the nuclear submarine force had been anticipated in the 1990s. By 1995, it was observed that a reduced production rate of nuclear submarines following increased build rates of the later Cold War would shrink the fleet irretrievably to dangerously low levels in a so-called attack submarine valley.[43] In fact, following a submarine commissioning holiday during which no boats were delivered to the Navy from 1996 to 2004, the associated workforce and supplier base shrank precipitously, raising alarms within the Navy's submarine community. A 2005 RAND study found that sustaining submarine design capacities at the existing two submarine shipyards (Northrup Grumman Newport News and Electric Boat) would be more cost effective than recapitalizing and training replacements in the future. The report also found that sustaining the workforce did not equate to experience without active submarine design and construction.[44]

After years of advocating for sufficient investment to secure both submarine production and the skilled workforce required for that production, the submarine force seems to have bent the curve by sustaining a two-a-year build rate for attack submarines with a view to a goal of sixty-six boats by 2048. In addition, the Navy began construction of the next strategic ballistic missile submarine (SSBN), the *Columbia* class, on October 1, 2020, with about 6 percent of construction complete due to aggressive advance construction necessitated by the program's importance. The first-in-class *Columbia* (SSBN 826) must begin delivery in FY 2027 to avoid any lapse in strategic deterrence capability as the aging *Ohio*-class SSBNs retire.[45] A major concern is the need to sustain attack submarine construction levels while avoiding shipyard delays that could be caused by prioritized construction of the *Columbia* class.

The most recent Navy long-range shipbuilding plan, released in December 2020, called for further increases in attack submarine production. To achieve the sought-after goal of seventy-two attack submarines by 2045, production will increase to three a year, requiring a $1.7 billion shipyard investment from FY 2022 to FY 2024.[46] After years of study and advocacy, the submarine force appears to have found the interval to sustain and judiciously expand the nuclear submarine industrial base. Specific lessons informing the build rate and industrial base sustainment, however, are unique to the submarine force and not easily transferrable to, say, the challenges of sustaining destroyer production. The production rates needed to sustain or grow the industrial base for other classes of warships are unique to each program and not generally known.

Invariably, new classes of ships will be required, either because of operational necessity or because technologies provide new design opportunities. Perhaps the best example of successful management of this transition is the Japanese Maritime Self-Defense Forces (JMSDF) submarine program. JMSDF has been building submarines at Kawasaki Heavy Industries and Mitsubishi Heavy Industries for decades, increasing their fleet from sixteen to twenty-two boats over the past twenty years while transitioning across three designs.[47] The Navy must consider future class transition in its planning for shipbuilding, in consultation with industry in order to avoid production disruptions and needless costs. A long-range production strategy can help to ensure that the Navy strikes the right balance on cost efficiencies and shipbuilding capacity. Failing this, costly gaps in shipbuilding will result in reduced infrastructure and workforce, as well as design inactivity that leads to the loss of highly trained naval architects who are not easily or quickly replaced.

The key to finding the optimum shipbuilding interval is having a clear target end strength so that industry can adjust to meet that demand. Each warship class is unique and places different demands on the sequencing of skilled workers across multiple shipbuilding programs. Additionally, without adequate shipbuilding work the industry and labor force will diminish, and at that point any hope of recapitalizing the nation's shipbuilding capacity evaporates. The lesson of the 2000s submarine force is that recovering skills and industrial capacities is more expensive in the long run than sustaining them. Moreover, time is a luxury the Navy does not have; in conflict, there will be no time to rebuild the skilled shipbuilding workforce required of a modern fighting fleet.

How the U.S. Navy plans and builds its fleet warrants focused attention and investment. This is particularly important given the time frames required to recapitalize shipbuilding infrastructure and design and build a larger modern fleet that can keep pace with maritime threats effectively. While doing so is a national imperative, it does not appear the Navy, shipbuilders, Congress, and the public are all on the same page. Perhaps a better understanding of the foundational principles involved in shipbuilding can help to bridge these divides and also help the nation recapture its maritime prowess and ensure that its maritime industry delivers warships on budget and on time. By focusing on best engineering design and construction principles, the Navy and shipbuilders will be better able to provide the nation with the Navy it needs. There are a few suggestions to ensure the nation's ability to meet its shipbuilding needs in an era of great power competition:

- Rebuild in-house naval design capacity to Cold War levels—approximately 1,200 engineers involved in design and the development of relevant specifications—through increased recruitment from industry and universities. This would better inform design requirements at the early stages of development in order to ensure design discipline throughout program development. Given the importance of unmanned ships to the future fleet, a significant portion of this expanded engineering staff should be dedicated to specialties associated with autonomous robotic systems and artificial intelligence. Targeted signing bonuses and lucrative tuition assistance should be employed by a dedicated team of NAVSEA recruiters charged with this task.

- Increase advanced educational opportunities for the Navy's civilian engineers and expand commercial industry's participation in concept formulation teams at the Navy's Center for Innovation in Ship Design to include nonmaritime industry. The Navy's Technical Warrant Holder provides an additional method to increase experienced workforce involved in engineering planning, certification of design, and performance assessments that can then be fed back into new design.[48]

- Designate life-of-program System Command (SYSCOM) leads early in the material solution analysis phase to inform new design by incorporating commonality with legacy system parts and life cycle sustainment. Associated updates to the Secretary of the Navy's instructions should stipulate specifically that SYSCOMs (NAVSEA and Naval Air Systems Command) must consider commonality with legacy systems in new design, mitigating the risk of cost overruns throughout life-cycle management, and minimizing production delays due to excessive concurrence.

- The Chief of Naval Operations should produce strategic development plans for future specific, key at-sea capabilities. The CNO must identify new technologies, their development, and the timelines for their employment on new classes of warships, as part of future thirty-year shipbuilding plans. Emphasis should be given to land-based prototyping that is followed by limited installation on current warships, to further refine designs and better inform total ownership costs of maintaining and operating future classes of warships. Candidates include plans for development and employment of rail guns and high-energy lasers on future warships.

- Congress can help by applying authorities granted to the National Sea-Based Deterrence Fund to the entirety of the Navy's shipbuilding budget. Additionally, any request for DoD reprogramming should include a stipulation that the secretary of defense ascertain that said funds would not be better reprogrammed into the Navy's shipbuilding program. This would enable Congress to ensure the adequate prioritization of resources used to build the Navy needed for great power competition while empowering sound engineering decision-making through more flexible shipbuilding budget structures.

- Moreover, Congress should require the Navy to incorporate into its annual long-range shipbuilding report production strategies that include transition to follow-on classes of ships. This assumes increased collaboration between shipbuilders and the Navy. Such effort can mitigate a repeat of the DDG-51-class 2005–10 building holiday that resulted in a 23 percent cost increase before production was resumed. Consideration should also be given to including Coast Guard long-range building plans with the intent of maximizing opportunities for system commonalities and associated cost savings.

## A Comprehensive National Maritime Initiative

During a July 17, 2017, Senate Armed Service Committee hearing, John Lehman, who served as Secretary of the Navy from 1981 to 1987, was asked to reflect on the Reagan-era buildup of naval forces and presence. At the time, his thinking was that a rapid buildup in forces and naval exercises would demonstrate the power of NATO to command the seas and that 90 percent of the needed deterrent power could be achieved in the effort's first year. Also important to his success as Secretary of the Navy was a clear articulation of the strategy and its risks to Congress, which earned him sustained bipartisan support for an expensive endeavor—building the six-hundred-ship navy. A forceful renewed naval presence left no doubt among friend and foe that the buildup was real and lasting.[49] Years later, statements of ex-Soviet leaders and declassified assessments indicate that the approach of President Reagan and Secretary Lehman was correct.[50] The question before the nation now is whether a similar feat can be replicated to affect China's and Russia's strategic calculations.

Getting the fleet needed for this task, however, depends on the expansion of shipyard capacity, the merchant fleet, and the maritime workforce.
In this competition with China and Russia, efficiencies could be gained by
coordinating shipbuilding with the U.S. Coast Guard. Like the Navy, the
Coast Guard confronts capacity challenges as demands grow for it to protect the Arctic, defend against illegal fishing, and increasingly deploy overseas in training missions that support the National Defense Strategy.[51] The
Coast Guard's future force structure is guided by its 2004 program of record
and Fleet Mix Analysis Phase 1 (2009) and Phase 2 (2011) studies, all of
which predate the current National Defense Strategy published in 2018.[52]
All these documents and associated thinking are in need of an update.

As both the Navy and the Coast Guard contend with the operational
demands of great power competition, there is precedent as well as operational necessity for collaboration in designing their fleets. In 2002, 2006, and
2013, for example, the two signed Joint National Fleet Policy Statements to
ensure that they can support each other and avoid redundancy. Also, the
president is authorized to align the Coast Guard under the Navy in wartime, and so they must be able to quickly operate together seamlessly. For
these reasons, it has been suggested at congressional hearings that both
services would benefit from a combined procurement plan. One such platform the Navy may find utility in is the Coast Guard's National Security
Cutter, which has a displacement of 4,500 tons and is in series production.[53] This would require a redesign, however, since the National Security
Cutter currently does not include an armory to store munitions like torpedoes or antiship missiles, needed for convoy or maritime patrols. While the
Navy, and to a lesser extent the Coast Guard, have garnered some needed
attention and resources to meet new challenges, the merchant fleet has not.
That is a vital unaddressed matter: the United States has become overly
reliant on foreign shippers and mariners to sustain the nation's economy
and meet military sealift needs in a crisis.

Annually, thousands of foreign-owned and operated ships conduct
U.S. trade that keeps the lights on, grocery stores stocked, and cars on the
road. To get some sense of how dependent the United States has become
on foreign shippers, consider that in 2015 there were 82,044 visits to U.S.
ports conducted by thousands of commercial vessels.[54] The U.S.-flagged

merchant vessels are the only ones that it could rely on in a crisis, and in July 2021 the number stood at 180, of which 157 were militarily useful.[55] Additionally, 93 percent of all commercial shipping produced in 2019 was by just three Northeast Asian nations—China, South Korea, and Japan. While two (Japan and South Korea) are allies, proximity to China in a conflict could preclude access to their commercial shipbuilding. According to 2020 data, China owned 6,869 merchant vessels measuring over a thousand tons, which comprised 13 percent of the world total.[56] The issue is not just supporting a military contingency overseas but against a foe such as China, sustaining a wartime economy for what could likely be a yearslong war. How did the United States get to this point?

In their book *The Abandoned Ocean*, authors Andrew Gibson and Arthur Donovan detail the rise and fall of U.S. shipping. Their detailed history stretches all the way back to colonial days, and a typical boom-bust pattern is clear in this critical sector of the U.S. economy since the 1600s. It is the accelerating bust since the end of the Cold War, however, and its consequences in great power competition that is most concerning. President George H. W. Bush's 1989 National Sealift Policy was intended to provide adequate shipping for national economic and security needs. To do this would have required coordination between the Departments of Defense and Transportation. But the August 1981 shift of the U.S. Maritime Administration (MARAD) from the Department of Commerce to Transportation meant the government's relationship would be regulatory and not as it was under Commerce with advocacy. Had this policy, as originally envisioned, been properly implemented by a senior interagency body, there may have been serious progress made. Around the same time, to determine the nation's shipping needs, Congress established the Commission on Merchant Marine and Defense, which met over 1986 to 1988. In its second report to Congress, it recommended the nation obtain a fleet of 650 oceangoing cargo ships to meet wartime military and economic needs.[57] Unfortunately, the end of the Cold War evaporated national security concerns that were driving interests in sustaining a U.S.-flagged merchant fleet.

Absent a clear national security prerogative and MARAD's focus on regulation, U.S. commercial shipbuilders and shipowners retreated from the marketplace. Even problems with securing shipping during the 1991 Gulf War couldn't turn this around. Despite incentives intended by the Merchant Marine Act of 1920, also known as the Jones Act, to ensure a fiducial merchant fleet available for war, it has withered and become uncompetitive with global shipping.[58] Statistics speak for themselves: the 2019 Turbo Activation 19-Plus exercise demonstrated that only 64 percent of the Ready Reserve Fleet was able to deploy on time. Moreover, the average age of these merchant ships is forty-five years, well over the industry end-of-life average of twenty years, and "DoD faces a gap of approximately 76 fuel tankers to meet surge sealift requirements."[59] This has occurred despite one hundred years of protections offered to U.S. shippers. Specifically, the Jones Act requires that shipping between U.S. ports be on ships built, owned, and manned by U.S. citizens. The result is that foreign shippers generally bypass Hawaii and Puerto Rico in favor of larger coastal ports as their U.S. debarkation point, causing shipping rates to these U.S. islands to be inflated and raising cost of living expenses there. The Jones Act, while protecting a narrow portion of U.S. seaborne trade, has not secured the merchant fleet needed by the Navy and a wartime national economy.

Moreover, market distortions caused by the Jones Act have worked against developing a competitive merchant marine. Instead U.S. commercial shipyards are more than 60 percent less efficient than overseas shipbuilders and are producing ships of limited value to the Navy's logistic needs (e.g., drafts too deep or unsuitable for austere ports) at a 700 percent price premium.[60] Further weakening the competitiveness of U.S.-flagged vessels, a 50 percent ad valorem duty on any nonemergency maintenance done overseas was imposed by the Tariff Act of 1930. It has had little positive effect; despite this duty, the cost of repairs at less modern U.S. shipyards is still cost prohibitive.[61] In fact, for a time, despite the ad valorem tax, it was economical for U.S. shippers to do repairs overseas. Eventually many shifted their ships to a flag of convenience and escaped the penalty altogether. Arguably it would have been better to have focused on improving the competitiveness of domestic shipyards; instead taxpayers saw shippers depart and shipbuilders close shop in the United States.

If you have the cash, buying commercial ships on the open market is a quick solution, but you still need a crew. The nation's experience with foreign crews indicates they would be reluctant to enter a war zone and may be precluded by their home country governments from serving on U.S. commercial vessels. Acting on the capacity side of this equation, Congress in fiscal year 2021 authorized purchase of up to nine foreign-built oceangoing vessels to make up for inadequate shipping.[62] Although access to shipping is critical in the early stages of conflict, it won't matter if there isn't a ready reserve force of trained U.S. merchant mariners to man them.[63] Today U.S. mariners are in short supply; in a sustained crisis there would be a shortfall of 15 percent of requirements (approximately two thousand mariners) in a group with an average age of forty-six years in 2020.[64] In addition, in 1951 there were 1,288 U.S. merchant ships.[65] Moreover, of large U.S.-flagged vessels that would be available for military use through the MSP stipend, none was produced in the United States.[66] Administrator Mark Buzby of MARAD, responsible for ensuring sealift for our military, warned in March 2020 that the merchant fleet is likely unable to deliver in a conflict and that, with only one shipyard able to build the needed logistic ships, the capacity to shift to needed production when necessary is questionable.[67] A first step in remedying this problem would be to repeal vestiges of the Tariff Act of 1930 requiring ad valorem duties on nonemergent repairs of U.S.-flagged vessels conducted overseas. This would enable U.S. shippers to become more competitive in the international marketplace by taking advantage of cheaper and more modern overseas facilities. Second, repealing the Jones Act would enable access to cheaper and more plentiful shipping in peacetime. Intended to boost U.S. shipbuilding and naval preparedness, the Jones Act has fallen woefully short of both, at a steep cost to American consumers.

After a century of being in force, however, simply revoking the Jones Act would likely be irresponsible. A plan is needed. Shipowners and shipbuilders accustomed to a protected market must be moved into global competition, while Congress and the president take on unfair practices by overseas shipbuilders, at the same time ensuring the Navy and the nation have access to the ships and crews needed in a crisis. This will require vigorously addressing unfair trade practices of foreign shipbuilders—notably Chinese state-owned enterprises. One example is China's state-owned COSCO. It rose to become the world's third-largest shipper in 2016, having benefited from billions in direct and indirect subsidies ($1 billion alone in 2014–15), favorable state financing, and regulatory barriers to competitors.[68] Working through the World Trade Organization is a given, but of the twenty-three cases the United States has brought against China since 2004, the results have been disappointing.[69] New approaches in economic statecraft will be needed as well as investment in a revitalized U.S. maritime industry. The United States should avoid playing "China's game" by matching subsidies and instead focus broadly on competitiveness while building a merchant maritime fleet able to support the nation during a conflict. The importance of this was made clear during the 1991 Gulf War. During that war, thirteen foreign-charted vessels refused to enter the war zone. Today in a conflict the United States would rely on military sealift, domestic shipping, America's allies, and contracted third parties to meet the military's need for 19.2 million square feet of capacity and eighty-six tankers.[70] To address any shortfall, MARAD has created several mechanisms, notably the MSP, to gain access to needed shipping. But to be clear, this does not address the shipping needed to sustain a wartime U.S. economy in a prolonged conflict.

The already mentioned MSP in 2020 provided stipends of $5.3 million per ship to sixty commercial cargo ships.[71] Expanding the MSP as Jones Act and Tariff Act protections are phased out could mitigate the loss of commercial shipbuilding while incentivizing shipbuilding that meets the Navy's needs and is more competitive in a global market. A Center for Strategic and Budgetary Assessments (CSBA) market analysis indicated that broadening MSP stipends for fuel tankers to $10 million a ship would meet the Navy's requirements.[72] Expanding MSP in this way would cost an additional $860 million annually over current stipends.

Managing this transition while ensuring adequate and available military sealift will require a period of government investment at a cost higher than $1 billion a year at least until 2035. Policy-makers will also need to explore other government-imposed tax and regulatory barriers to U.S. maritime industry competitiveness. U.S. shipping has been an engine for innovation in shipping and can again. U.S. shippers such as Malcom

McLean in 1956 revolutionized maritime trade when he introduced container shipping, greatly speeding the movement of products and reducing the likelihood of damage or pilferage seen in bulk shipping. Other innovations included the Car Identification System, double-stack railcars, and huge post-Panamax containerships. Containerization was revolutionary, not for its new ships but because it integrated sealift with intermodal movement of goods from source to destination, not just between ports. Amid COVID pandemic shutdowns and a grounding that closed off the Suez Canal in March 2021, shipping backlogs and rising prices point to the need while new technologies offer the potential for a new revolution in shipping. Can the United States position itself to take the lead here?

To regain a competitive edge and make gains in the global maritime marketplace, a new approach is needed, and the Navy will have a central role. Rather than duties and subsidies, the Navy must forge new partnerships with industry to develop new capabilities, while growing entrants in the maritime sector. During an October 2021 panel discussion at the Heritage Foundation, William Roper laid out a potential framework for doing this, called a market bridge.[73] The idea builds on his eight years of experience at the DoD as director of the Strategic Capabilities Office and Assistant Secretary of the Air Force for Acquisition, Technology, and Logistics. Roper saw the military as an incubator for innovation for new capabilities with wider market potential that could entice greater partnering with industry—industry that at times was loath to work with the military, especially in Silicon Valley. His test case was the Air Force's Agility Prime initiative to develop electric vertical takeoff and landing craft (eVTOL), which is producing prototypes with only $25 million in federal funding for a project expected to cost more than $100 million. Investors were attracted for two reasons: (1) The military provided a proven safety certification process and permissive regulatory environment in which to perfect the technology. (2) The military provided a favorable value proposition in that investors could develop and then sell these eVTOLs to the military, whose operations further mature the technology. Finally, the product (eVTOL) market fit was ideal for such an endeavor—drones and manned eVTOLs that could be used for military and commercial transport and logistics. Roper says to achieve effective market bridges, military

246 | CHAPTER 8

acquisition will have to focus more on providing opportunities for collaborative development of promising new technologies.

For the Navy and commercial shipping, the logistic backlogs and barren grocery store shelves of 2021 provide an opportunity for developing new approaches and capabilities. One cause of the U.S. logistic backlog was a dearth of truck drivers encouraged to stay home during the COVID pandemic, even as demand surged. The thin margins of a containerized shipping industry meant that one delay compounded onto another, resulting in historic backlogs of ships at U.S. ports. This problem—moving cargo from ship to shore—was appreciated by the Navy earlier. The Military Sealift Command, not wanting to be beholden to foreign overland transport, has purchased roll-on/roll-off ships for moving military equipment that it drives off the ship and takes to the frontline. As the Navy looks to distribute its forces and increase mobility while under Chinese threat, it needs the ability to move material quickly to and from land without the benefit of ports and airfields. At the same time, additive manufacturing will desegregate production widely and will place new strains by adding many more hubs to existing logistics networks. Connecting these hubs and moving material to shifting destinations without ports and airfields is the challenge. Partnering with the Navy to solve its first island chain logistics and operational challenges has the potential of opening new approaches to commercial shipping. So rather than trying to play the current shipping game better, apply a Blue Ocean approach and shift the competition.

This is where Roper's market bridges come in. The Navy needs new ways of quickly moving material to shore, while U.S. industry needs better options for taking advantage of additive manufacturing and transport not prone to backlogs. A market bridge provides the setting for drawing new entrants into the defense sector with their investment dollars and technical competencies. Development under a military regulatory umbrella and the promise of an assured military customer if the capability works are proving enticing to start-up companies.[74] Such an approach would likely work in solving the nation's logistic challenge, but could just as easily apply to developing promising innovations in bioengineering, quantum sensing, and high-energy lasers.

Innovation alone, however, will neither save the U.S. shipping industry nor deliver the sealift the nation needs. The shortfall in available merchant mariners to man logistic ships during war has not improved despite Jones Act requirements for U.S.-crewed domestic ships and an $8,000-per-year Student Incentive Payment (SIP) with subsequent obligated merchant marine service.[75] To increase the incentives to attract and retain new maritime industry hires—specifically, to crew U.S.-flagged commercial vessels—the current three-year commitment to service in the merchant marine could be extended to five years with an increased SIP of $12,000 a year. Stipends for vocational training in maritime skills with commitments to grow a skilled U.S. workforce for the merchant marine as well as a U.S.-flagged commercial fleet are also part of the solution.

To grow the number of U.S. merchant mariners, MARAD has sought expanded training capacity with new training vessels ($300 million appropriated in 2019) along with more instructors and more schools (e.g., $100 million for an additional State Maritime Academy).[76] To ensure that such investments are having the desired effect, an achievable and concrete goal is needed. Such a goal would be to train and sustain a reserve force adequate for manning 120 percent of the need for wartime operations. This would require a reserve mariner force of 16,329, or 4,561 more than the current inventory of 11,768. No matter how big the schools and training fleet, if there are no jobs for U.S. merchant mariners the effort will be pointless. Today the majority of such jobs are related to Jones Act–protected intra–United States shipping—which has failed in growing the numbers of mariners needed.

If the nation hopes to have the needed number of citizens working in the shipping sector available for call-up during a crisis, more is needed than the Jones Act. One proposal would see a bonus paid to U.S. mariners working on foreign and U.S.-flagged vessels in a reserve merchant marine status. Receiving such a bonus carries the obligation to serve when called, remain physically ready for sea service, and remain proficient as a certified mariner. Keeping U.S. citizens active in seafaring mitigates against losing perishable skills that require six months to two years to acquire. Without U.S.-flagged oceangoing vessels to work on board, the demand for U.S. merchant mariners has dwindled, replaced by cheaper foreign labor.

# Chart 12. Planning for the Future: Key Initiatives for the U.S. Navy

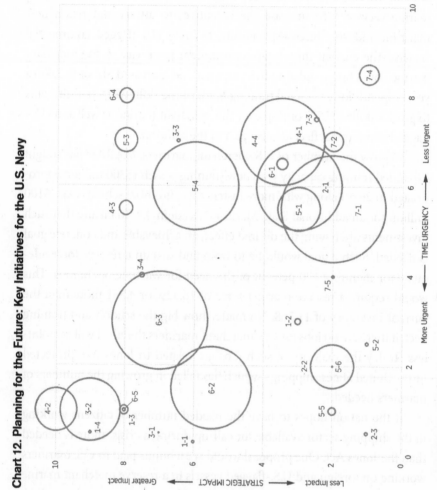

Circle size =
Resources and
duration of effort
required

SOURCE: Author's analysis, based on his article "Rebuilding America's
Military Project: United States Navy," p. 22–50.

# Table 3. Planning for the Future: Key Initiatives for the Navy (details)

| Label | Initiative | Time Urgency 0-10 | Strategic Impact 0-10 | Resources + Duration of Effort Required 0-30,000 |
|---|---|---|---|---|
| | **DEVELOP A UNIFYING NARRATIVE DRIVEN BY VISIONARY LEADERS** | | | |
| 1-1 | Articulate Vision | 0.3 | 6.0 | 20 |
| 1-2 | Educate Leaders | 3.0 | 3.0 | 100 |
| 1-3 | Develop Leaders | 1.0 | 8.0 | 200 |
| 1-4 | Promote Dynamic Leaders | 0.5 | 9.0 | 15 |
| | **ACCELERATE A NEW FLEET DESIGN FOR CONTESTED OPERATIONS** | | | |
| 2-1 | Increase Shipyard Capacity | 6.0 | 3.0 | 20,000 |
| 2-2 | Expand Shipyard Workforce | 2.0 | 2.0 | 5,000 |
| 2-3 | Identify Systemic Issues | 0.5 | 1.0 | 20 |
| | **EXPAND SHIPYARD CAPACITY** | | | |
| 3-1 | Reform Global Force Management | 0.5 | 7.0 | 2 |
| 3-2 | Dedicate Task Forces in Eastern Mediterranean and South China Sea | 1.0 | 9.0 | 10,000 |
| 3-3 | More Non-Lethal Options | 7.0 | 6.5 | 20 |
| 3-4 | New Concept of Operations Exercises | 4.0 | 7.5 | 50 |
| | **EMPHASIZE PERSISTENT OPERATIONS IN DECISIVE THEATERS** | | | |
| 4-1 | Doctrinal Training | 7.0 | 3.0 | 20 |
| 4-2 | Large Scale Exercise | 1.0 | 10.0 | 5,000 |
| 4-3 | International Training Missions | 5.5 | 8.0 | 500 |
| 4-4 | Grow Manning | 7.0 | 3.5 | 20,000 |
| | **FOCUS ON TRADITION WHILE BUILDING NEW CORE COMPETENCIES** | | | |
| 5-1 | Base Resiliency Plan | 5.5 | 3.0 | 5,000 |
| 5-2 | Review Title 10 | 2.5 | 1.0 | 20 |
| 5-3 | Logistic Force Pacific | 7.0 | 8.0 | 1,500 |
| 5-4 | Base Recapitalization Fund | 6.0 | 6.0 | 20,000 |
| 5-5 | Embed Department of Navy Personnel at the Development Finance Corporation | 1.0 | 2.0 | 120 |
| 5-6 | Add Department of Defense Assessment in Congressionally Mandated Development Finance Corporation Reports | 2.0 | 2.0 | 3 |
| | **SECURE AND ENHANCE AN IMPROVED NAVAL FORCE POSTURE** | | | |
| 6-1 | Develop and Utilize Global Scaled Modeling and Simulation | 6.5 | 3.5 | 300 |
| 6-2 | Design and Build New Class of Tenders | 1.5 | 5.5 | 18,000 |
| 6-3 | New Class of Warships Optimized for First Island Chain Operations | 3.0 | 7.0 | 25,000 |
| 6-4 | Upgrade Small Surface Combatants for Gray Zone Operations | 8.0 | 8.0 | 600 |
| 6-5 | Deploy Non-Lethal Gear on Forward Deployed Ships | 1.0 | 8.0 | 20 |
| | **IMPLEMENT A COMPREHENSIVE NATIONAL SHIPBUILDING PLAN** | | | |
| 7-1 | National Maritime Program | 5.5 | 2.0 | 30,000 |
| 7-2 | Incentivize Maritime Recruiting | 7.0 | 2.0 | 1,000 |
| 7-3 | Deregulate Shipping | 7.5 | 2.5 | 50 |
| 7-4 | Reform Design Factory | 8.5 | 1.0 | 1,000 |
| 7-5 | Establish a Shipbuilding Department of Defense Capital Account | 4.0 | 2.0 | 12 |

The complexity and interdependencies of U.S. shipbuilding and merchant marines make a national maritime revitalization program appropriate. A February 2020 U.S. Department of Transportation report, *Goals and Objectives for a Stronger Maritime Nation*, is a partial response to a 2014 congressional request for a national maritime strategy. An implementation plan was scheduled to follow in early 2021, but the seven years it has taken to get to this point is unacceptable. A national maritime strategy should complement the Navy's SIOP for public shipyards and be resourced to assist industry in becoming more competitive internationally.

If the nation is to obtain needed maritime security, it will have to reconstitute a competitive commercial maritime sector that can sustain it in a long war with China. This will require partnerships with local waterfront communities, shipbuilders, shipping companies, Congress, and the executive branch. To grow the infrastructure and workforces needed, the nation will have to encourage young people to enter this sector while viewing them as national assets that could be called on in a crisis. Subsidies have not helped grow the type of commercial shipping the military needs; a new approach is required, focusing on competition. Only the United States levies dues on U.S.-flagged shippers that do repairs overseas and taxes shippers engaged in international trade. In simplest terms, laws such as the Jones Act must be changed to make owning and operating oceangoing ships in the United States once again advantageous. Due to the complexities and many interest groups involved, a national maritime initiative is needed and appropriate. It should be led by a congressionally directed independent Maritime Administration with a mandate to regulate as well as advocate for a merchant marine that meets the nation's wartime economic and military needs.

# CHAPTER 9

# Developing Leaders for Great Power Competition

————— ⊗⊗⊗ —————

*The luxuries of the present are the necessities of the future.*

—Adm. Jackie Fisher, RN, in a letter to
Winston Churchill, January 16, 1912

**B**efore the U.S. Navy can meet the challenges of today's great power competition, execute naval statecraft, and incorporate future technological advances a foundational issue must be addressed. Progress on the previous imperatives is predicated on having the right leadership at both sea and headquarters. This leadership will be foundational in invigorating the force structure that is being built and that is required to compete with or fight against China and Russia. President Ronald Reagan's Secretary of the Navy, John Lehman, successfully led the Navy, and the industry supporting it, toward a six-hundred-ship force, a relevant lesson of leadership needed for the task before the Navy today.

President Reagan promised a robust increase in defense spending, with which to build a larger military capable of doing more, including its naval forces. He confronted the Soviet-declared, expansionist Brezhnev Doctrine and made clear his intention to pursue a "forward strategy." In addition to pursuing declared policies, he also intended to launch a highly classified program to exploit Soviet economic, political, military, and psychological vulnerabilities. In his book *Oceans Ventured*, Secretary Lehman lays out the importance of a well-thought-out strategy and the importance of working with Congress—important lessons for any future Secretary of the Navy.[1]

In November 1976, a bipartisan group formed an advocacy group under the resurrected name the Committee on the Present Danger. For the next four years it published papers, its members gave speeches, it organized conferences, and it lobbied for rebuilding American nuclear, land, and naval forces. It included thirty-three Republican and Democratic members, many of whom later served in the Reagan administration. Its yearlong study produced National Security Decision Memorandum 344, "Navy Shipbuilding Program," on January 18, 1977. To quote Secretary Lehman, "Coming two days before the inauguration of President Jimmy Carter, the study may have made the Navy's heart beat faster, but it had no chance of enactment." Meanwhile, the U.S. Navy's fleet shrunk precipitously from 751 active warships and 19 carriers to 521 active warships and 12 carriers by 1981. The Soviet Union was not slow in taking advantage of this radically fading naval deterrence, fomenting revolution in Central America and establishing a forward naval presence in the South China Sea at former U.S. bases in Vietnam.

Carter's defense secretary, inordinately fearful of losing carriers in wartime, believed they had to be kept at least "1,500 nautical miles from Soviet land bases" if they were to survive long enough to win in a naval war. Otherwise his chief concern was that resupply of forward allies by convoy must be able to take place thirty days after a conflict started. To ensure the Navy's views informed future force structure decisions, it organized a major policy and strategy study, to be conducted at the Naval War College and in Washington under the leadership of Bing West, who would serve in the Reagan Pentagon. The study was called Sea Plan 2000 and had momentous effect. The analysis tallied Army, Air Force, and Coast Guard forces available to support naval operations, as well as allied naval and air forces that could be counted on, and finally calculated Navy and Marine Corps force levels required to deter threats. Ironically, this comprehensive plan, undertaken and paid for by the Carter Pentagon, became one of the main sources for fleshing out Ronald Reagan's naval policy initiative, and was a critical part of his campaign platform.

In 1980, Reagan's chief foreign policy adviser Richard V. Allen organized his team of experts, including congressional and Pentagon budget experts working on their own time, to prepare a detailed new defense budget and a budget supplemental for additional funding. It would include a new exercise—Ocean Venture '81, a massive naval operation into the North Atlantic, which the Soviets viewed as within their maritime sphere of influence. It was approved by Reagan before his inauguration and launched just seven months after he entered the White House. In March 1982, Atlantic Fleet commander Admiral Train and Striking Fleet commander Vice Admiral Lyons briefed members of Congress and staff on Ocean Venture '81. It was important that Congress learn firsthand what the Navy had just done, and why and how. Congressional support for the Reagan shift in U.S. foreign and military strategy was essential, and here was a real-world example of the Reagan strategy in action. Updated and refined, these exercises under different names were repeated every year thereafter, until the Soviet Union and its navy collapsed at the end of the decade.

Using data as of November 1985, the CIA's Office of Soviet Analysis concluded in a declassified secret analysis that the Soviets had perceived a marked U.S. increase in emphasis on sea power and an increased and rapidly developing threat to the Soviet Union from the sea. In the CIA's analysis, the Soviets viewed U.S. aircraft carriers as increasingly capable and survivable in the Norwegian Sea and northwestern Pacific.

Various cracks in the Navy's institutional hull must be addressed before beginning to build it for great power competition. As it was for Lehman, an invigorated relationship with Congress and the electorate is required to rethink the Navy's role and overhaul outdated operational and bureaucratic frameworks. Building the Navy the nation needs for a new era will take years of sustained effort, investment, and flexibility to adjust as conditions change and competitors react. Such a comprehensive endeavor requires that several key imperatives be addressed.

## The Right Narrative Can Unify and Empower Visionary Naval Leaders

The closest thing the Navy has to a comprehensive vision of its future is the combination of a thirty-year shipbuilding plan,[2] an Integrated Naval Force Structure Assessment (INFSA),[3] and A Design for Maintaining Maritime Superiority.[4] Despite the Design's focus on delivering "High Velocity" results, it was more about long-standing initiatives representing managed incremental change than it was about winning great power competition.[5]

In an unusual move, after a meeting with the Navy's leadership in February 2020, the secretary of defense delayed the congressionally mandated release of the thirty-year shipbuilding plan and the INFSA because of concerns that they would be cost prohibitive and did not support the goal of achieving a 355-ship fleet by 2034.[6] Despite the publication of a series of groundbreaking naval strategies since the end of the Cold War, the Navy has consistently shrunk since 1991 to a low of only 279 ships in 2007, unable to exceed 300 ships ever since.[7] Then in December 2020, the Navy released both its latest thirty-year shipbuilding plan for a fleet that could reach 546 ships by 2045[8] and a new naval strategy called *Advantage at Sea*.[9] Both argue for a Navy able to compete with China and Russia, but the timing of their release at the end of the Trump administration means it is doubtful ever to have any enduring impact.

Better timing and articulation of a future force design informed by a new strategic framework is critical to navigating changing political realities, while simultaneously enabling deeper collaboration with industry and across the whole of Congress. Without an accessible vision, however, the effort to expand the fleet above 300 ships will falter. The consequences were playing out during the fiscal year 2023 budget, which could see the Navy further shrink to 280 ships by the critical year of 2027.[10]

At the same time, the tempo of great power competition affords a large organization like the Navy fewer opportunities to learn and adapt. This places a premium on correct metrics for identifying leaders with the right balance of judgment and initiative. Of these, initiative is arguably harder to instill in a large organization because it requires years of cultural change. What's more, initiative pursued too freely can lead to waste and institutional confusion; conversely, initiative that is too constrained may miss opportunities, begetting catastrophic consequences. Getting the balance right is an imperative. British admiral Horatio Nelson was a leader who got it right. Having trained and selected many of his ships' captains, he issued a pivotal memo twelve days before the October 1805 Battle of Trafalgar, communicating his vision for the impending battle. He explained to his captains in detail how he expected his adversary, France's fleet, to fight and how his fleet would operate. The British went on to sink or capture 67 percent of the French fleet, losing not a single ship in the process. Nelson had enabled his forces to operate coherently while still acting with great initiative independently, thereby winning a historic victory.

Great power competitors are changing the peacetime status quo by acting below the U.S. threshold for conflict. To push back effectively, the Navy needs leaders steeped in great power competition who can be the "captains of change", as the Navy embarks on a reimagination of its role. The first task should be to publish a modern version of Nelson's Trafalgar memorandum with its coherent vision of how day-to-day operations and long-term resourcing decisions will come together. CNO Admiral Gilday's NAVPLAN released in January 2021 is a good start and was improved on in an update released in July 2022, but it must still better describe how the Navy will be postured to respond to the expected countermoves of China and Russia.[11] Visionary leadership will be critical to draw out, retain, and promote the very best innovative and creative minds. Without such a vision, the Navy will continue the post–Cold War tendency of managing a shifting status quo and its underlying competition, eventually ceding maritime leadership in the process.

## Required Focus on Tradition While Building New Core Competencies

"It is by no means enough that an officer of the Navy should be a capable mariner. He must be that, of course, but also a great deal more."[12] U.S. Revolutionary War naval hero John Paul Jones' immortal words are memorized by every plebe (first-year student) at the Naval Academy. The quote goes on to stress the characteristics of an effective naval officer, but its admonition to be more than a capable mariner has added emphasis in today's era of great power competition. The officers and sailors of the Navy today often operate in contested waters, making their skills as mariners and ability to place their actions into a global context strategically important. For this reason, the Navy must

- allow commanding officers more discretionary time to train their crews,
- continue to focus on retention and invigorated recruiting to man the Navy of the future,
- train and exercise with a view to great power competition and future war, and

- leverage the resources of the Navy reserve and naval militia more effectively.

With respect to personnel readiness, the Navy's 2018 *Design for Maintaining Maritime Superiority* emphasized several core attributes: integrity, accountability, initiative, and toughness. To be sustained and strengthened, however, these foundational attributes, like muscle, must be exercised and tested. In December 2019, shortly after assuming his responsibilities as CNO, Adm. Michael M. Gilday issued a fragmentary order (FRAGO) reiterating the importance of these attributes.[13] Those attributes will be critical in a more dispersed fleet, where commanding officers' discretion will be of strategic importance while operating in competition with China and Russia. Sadly, as operational requirements weigh on a smaller fleet, precious little time remains for crews to learn their ships and give junior officers the time to build confidence as mariners. A larger fleet makes it possible for more ships to distribute the operational demands; today a third of the Navy's ships are typically at sea, and the ensuing high operational tempo has been detrimental.

The collisions involving destroyers *McCain* and *Fitzgerald* claimed the lives of seventeen sailors during two unrelated routine "independent steaming" operations in the Western Pacific. The Chinese were quick to exploit these incidents by charging that the U.S. Navy was unsafe and should not be operating in the Western Pacific—hardly surprising for Chinese propaganda but tough for a proud Navy to stomach. Subsequent Navy reviews identified several broad institutional recommendations, most notably that "the creation of combat ready forces must take equal footing with meeting the immediate demands of Combatant Commanders."[14] In short, the commanding officers, while held accountable to the readiness of their crews, must also be given the time and resources to ensure adequate training and familiarity with their ships.

Another finding was that each ship must be fully manned. For the 355-ship fleet planned for 2034, the Navy assessed that its end-strength manpower would have to grow by approximately 35,000 sailors.[15] Funding has supported this, with the FY 2021 budget continuing an increase in active-duty manning by an additional 7,300 sailors.[16] If this growth is not sustained, overworked sailors and officers on undermanned ships will vote with their feet. Recent trends in the accession of new sailors and officers have been positive, but whether this can be sustained remains to be seen. Growing the fleet without consideration of the crews runs the risk of creating a hollow force—ships undermanned and underresourced to undertake required training. Attempts to make existing personnel counts go further by reducing needed manning on a by-ship basis have been stymied by the manpower-intensive designs of current ships. Future classes of unmanned and optionally manned ships may provide less reliance on manning and allow for a larger fleet with modest growth in overall personnel.

There will always, however, be sailors maintaining and officers commanding warships—unmanned, manned, or optionally manned. The Navy has renewed interest in senior officer training to help these future naval leaders put in context their actions in great power competition. Specifically, to improve understanding of our rivals, former secretary of defense Mark Esper directed the National Defense University (NDU) to devote 50 percent of the coursework of senior officers to China. While helpful, it is too narrowly focused and fails to take proper account of Russia's role in great power competition. Nor does it necessarily focus on the group making the majority of day-to-day operational decisions: commanding officers. They typically do not attend NDU before their command tours.

The officers and sailors at sea making strategic decisions must also increasingly coordinate their actions with regional partners and allies. This will require a higher degree of cultural and linguistic familiarity than in the recent past. If the Navy is to practice more strategically impactful combined activities on shore and at sea with partner navies, it needs new skills. In 2006, the Navy established the Foreign Area Officer (FAO) community comprising a cadre of mid- to senior-level officers with language and regional expertise. Josh Taylor, who has served in various posts at embassies and joint command headquarters, has argued that FAO officers with operational and regional experience provide the Navy an unmatched combination of skills and knowledge perfect for building access and enhancing partner navy capabilities.[17] These skills include the sale or transfer of naval equipment to partner navies, overseeing training in its use, and performing combined exercises. Their in-country experience is also key to establishing the personal networks that smooth port visits and make dignitary visits productive in reaching agreements and treaties. As the competition with China and Russia heats up over access to ports and customers for arms sales, there will be an increased emphasis on the type of skills the FAOs have and the networks they have built.

Across all regions, it is U.S. alliances that are the greatest asset, but they must be modernized in order to remain relevant in a dynamic security environment.[18] Consider recent efforts in the Philippines, where Japan has joined U.S. efforts to improve the Philippine coast guard and navy.[19] This has only been possible because Japan has made legislative and constitutional adjustments for a proactive regional role. Critical in this Japanese endeavor has been the 2015 revision of U.S.-Japan Defense Guidelines and constitutional reinterpretations allowing collective self-defense. Both nations, moreover, have committed to active and continuous coordination of national policy and military operations through the Alliance Coordination Mechanism and the Bilateral Enterprise, both established in 2015. While the alliance with Japan is rapidly evolving, more is needed to modernize and network other alliances to best confront today's threats together.

Moreover, China's increasingly provocative and aggressive actions are driving new strategic partnerships and energizing old partners. The QUAD, made up of the United States, Japan, India, and Australia, mostly languished after its abortive 2008 formation but has gained renewed energy since 2017. Most notably, the QUAD, for only the second time and within a year of the first, held a summit in Tokyo addressing common security concerns.[20] As leaders met in Tokyo, in a provocative manner signaling displeasure, Russian and Chinese aircraft and warships operated together and circumnavigated the home islands of Japan. And in September 2021 a new endeavor was announced called AUKUS, intended to invigorate security collaboration between the United States, the United Kingdom, and Australia; its most notable component was the development of an Australian nuclear submarine.[21] Without China's increasing bellicoseness and Russia's invasion of Ukraine, these efforts would likely not have occurred. Yet success in these endeavors is far from assured. To achieve stronger naval partnerships and foster greater allied combined operations, the Navy will have to better utilize access to partner nation leadership and the resources of other agencies within government.

When it comes to executing naval statecraft, the Navy must be an active and oftentimes leading member of an interagency effort. This effort requires using five levers of naval statecraft: posture, presence, partner capacity building, treaties and agreements, and information operations. For the Navy to gain and, if needed, modernize ports and airfields, it will have to work more closely with the DFC and civil engineering firms. A presence that matters necessitates longer dwell times in regions with forces conducting operations, tailored to impact the thinking of leaders in Beijing and Moscow. This will require concerted planning at least a year before execution, with the involvement of the intelligence agencies, the State Department, and the DoD, all coordinated through the NSC. During the Cold War, the Reagan White House did this through a National Security Planning Group. To function effectively, any future such group would need the president's endorsement, as was the case with President Reagan's 1983 National Security Decision Directive #75 regarding the Soviet Union.[22] Partner capacity building will require actively working with industry to tailor capabilities appropriate to the advancing of U.S. interests. These include capabilities like diesel submarines or small coastal patrol boats not well suited to use in the U.S. Navy and therefore not built in the United States. At the same time, meeting defense needs of partners should include developing new leasing mechanisms and associated in-country training and maintenance missions.

To get a sense of what this could be, imagine Indonesia leasing or buying sensor time of several maritime patrol aircraft based on Natuna Island in the South China Sea, but the aircraft are operated by U.S. crews. For partner nations limited in resources and personnel, such a hybrid approach, involving the leasing of intelligence-collection platforms and maritime patrol platforms, would speed capacities to decisive theaters in a way that benefits both the host and the United States. Treaties and agreements with partner nations are in the purview of the State Department, but the Navy is going to have to campaign proactively for agreements supporting its interests in arenas it has generally not entered—economics, infrastructure, and developmental aid. Finally, the Navy has in recent years made good use of the information domain, notably working with the press and the State Department's Global Engagement Center to expose

Chinese militarization of the South China Sea. To affect the strategic calculations of leadership in Moscow and Beijing, however, a new, disciplined approach, enabled by the intelligence agencies and special forces, and supported by forward naval presence, will be required. This would expand the focus of such forward operations from deterrence or crisis response, to actively changing the thinking of targeted leaders in which naval presence is one element—such as undermining the confidence of Chinese political leaders in their own military commanders, triggering Chinese diplomatic responses that further alienate the CCP from its neighbors, or implementing active measures that undermine CCP influence networks abroad. All of this requires a new way of thinking and conceptualizing the Navy's role in great power competition.

On top of this, the Navy does not have a doctrine for peacetime competition, nor does it train to conduct aggressive peacetime operations independently, or with partner navies.[23] Given that our competitors are willing to risk collisions and damage to their ships, our crews must train to respond, and ships should be appropriately equipped. In dealing with nonmilitary Chinese vessels, especially the maritime militia, our ships have little capability to stand their ground when swarmed by such vessels. As Hunter Stires points out in his award-winning naval essay "Win without Fighting," new tools are necessary to contest the maritime insurgency that China is waging in the South China Sea.[24] Leveraging the Marine Corps' efforts in crowd control by field testing and deploying nonlethal Active Denial Systems based on microwave and acoustic technologies requires new thinking, not just new capabilities.[25] As such, priority should be given to developing new concepts of operation as well as capabilities to prepare commanding officers for operating in waters where they will encounter the Chinese maritime militia.

To date, there has been little dedicated effort toward exercising with partner navies or coast guards to practice effective measures to counter the tactics that the Chinese Coast Guard (e.g., shouldering) and Chinese maritime militia (e.g., swarming) often employ. While some partner navies and coast guards (e.g., Japan's) undoubtedly have invaluable experience, the Navy would serve itself well by building on these partners' lessons as it develops new tactics and capabilities to neuter Chinese echelon defense or "cabbage" strategy. New technologies, and the operational lessons of part-ner maritime forces can greatly benefit a naval peacetime theory of victory.

Training and exercising crews on the operational doctrines required in great power competition and modern naval warfare will be critical in ensuring that they respond as if it were second nature in a crisis.

China and Russia are changing the way the Navy will have to fight. The Navy's DMO concept aims to complicate an adversary's targeting by disag-gregating the fleet. The Marine Corps' operational concepts, LOCE and EABO, call for smaller and more dispersed Marine units conducting mis-sions that range from scouting (intelligence, surveillance, and reconnais-sance) to coastal defense to forward arming and refueling points (FARPs) for vertical takeoff and landing F-35B operations. Likewise, the Army's evolving Multi-domain Operations (MDO) concept will be enabled by invigorated investment in ground-launched cruise and ballistic missiles. For a theory of victory in a great power war to work, Navy ships will have to operate with allies and other U.S. forces. And as these untested concepts of operation mature, so too will the demands on the Navy's future officers and sailors. Sadly, in-the-field testing and evolution of these concepts of operations has progressed slowly.

Field tests of such concepts, with the crews expected to execute them, have been urgently needed for some time, especially to inform resource decisions such as what weapon or ship design to purchase. One example is the Navy's Large-Scale Exercise (LSE) announced in 2018 and origi-nally scheduled to occur in 2020 but delayed until summer 2021 because of concerns related to the COVID-19 pandemic. When executed, the LSE provided valuable field experience, especially regarding integration with unmanned systems.[26] Notable was the twelve days during the LSE that con-nected naval operations globally, merging the real world with virtual plat-forms to accelerate operational learning. This is good news, but hopefully the next LSE will take place sooner, rather than under the Navy's stated three-year periodicity.

In late April 2021, the Navy conducted its first multiplatform manned/unmanned fleet experiment, Integrated Battle Problem 21 (UxS IBP21). This fleet experiment brought together the Navy's *Zumwalt* destroyer and unmanned MUSVs with a range of sensitive air and undersea unmanned platforms. The intent was to mature the technologies and techniques required for effective manned/unmanned naval operations.[27] On the heels of IBP21, the Navy reached a milestone in September 2021 when its Ghost Fleet—the Navy's small fleet of unmanned surface ships—launched and hit a target with an SM-6 missile.[28] After spending years in a laboratory, and in controlled, at-sea navigational tests, unmanned ships are now deploying. That same year, the Navy established Task Force 59, composed of unmanned platforms in the Persian Gulf, where this task force will come into contact with hostile forces.[29] Lessons learned this way will greatly accelerate the adoption of unmanned platforms into the wider Navy by proving their utility under real-world challenges.

In the future, LSE and other such exercises must explore the synthesis of DMO with EABO and MDO to generate significant learning, not unlike that created by exercise Nifty Nugget, conducted over twenty-one days in October 1978 to test the logistics systems that were assumed capable of supporting a war in Europe. The immediate results were ugly: they revealed that the United States was not ready to execute its plans to sustain a major war in Europe. By effectively challenging key operational planning assumptions, Nifty Nugget led to realistic looks at the domestic industrial base, airlift and sealift deficiencies, and resourcing of biennial mobilization exercises. Such an exercise and what is sure to be hard learning should be welcomed as the Navy looks to develop new forces and operational constructs to compete with China and Russia.

In a time of sharpening competition, there are also some latent capacities available to the Navy: notably, the Navy reserves and the little-known state naval militias. The impact of COVID-19 on maintenance at the Navy's four public shipyards, for example, led to the activation of 1,629 reservists to backfill the quarter of the civilian workforce deemed "high risk" for health reasons. Such actions have helped the Navy conduct maintenance on schedule and are testament to the Navy's resilience when utilizing its reserve forces. The largest and perhaps most recognizable element of the reserves is the Selected Reserve (SELRES), made up of individuals who provide periodic support to active units and others who perform in a full-time or activated role.[30] As of March 2020, there were 59,641 SELRES (10,153 full-time support); 44,176 Individual Ready Reserve ready for recall; and

167 reserve aircraft manned by reserves.[31] Reserve aircraft are critical in both peacetime and war because of their high utilization as the Navy's only organic intertheater air logistics platform.[32] Unfortunately, reserve infrastructure is antiquated, with an average age of forty-three years and over 20 percent deemed substandard. To continue providing air logistic support that saves the Navy almost $1 billion annually, the Navy must eventually replace the reserves' twenty-five C-130 airplanes.[33] To grow the Navy in the coming decade, better employment of the reserves will be required, and this means investing in their equipment to remain relevant in supporting the active-duty Navy.

Interestingly, the reserves do not operate any of their own ships, unlike state naval militia. Like the better-known and larger National Guard, the naval militia is a state entity that supports a range of state defense and disaster response. After the establishment of the naval reserve in 1915, the role of naval militias waned until the attacks of September 11, 2001. Following those attacks, New York and New Jersey naval militias played a notable role, ferrying people fleeing lower Manhattan and bringing in first responders. Because of its experience and capability, the naval militia is well positioned to support capacity building and training with key partner nations through the National Guard's State Partnership Program (SPP).[34] Established by Title 10 of the United States Code, the SPP engages with seventy-eight countries' military, security, and other governmental organizations.[35] SPP engagements are broader in scope than military-to-military engagements, with the same units and people often routinely training with the same partner nation's units. This recurring personal connection fosters a degree of interoperability and trust unique in military exercises. Typically, active-duty military units that conduct exercises and training with a partner nation don't return, making any person-to-person team building of short effect. The few states with active naval militias (Alaska, New York, New Jersey, Ohio, and South Carolina) could be prime candidates for greater participation by those militia in SPP activities to enhance maritime cooperation.

Competing in day-to-day operations that carry strategic implications against China and Russia will place added strains on the crews of the Navy's warships. This includes operating unmanned warships, employing nonlethal capabilities in new ways to prevail in gray-zone activities, and employing reserve forces more fully. Training can help prepare sailors for these rigors, while inculcating officers in a new theory of victory. Still, this will not lessen the need for proficiency in seamanship, or the need for building unit cohesion before engaging China or Russia. Naval statecraft in modern great power competition requires long-term investing and nurturing of new naval leaders through education and practice to succeed in this new era.

# Conclusion
## Sailing Directions

*For in this modern world, the instruments of warfare are not solely for waging war. Far more importantly, they are the means for controlling peace. Naval officers must therefore understand not only how to fight a war, but how to use the tremendous power which they operate to sustain a world of liberty and justice, without unleashing the powerful instruments of destruction and chaos that they have at their command.*

—Adm. Arleigh Burke, CNO, August 1, 1961,
Change of Command Address at Annapolis

The fleet design offered in the previous chapters can provide the nation a maritime force designed to contest Russian and Chinese theories of victory. Naval statecraft provides the framework for employing today's navy to greater effect as the fleet grows, and builds the competencies needed in the future. Importantly, together the future fleet design and naval statecraft set the foundation for a new model navy that will employ fourth and fifth industrial revolution technologies. Pursuing such a force design will necessarily shape future concepts of operations and inform research and development optimally for competition with these great power rivals. Naval statecraft, by merging economic, diplomatic, and military strategies, will mean a paradigm shift in governance. On this, there is special urgency to develop a new whole-of-government gray-zone concept of operation and field naval capabilities to better compete in the day-to-day interactions with the Chinese and Russian maritime forces. One important aim is reversing the erosion of the rules-based maritime order, starting with decisive theaters—the Eastern Mediterranean and South China Sea.

An invigorated peacetime competition, backed by an improving capacity to fight the most likely war scenario, is, in fact, the best deterrent. This will require expanding the nation's maritime industrial capacity to sustain and recapitalize the fleet in case of a major war. Not doing this could lead to the United States fighting one war with China or Russia, only to lose the next before it can recover from wartime losses in a pyrrhic victory. Our rivals undoubtedly know this, as they make speed in getting ships back to sea from damage and maintenance, as well as build new ships. Addressing this national weakness is a strategic imperative. It is also especially important in deterring China, whose navy is backed by massive shipbuilding capacity, enabling it to rebound from losses inflicted. Rebuilding America's maritime power requires a concerted, sustained national effort.

## The Bottom Line

The goal of this book is to provide a framework for effectively competing with China and Russia, safeguarding U.S. national interests and the global rules-based maritime order. Achieving this with acceptably measured risk requires acting strategically in impactful day-to-day actions. Doing this also contributes to avoiding a disastrous major global war. Should that goal fail, the Navy must be postured and armed to win a major war quickly, while retaining deep industrial reserves for a long war. At the beginning of the 2020s, to many who follow events in Asia, a conflict seems to be approaching ominously. The most likely and dangerous wartime scenario would be fought with China over Taiwan, as Russia embarked on opportunistic adventures elsewhere. To avoid that outcome, the nation in concert with like-minded partners and allies must act urgently. For the United States this means:

1. *Employ Naval Statecraft.* To compete with China and Russia effectively the nation must bring to bear all its influence and power. That is the framework of naval statecraft, centered on the nation's advantages and interests in the maritime. It means new policies, authorities bridging various agencies in government (e.g., Departments of Defense, State, and Commerce), and naval capabilities to better compete in peacetime.

2. *Focus on Influencing Rival Decision-Makers.* Invigorate insights from the wider intelligence community to shape and time how the Navy deploys. The goal is to maximize the strategic impact of naval presence, notably by affecting national leadership calculations in Beijing and Moscow.

3. *Emphasize Numbered Fleets.* To best employ limited resources, the Navy must embrace an architecture based on the maritime and move away from the Goldwater-Nichols-era architecture of geographic combatant commands. This would see the Navy become a functional command for global maritime operations, akin to Space Command. Likewise, this would include reestablishing the First Fleet in the South China Sea, redrawing areas of responsibility for each numbered fleet according to eight maritime theaters, and rethinking the relationship between the Joint Staff and the Navy regarding allocation and deployment of maritime forces globally.

4. *Execute a National Maritime Initiative.* To address shipyard insufficiencies encountered sustaining the fleet of 296 ships in 2021 will require added capacity. This includes growing a highly skilled maritime workforce, and capital investments such as new dry docks. To build and sustain the 575 ships the fleet needs requires addressing several foundational imperatives. Given the threat from China called out by Admiral Davidson in 2021, building this fleet necessitates immediate action through 2027, without which would leave China undeterred from waging war over Taiwan. This naval buildup would have to be sustained through 2035, as a third of the Navy's warships age out of service by 2030. Building this fleet requires treating the nation's maritime industrial sector as a strategic asset. As such, after decades of atrophy with shrinking capacity and lost competitiveness, there is an urgent need to grow the merchant marine to support the nation's economy in a prolonged war. All told, building this fleet and recapitalizing the nation's needed maritime sector capacity would cost approximately $160 billion and more than thirteen years to accomplish.

5. *Build a New Model Navy.* Securing U.S. interests out to 2050 entails actions and investments informed by several macro trends. The rise of

megacities in the Indo-Pacific will place greater demand on shipping and maritime security, while additive manufacturing may mitigate the need to ship large fabricated machinery across those routes. Reliance on shipping, however, will persist well into the future in the transport of energy resources (e.g., LNG), food, and military equipment and supplies. At the same time, advances in material engineering, bioengineering, and artificial intelligence offer a potential revolution in shipping and naval affairs that the Navy must harness to remain relevant in 2050.

For the nation to prevail in this era's great power competition, progress is needed in all of the above focus areas. To get institutions moving in the right direction, early successes are necessary to kickstart what promises to be a decades-long endeavor.

## Sailing Directions

Strategies, by design, involve long-term time horizons that too often lead to admiration but not action. To overcome this and execute through to 2035 the recommendations made here, a plan for action is needed—in naval parlance, sailing directions. Readily understood by mariners, sailing directions provide critical details and warnings of danger along a charted course.[1] To participate effectively in great power competition, the Navy must accomplish two corporate objectives as it moves ahead:

1. Retain public confidence while better competing in the peacetime day-to-day contest with China and Russia.
2. Develop and build a fleet that can win wars and be reconstituted quickly during and between wars.

To ensure the wisest use of its limited resources, the Navy must synchronize with and leverage disparate government activities in new ways: a naval statecraft approach.[2] As the Navy invests in and deploys military operations, shipyards, and advanced technologies, and strengthens alliances, China and Russia will act. As they attempt to stop or delay any effort that confounds their own strategies, the nation must anticipate this while maintaining strategic focus. To get the Navy under way on this comprehensive national maritime program, the following course is recommended.

*Day One:* Issue a modern Trafalgar memorandum.

From the outset the nation must be made aware of the risks and long-term plan to regain maritime prowess. A modern version of Lord Nelson's Trafalgar memo, addressed to the nation, can provide an overarching narrative. It must explain the rationale for the policies and budgets of a national maritime initiative, as well as the potential reactions from rivals. This would encourage unity of effort across government, but to do so it will need an organizational framework and authority. A clear commitment from the president is imperative, as well as the naming of a leader charged with overseeing and ensuring coherent policy execution, the mission being to drive robust local community engagement and congressional, industry, and U.S. government action. Helping the secretary of defense reform internal processes (e.g., GFM and the Global Posture Executive Council) to be timelier will be key, while delivering strategic results most effectively coordinated across government agencies.

Because it represents the largest budget demand and urgency for forward naval presence, the Navy must deliver early, with visible results in order to sustain bureaucratic and political momentum. The Secretary of the Navy will play a critical role in engaging and gaining Congress' commitment in law to a larger fleet of 575 ships. As the senior uniformed naval officer, the Chief of Naval Operations will also play a critical role. As such, the CNO's early and clear elucidation of how the Navy will engage China and Russia in a global maritime competition will provide assurance of the military viability of naval statecraft and the fleet being built. Such a teaming of president, Secretary of the Navy, and CNO is not new, having been important in resourcing the six-hundred-ship naval buildup of the 1980s.

At that time, the Navy consumed an average of 34.3 percent of a defense budget that averaged 5.8 percent of the nation's GDP. Today, despite efforts to grow to 355 ships since 2016, the Navy averages only 29 percent of a defense budget that accounts for only 3.2 percent of GDP. Had the Navy maintained a flat budget and not been squeezed for a peace dividend, its budget would have been $49 billion larger in 2021. Moreover, representing a decades-long divestment of naval power, from 1989 to 2020 the Navy has contributed over $1.2 trillion toward the so-called peace dividend.[3] The case must be made that to reverse trends and grow the Navy, a major recapitalization effort is needed. There must be restructuring and reconceptualization of naval operations, guided by naval statecraft. Finally, frequent frank dialogue with Congress is critical in sustaining the resources to build the fleet that will be the foundation of a new model Navy between now and 2050.

Enabling the robust and discreet dialogue with Congress and its staffers that is needed will mean the establishment of a task-specific forum will be required with the Department of the Navy. This could be done by establishing a Regain Maritime Leadership Commission consisting of the Departments of Defense, Transportation, and Homeland Security along with leaders from industry and waterfront communities. This commission would be charged with assessing and recommending legislative actions to regain global maritime competitiveness. Such gospels as the Jones Act, Tariff Act of 1930, Goldwater-Nichols Act, and U.S. Code Title 10 would all be scrutinized with an eye to replacement by a new framework for great power competition.

*Waypoint One*: Within six months, demonstrate resolve in an invigorated forward strategy.
It is critical that actions follow words to bolster U.S. credibility overseas and assure Congress that investment in a national maritime program will be effective. The clearest way to do this, as Secretary of the Navy Lehman realized in the 1980s Ocean Venture exercises, is an operational demonstration. The Soviets then, like the Chinese during the first year of President Obama's 2012 Rebalance to the Asia-Pacific, did not believe in the sustainability of the newly invigorated policy. But within eight months of Reagan's inauguration, the Sixth Fleet sailed into the North Atlantic in operation Ocean Venture. The exercise got the attention of the Soviets, NATO, and Washington.

The Secretary of Navy should establish standing South China Sea and Eastern Mediterranean task forces in consultation with the secretary of defense. This ensures a minimum allocation of forces to effect an invigorated competitive strategy with China and Russia where it matters most. To firmly establish these task forces, large joint exercises should be held on their stand-up, with select exercise forces remaining in theater as part of an associated task force. In the Western Pacific, the South China Sea task force would demonstrate expeditionary sea-denial naval operations in concert with exercises demonstrating concepts, like the Army's MDO and the Marine Corps' EABO. The preference would be for this to be coordinated with longer-duration Army Pacific Pathways deployments. If the timing is right, it could see partner nations like Malaysia, the Philippines, and Indonesia invite U.S. forces to train and operate in meaningful ways across the first island chain. A similar effort could follow in the Eastern Mediterranean, effecting greater partnering by Turkey, Lebanon, Tunisia, Egypt, and Cyprus.

Getting shipbuilders and shipowners on board and making early capital investments to expand capacity will be critical in this national maritime program. In consultation with industry and Congress, the Secretary of the Navy will have to surge investments to grow shipbuilding capacity and accelerate the design of several new classes of ships. Additionally, a concerted effort with the Department of Transportation's MARAD will have to begin expanding the merchant marine fleet. This can be done by international market purchases and domestic commercial ship orders, the intent being to mitigate the nation's reliance on foreign shippers in a crisis. Sadly, the inactive fleet in 2021 was assessed as being of marginal operational value to the Navy and does not offer a ready naval reserve capacity to be tapped.[4]

Finally, the CNO should begin planning for a global large-scale exercise encompassing the Western Pacific and Eastern Mediterranean, and it should begin exercising coordination between task forces in these two decisive theaters. This exercise should follow shortly after independent exercises detailed above in both decisive theaters, and would achieve two objectives: the testing of global operational coordination and signal commitment to a forward strategy. The CNO should also conduct a live-fire field test of a manned/unmanned task force and invite key congressional leaders to observe. Gaining congressional support in this important field of naval warfare is critical. The development of unmanned naval platforms plays a critical role in future force design, by cost-effectively growing the fleet with platforms that can be produced faster, at more shipyards, and in greater numbers than conventionally manned warships.

*Waypoint Two*: Within two years, focus on institutions and prioritize growth in capacity.

As the effort enters its second year, the Navy will have to shift focus to the institutionalization of reforms and operations that have proven to be effective. Topping the list is ensuring the continuity of annual large-scale exercises, fleet experiments, and new joint exercises in the first island chain.

To support this effort, the national security adviser should establish a new, operationally focused maritime coordinating body within the NSC to oversee the proactive strategic activities of forward naval forces while also seizing on opportunities such as the Republic of Palau's and Papua New Guinea's Manus Island invitation to U.S. forces. This NSC body would in effect become the executive of naval statecraft by coordinating economic development, military posture, and presence operations with diplomacy.

At the same time, the Secretary of the Navy and the CNO must work to institutionalize changes to deployment patterns and operations. This will require identifying pragmatic and energetic uniformed leaders ready to operate across the institutional seams of military operations, diplomacy, and economic development. Once effective captains of change are found, efforts to rotate them into new positions must be resisted, while ensuring they remain competitive for promotion. At the same time, it should be expected that China and Russia will have made attempts at operational countermeasures and sharpening regional influence campaigns. With this in mind, these captains of change and veterans of naval statecraft would be positioned to sustain pushback energetically and effectively.

To sustain a global and comprehensive maritime competition with China and Russia, the Navy and Coast Guard partnership will be important. The Navy can benefit by advocating for Coast Guard force structure increases (i.e., National Security Cutters) and would be well served by incorporating Coast Guard capacities into its strategic and operational planning. By leveraging the Coast Guard's unique skill sets and access to maritime police forces overseas, the Navy would gain more opportunities and options in the execution of naval statecraft. For example, a larger Coast Guard presence in the Central Pacific and the Caribbean–Gulf of Guinea maritime corridor can better address Chinese illegal fishing and prevent encroachment on our nation's exclusive economic zones, notably in the

Pacific, and harden Pacific island nations against Chinese debt diplomacy. Joint Interagency Task Force South (JIATF-S) provides an example of what such a joint force can accomplish in complicating illicit maritime activities.[5] Likewise, an expanded Coast Guard presence based in American Samoa as part of a JIATF Central Pacific could serve similar purposes, focusing on countering illegal fishing while recapitalizing ports and airfields across the South and Central Pacific to sustain its presence, which is important in securing sea-lanes and U.S. EEZs.

Additionally, it will be increasingly important for the Navy to incorporate other military services into a naval statecraft approach. This can be done by inviting service secretaries and uniformed service chiefs to conduct campaign analysis and maritime war games. The Naval War College in Newport, Rhode Island, has held similar events, which should be continued and expanded. The findings of these war games often inform future resourcing decisions, and having a unified approach to such analysis can ensure better alignment of investments and unity of effort. Moreover, these studies provide valuable insight into the efficacy of naval statecraft and needed adjustments to the national maritime program, detailed in chapter 8. Findings regarding the industrial base should be shared with Congress to inform and foster an active relationship with key members of Congress (another Secretary Lehman lesson from the Reagan buildup).

Finally, the secretary of defense, in concert with the wider intelligence community, should establish a strategic communications and counter-intelligence task force. This group would be charged with coordinating actions thwarting Chinese and Russian influence campaigns, and counter-ing activities aimed at undermining the national maritime program. This would include educating the public about and exposing foreign influence campaigns before they can have negative impacts.

*Waypoint Three*: Within three years, begin realizing posture changes and industry adjustments.

Within the first three years of this national maritime initiative, it should be no surprise that China and Russia would have conducted several aggressive challenges to test U.S. resolve. These challenges possibly include use of mar-itime militia to ram U.S. or allied navy ships, use of warning shots resulting in limited casualties, and potentially even the capture of U.S.-flagged vessels. Such eventualities must be anticipated and countered aggressively and early to prevent repetition. To ensure crews are ready for this, the Navy should require training in new "gray-zone" concepts of operations, and the installation of nonlethal equipment on all ships deploying in proximity to Chinese and Russian maritime forces. Success in this regard can condition partner nations, as well as China and Russia, to a renewed U.S. presence as a fact of life, ushering in a "new normal" favorable to U.S. interests. Rivals will aim to cause an embarrassment that undercuts political support for investing in a larger Navy and the overarching naval statecraft approach.

The U.S. reliance on foreign shipping, especially Chinese, poses a potential weakness that can be exploited. Anticipating this, to mitigate the potential of a Chinese boycott of shipping to the United States, the Secretary of the Navy and the Secretary of Transportation must ensure a minimum merchant marine force on hand to meet the Navy's needs in wartime. Likewise, merchant marine options and plans for national wartime economic support will be needed. This effort can build on the Department of Transportation's implementation plan for a national maritime strategy.

Finally, the Secretary of the Navy and the CNO must bolster and expand civilian shipyards' skilled workforces and naval architect design capacity. If early efforts to expand the Navy's in-house ship design capacity to Cold War levels are succeeding, it should be visible by this time. This expanded engineering capacity will be important to ensure wise use of resources and effective ship design important to meeting an aggressive timeline of growing the Navy to 575 ships by 2035. To sustain a growing fleet, greater shipyard capacities are needed urgently, and a tangible example of this expanded capacity will be required to sustain political support. For this reason, an unmistakable signal of the commitment to a larger fleet would be to break ground on a fifth public shipyard, ideally on the West Coast.

*Waypoint Four*: Within four years, institutionalize great power competitive processes.
Sustaining a decade-plus national maritime program requires institutionalizing processes and training that are required of a great power

competition mindset. The Secretary of the Navy should therefore review and submit proposals to improve the Navy's ability to participate in great power competition (e.g., revision of U.S. Code Title 10 and associated national security laws) to the secretary of defense for consideration by Congress. Specifically, regulations should be removed or revised if they fail to encourage greater coordination across economic, diplomatic, and military agencies. Reaching this fourth waypoint sets the nation and the Navy on a course for effective great power competition.

## Theory of Victory

Since the end of the Cold War, assumptions based on U.S. preeminent military and economic power have encouraged generally passive or reactive national security policies. This must change, and it will not be easy. It has been over thirty years since the United States had to contend with the Soviet Union, the great power competitor in the Cold War. A theory of victory in this era's great power competition requires that the Navy be able both to field a war-winning fleet and to compete aggressively in the peacetime. As Elbridge Colby, who led the team that built the 2018 National Defense Strategy, stressed at a 2019 congressional hearing, our theory of victory must target our adversaries' weaknesses, undermine their theory of victory and especially prevent their ability to win tactical victories by fiat.[6]

The key to success in great power competition will be the ability to seize the initiative in an energetic approach toward a Free and Open Indo-Pacific and a global maritime strategy. Naval statecraft provides a framework for the Navy's active role in this undertaking. Executing such a program is ambitious, admittedly, but the consequences of not rising to the challenge are dire. To avoid ceding the world's maritime and associated prosperity away from future generations requires a unity of effort across the executive branch and Congress. Otherwise, the effort to build the Navy needed will falter in the headwinds of a questioning legislature, a distracted leadership, and a confused electorate.

In the final analysis, and chance aside, the outcome of a future major war will be determined before the fighting actually starts: the nation with the better-postured, better-resourced, and better-trained fleet is the nation that wins. Ensuring that the Navy remains ready, vigilant, and postured forward is the best way to deter war and perpetuate the rules-based order that has safeguarded the liberty and prosperity of ourselves and others for decades.

# NOTES

## Introduction

1. Bill Bostock, "Vietnam Pulled Dreamworks' 'Abominable' Movie Because It Used a Map Staking China's Claim over the Disputed South China Sea," *Business Insider*, October 15, 2019, https://www.businessinsider.com/abom inable-dreamworks-movie-vietnam-ban-south-china-sea-map-2019-10 (accessed June 6, 2021).

2. Kevin Burwick, "Top Gun 2 Controversy Ignites over Missing Flags on Maverick's Jacket," *Movie Web*, July 22, 2019, https://movieweb.com/top-gun -2-maverick-jacket-controversy-taiwanese-flag/ (accessed June 6, 2021).

3. Matt Goldberg, "MGM Doesn't Want *Red Dawn* Remake to Piss Off China; Will Piss Off North Korea Instead," *Collider*, March 16, 2011, https://collider. com/red-dawn-remake-china-north-korea/ (accessed June 6, 2021).

4. Wayne Ma, "Marriott Employee Roy Jones Hit 'Like.' Then China Got Mad," *Wall Street Journal*, March 3, 2018.

5. Michael McCann, "LeBron's China Comments and the Financial Fallout for the NBA, US," *Sports Illustrated*, October 15, 2019, https://www.si.com /nba/2019/10/15/lebron-james-nba-china-financial-fallout (accessed April 1, 2020).

6. Nate Schenkkan and Isabel Linzer, "Out of Sight, Not Out of Reach," Freedom House, February 2021, pp. 1, 11, 15, 27, https://freedomhouse.org/sites /default/files/2021-02/Complete_FH_TransnationalRepressionReport 2021_rev020221.pdf (accessed June 6, 2021).

7. Francis Fukuyama, *The End of History and the Last Man* (New York: Free Press, 1992).

8. Seva Gunitsky, *Aftershocks: Great Powers and Domestic Reforms in the Twentieth Century* (Princeton, NJ: Princeton University Press, 2017), 4.

9. Evan Osnos, "The Future of America's Contest with China," *New Yorker*, January 6, 2020, https://www.newyorker.com/magazine/2020/01/13/the-fu ture-of-americas-contest-with-china (accessed March 26, 2020).

10. Francis Fukuyama, "Against the New Pessimism," *Commentary*, February 1994, https://www.commentary.org/articles/francis-fukuyama-2/against-the- new-pessimism/ (accessed August 15, 2022).

11. Kurt M. Campbell and Jake Sullivan, "Competition without Catastrophe: How America Can Both Challenge and Coexist with China," *Foreign Affairs*, September/October 2019, https://www.foreignaffairs.com/articles/china /competition-with-china-without-catastrophe (accessed August 15, 2022).

12. Mark D. Miles and Charles R. Miller, "Global Risks and Opportunities," JFQ, no. 94, 3rd quarter 2019, https://ndupress.ndu.edu/Portals/68/Documents /jfq/jfq-94/jfq-94_86-91_Miles-Miller.pdf?ver=2019-07-25-162025-130 (accessed July 27, 2020).

13. Derek Leebaert, *The Fifty-Year Wound: The True Price of America's Cold War Victory* (Boston: Little, Brown, 2002).

14. Patrick M. Cronin and Ryan Neuhard, "Total Competition: China's Challenge in the South China Sea," Center for a New American Security, January 8, 2020.

15. Lionel Giles, *Sun Tzu on the Art of War* (Tokyo: Tuttle, 2008), 10.

16. Testimony by Elbridge A. Colby in *Senate Armed Services Committee Hearing on Implementation of the National Defense Strategy*, January 29, 2019, pp. 3–4, https://www.armed-services.senate.gov/imo/media/doc/Colby_01-29-19 .pdf (accessed June 29, 2021).

17. Henry J. Hendrix, *To Provide and Maintain a Navy* (Annapolis: Focsle, 2020), 75.

18. Josh Chin, "China Spends More on Domestic Security as Xi's Powers Grow," *Wall Street Journal*, March 6, 2018, https://www.wsj.com/articles /china-spends-more-on-domestic-security-as-xis-powers-grow-1520 358522 (accessed May 30, 2021).

19. Alfred Thayer Mahan, *The Influence of Sea Power upon History* (Boston: Little, Brown and Company, 1894).

20. Julian Stafford Corbett, *Some Principles of Maritime Strategy* (London: Longmans, Green and Company, 1911).

21. Terry L. Deibel, *Foreign Affairs Strategy: Logic for American Statecraft* (New York: Cambridge University Press, 2007).

22. Graham Allison's 1969 analysis of the Cuban Missile Crisis.

23. Subcommittees on Seapower and Projection Forces and Asia, the Pacific, Central Asia, and Nonproliferation Joint Hearing: "Maritime Security in the Indo-Pacific and the UN Convention for the Law of the Sea," April 29, 2021, https://armedservices.house.gov/hearings?ID=0FD6CE11-21C7-40B4-9A8A-46D1EDF68595 (accessed May 30, 2021).

24. John Grady, "Analyst: China Exceeded Expectations in Speed of Naval Growth," USNI News, September 10, 2020, https://news.usni.org/2020/09/10 /analyst-china-exceeded-expectations-in-speed-of-naval-growth?utm _source=USNI+News&utm_campaign=5479b952bd-USNI_NEWS_ DAILY&utm_medium=email&utm_term=0_0dd4a1450b-5479b952bd-231 849665&mc_cid=5479b952bd&mc_eid=1f01aea19e (accessed November 19, 2020).

25. The "Fat Leonard" scandal is a corruption scandal and ongoing investigation within the U.S. Navy involving ship support contractor Glenn Defense Marine Asia (GDMA), a subsidiary of the Glenn Marine Group. At the heart of the scandal was GDMA, run by Leonard Glenn Francis, a Malaysian national known as Fat Leonard for his then 350-plus-pound weight. Leonard bought access to sensitive ship schedules and favoritism for contracting multimillion-dollar ship support deals. Craig Whitlock called the scandal "perhaps the worst national-security breach of its kind to hit the Navy since the end of the Cold War." Craig Whitlock, "The Man Who Seduced the 7th Fleet," *Washington Post*, May 27, 2016, https://www.washingtonpost .com/sf/investigative/2016/05/27/the-man-who-seduced-the-7th-fleet/ (accessed November 19, 2020).

## Chapter 1. Naval Statecraft

1. Melanie W. Sisson, James A. Siebens, and Barry M. Blechman, "Coercion in the Past, and the Future of Competition," in *Military Coercion and US Foreign Policy: The Use of Force Short of War* (London: Routledge, 2020), 168–69, 171, 173.

2. Dean Cheng, "Challenging China's 'Wolf Warrior' Diplomats," Heritage Foundation *Backgrounder* no. 3504, July 6, 2020, https://www.heritage.org /asia/report/challenging-chinas-wolf-warrior-diplomats.

3. Dan Straub and Hunter Stires, "Littoral Combat Ships for Maritime COIN," U.S. Naval Institute *Proceedings* 147, no. 1 (January 2021), https://www.usni .org/magazines/proceedings/2021/january/littoral-combat-ships-maritime-coin (accessed February 17, 2022).

4. Blake Herzinger, "Learning in the South China Sea: The U.S. Response to the West Capella Standoff," *War on the Rocks*, May 18, 2020, https://waron therocks.com/2020/05/learning-in-the-south-china-sea-the-u-s-response-to-the-west-capella-standoff/ (accessed November 21, 2020).

5. Diana Stancy Correll, "Nimitz, Reagan Carrier Strike Groups Pick Up Dual-Carrier Exercises in South China Sea Again," *Navy Times*, July 17, 2020, https://www.navytimes.com/news/your-navy/2020/07/17/nimitz-reagan-carrier-strike-groups-pick-up-dual-carrier-exercises-in-south-china-sea-again/ (accessed November 21, 2020).

6. Press statement by Michael A. Pompeo, Secretary of State, "U.S. Position on Maritime Claims in the South China Seas," Department of State, July 13, 2020, https://2017-2021.state.gov/u-s-position-on-maritime-claims-in-the-south-china-sea/index.html (accessed December 13, 2021).

7. Radio Free Asia, "Indonesian Navy Conducts Major Exercise amid South China Sea Tensions," July 22, 2020, https://www.rfa.org/english/news/china /indonesia-southchinasea-07222020212724.html (accessed November 21, 2020); Republic of the Philippines, Department of Foreign Affairs, "Statement

of Secretary of Foreign Affairs Teodoro L. Locsin, Jr. on the 4th Anniversary of the Issuance of the Award in the South China Sea Arbitration," July 12, 2020, https://dfa.gov.ph/dfa-news/statements-and-advisoriesupdate/27140-state ment-of-secretary-of-foreign-affairs-teodoro-l-locsin-jr-on-the-4th- anniversary-of-the-issuance-of-the-award-in-the-south-china-sea-arbi tration (accessed November 21, 2020); Permanent Mission of Malaysia to the United Nations, Note Verbale "with reference to the Note Verbale CML/14/2019 dated 12 December 2019 by the Permanent Mission of the People's Republic of China to the United Nations to the Secretary-General," July 29, 2020, https://www.un.org/Depts/los/clcs_new/submissions_files /mys_12_12_2019/2020_07_29_MYS_NV_UN_002_OLA-2020-00373 .pdf (accessed November 21, 2020).

8. Sharon Sean, Hoang Thi Ha, Melinda Martinus, and Pham Thi Phuong Thao, "The State of Southeast Asia: 2021 Survey Report," ASEAN Studies Center, February 10, 2021, https://www.iseas.edu.sg/category/articles-commentaries /state-of-southeast-asia-survey/ (accessed December 16, 2021).

9. U.S. Department of State, *A Free and Open Indo-Pacific: Advancing a Shared Vision*, November 4, 2019, https://www.state.gov/wp-content/uploads /2019/11/Free-and-Open-Indo-Pacific-4Nov2019.pdf (accessed November 21, 2020).

10. Shayerah Ilias Akhtar and Marian L. Lawson, "BUILD Act: Frequently Asked Questions about the New US International Development Finance Corpo- ration," Congressional Research Service Report for Members and Commit- tees of Congress no. R45461, January 15, 2019, https://fas.org/sgp/crs/misc /R45461.pdf (accessed August 25, 2020).

11. Daniel Egel, Adam R. Grissom, John P. Godges, Jennifer Kavanagh, and Howard J. Shatz, "Estimating the Value of Overseas Security Commitments," RAND Corporation, 2016, pp. x–xi, 51, 63, 86–87, https://www.rand.org /pubs/research_reports/RR518.html (accessed October 25, 2021).

12. Jen Judson, "Head of US Army Pacific Command Talks Multi-domain Challenges in the Region," *Defense News*, November 25, 2018, https://www .defensenews.com/interviews/2018/11/26/head-of-us-army-pacific-com mand-talks-multidomain-challenges-in-the-region/ (accessed November 27, 2021).

13. Embassy of Ethiopia in Brussels, "Railway Development in Ethiopia," Janu- ary 6, 2017, https://ethiopianembassy.be/railway-development-in-ethiopia/ (accessed November 21, 2020). An editorial note reflects that "this article was originally published in the 4th issue (October 2016) of the *Ethiopian Messenger*, the quarterly magazine of the Embassy of Ethiopia in Brussels."

14. Alexander Cooley, *Base Politics: Democratic Change and the US Military Overseas* (Ithaca, NY: Cornell University Press, 2008), 3.

15. Remarks by President Biden on America's Place in the World, February 4, 2021, https://www.whitehouse.gov/briefing-room/speeches-remarks/2021/02/04/remarks-by-president-biden-on-americas-place-in-the-world/ (accessed April 1, 2021).

16. Cooley, *Base Politics*, 269–73.

17. Agreement between the Government of the Republic of the Philippines and the Government of the United States of America on Enhanced Defense Cooperation, April 28, 2014, https://www.officialgazette.gov.ph/downloads/2014/04apr/20140428-EDCA.pdf (accessed March 23, 2021).

18. Guillaume Lavallee, "US Special Forces Back Philippine Troops in Marawi," Agence France-Presse, June 10, 2017, https://www.rappler.com/nation/us-special-forces-help-ph-troops-marawi (accessed March 23, 2021).

19. Jason Hung, "China's Swift Power Grows in the Philippines," *The Diplomat*, February 26, 2021, https://thediplomat.com/2021/02/chinas-soft-power-grows-in-the-philippines/ (accessed March 25, 2021).

20. Observatory of Economic Complexity, https://oec.world/en/profile/country/phl (accessed March 25, 2021).

21. Raissa Robles, "Philippines Sends Navy on 'Sovereignty Patrols' to South China Sea amid Fears Whitsun Reef Is 'Scarborough Shoal 2.0,'" *South China Morning Post*, March 25, 2021, https://www.scmp.com/week-asia/politics/article/3126997/philippines-sends-navy-sovereignty-patrols-south-china-sea-amid (accessed March 29, 2021).

22. Karen Lema, "Philippines' Duterte Tells US 'You Have to Pay' If It Wants to Keep Troop Deal," Reuters, February 12, 2021, https://www.reuters.com/article/us-philippines-usa-defence/philippines-duterte-tells-u-s-you-have-to-pay-if-it-wants-to-keep-troop-deal-idUSKBN2AC1K2 (accessed April 1, 2021).

23. Seth Robson, "Australian Shipbuilder Teams with US Firm in Bid to Take Over Subic Bay Shipyard," *Stars and Stripes*, June 20, 2020, https://www.stripes.com/news/pacific/australian-shipbuilder-teams-with-us-firm-in-bid-to-take-over-subic-bay-shipyard-1.633908 (accessed March 25, 2021).

24. James Roberts and Brett Schaefer, "The BUILD Act's Proposed US Development Finance Corporation Would Supersize OPIC, But Not Improve It," Heritage Foundation Backgrounder no. 3312, May 2, 2018, https://www.heritage.org/international-economies/report/the-build-acts-proposed-us-development-finance-corporation-would (accessed April 1, 2021).

25. Joseph R. Biden, "Interim National Security Strategic Guidance," White House, March 2021, https://www.whitehouse.gov/wp-content/uploads/2021/03/NSC-1v2.pdf (accessed March 29, 2021).

26. Jacob Parakilas, "The China-US Arms Trade Arms Race," *The Diplomat*, August 6, 2021, https://thediplomat.com/2021/08/the-china-us-arms-trade-arms-race/ (accessed October 29, 2021).

27. Stockholm International Peace Research Institute, "Arms Exports from United States, 2000–2020," SIPRI, October 29, 2021, https://armstrade.sipri.org/armstrade/html/export_values.php (accessed October 29, 2021).

28. Center for International Policy, "Security Assistance Monitor," CIP, database of years 2012–20, https://securityassistance.org/security-sector-assistance/ (accessed October 29, 2021).

29. Claudette Roulo, "Japan, Australia to Provide F-35 Maintenance Sites in Pacific Region," *DoD News*, December 17, 2014, https://www.defense.gov/News/News-Stories/Article/Article/603831/ (accessed October 29, 2021).

30. "SM-3 Cooperative Development (SCD) Project," Missile Defense Agency, February 2016, p. 1, https://www.globalsecurity.org/military/library/budget/fy2017/dod-peds/U_0604881C_4_PB_2017.pdf (accessed October 29, 2021).

31. Floyd Whaley, "U.S. Reaffirms Defense of Philippines in Standoff with China," *New York Times*, May 1, 2012, https://www.nytimes.com/2012/05/02/world/asia/us-reaffirms-defense-of-philippines-in-standoff-with-china.html (accessed February 21, 2022).

32. Michael Green, Kathleen Hicks, Zack Cooper, John Schaus, and Jake Douglas, "Counter-coercion Series: Scarborough Shoal Standoff," Center for Strategic and International Studies, Asia Maritime Transparency Initiative, May 22, 2017, https://amti.csis.org/counter-co-scarborough-standoff/ (accessed December 6, 2020); Permanent Court of Arbitration, "The South China Sea Arbitration (The Republic of Philippines v. The People's Republic of China," https://pca-cpa.org/en/cases/7/ (accessed December 30, 2020); Sam LaGrone, "Confusion Continues to Surround U.S. South China Sea Freedom of Navigation Operation," USNI News, updated November 6, 2015, https://news.usni.org/2015/11/05/ confusion-continues-to-surround-u-s-south-china-sea-freedom-of-navigation-operation (accessed February 3, 2022).

33. Sam LaGrone, "Confusion Continues to Surround US South China Sea Freedom of Navigation Operation," USNI News, updated November 6, 2015, https://news.usni.org/2015/11/05/confusion-continues-to-surround-u-s-south-china-sea-freedom-of-navigation-operation (accessed December 6, 2020).

34. Michael M. Phillips, "China Seeks First Military Base on Africa's Atlantic Coast, US Intelligence Finds," *Wall Street Journal*, December 5, 2021, https://www.wsj.com/articles/china-seeks-first-military-base-on-africas-atlantic-coast-u-s-intelligence-finds-11638726327 (accessed December 20, 2021).

35. U.S. Africa Command press release, "Obangame Express," March 2021, https://www.africom.mil/what-we-do/exercises/obangame-express (accessed December 20, 2021).

36. Ian Ralby, "Looking Past Gulf of Guinea Piracy: Chinese Twins, 'Ghanaian' Fishing, and Domain Awareness," CIMSEC, March 17, 2021, https://cimsec.org/looking-past-gulf-of-guinea-piracy-chinese-twins-ghanaian-fishing-and-domain-awareness/ (accessed December 20, 2021).

37. Ganapathiraju Pramod, "Global Evaluation of Fisheries Monitoring Control and Surveillance in 84 Countries," IUU Risk Intelligence, Policy Report 1, no. 1 (December 2019), https://iuuriskintelligence.com/wp-content/uploads /2019/12/Equatorial-Guinea-country-Report-Global-Fisheries-MCS-Report-2019.pdf (accessed December 21, 2021).

## Chapter 2. Competition to Rule the Seas

1. Joint Declaration of the Government of the United Kingdom of Great Britain and Northern Ireland and the Government of the People's Republic of China on the Question of Hong Kong, pp. 61–62, para. 3.12, https://treaties.un.org /doc/Publication/UNTS/Volume%201399/v1399.pdf (accessed August 19, 2021).

2. For the article in the original Russian, see Valery Gerasimov, "The Value of Science Is in the Foresight," *Military-Industrial Kurier (VPK)*, February 16, 2013, https://www.vpk-news.ru/articles/14632 (accessed December 3, 2020). For an English-language translation, see *Military Review* 96, no. 1 (January–February 2016): 23–29, https://www.armyupress.army.mil/Portals/7/military -review/Archives/English/MilitaryReview_20160228_art001.pdf (accessed December 3, 2020).

3. See Shane R. Reeves and David Wallace, "The Combatant Status of the 'Little Green Men' and Other Participants in the Ukraine Conflict," U.S. Naval War College, *International Law Studies* 91 (2015): 362–401, https://digital-com mons.usnwc.edu/cgi/viewcontent.cgi?article=1321&context=ils (accessed November 19, 2020).

4. Eugene Rumer, "The Primakov (Not Gerasimov) Doctrine in Action," Carnegie Endowment for International Peace, June 2019, https://carnegieen dowment.org/files/Rumer_PrimakovDoctrine_final1.pdf (accessed November 19, 2020).

5. Gen. Valery Gerasimov, as reported by the Russian Academy of Military Sciences, March 24, 2018. See Julian Lindley-French, "Complex Strategic Coercion and Russian Military Modernization," Canadian Global Affairs Institute *Policy Perspective*, January 2019, p. 1, https://d3n8a8pro7vhmx .cloudfront.net/cdfai/pages/4117/attachments/original/1548354852 /Complex_Strategic_Coercion_and_Russian_Military_Modernization .pdf?1548354852 (accessed November 19, 2020).

6. Vladimir Putin, "On the National Security Strategy of the Russian Federation," July 2, 2021, http://ips.pravo.gov.ru:8080/default.aspx?pn=00012 02107030001 (accessed August 19, 2021).

7. Anna Borshchevskaya, "Shifting Landscape: Russia's Military Role in the Middle East," Washington Institute for Near East Policy, *Policy Note* no. 68, September 2019, p. 2, https://www.washingtoninstitute.org/uploads/Docu ments/pubs/PolicyNote68.pdf (accessed November 19, 2020).

8. Yuras Karmanau, "Naval Base in Syria Anchors Russia to Mediterranean," *Navy Times*, September 26, 2019, https://www.navytimes.com/news/your-navy/2019/09/27/naval-base-in-syria-anchors-russia-to-mediterranean/ (accessed November 19, 2020).

9. Thomas Wright, "Russia: What's Old Is New Again," in *Military Coercion and US Foreign Policy: The Use of Force Short of War*, ed. Melanie W. Sisson, James A. Siebens, and Barry M. Blechman (London: Routledge, 2020), 133.

10. Vladimir Isachenkov, "Russia to Establish Navy Base in Sudan for at Least 25 Years," Associated Press, December 8, 2020, https://apnews.com/article/international-news-sudan-moscow-africa-russia-0e1932a384bba427e13 e590a4ac7a1f8 (accessed December 29, 2020).

11. International Institute for Strategic Studies, *The Military Balance 2019: The Annual Assessment of Global Military Capabilities and Defence Economics* (London: Routledge, 2019), 195–209.

12. U.S. Navy, Office of Naval Intelligence, *The Russian Navy: A Historic Transition*, December 2015, pp. 15–29, https://www.oni.navy.mil/Portals/12/Intel %20agencies/russia/Russia%202015print.pdf?ver=2015-12-14-082038-923 (accessed November 19, 2020).

13. U.S. Defense Intelligence Agency, *Russia Military Power: Building a Military to Support Great Power Aspirations* (Washington: U.S. Defense Intelligence Agency, 2017), 66, https://www.dia.mil/Portals/27/Documents/News/Mili tary%20Power%20Publications/Russia%20Military%20Power%20 Report%202017.pdf?ver=2017-06-28-144235-937 (accessed November 19, 2020).

14. Dakota L. Wood, ed., *2020 Index of US Military Strength* (Washington: Heritage Foundation, 2020), 219, https://www.heritage.org/sites/default /files/2019-11/2020_IndexOfUMilitaryStrength_WEB.pdf (accessed December 3, 2020).

15. Mike Yeo, "Indonesia Calls Russian Bombers Visit Part of Navigation Exercise," *Defense News*, December 6, 2017, https://www.defensenews.com /air/2017/12/06/indonesia-calls-russian-bombers-visit-part-of-navigation-exercise/ (accessed August 19, 2021).

16. "Russian and Chinese Bombers Fly Joint Patrol over Pacific," AP News, December 22, 2020, https://apnews.com/article/beijing-vladimir-putin-moscow-russia-east-china-sea-dfe0b31a067eea6311109922c1c263aa (accessed August 19, 2021).

17. Sam LaGrone, "Australian MoD: Russian Surface Group Operating Near Northern Border," USNI News, November 12, 2014, https://news.usni .org/2014/11/12/australian-mod-russian-surface-group-operating-near-northern-border (accessed August 19, 2021).

18. William Cole, "Russian Naval Exercise Ends as Spy Ship Remains in Hawaii Area," *Star Advertiser*, June 21, 2021, https://www.staradvertiser

.com/2021/06/21/breaking-news/navy-conducts-drills-near-hawaii-as-rus sian-spy-ship-cruises-north-of-oahu/ (accessed August 19, 2021).

19. Vladimir Putin, "Strategy for the Development of the Arctic Zone of the Russian Federation and National Security for the Period up to 2035," President of Russian Federation, October 26, 2020, https://docs.cntd.ru/document/566091182 (accessed August 19, 2021).

20. Vladimir Putin, "State Policy of the Russian Federation in the Arctic for the Period up to 2035," President of the Russian Federation, March 5, 2020, https://docs.cntd.ru/document/564371920?marker=6560IO (accessed August 19, 2021).

21. China Power, "How Does China's First Aircraft Carrier Stack Up?," Center for Strategic and International Studies, December 9, 2015, https://chinapower .csis.org/aircraft-carrier/ (accessed August 20, 2021).

22. Jamie Seidel, "Russian Aircraft Carrier Damaged in Dry Dock Accident," October 31, 2018, https://www.news.com.au/technology/innovation/mili tary/hole-ripped-in-russian-carriers-side/news-story/90917c29698ed02b03 780f35ba01db8c (accessed August 20, 2021).

23. Martin Manaranche, "Russian Aircraft Carrier to Rejoin the Fleet in Late 2023," Naval News, June 24, 2021, https://www.navalnews.com/naval-news/2021/06/russian-aircraft-carrier-to-rejoin-the-fleet-in-late-2023/ (accessed August 20, 2021).

24. Pierre Tran, "Mistral Dispute with Russia Settled, France Eyes Exports," Defense News, August 9, 2015, https://www.defensenews.com/naval/2015 /08/09/mistral-dispute-with-russia-settled-france-eyes-exports/ (accessed August 20, 2021).

25. Lorenzo Tual, "Russian Making Progress On Improved Ivan Gren-Class Landing Ships," Naval News, June 18, 2021, https://www.navalnews.com /naval-news/2021/06/russian-making-progress-on-improved-ivan-gren-class-landing-ships/ (accessed August 20, 2021).

26. David Axe, "Russia's New Assault Ship Might Look Familiar—Especially to the French," Forbes, May 28, 2020, https://www.forbes.com/sites/davi daxe/2020/05/28/russias-new-assault-might-look-familiar-especially-to-the-french/?sh=6016fb1c734c (accessed August 20, 2021).

27. Igor Delano, "Russia's Black Sea Fleet: Toward a Multi-regional Force," Center for Naval Analyses, June 5, 2019, p. 8, https://www.cna.org/CNA_ files/PDF/IOP-2019-U-020190-Final.pdf (accessed August 20, 2021).

28. Ihor Kabaneko, "Russia's Shipbuilding Program: Postponed Blue-Water Ambitions," Real Clear Defense, April 4, 2020, https://www.realcleardefense .com/articles/2018/04/20/russias_shipbuilding_program_postponed_blue-water_ambitions_113347.html (accessed August 20, 2021).

29. Alexey Rakhmanov, president of United Shipbuilding Corporation (USC), talks to the state of Russia's shipbuilding industry, Energy Year, February 25, 2020,

https://theenergyyear.com/articles/growth-in-russias-shipbuilding/?cn-re
loaded=1 (accessed August 20, 2021).

30. Borshchevskaya, "Shifting Landscape," 10.

31. Testimony of Kimberly Marten, "The GRU, Yevgeny Prigozhin, and Russia's Wagner Group: Malign Russian Actors and Possible US Responses," Subcommittee on Europe, Eurasia, Energy, and the Environment United States House of Representatives, July 7, 2020, pp. 3–5, https://docs.house.gov/meetings /FA/FA14/20200707/110854/HHRG-116-FA14-Wstate-MartenK -20200707.pdf (accessed August 22, 2021).

32. Paige Montfort, "Band of Brothers: The Wagner Group and the Russian State," Center for Strategic and International Studies, September 21, 2020, https://www.csis.org/blogs/post-soviet-post/band-brothers-wagner-group-and-russian-state (accessed August 22, 2021).

33. Harley Balzer, "Public Opinion Paradoxes? Russians Are Increasingly Dubious about the Cost of Putin's Foreign Policies," PONARS Eurasia, May 2019, pp. 4–6, https://www.ponarseurasia.org/WFP-content/uploads/attachments /Pepm595_Balzer_May2019_0.PDF (accessed August 22, 2021).

34. Thomas Gibbons-Neff, "How a 4-Hour Battle between Russian Mercenaries and US Commandos Unfolded in Syria," *New York Times*, May 24, 2018.

35. Ilya Barabanov and Nader Ibrahim, "The Lost Tablet and the Secret Documents: Clues Pointing to a Shadowy Russian Army," BBC News, August 11, 2021, https://www.bbc.co.uk/news/extra/8iaz6xit26/the-lost-tablet-and-the-secret-documents (accessed August 22, 2021).

36. Eric Sof, "7 Contractors from Wagner Group Killed in an Ambush in Mozambique," *Spec Ops Magazine*, https://special-ops.org/7-contractors-from-wag ner-group-killed/ (accessed August 22, 2021).

37. Philip Short, *Mao: A Life* (New York: Henry Holt and Company, 1999), 119–20.

38. Short, 419.

39. Office of the Secretary of Defense, *Annual Report to Congress: Military and Security Developments involving the People's Republic of China 2019* (Washington: U.S. Department of Defense, 2019), iii, 14, 83–85, https:// media.defense.gov/2019/May/02/2002127082/-1/-1/1/2019%20CHINA%20 MILITARY%20POWER%20REPORT%20(1).PDF (accessed November 19, 2020).

40. Shelley Rigger, *Why Taiwan Matters: Small Island, Global Powerhouse* (New York: Rowman & Littlefield, 2011), 143–46.

41. Kat Devlin and Christine Huang, "In Taiwan, Views of Mainland China Mostly Negative," Pew Research Center, May 12, 2020, https://www.pewre search.org/global/2020/05/12/in-taiwan-views-of-mainland-china-mostly-negative/ (accessed August 24, 2021).

NOTES TO PAGES 51–53 | 287

42. John F. Cooper, *China's Foreign Aid and Investment Diplomacy*, vol. 2: *History and Practice in Asia, 1950–Present* (London: Palgrave Macmillan, 2016), 165–67.

43. Scott W. Harold, Lyle J. Morris, and Logan Ma, "Countering China's Efforts to Isolate Taiwan Diplomatically in Latin America and the Caribbean: The Role of Development Assistance and Disaster Relief," RAND Corporation, 2019, https://www.rand.org/content/dam/rand/pubs/research_reports/RR2800/RR2885/RAND_RR2885.pdf (accessed August 25, 2021).

44. Alex Joske, "The Party Speaks for You: Foreign Interference and the Chinese Communist Party's United Front System," Australian Strategic Policy Institute, June 2020, pp. 10–13, https://s3-ap-southeast-2.amazonaws.com/ad-aspi/2020-06/The%20party%20speaks%20for%20you_0.pdf?VersionId=gFHuXyYMR0XuDQOs.6JSmrdyk7MraIcN (accessed August 25, 2021).

45. U.S. Senate, Permanent Subcommittee on Investigations, Committee on Homeland Security and Governmental Affairs, "Threats to the US Research Enterprise: China's Talent Recruitment Plans," November 2019, pp. 1–2, 35, 37–38, https://www.hsgac.senate.gov/imo/media/doc/2019-11-18%20PSI%20Staff%20Report%20-%20China's%20Talent%20Recruitment%20Plans.pdf (accessed August 25, 2021).

46. Rob Schmitz, "Australia and New Zealand Are Ground Zero for Chinese Influence," NPR: *All Things Considered*, October 2, 2018, https://www.npr.org/2018/10/02/627249909/australia-and-new-zealand-are-ground-zero-for-chinese-influence (accessed August 1, 2022).

47. Iain Robertson, "Chinese Messaging across the Strait China-Friendly Narratives and the 2020 Taiwan Presidential Election," Atlantic Council, December 2020, pp. 8, 11, https://www.atlanticcouncil.org/wp-content/uploads/2020/12/China-Taiwan-FINAL.pdf (accessed August 25, 2021).

48. Joske, "The Party Speaks for You," 6–7.

49. Wayne Ma, "Marriott Employee Roy Jones Hit 'Like.' Then China Got Mad," *Wall Street Journal*, March 3, 2018.

50. Joseph Marks, "The Cybersecurity 202: US Officials: It's China Hacking That Keeps Us Up at Night," *Washington Post*, March 6, 2019.

51. Office of the Secretary of Defense, *Annual Report to Congress: Military and Security Developments involving the People's Republic of China 2019*, 112–13.

52. Michael McCann, "LeBron's China Comments and the Financial Fallout for the NBA, US," *Sports Illustrated*, October 15, 2019, https://www.si.com/nba/2019/10/15/lebron-james-nba-china-financial-fallout (accessed April 1, 2020).

53. Zach Dorfman, "The Disappeared: China's Global Kidnapping Campaign Has Gone On for Years. It May Now Be Reaching inside US Borders," *Foreign Policy*, March 29, 2018, https://foreignpolicy.com/2018/03/29/the-disappeared-china-renditions-kidnapping/ (accessed December 20, 2020).

54. Damien Cave and Jacqueline Williams, "Australian Politics Is Open to Foreign Cash, and China Has Much to Gain," *New York Times*, June 6, 2017, https://www.nytimes.com/2017/06/06/world/australia/china-political-influence-campaign-finance.html?referringSource=articleShare (accessed August 26, 2021).

55. Australia's Foreign Relations (State and Territory Arrangements) with consequential amendments to bill, https://www.aph.gov.au/Parliamentary_Business/Bills_Legislation/Bills_Search_Results/Result?bId=r6595; Foreign Influence Transparency Scheme Act 2018, https://www.legislation.gov.au/Details/C2018A00063 (both accessed August 26, 2021).

56. Renju Jose, "Australia Reviewing Lease of Darwin Port to Chinese Firm—Source," Reuters, May 2, 2021, https://www.reuters.com/world/asia-pacific/australia-review-lease-port-chinese-firm-media-report-2021-05-02/ (accessed August 26, 2021).

57. Ethan Meick and Nargiza Salidjanova, "China's Response to US-South Korean Missile Defense System Deployment and its Implications," US-China Economic and Security Review Commission, p. 7, https://www.uscc.gov/sites/default/files/Research/Report_China's%20Response%20to%20THAAD%20Deployment%20and%20its%20Implications.pdf (accessed August 26, 2021).

58. Victoria Kim, "When China and US Spar, It's South Korea That Gets Punched," *Los Angeles Times*, November 19, 2020, https://www.latimes.com/world-nation/story/2020-11-19/south-korea-china-beijing-economy-thaad-missile-interceptor (accessed August 26, 2021).

59. "Action Plan on the Belt and Road Initiative," State Council of the PRC, March 30, 2015, http://english.www.gov.cn/archive/publications/2015/03/30/content_281475080249035.htm (accessed August 26, 2021).

60. Michele Ruta, "Belt and Road Economics: Opportunities and Risks of Transport Corridors," World Bank, 2019, https://openknowledge.worldbank.org/bitstream/handle/10986/31878/9781464813924.pdf (accessed August 26, 2021).

61. Silvia Amaro, "China Bought Most of Greece's Main Port and Now It Wants to Make It the Biggest in Europe," CNBC, November 15, 2019, https://www.cnbc.com/2019/11/15/china-wants-to-turn-greece-piraeus-port-into-europe-biggest.html (accessed August 26, 2021).

62. "Dry Dock Services," Piraeus Port Authority, https://www.olp.gr/en/services/dry-dock-department (accessed August 26, 2021).

63. Geoffrey F. Gresh, *To Rule Eurasia's Waves: The New Great Power Competition at Sea* (New Haven, CT: Yale University Press, 2020), loc. 1352–84.

64. Tasos Kokkinidis, "China's Cosco Tightens Grip on Piraeus Port by Raising Stake to 67%," *Greek Reporter*, August 22, 2021, https://greekreporter.com/2021/08/22/china-cosco-tightens-grip-piraeus-port/ (accessed September 2, 2021).

65. Ahmed Shafiq and Zhang Xu, "Five Years On, Suez Flagship Project Tells Story of Dynamic China-Egypt Cooperation," Xinhua, January 24, 2021, http://www.xinhuanet.com/english/2021-01/24/c_139693564.htm (accessed August 26, 2021).

66. Junaid Ashraf, "String of Pearls and China's Emerging Strategic Culture," *Strategic Studies* 37, no. 4 (2017): 166–81, https://www.jstor.org/stable/485 37578 (accessed August 26, 2021).

67. Saeeduddin Faridi, "China's Ports in the Indian Ocean," Gateway House: Indian Council on Global Relations, August 19, 2021, https://www.gate wayhouse.in/chinas-ports-in-the-indian-ocean-region/?utm_source =MadMimi&utm_medium=email&utm_content=Afghanistan%3A+Limi ted+options+for+regional+powers+%7C+China%27s+ports+in+the+Indi an+Ocean+%7C+Afghan+Hindus+%26+Sikhs+under+attack+%7C+Afgh anistan%3A+Development+against+the+odds+%7C+Mafia-nation%3 A+State+capture+by+criminal+syndicates&utm_campaign=20210818_ m164406509_Weekly+Briefing+2021+%281%29&utm_term=China_27s+ ports+in+the+Indian+Ocean (accessed August 26, 2021).

68. Briefing with Senior State Department Officials to Traveling Press, U.S. Department of State, May 4, 2021, https://www.state.gov/briefing-with-senior-state-department-officials-to-traveling-press/ (accessed August 26, 2021).

69. Maria Abi-Habib, "How China Got Sri Lanka to Cough Up a Port," *New York Times*, June 25, 2018, https://www.nytimes.com/2018/06/25/world/asia/china -sri-lanka-port.html?referringSource=articleShare (accessed August 27, 2021).

70. Peter Cai, "Understanding China's Belt and Road Initiative," Lowy Institute, March 22, 2017, https://www.lowyinstitute.org/publications/understanding-belt-and-road-initiative (accessed August 27, 2021).

71. David Dollar, "Order from Chaos: Seven Years into China's Belt and Road," October 1, 2020, https://www.brookings.edu/blog/order-from-chaos/2020/10 /01/seven-years-into-chinas-belt-and-road/ (accessed August 27, 2021).

72. David Shambaugh, *Modernizing China's Military: Progress, Problems, and Prospects* (Berkeley: University of California Press, 2002), 69–74, 83–89, 105–7.

73. Saad Rahim, "China's Energy Strategy toward the Middle East," in *China's Energy Strategy: The Impact on Beijing's Maritime Policies* (Annapolis: Naval Institute Press, 2008), 146–51.

74. Michael A. McDevitt, *China as a Twenty-First-Century Naval Power* (Annapolis: Naval Institute Press, 2020), 159.

75. "Annual Report on the Military Power of the People's Republic of China," May 29, 2004, pp. 23–24, 39–40, https://www.globalsecurity.org/military/ library/report/2004/d20040528prc.pdf (accessed August 29, 2021).

76. Bernard D. Cole, "China's Military and Security Activities Abroad," Testimony before the U.S.-China Economic and Security Review Commission, March 4, 2009, pp. 2, 4–6, https://www.uscc.gov/sites/default/files/3.4.09Cole.pdf (accessed August 30, 2021).

77. Ronald O'Rourke, "China Naval Modernization: Implications for US Navy Capabilities—Background and Issues for Congress," Congressional Research Service, August 3, 2021, pp. 2–3, 8, 10, https://sgp.fas.org/crs/row/RL33153 .pdf (accessed August 30, 2021).

78. Office of the Secretary of Defense, *Annual Report to Congress: Military and Security Developments involving the People's Republic of China 2020* (Washington: U.S. Department of Defense, 2020), i–ii, https://media.defense. gov/2020/Sep/01/2002488689/-1/-1/1/2020-DOD-CHINA-MILITARY- POWER-REPORT-FINAL.PDF (accessed August 30, 2021).

79. Michael S. Chase et al., "China's Incomplete Military Transformation: Assessing the Weaknesses of the People's Liberation Army (PLA)," RAND, 2015, pp. 69–74, https://www.rand.org/pubs/research_reports/RR893.html (accessed August 30, 2021).

80. David M. Finkelstein, "Breaking the Paradigm: Drivers behind the PLA's Current Period of Reform," in *Chairman Xi Remakes the PLA* (Washington: National Defense University Press, 2019), 48–52.

81. James Mulvenon, "To Get Rich Is Unprofessional: Chinese Military Corruption in the Jiang Era," *China Leadership Monitor*, vol. 6, Hoover Institute, June 5, 2003, pp. 23, 25–26, https://www.hoover.org/sites/default/files /uploads/documents/clm6_jm.pdf (accessed August 30, 2021).

82. Eric Heginbotham, "Chinese Views of the Military Balance in the Western Pacific," China Maritime Studies Institute, *China Maritime Report*, no. 14 (June 2021): 11–13, https://digital-commons.usnwc.edu/cgi/viewcontent.cgi ?article=1013&context=cmsi-maritime-reports (accessed August 30, 2021).

83. Timothy Heath and Andrew S. Erickson, "Is China Pursuing Counter-intervention?," *Washington Quarterly* 38, no. 3 (Fall 2015): 143–56, https:// www.andrewerickson.com/2015/11/is-china-pursuing-counter-interven tion/ (accessed November 19, 2020).

84. Oriana Skylar Mastro, "The Taiwan Temptation: Why Beijing Might Resort to Force," *Foreign Affairs*, July/August 2021, https://www.foreignaffairs.com /articles/china/2021-06-03/china-taiwan-war-temptation (accessed August 30, 2021).

85. David Hambling, "China Converts Car Ferries for Amphibious Assault," *Forbes*, July 27, 2021, https://www.forbes.com/sites/davidhambling/2021/07 /27/china-converts-car-ferries-for-amphibious-assault/?sh=436ecdbf3a04 (accessed August 30, 2021).

86. Testimony by Elbridge A. Colby in *Senate Armed Services Committee Hearing on Implementation of the National Defense Strategy*, January 29, 2019,

https://www.armed-services.senate.gov/imo/media/doc/Colby_01-29-19
.pdf (accessed August 30, 2021).

87. David Sacks, "What Xi Jinping's Major Speech Means for Taiwan," Council
on Foreign Relations, July 6, 2021, https://www.cfr.org/blog/what-xi-jinpings
-major-speech-means-taiwan (accessed August 30, 2021).

88. Ryan D. Martinson, "Echelon Defense: The Role of Sea Power in Chinese
Maritime Dispute Strategy," CMSI Red Books, Study No. 15 (May 2018),
3–4, 13, 53–54, 57, 97, https://digital-commons.usnwc.edu/cgi/viewcontent
.cgi?article=1014&context=cmsi-red-books (accessed September 4, 2021).

89. Yuli Yang, "Pentagon Says Chinese Vessels Harassed US Ship," CNN,
March 9, 2009, http://www.cnn.com/2009/POLITICS/03/09/us.navy.china
/index.html (accessed September 4, 2021).

90. Kawashima Shin, "The Senkaku Crisis in Perspective: An Interview with
Former Chief Cabinet Secretary Sengoku Yoshito," Nippon.com, December
5, 2017, https://www.nippon.com/en/currents/d00365/?pnum=2 (accessed
September 4, 2021).

91. Keith Bradsher, "Amid Tension, China Blocks Vital Exports to Japan," *New
York Times*, September 22, 2010, https://www.nytimes.com/2010/09/23
/business/global/23rare.html (accessed September 4, 2021).

92. Wu Jiao, "Premier Wen Urges Japan to Release Captain," *China Daily*, September 22, 2021, http://www.chinadaily.com.cn/china/2010-09/22/content_
11337158.htm (accessed September 4, 2021).

93. Michael Green, Kathleen Hicks, Zack Cooper, John Schaus, and Jake
Douglas, "Counter-coercion Series: Senkaku Islands Nationalization Crisis,"
Asia Maritime Transparency Initiative, June 14, 2017, https://amti.csis.org
/counter-co-senkaku-nationalization/ (accessed September 4, 2021).

94. See Andrew Erickson's website for China analysis from original sources:
Andrew S. Erickson, "China's Maritime Militia: What It Is and How to Deal
with It," June 24, 2016, https://www.andrewerickson.com/2016/06/chinas-
maritime-militia-what-it-is-and-how-to-deal-with-it/ (accessed September
5, 2021).

95. Conor M. Kennedy and Andrew S. Erickson, "China's Third Sea Force,
the People's Armed Forces Maritime Militia: Tethered to the PLA," China
Maritime Studies Institute, *China Maritime Report*, no. 1 (March
2017): 6, 9–10, https://digital-commons.usnwc.edu/cgi/viewcontent.cgi
?article=1000&context=cmsi-maritime-reports (accessed September 5, 2021).

96. Zachary Haver, "Sansha City in China's South China Sea Strategy: Building a
System of Administrative Control," China Maritime Studies Institute, *China
Maritime Report*, no. 12 (2021): 8, 38–40, https://digital-commons.usnwc
.edu/cgi/viewcontent.cgi?article=1011&context=cmsi-maritime-reports
(accessed September 5, 2021).

97. Patrick Böhler, "China's Coast Guard Rams Fishing Boat to Free It from Indonesian Authorities," *New York Times*, March 16, 2016, https://www.nytimes.com/2016/03/22/world/asia/indonesia-south-china-sea-fishing-boat.html (accessed September 5, 2021).

98. Arlina Arshad, "Chinese Coast Guard Tried to Intervene during Trawler's Seizure," *Straits Times*, May 31, 2016, https://www.straitstimes.com/asia/chinese-coast-guard-tried-to-intervene-during-trawlers-seizure (accessed September 5, 2021).

99. Ryan D. Martinson, "East Asian Security in the Age of the Chinese Mega-Cutter," CIMSEC, July 3, 2015, https://cimsec.org/tag/chinese-cutter/ (accessed September 5, 2021).

100. Trey Yingst and Yonat Friling, "Chinese Fishing Fleets Caught in Galapagos Islands Violating Ecuadorian Sovereignty," Fox News, September 30, 2020, https://www.foxnews.com/world/chinese-fishing-fleets-caught-in-galapagos-islands-violating-ecuadorian-sovereignty (accessed September 5, 2021).

101. Huseyin Erdogan, "China Invokes 'Cabbage Tactics' in South China Sea," Anadolu Agency, March 25, 2015, https://www.aa.com.tr/en/economy/china-invokes-cabbage-tactics-in-south-china-sea/63892 (accessed November 20, 2020).

102. Kennedy and Erickson, "China's Third Sea Force."

103. Chin Han Wong, "China a No-Show at Joint Military Safety Meeting with US," *Wall Street Journal*, December 17, 2020, https://www.wsj.com/articles/u-s-stood-up-by-china-at-military-safety-meeting-11608199871?st=q185ognuecl300z&reflink=article_copyURL_share (accessed September 9, 2021).

104. "Code for Unplanned Encounters at Sea," USNI News, June 17, 2014, https://news.usni.org/2014/06/17/document-conduct-unplanned-encounters-sea (accessed September 9, 2021).

105. Demetri Sevastopulo and Kathrin Hille, "US Warns China on Aggressive Acts by Fishing Boats and Coast Guard," *Financial Times*, April 28, 2019, https://www.ft.com/content/ab4b1602-696a-11e9-80c7-60ee53e6681d (accessed September 11, 2021).

106. Bureau of Oceans and International Environmental and Scientific Affairs, "Limits in the Sea: Maritime Claims in the South China Sea," U.S. Department of State, December 5, 2014, pp. 1, 23–24, https://2009-2017.state.gov/documents/organization/234936.pdf (accessed September 11, 2021).

107. "The South China Sea Arbitration (The Republic of Philippines v. The People's Republic of China)," case no. 2013–19, https://pca-cpa.org/en/cases/7/ (accessed September 11, 2021).

108. Sam LaGrone, "US Destroyer Comes within 12 Nautical Miles of Chinese South China Sea Artificial Island, Beijing Threatens Response," USNI News, October 27, 2015, https://news.usni.org/2015/10/27/u-s-destroyer-comes-within-12-nautical-miles-of-chinese-south-china-sea-artificial-island-beijing-threatens-response (accessed September 11, 2021).

109. U.S. White House Press Secretary, "Joint Press Conference with President Obama and Prime Minister Abe of Japan," April 24, 2014, https://obama whitehouse.archives.gov/the-press-office/2014/04/24/joint-press-confer ence-president-obama-and-prime-minister-abe-japan (accessed September 11, 2021).

110. Video of P-3 engaged with PLA air control station in South China Sea, May 21, 2015, YouTube, https://youtu.be/OaKbZW0pqkM (accessed September 11, 2021).

111. Commander, U.S. Pacific Fleet Australian Strategic Policy Institute Canberra, Australia, Adm. Harry B. Harris Jr., March 31, 2015, https://www.cpf.navy .mil/leaders/harry-harris/speeches/2015/03/ASPI-Australia.pdf (accessed September 11, 2021).

112. David H. Berger, "Maritime Security Dialogue: An Update on the Marine Corps with Commandant Gen. David H. Berger," Center for Strategic and International Studies, September 2, 2021, https://www.csis.org/analysis/mar itime-security-dialogue-update-marine-corps-commandant-gen-david-h-berger (accessed September 11, 2021).

113. U.S. Navy, Office of Naval Intelligence, *The PLA Navy: New Capabilities and Missions for the 21st Century* (Washington: Office of Naval Intelligence, 2015), 5, 9–11, https://www.oni.navy.mil/Portals/12/Intel%20agencies/China _Media/2015_PLA_NAVY_PUB_Print.pdf?ver=2015-12-02-081247-687 (accessed November 19, 2020).

114. Kyle Mizokami, "Peace Ark: Onboard China's Hospital Ship," USNI News, July 23, 2014, https://news.usni.org/2014/07/23/peace-ark-onboard-chinas-hospital-ship (accessed November 19, 2020).

115. U.S. Defense Intelligence Agency, *China Military Power: Modernizing a Force to Fight and Win* (Washington: U.S. Defense Intelligence Agency, 2019), 33, 63–80, https://www.dia.mil/Portals/27/Documents/News/Military%20 Power%20Publications/China_Military_Power_FINAL_5MB_20190103 .pdf (accessed November 20, 2020).

116. "Chinese Coast Guard Ships Depart for North Pacific on Law Enforce-ment Mission," *Global Times*, July 31, 2021, https://www.globaltimes.cn /page/202107/1230140.shtml (accessed September 11, 2021).

117. Office of the Secretary of Defense, *Military and Security Developments involving the People's Republic of China 2020*, 44–49.

118. A "black swan" event is one that defies normal expectations or, because of conventional bias, is considered to be impossible. Though the concept origi nated during Roman times, it was popularized in Nassim Nicholas Taleb, *The Black Swan: The Impact of the Highly Improbable* (New York: Random House, 2007).

119. Xinhua, "China, Russia Agree to Upgrade Relations for New Era," June 6, 2019, http://www.xinhuanet.com/english/2019-06/06/c_138119879.htm (accessed November 20, 2020).

120. Jeremy Page, "China Promises Further Military Cooperation with Russia," *Wall Street Journal*, updated July 24, 2019, https://www.wsj.com/articles/china-promises-further-military-cooperation-with-russia-11563973937 (accessed November 20, 2020).

121. Anton Tsvetov, "Russia's Tactics and Strategy in the South China Sea," Center for Strategic and International Studies, Asia Maritime Transparency Initiative, November 1, 2016, https://amti.csis.org/russias-tactics-strategy-south-china-sea/ (accessed November 20, 2020).

122. Andrew Chatzky and James McBride, "China's Massive Belt and Road Initiative," Council on Foreign Relations *Backgrounder*, last updated January 28, 2020, https://www.cfr.org/backgrounder/chinas-massive-belt-and-road-initiative (accessed November 20, 2020).

## Chapter 3. Global Maritime 2050

1. "Ice Free Arctic Summers Likely Sooner Than Expected," U.S. Department of Commerce, dated April 2, 2009, http://www.noaanews.noaa.gov/stories2009/20090402_seaice.html (accessed January 27, 2011).

2. "Predicting the Future of Arctic Ice," National Oceanic and Atmospheric Administration, February 28, 2020, https://www.ncei.noaa.gov/news/arctic-ice-study (accessed July 31, 2021).

3. "Nuclear Icebreakers Clear Path for Gas Shipment," *World Nuclear News*, August 17, 2010.

4. International Maritime Organization, *International Code for Ships Operating in Polar Waters*, pp. 16–18, https://wwwcdn.imo.org/localresources/en/MediaCentre/HotTopics/Documents/POLAR%20CODE%20TEXT%20AS%20ADOPTED.pdf (accessed August 1, 2021).

5. As of July 2021 the Arctic Council members are Canada, Denmark, Finland, Iceland, Norway, Russian Federation, Sweden, and the United States. Observer nations include France, Germany, Italy, Japan, Netherlands, People's Republic of China, Poland, India, South Korea, Singapore, Spain, Switzerland, and United Kingdom. "Who We Are," Arctic Council, https://arctic-council.org/en/ (accessed August 1, 2021).

6. Kyle Mizokami, "Russia's Nuclear-Powered Icebreaker Is a Step Toward Military Domination," *Popular Mechanics*, September 24, 2020, https://www.popularmechanics.com/military/navy-ships/a34128219/russia-nuclear-powered-icebreaker-arktika/ (accessed August 1, 2021).

7. Gleb Stolyarov, "Russia to Build First LNG-Powered Icebreakers for Arctic Sea Route," Reuters, July 23, 2021, https://www.reuters.com/article/us-russia-rosatom-icebreakers-idAFKBN2ET1V3 (accessed August 1, 2021).

8. Andrew Von Ah, "Maritime Infrastructure: A Strategic Approach and Interagency Leadership Could Improve Federal Efforts in the US Arctic,"

Government Accountability Office, April 2020, pp. 14, https://www.gao.gov/assets/gao-20-460.pdf (accessed August 1, 2021).

9. Alison Weisburger, "Lessons from the Russian Fuel Tanker Resupply of Nome, Alaska," January 6, 2012, https://www.thearcticinstitute.org/lessons-russian-fuel-tanker-resupply-nome/ (accessed September 28, 2021); "Nome, Alaska, Finally Gets Russian Tanker Fuel," CBS News, January 16, 2012, https://www.cbsnews.com/news/nome-alaska-finally-gets-russian-tanker-fuel/ (accessed September 28, 2021).

10. Acquisition Directorate, "Polar Security Cutter," U.S. Coast Guard, https://www.dcms.uscg.mil/Our-Organization/Assistant-Commandant-for-Acquisitions-CG-9/Programs/Surface-Programs/Polar-Icebreaker/ (accessed September 28, 2021).

11. RADM David Gove (USN), "Arctic Melt: Reopening a Naval Frontier," U.S. Naval Institute *Proceedings* 135, no. 2 (February 2009), http://www.usni.org/magazines/proceedings/2009-02/arctic-melt-reopening-naval-frontier (accessed January 6, 2011).

12. U.S. Coast Guard, "Polar Security Cutter," https://www.dcms.uscg.mil/Our-Organization/Assistant-Commandant-for-Acquisitions-CG-9/Programs/Surface-Programs/Polar-Icebreaker/ (accessed August 1, 2021).

13. "GAC Establishes New Base on Svalbard Archipelago," *Marketline*, October 28, 2009.

14. "Arctic Shipping 2030: From Russia with Oil, Stormy Passage, or Arctic Great Game?," Norshipping-07, http://www.econ.no (accessed December 20, 2010).

15. "El Faro Sinking: Poor Seamanship in the Spotlight," Safety4Sea, September 25, 2019, https://safety4sea.com/cm-el-faro-sinking-poor-seamanship-on-the-spotlight/?__cf_chl_jschl_tk__=pmd_893832f40b7b16ab5099fa0ebf6f5f c4f37cc368-1627950177-0-gqNtZGzNAg2jcnBszQeO (accessed August 2, 2021).

16. J. P. Kossin, K. A. Emanuel, and G. A. Vecchi, "The Poleward Migration of the Location of Tropical Cyclone Maximum Intensity," *Nature*, May 14, 2014, pp. 349–52, https://www.nature.com/articles/nature13278 (accessed July 30, 2021).

17. Geophysical Fluid Dynamics Laboratory, "Global Warming and Hurricanes: An Overview of Current Research Results," National Oceanic and Atmospheric Administration, March 29, 2021, https://www.gfdl.noaa.gov/global-warming-and-hurricanes/ (accessed July 30, 2021).

18. Hariesh Manaadiar, "Five Adverse Effects of Climate Change on Maritime Transport," Shipping and Freight Resource, October 2, 2019, https://www.shippingandfreightresource.com/5-adverse-effects-of-climate-change-on-maritime-transport/ (accessed July 30, 2021).

19. Keith Wagner, "Climate Change and Shipping," *Maritime Executive*, January 4, 2017, https://www.maritime-executive.com/features/climate-change-and-shipping (accessed July 30, 2021).

20. Ian Ralby, "Evolution of the Fleet: A Closer Look at the Chinese Fishing Vessels off the Galapagos," Center for International Maritime Security, October 19, 2020, https://cimsec.org/evolution-of-the-fleet-a-closer-look-at-the-chinese-fishing-vessels-off-the-galapagos/ (accessed July 30, 2021).

21. William W. L. Cheung, Vicky W. Y. Lam, Jorge L. Sarmiento, Kelly Kearney, Reg Watson, Dirk Zeller, and Daniel Pauly, "Large-Scale Redistribution of Maximum Fisheries Catch Potential in the Global Ocean under Climate Change," *Global Change Biology*, May 6, 2009, pp. 5–6, http://www.indiaenvironmentportal.org.in/files/Large-scale%20redistribution%20of%20maximum%20fisheries.pdf (accessed July 30, 2021).

22. Marine Stewardship Council, "Climate Change Is Having a Profound Impact on Our Oceans and Marine Life. Its Effects Are Changing the Distribution of Fish Stocks and Their Food," https://www.msc.org/what-we-are-doing/oceans-at-risk/climate-change-and-fishing (accessed July 30, 2021).

23. Reece Shaw, "A Primer on the Effect of the Panama Canal Expansion on World Commerce," AAPA Facilities Engineering Seminar, November 7, 2007, San Diego, CA.

24. "Impact of the Panama Canal Expansion on the United States Intermodal System," U.S. Department of Agriculture, January 2010.

25. Eduardo Lugo, "The Impact of the Panama Canal Expansion and Shipping Strategies on the Caribbean Port Industry," Market Research and Analysis Panama Canal Authority, http://www.portguadeloupe.com/fr_save/images/document/presentlugo.pdf?d4dad6935f632ac35975e3001dc7bbe8=39000741780e92b3246e8d5cb6a0acf5 (accessed January 5, 2011).

26. Based on lectures and discussions at Naval War College with commercial shipping business leaders on the likely impact on shipping patterns of the Panama Canal expansion, Newport, Rhode Island, on December 8–9, 2010.

27. Greg Miller, "Inside Box Shipping's Caribbean Transshipment Triangle," *Freight Waves*, July 11, 2019, https://www.freightwaves.com/news/inside-container-shippings-caribbean-transshipment-triangle (accessed August 1, 2021).

28. "Panama Canal Expansion and the Global Economy," Global Envision, http://www.globalenvision.org/library/3/1339 (accessed October 13, 2010).

29. "Multiple Ship Groundings and Collisions Send Suez Canal into Chaos," *Ship Technology*, July 17, 2018, https://www.ship-technology.com/news/suez-canal-grinds-to-a-halt-after-multi-ship-groundings-collisions/ (accessed July 25, 2021).

30. Patrick Kingsley, Ronen Bergman, Farnaz Fassihi, and Eric Schmitt, "Israel's Shadow War with Iran Moves Out to Sea," *New York Times*, March 26,

2021, https://www.nytimes.com/2021/03/26/world/middleeast/israel-iran-shadow-war.html (accessed July 25, 2021).

31. Yaron Steinbuch, "US Official Says Buildup of Russian Forces Near Ukraine Is 'Concerning,'" *New York Post*, March 31, 2021, https://nypost.com /2021/03/31/us-official-buildup-of-russian-troops-near-ukraine-is-conc erning/ (accessed July 25, 2021).

32. Courtesy Story, "15th MEU Concludes Support to Operation Inherent Resolve," U.S. Marine Corps, April 3, 2021, https://www.15thmeu.marines .mil/News/News-Article-Display/Article/2560520/15th-meu-concludes-support-to-operation-inherent-resolve/ (accessed July 25, 2021).

33. "USNI News Fleet and Marine Tracker," USNI News, March 29, 2021, https://news.usni.org/2021/03/29/usni-news-fleet-and-marine-tracker-march-29-2021 (accessed July 25, 2021).

34. John Bowden, "Pentagon: Suez Canal Stoppage May Impact Transit of Military Vessels," *The Hill*, March 28, 2021, https://thehill.com/policy/defense /navy/545292-pentagon-suez-canal-stoppage-may-impact-transit-of-mili tary-vessels (accessed July 25, 2021).

35. Amira El-Fekki, Summer Said, and Rory Jones, "Ship Stuck in the Suez Canal Is Freed," *Wall Street Journal*, March 29, 2021, https://www.wsj.com/articles/ ship-blocking-suez-canal-is-partially-freed-11616989503 (accessed July 25, 2021).

36. Rene Wagner and Christian Kraemer, "Suez Canal Blockage Could Cost $6 Billion to $10 Billion in Lost Trade," Reuters, March 26, 2021, https://www .reuters.com/article/us-egypt-suezcanal-ship-costs-idUSKBN2BI261#:~:tex t=BERLIN%2520%2528Reuters%2529%2520-%2520The%2520container% 2520ship%2520blocking%2520the,to%25200.4%2520percentage%2520poin ts%2520off%2520annual%2520trade%2520growth (accessed July 25, 2021).

37. Delmy L. Salin, "Impact of Panama Canal Expansion on the US Intermodal System," U.S. Department of Agriculture, January 2010, pp. 2, 8, https:// www.ams.usda.gov/sites/default/files/media/Impact%20of%20Panama%20 Canal%20Expansion%20on%20the%20US%20Intermodal%20System.pdf (accessed July 25, 2021).

38. Sam LaGrone, "Eisenhower Strike Group Now in Middle East after Suez Canal Transit" (video), USNI News, April 2, 2021, https://news.usni.org /2021/04/02/eisenhower-strike-group-entering-the-middle-east-after-suez-canal-transit (accessed July 25, 2021).

39. "Annual Report," Panama Canal Authority, September 30, 2020, p. 38, https://www.pancanal.com/eng/general/reporte-anual/2020-Annual Report.pdf (accessed July 25, 2021); "OECD Development Pathways, Multi-dimensional Review of Panama," Organization for Economic Cooperation and Development (OECD), October 11, 2017, https://www.oecd -ilibrary.org/sites/9789264278547-7-en/index.html?itemId=/content /component/9789264278547-7-en (accessed July 25, 2021).

40. "ALP Guard," ALP Maritime Services, https://www.alpmaritime.com/fleet/alp-guard (accessed July 25, 2021).

41. Mat Youkee, "The Panama Canal Could Become the Center of the US-China Trade War," *Foreign Policy*, May 7, 2019, https://foreignpolicy.com/2019/05/07/the-panama-canal-could-become-the-center-of-the-u-s-china-trade-war/ (accessed July 25, 2021).

42. Briefing Room, "Fact Sheet: The American Jobs Plan," White House, March 31, 2021, https://www.whitehouse.gov/briefing-room/statements-releases/2021/03/31/fact-sheet-the-american-jobs-plan/ (accessed July 25, 2021).

43. Matthew Chambers and Mindy Liu, "Maritime Trade and Transportation by the Numbers," Bureau of Transportation Statistics, March 7, 2021, https://www.bts.gov/archive/publications/by_the_numbers/maritime_trade_and_transportation/index (accessed July 25, 2021).

44. Grant Eskelsen, Adam Marcus, and W. Kenneth Ferree, *The Digital Economy Fact Book, 2008–2009*, 10th ed. (Washington: Progress and Freedom Foundation, 2009). Information for these e-commerce figures is taken from the U.S. Census Bureau, https://www.census.gov/retail/ecommerce/historic_releases.html (accessed August 2, 2022).

45. U.S. Bureau of Economic Analysis, "Digital Economy," p. 2, https://www.bea.gov/system/files/2021-06/DE%20June%202021%20update%20for%20web%20v3.pdf (accessed August 4, 2021).

46. Federal Communication Commission, "Improving Outage Reporting for Submarine Cables and Enhanced Submarine Cable Outage Data," GN docket no. 15–206, June 24, 2016, p. 4.

47. James Griffiths, "The Global Internet Is Powered by Vast Undersea Cables. But They're Vulnerable," CNN, July 26, 2019, https://www.cnn.com/2019/07/25/asia/internet-undersea-cables-intl-hnk/index.html (accessed August 4, 2021).

48. David E. Sanger and Eric Schmitt, "Russian Ships Near Data Cables Are Too Close for US Comfort," *New York Times*, October 25, 2015, https://www.nytimes.com/2015/10/26/world/europe/russian-presence-near-undersea-cables-concerns-us.html?_r=0 (accessed August 4, 2021).

49. Rishi Sunak, *Undersea Cables: Indispensable, Insecure* (London: Policy Exchange, 2017), 6–7, https://policyexchange.org.uk/wp-content/uploads/2017/11/Undersea-Cables.pdf (accessed August 4, 2021).

50. H. I. Sutton, "Russia's Suspected Internet Cable Spy Ship Vanishes off the Americas," *Forbes*, November 19, 2019, https://www.forbes.com/sites/hisutton/2019/11/19/russias-suspected-internet-cable-spy-ship-vanishes-off-the-americas/?sh=7f1737e762c1 (accessed August 4, 2021).

51. Sherry Sontag and Christopher Drew, *Blind Man's Bluff: The Untold Story of American Submarine Espionage* (New York: Public Affairs, 1998), 252–53, 342.

52. Nadia Schadlow and Brayden Helwig, "Protecting Undersea Cables Must Be Made a National Security Priority," *Defense News*, July 1, 2020, https://www .defensenews.com/opinion/commentary/2020/07/01/protecting-undersea-cables-must-be-made-a-national-security-priority/ (accessed August 4, 2021).

53. Helena Martin, "Undersea Espionage: Who Owns Underwater Internet Cables?," *McGill International Review*, September 29, 2019, https://www .mironline.ca/undersea-espionage-ownership-of-underwater-internet-cables/ (accessed August 4, 2021).

54. Submarine Cable Map, TeleGeography, https://www.submarinecablemap .com (accessed August 4, 2021).

55. United Nations Education, Scientific and Cultural Organization, "Megacities Worldwide," https://en.unesco.org/events/eaumega2021/megacities (accessed August 7, 2021).

56. Daniel Hoornweg and Kevin Pope, *Socioeconomic Pathways and Regional Distribution of the World's 101 Largest Cities* (Toronto: Global Cities Institute, 2014), 9, https://shared.ontariotechu.ca/shared/faculty-sites/sustainability -today/publications/population-predictions-of-the-101-largest-cities-in-the-21st-century.pdf (accessed August 7, 2021).

57. Fransua Vytautas Razvadauskas, "Megacities: Developing Country Domination," Euromonitor International, August 2018, pp. 6–8, http://go.euromonitor. com/rs/805-KOK-719/images/MegacitiesExtract.pdf?mkt_tok=eyJpIjo iTkdFNFpUWTROVFZsTWpNMCIsInQiOiJ6NGs0d1RNa2VMVjRQQn hHY1VmM3I0aXNEczU1Q1F3TnAyd1lZVHlQR21DSDNzMkVFV lpMMUNRejBLeStkalZFcGlxWDd4SXRKQ3AxemJKN3pFb1c4R2prY zJBdFRRQTZxZEhFSlVMNm84ZXJPVWU5aEI5OVlhdndSSTV6dml weSJ9 (accessed August 7, 2021).

58. Donald Rutherford, *Economics: The Key Concepts* (Routledge, London, 2007). Either by Keynesian theories regarding consumption or by Milton Friedman's permanent income hypothesis, a greater supply of capital results from increased disposable income free for investment/savings or consumption.

59. Hong Kong Business Advisory, "Risks and Considerations for Businesses Operating in Hong Kong," July 16, 2021, https://content.govdelivery .com/attachments/USSTATEBPA/2021/07/16/file_attachments/1881144 /Risks%20and%20Considerations%20for%20Businesses%20Operating%20 in%20Hong%20Kong.pdf (accessed August 8, 2021).

60. "Investors Worry about Labor Costs," *Global Times*, June 19, 2010.

61. Dexter Roberts, "Why Factories Are Leaving China," *Bloomberg Businessweek*, May 13, 2010.

62. "Migrant Workers in China," *China Labor Bulletin*, http://www.clb.org.hk /en/node/100259 (accessed December 7, 2010).

63. Bureau of Conflict and Stabilization Operations, "2021 Report to Congress Pursuant to Section 5 of the Elie Wiesel Genocide and Atrocities Prevention Act of 2018 (P.L. 115–441)," U.S. Department of State, July 12, 2021, https://www.state.gov/2021-report-to-congress-pursuant-to-section-5-of-the-elie-wiesel-genocide-and-atrocities-prevention-act-of-2018 (accessed August 7, 2021).

64. M. Szmigiera, "Manufacturing Labor Costs per Hour for China, Vietnam, Mexico from 2016 to 2020," Statistica, March 30, 2021, https://www.statista.com/statistics/744071/manufacturing-labor-costs-per-hour-china-vietnam-mexico/#:~:text=Published%20by%20M.%20Szmigiera%2C%20Mar%2030%2C%202021%20In,in%20Vietnam.%20Manufacturing%20jobs%20in%20the%20United%20States (accessed August 7, 2021).

65. The impact and insidiousness of illicit trade is extensively detailed in Moises Naim's 2005 book *Illicit* (New York: Anchor Books, 2006).

66. UN Office on Drugs and Crime (UNODC), *World Drug Report 2010* (United Nations Publication, Sales No. E.10.XI.13), 70, 100–101, 233–35, https://www.unodc.org/documents/wdr/WDR_2010/World_Drug_Report_2010_lo-res.pdf (accessed October 19, 2020). Since 2007 there have been widespread reports of his connection to narcotics trafficking, and he was suspected of attempts to silence reporters with death threats. In August 2008 the Head of the Navy in Guinea-Bissau (Bubo Na Tchuto) was implicated in an attempted coup and fled the country, only to return in April 2010. While sheltered in the UN mission, soldiers loyal to him took the Prime Minister hostage, replacing him, and subsequently Bubo Na Tchuto was named as his aide.

67. "Ownership and Control of Ships," Organization for Economic Co-operation and Development, March 2003.

68. Southern Command web page, http://www.southcom.mil/AppsSC/pages/counterNarco.php (accessed January 26, 2011).

69. James White, "Extraordinary 100ft Submarine Used by Colombian Drug-Runners Discovered in Remote Jungle," July 4, 2010, http://www.dailymail.co.uk/news/worldnews/article-1291900/Police-discover-extraordinary-100ft-submarine-used-Colombian-drug-runners-smuggle-cocaine.html (accessed January 26, 2011). A second fully submersible craft was discovered in Colombia in February 2011, representing an ongoing effort by the smugglers to use this technology. "Drug Smuggling Submarine Seized in Colombia," *Huffington Post*, February 15, 2011.

70. "Improving Security Policy in Colombia," *International Crisis Watch*, June 29, 2010, http://www.crisisgroup.org/~/media/Files/latin-america/colombia/B23%20Improving%20Security%20Policy%20in%20Colombia.ashx (accessed January 26, 2011).

71. "The World Factbook," Central Intelligence Agency, https://www.cia.gov/library/publications/the-world-factbook/fields/2086.html (accessed January 26, 2011).

72. "International Narcotics Control Strategy Report," U.S. Department of State, vol. 1, March 2010.

73. *World Drug Report 2010.*

74. "Human Trafficking: The Facts," UN Global Initiative to Fight Human Trafficking, http://www.unglobalcompact.org/docs/issues_doc/labour/Forced _labour/HUMAN_TRAFFICKING_-_THE_FACTS_-_final.pdf (accessed January 26, 2011).

75. USAID, *ASEAN Wildlife Enforcement Network,* undated brochure, http:// usaid.eco-asia.org/files/fact_sheets/ASEAN_WEN.pdf (accessed January 26, 2011).

76. Liana Wyler, "International Illegal Trade in Wildlife: Threat and US Policy," Congressional Research Service Report for Congress, August 22, 2008.

77. John Grady, "Threats to Merchant Ships Growing; Mariners Face Pirates, Lethal Drones," USNI News, August 5, 2021, https://news.usni .org/2021/08/05/threats-to-merchant-ships-growing-mariners-face-pirates-lethal-drones (accessed August 9, 2021).

78. Lauren Ploch, Christopher M. Blanchard, Ronald O'Rourke, R. Chuck Mason, and Rawle O. King, "Piracy off the Horn of Africa," Congressional Research Service, April 27, 2011, pp. 4, https://fas.org/sgp/crs/row/R40528 .pdf (accessed August 9, 2021).

79. Regional Cooperation Agreement on Combating Piracy, "Executive Director's Report 2020," p. 8, https://www.recaap.org/resources/ck/files/reports /ED%20Report/ED's_Report_2020_FINAL.pdf (accessed August 9, 2021).

80. International Maritime Bureau Reporting Center, "Piracy and Armed Robbery Prone Areas and Warnings," August 9, 2021, https://www.icc-ccs .org/index.php/piracy-reporting-centre/prone-areas-and-warnings (accessed August 9, 2021).

81. "International Trade Statistics 2010," World Trade Organization, https://www .wto.org/english/res_e/statis_e/its2010_e/its10_toc_e.htm (accessed August 2, 2022); *World Drug Report 2010.*

82. William Komiss and LaVar Huntzinger, "An Economic Impact Assessment of Maritime Oil Chokepoints," Center for Naval Analyses, March 2011, https:// www.cna.org/reports/2011/D0024669.A1.pdf (accessed August 2, 2022).

83. Roderick Eggert, "Critical Minerals and Emerging Technologies," Issues in Science and Technology, http://www.issues.org/26.4/eggert.html (accessed December 7, 2010).

84. "The Principal Rare Earth Elements Deposits of the United States—a Summary of Domestic Deposits and a Global Perspective," Scientific Investigations Report No. 5220, U.S. Geological Survey and U.S. Department of the Interior (2010).

85. "The Principal Rare Earth Elements Deposits of the United States."

86. Marc Humphries, "Rare Earth Elements: The Global Supply Chain," Congressional Research Service, December 16, 2013, https://sgp.fas.org/crs/natsec/R41347.pdf (accessed August 2, 2022).

87. Humphries, 2–3.

88. Jake Sullivan and Brian Reese, "Building Resilient Supply Chains, Revitalizing American Manufacturing, and Fostering Broad-Based Growth," White House, June 2021, pp. 158–59, https://www.whitehouse.gov/wp-content/uploads/2021/06/100-day-supply-chain-review-report.pdf (accessed March 23, 2022).

89. Humphries, "Rare Earth Elements," 1, 17–18.

90. Briefing Room, "Executive Order on America's Supply Chains," White House, February 24, 2021, https://www.whitehouse.gov/briefing-room/presidential-actions/2021/02/24/executive-order-on-americas-supply-chains/ (accessed July 25, 2021).

91. "Oil Dependence and US Foreign Policy 1850–2017," Council on Foreign Relations, https://www.cfr.org/timeline/oil-dependence-and-us-foreign-policy (accessed July 25, 2021).

92. H. I. Sutton, "Spate of Attacks on Ships in Middle East Points to Iran-Backed Group," USNI News, January 6, 2021, https://news.usni.org/2021/01/06/spate-of-attacks-on-ships-in-middle-east-points-to-iran-backed-group (accessed July 25, 2021).

93. David Vergun, "Freedom of Navigation in South China Sea Critical to Prosperity, Says Indo-Pacific Commander," U.S. Department of Defense, November 23, 2019, https://www.defense.gov/Explore/News/Article/Article/2025105/freedom-of-navigation-in-south-china-sea-critical-to-prosperity-says-indo-pacif/ (accessed July 25, 2021).

94. "Assessing and Strengthening the Manufacturing and Defense Industrial Base and Supply Chain Resiliency of the United States," Report to President Donald J. Trump by the Interagency Task Force in Fulfillment of Executive Order 13806, September 2018, https://media.defense.gov/2018/Oct/05/2002048904/-1/-1/1/ASSESSING-AND-STRENGTHENING-THE-MANUFACTURING-AND%2520DEFENSE-INDUSTRIAL-BASE-AND-SUPPLY-CHAIN-RESILIENCY.PDF; and Office of the Secretary of Defense for Industrial Policy, "Industrial Capabilities Report to Congress," January 2021, https://media.defense.gov/2021/Jan/14/2002565311/-1/-1/0/FY20-INDUSTRIAL-CAPABILITIES-REPORT.PDF (both accessed July 25, 2021).

95. *Onshoring* is a term used in the business world to mean the practice of transferring a business operation that was moved overseas back to the country originally established.

96. Maiya Clark, "Revitalizing the National Defense Stockpile for an Era of Great Power Competition," Heritage Foundation, January 4, 2022, https://www

.heritage.org/defense/report/revitalizing-the-national-defense-stockpile-era-great-power-competition (accessed March 23, 2022).

97. "Strategic Initiatives," Office of Commercial and Economic Analysis, https://www.afocea.com/strategic-research (accessed July 26, 2021).

98. Mike Colias, "Ford Expected to Slash Vehicle Production over Chip Shortage," *Wall Street Journal*, February 4, 2021, https://www.wsj.com/articles/fords-2021-to-do-list-is-topped-by-fixing-quality-problems-11612450536?st=3tthqcc56ei1n8f&reflink=article_email_share (accessed July 26, 2021).

99. Semiconductor Industry Association, "2020 State of the US Semiconductor Industry," p. 8, https://www.semiconductors.org/wp-content/uploads/2020/06/2020-SIA-State-of-the-Industry-Report.pdf (accessed July 26, 2021).

100. Office of the Secretary of Defense for Industrial Policy, "Industrial Capabilities Report to Congress," January 2021, pp. 75–79, https://media.defense.gov/2021/Jan/14/2002565311/-1/-1/0/FY20-INDUSTRIAL-CAPABILITIES-REPORT.PDF (accessed July 25, 2021).

101. "Mineral Commodity Summaries 2021," U.S. Geological Survey, January 29, 2021, pp. 178–79, https://pubs.usgs.gov/periodicals/mcs2021/mcs2021.pdf (accessed July 26, 2021).

102. "Mineral Commodity Summaries 2021," 174–77.

103. "Mineral Commodity Summaries 2021," 20–21, 30–31.

104. Nathan Bomey, "Trump Administration Imposes Aluminum Tariffs on $2B Imports from 18 Countries," *USA Today*, October 9, 2020, https://www.usatoday.com/story/money/2020/10/09/aluminum-tariffs-trump-administration-commerce-department/5938522002/ (accessed July 26, 2021).

105. Brandon S. Tracy, "An Overview of Rare Earth Elements and Related Issues for Congress," Congressional Research Service, November 24, 2020, pp. 15–16, https://www.everycrsreport.com/files/2020-11-24_R46618_6639173333b5877128b3af8449e1c1d88a16f327.pdf (accessed July 26, 2021).

106. Frank Gottron, "National Stockpiles: Background and Issues for Congress," Congressional Research Service, June 15, 2020, https://fas.org/sgp/crs/natsec/IF11574.pdf (accessed July 26, 2021).

107. Bryan Clark and Dan Whiteneck, "Strategic Choices at the Tipping Point," U.S. Naval Institute Proceedings 137, no. 2 (February 2011), https://www.usni.org/magazines/proceedings/2011/february/strategic-choices-tipping-point (accessed August 2, 2022).

108. G20, "About the G20," https://www.g20.org/about-the-g20.html (accessed July 25, 2021).

109. U.S. Department of State, Department of the Treasury, Department of Commerce, and Department of Homeland Security, "Risks and Considerations for Businesses Operating in Hong Kong," July 16, 2021, https://home.treasury.gov/system/files/126/20210716_hong_kong_advisory.pdf (accessed July 25, 2021).

110. *BRIC* refers to the grouping of Brazil, Russia, India, and China in a quad of what seemed to be common cause on economic policies as early as 2006. South Africa joined this unofficial group, now known as the BRICS, in December 2010. The group has met annually since 2009.

111. Sir Halford John Mackinder (an early exponent of geopolitics), "The Geographical Pivot of History," *Geographical Journal* 23, no. 4 (April 1904); Robert Kagan, *The Revenge of Geography* (New York: Random House, 2012).

112. "No bucks, no Buck Rogers," from the book *The Right Stuff*, means that without an adequate budget the nascent U.S. space program wouldn't have been able to get a man into space. Tom Wolfe, *The Right Stuff* (New York: Picador, 1979).

113. For more information about Robert Lucas and Paul Romer's economic theory of endogenous growth, see Philippe Aghion and Peter W. Howitt, *Endogenous Growth Theory* (Cambridge, MA: MIT Press, 1997).

114. Dominick Salvatore, *International Economics*, 8th ed. (New York: John Wiley & Sons, 2004), 360–61, 374–77.

115. Gabriel J. Felbermayr and Friederike Niepmann, "Globalization and the Spatial Concentration of Production," *World Economy* 33 (May 2010): 680–709.

116. Akio Imai, Stratos Papadimitriou, and Koichi Shintani, "Multi-port vs. Hub-and-Spoke Port Calls by Container Ships," *Transportation Research Part E* 45, no. 5 (January 2009): 740–57.

117. Sabine Limbourg and Bart Jourquin, "Optimal Rail-Road Container Terminal Locations on the European Network," *Transportation Research Part E* 45, no. 4 (July 2009): 551–63. Port rankings taken from U.S. Bureau of Census, U.S. Merchandise Trade, Selected Highlights (Report FT 920), *AAPA Advisory*, March 8, 2010.

118. Dean Jones, Brian Levine, and Linda Nozick, "Estimating an Origin-Destination Table for United States Imports or Waterborne Containerized Freight," *Transportation Research Part E* 45, no. 4 (July 2009): 611–26.

## Chapter 4. Decisive Theaters

1. Daniel Hartnett, "The Father of the Modern Chinese Navy—Liu Huaqing," Center for International Maritime Security, October 8, 2014, https://cimsec .org/father-modern-chinese-navy-liu-huaqing/#_ftn8 (accessed September 12, 2021).

2. C. J. Jenner, "Facing China's Sea Power: Strategic Culture and Maritime Strategy," Asia Maritime Transparency Initiative, May 19, 2019, https://amti .csis.org/facing-chinas-sea-power-strategic-culture-maritime-strategy / (accessed September 12, 2021).

3. Peter D. Haynes, *Toward a New Maritime Strategy: American Naval Thinking in the Post–Cold War Era* (Annapolis: Naval Institute Press, 2015), 245–46.

4. Daniel Hoornweg and Kevin Pope, "Socioeconomic Pathways and Regional Distribution of the World's 101 Largest Cities," University of Ontario Institute of Technology, January 2014, pp. 9–20, https://shared.ontariotechu .ca/shared/faculty-sites/sustainability-today/publications/population-pre dictions-of-the-101-largest-cities-in-the-21st-century.pdf (accessed September 19, 2021).

5. U.S. Energy Information Administration, "Annual Energy Outlook 2021," Department of Energy, February 2021, pp. 3, 21–23, https://www.eia.gov /outlooks/aeo/pdf/AEO_Narrative_2021.pdf (accessed September 20, 2021).

6. Department of Energy, Republic of the Philippines, "Oil Supply/Demand Report 1H 2019 vs 1H 2018," June 2019, https://www.doe.gov.ph/down stream-oil/oil-supplydemand-report-1h-2019-vs-1h-2018?ckattempt=1 (accessed September 19, 2021); OEC, "Crude Petroleum in South Korea," https://oec.world/en/profile/bilateral-product/crude-petroleum/reporter /kor (accessed September 19, 2021); World Integrated Trade Solution, "Japan Oils; Petroleum Oils and Oils Obtained from Bituminous Minerals, Crude Imports by Country in 2019," World Bank, https://wits.worldbank.org/trade /comtrade/en/country/JPN/year/2019/tradeflow/Imports/partner/ALL /product/270900 (accessed September 19, 2021).

7. Christof Rühl, "The Five Global Implications of Shale Oil and Gas," *Energy Post*, January 10, 2014, http://energypost.eu/five-global-implications-shale-revolution/ (accessed December 2, 2016).

8. Abhijit Singh, "Anti-submarine Operations in the Indian Ocean," *The Diplomat*, September 9, 2015, http://thediplomat.com/2015/09/anti-subma rine-operations-in-the-indian-ocean/ (accessed on April 21, 2016).

9. Office of the Secretary of Defense, *Annual Report to Congress: Military and Security Developments involving the People's Republic of China 2020* (Washington: U.S. Department of Defense, 2020), 133–34, 170, https://media .defense.gov/2020/Sep/01/2002488689/-1/-1/1/2020-DOD-CHINA-MILI TARY-POWER-REPORT-FINAL.PDF (accessed September 19, 2021).

10. James Griffiths, "India's Modi Responds to 'Violent Face-Off' with China over Himalayan Border," CNN, June 18, 2020, https://www.cnn.com/2020/06/17 /asia/china-india-himalayas-conflict-intl-hnk/index.html (accessed September 19, 2021).

11. "Top Trading Partners," U.S. Census Bureau, July 2021, https://www.census .gov/foreign-trade/statistics/highlights/top/top2107yr.html (accessed September 19, 2021).

12. Jayshree Bajoria and Esther Pan, "The US-India Nuclear Deal," Council on Foreign Relations, November 5, 2010, https://www.cfr.org/backgrounder/us-india-nuclear-deal (accessed September 19, 2021).

13. Migration Policy Institute, "The Indian Diaspora in the United States," Aspen Institute, February 2014, https://www.aspeninstitute.org/wp-content /uploads/files/content/docs/RAD/India_Profile.pdf (accessed September 19, 2021).

14. People's Republic of Bangladesh v. Republic of India, 2010–16 (Permanent Court of Arbitration 2014), https://pca-cpa.org/en/cases/18/ (accessed September 19, 2021).

15. Ministry of External Affairs, Government of India, "Act East: India's ASEAN Journey," November 10, 2014, https://www.mea.gov.in/in-focus-article.htm ?24216/Act+East+Indias+ASEAN+Journey (accessed September 19, 2021).

16. "Quad Leaders' Joint Statement: 'The Spirit of the Quad,'" White House Briefing Room, March 12, 2021, https://www.whitehouse.gov/briefing-room/statements-releases/2021/03/12/quad-leaders-joint-statement-the-spirit-of-the-quad/ (accessed September 19, 2021).

17. Jim Garamone, "US Officials Seek to Boost Arms Sales to India," Defense Security Cooperation Agency, September 6, 2018, https://www.dsca.mil /news-media/news-archive/us-officials-seek-boost-arms-sales-india (accessed September 21, 2021).

18. Diego Lopes da Silva, Nan Tian and Alexandra Marksteiner, "Trends in World Military Expenditure," Sipri Fact Sheet, April 2021, pp. 2–4, 7, https:// sipri.org/sites/default/files/2021-04/fs_2104_milex_0.pdf (accessed September 20, 2021).

19. John Lehman, *Oceans Ventured: Winning the Cold War at Sea* (New York: W. W. Norton, 2018), 99–103, 145–46.

20. Magnus Nordenman, *The New Battle for the Atlantic: Emerging Naval Competition with Russia in the Far North* (Annapolis: Naval Institute Press, 2019), 158–63.

21. James Foggo III, "The Fourth Battle of the Atlantic," U.S. Naval Institute *Proceedings* 142, no. 6 (June 2016), https://www.usni.org/magazines/pro ceedings/2016/june/fourth-battle-atlantic (accessed September 24, 2021).

22. "Russian Nuclear Submarines Step Up Patrols over Past Year—Navy Commander," Sputnik International, March 19, 2015, https://sputniknews .com/20150319/1019714161.html (accessed September 24, 2021).

23. Press Office, "2nd Fleet Declares Full Operational Capability," U.S. Navy Public Affairs Office, December 31, 2019, https://www.navy.mil/Press-Office /Press-Releases/display-pressreleases/Article/2237734/2nd-fleet-declares-full-operational-capability/ (accessed September 24, 2021).

24. "Royal Air Force Receives Sixth Poseidon Maritime Patrol Aircraft," Defense Brief, September 21, 2021, https://defbrief.com/2021/09/22/royal-air-force-receives-sixth-poseidon-maritime-patrol-aircraft/ (accessed September 24, 2021).

25. Sebastian Sprenger, "Next-Gen Tech Investments, Platform Upgrades Lead France's 2022 Defense Budget," *Defense News*, September 22, 2021, https://www.defensenews.com/global/europe/2021/09/22/next-gen-tech-investments-platform-upgrades-lead-frances-2022-defense-budget/ (accessed September 26, 2021); "Budget de l'État Dépenses par mission," https://www.budget.gouv.fr/budget-etat/mission (accessed September 26, 2021).

26. Frank Bakke-Jensen, "The Defence of Norway Capability and Readiness: Long Term Defence Plan 2020," Norwegian Ministry of Defence, 2020, pp. 14, 18, https://www.regjeringen.no/contentassets/7d48f0e5213d48b9a0b8e100c608bfce/long-term-defence-plan-norway-2020---english-summary.pdf (accessed September 26, 2021).

27. Maria Sheehan and Sarah Marsh, "Germany to Increase Defense Spending in Response to Putin's War—Schulz," Reuters, February 27, 2022, https://www.reuters.com/business/aerospace-defense/germany-hike-defense-spending-scholz-says-further-policy-shift-2022-02-27/ (accessed March 24, 2022).

28. "Terceira: US to Reduce Military Presence at Lajes Air Field—Azores," Portuguese American Journal, November 24, 2012, https://portuguese-american-journal.com/terceira-u-s-to-reduce-military-presence-in-lajes-air-field-azores/ (accessed September 26, 2021).

29. National Command Center, "Global MOTR Coordination Center," Department of Homeland Security, September 8, 2011, https://www.dhs.gov/global-motr-coordination-center-gmcc (accessed September 26, 2021).

30. Bureau of International Security and Nonproliferation, "Proliferation Security Initiative," U.S. Department of State, https://www.state.gov/proliferation-security-initiative/ (accessed September 26, 2021).

31. U.S. Customs and Border Protection, "CSI: Container Security Initiative," Department of Homeland Security, May 31, 2019, https://www.cbp.gov/border-security/ports-entry/cargo-security/csi/csi-brief (accessed September 26, 2021).

32. "Arctic Monitoring and Assessment Programme," Arctic Council, https://www.amap.no/about/geographical-coverage (accessed September 29, 2021).

33. "Alaska's Fishing Industries," Resource Development Center of Alaska, 2018, https://www.akrdc.org/fisheries (accessed September 28, 2021).

34. "Chinese Coast Guard Wraps Up Fishery Patrol in North Pacific," Xinhua Net, August 31, 2021, http://www.news.cn/english/2021-08/31/c_1310159364.htm (accessed September 28, 2021); Public Affairs News Release, "Coast Guard Crews Remain Vigilant during Operations in the Arctic Region," U.S. Coast Guard District 17, September 13, 2021, https://content.govdelivery.com/accounts/USDHSCG/bulletins/2f100cd (accessed September 28, 2021).

35. Jon McCracken, "Russian Military Activity in the EEZ," North Pacific Fishery Management Council, October 20, 2021, https://www.npfmc.org/russian-military-activity/ (accessed September 28, 2021).

36. Testimony of Stephanie Madsen Executive Director, At-Sea Processors Association, "US Coast Guard Capabilities for Safeguarding National Interests and Promoting Economic Security in the Arctic," before the U.S. Senate Committee on Commerce, Science, and Transportation Subcommittee on Security, September 22, 2020, https://meetings.npfmc.org/CommentReview/DownloadFile?p=ea62a3ee-a32b-4eec-bf3b-a12f68d35a83.pdf&fileName=200922%20Stephanie%20Madsen%20Testimony%20for%20US%20Senate%20Commerce%20Committee%20Security%20Subcommittee.pdf (accessed September 28, 2021).

37. United Nations, "Convention on the Law of the Sea," December 10, 1982, part 4, articles 56–57, https://www.un.org/Depts/los/convention_agreements/texts/unclos/part5.htm (accessed September 29, 2021).

38. "Law of the Sea: Military Activities in an EEZ," Fletcher School, https://sites.tufts.edu/lawofthesea/chapter-4/ (accessed September 29, 2021).

39. United Nations, "Convention on the Law of the Sea," December 10, 1982, part 7, article 87, and part 16, articles 300–301, https://www.un.org/depts/los/convention_agreements/texts/unclos/UNCLOS-TOC.htm (accessed September 29, 2021).

40. Hyun-soo Kim, "Military Activities in the Exclusive Economic Zone: Preventing Uncertainty and Defusing Conflict," *International Law Studies* 80 (2006): 261, https://digital-commons.usnwc.edu/cgi/viewcontent.cgi?article=1265&context=ils (accessed September 29, 2021).

41. "Alaska's Oil and Gas Industry," Resource Development Council for Alaska, https://www.akrdc.org/oil-and-gas (accessed September 29, 2021).

42. U.S. Energy Information Administration, "Natural Gas Explained," May 26, 2021, https://www.eia.gov/energyexplained/natural-gas/use-of-natural-gas.php and "Oil and Petroleum Products Explained," May 10, 2021, https://www.eia.gov/energyexplained/oil-and-petroleum-products/use-of-oil.php (accessed September 29, 2021).

43. United Nations, "Convention on the Law of the Sea," December 10, 1982, part 6, articles 76–77, https://www.un.org/depts/los/convention_agreements/texts/unclos/part6.htm (accessed September 2021).

44. Steven Groves, "Accession to Convention on the Law of the Sea Unnecessary to Advance Arctic Interests," Heritage Foundation, June 26, 2014, pp. 8–12, http://thf_media.s3.amazonaws.com/2014/pdf/BG2912.pdf (accessed September 29, 2021); "Partial Revised Submission by the Russian Federation to Commission on the Limits of the Continental Shelf (CLCS) Outer Limits of the Continental Shelf beyond 200 Nautical Miles from the Baselines," August 3, 2015, pp. 10, 23, 30, https://www.un.org/depts/los/clcs_new/submissions_files/rus01_rev15/2015_08_03_Exec_Summary_English.pdf (accessed September 29, 2021).

45. "The Canada-US Defence Relationship," Government of Canada, December 2014, https://www.canada.ca/en/news/archive/2014/12/canada-defence-rela tionship.html#:~:text=The%20United%20States%20is%20Canada%27s%20 most%20important%20ally,with%20greater%20security%20than%20 could%20be%20achieved%20individually (accessed September 29, 2021).

46. Joint Statement on NORAD Modernization, Canada National Defence, August 14, 2021, https://www.canada.ca/en/department-national-defence/ news/2021/08/joint-statement-on-norad-modernization.html (accessed September 30, 2021).

47. Ministry of the Interior National Immigration Agency, Republic of China (Taiwan), August 23, 2021, https://www.immigration.gov.tw/5385/7344/7350 /外僑居留/?alias=settledown (accessed October 2, 2021).

48. "Immigrant and Emigrant Populations by Country of Origin and Destination," Migration Policy Institute, https://www.migrationpolicy.org/programs /data-hub/charts/immigrant-and-emigrant-populations-country-ori gin-and-destination (accessed October 2, 2021); Population Division, "International Migrant Stock," United Nations, 2020, https://www.un.org /development/desa/pd/content/international-migrant-stock (accessed October 2, 2021).

49. "Top Trading Partners," U.S. Census Bureau, July 2021, https://www.census .gov/foreign-trade/statistics/highlights/toppartners.html (accessed October 2, 2021).

50. James Harrigan, "The Impact of the Asia Crisis on US Industry: An Almost-Free Lunch?," *Economic Policy Review*, September 2020, p. 79, https://www .newyorkfed.org/medialibrary/media/research/epr/00v06n3/0009harr .pdf#:~:text=The%20impact%20of%20the%20Asia%20crisis%20on%20 US,fast%20that%20the%20value%20of%20exports%20actually%20fell (accessed October 2, 2021).

51. "Historical GDP by Country: Statistics from the World Bank," KNOEMA, March 29, 2021, https://knoema.com/mhrzolg/historical-gdp-by-country-statistics-from-the-world-bank-1960-2019 (accessed October 2, 2021).

52. Letter from the Permanent Representative of the Republic of Korea to the United Nations addressed to the President of the Security Council, June 4, 2010, http://www.securitycouncilreport.org/atf/cf/%7B65BFCF9B-6D27-4E9C-8CD3-CF6E4FF96FF9%7D/DPRK%20S%202010%20281%20 SKorea%20Letter%20and%20Cheonan%20Report.pdf (accessed October 2, 2021).

53. "South Korean Civilians Were Killed in Artillery Barrage," *New York Post*, November 24, 2010, https://nypost.com/2010/11/24/south-korean-civilians-were-killed-in-artillery-barrage/ (accessed October 2, 2021).

54. D. Sean Barnett, Yvonne K. Crane, Gian Gentile, Timothy M. Bonds, Dan Madden, and Katherine Pfrommer, "North Korean Conventional Artillery a Means to Retaliate, Coerce, Deter, or Terrorize Populations," RAND Corporation, 2020, pp. 14–15, 18–19, https://www.rand.org/pubs/research_reports/RRA619-1.html (accessed October 2, 2021).

55. Statement of Gen. Robert B. Abrams, Commander, United Nations Command; Commander, United States–Republic of Korea Combined Forces Command; and Commander, United States Forces Korea before the House Armed Services Committee Fiscal Year 2022, March 3, 2021, p. 8, https://docs.house.gov/meetings/AS/AS00/20210310/111316/HHRG-117-AS00-Bio-AbramsR-20210310.pdf (accessed October 2, 2021).

56. Mitch Shin, "South Korea and US Reach Agreement on Defense Cost Sharing," *The Diplomat*, March 8, 2021, https://thediplomat.com/2021/03/south-korea-and-us-reach-agreement-on-defense-cost-sharing/ (accessed October 2, 2021).

57. Isabel Reynolds and Emi Nobuhiro, "Hong Kong's Fate Spurs Japan to Speak Up about Defending Taiwan," *Japan Times*, August 3, 2021, https://www.japantimes.co.jp/news/2021/08/03/national/japan-china-taiwan-shift/ (accessed October 2, 2021).

58. "Host Nation Support," Japan Ministry of Foreign Affairs, March 8, 2021, https://www.mofa.go.jp/region/n-america/us/security/hns.html (accessed October 2, 2021).

59. Office of the Secretary of Defense, *Annual Report to Congress: Military and Security Developments involving the People's Republic of China 2020* (Washington: U.S. Department of Defense, 2020), 162, https://media.defense.gov/2021/Nov/03/2002885874/-1/-1/0/2021-CMPR-FINAL.PDF (accessed December 9, 2021).

60. Inder Singh Bisht, "Russia to Deploy Submarine Armed with Nuclear Drone in Pacific," *Defense Post*, April 7, 2021, https://www.thedefensepost.com/2021/04/07/russia-submarine-nuclear-drone-pacific/ (accessed October 2, 2021); TASS Russian News Agency, "Russia's Pacific Fleet to Get 15 New Vessels in 2020," *Naval News*, May 29, 2020, https://www.navalnews.com/naval-news/2020/05/russias-pacific-fleet-to-get-15-new-vessels-in-2020/ (accessed October 2, 2021).

61. Ross Babbage, "Countering China's Adventurism in the South China Sea: Strategy Options for the Trump Administration," Center for Strategic and Budgetary Assessments, December 14, 2016, http://csbaonline.org/research/publications/countering-chinas-adventurism-in-the-south-china-sea-strategy-options-for-t (accessed on December 26, 2016).

62. "UK Conducts UN Sanctions Enforcement to Counter North Korea's Weapons Programmes" (press release), U.K. Ministry of Defence, September 26, 2021,

https://www.gov.uk/government/news/uk-conducts-un-sanctions-enforce ment-to-counter-north-koreas-weapons-programmes (accessed October 2, 2021).

63. "Russia Defends Sending Troops to Venezuela to Back Up Nicolas Maduro after Warning from Pompeo," CBS News, March 27, 2019, https://www .cbsnews.com/news/russia-venezuela-troops-back-up-nicolas-maduro-mike-pompeo-warning/ (accessed October 3, 2021).

64. John E. Herbst and Jason Marczak, "Russia's Intervention in Venezuela: What's at Stake?," Atlantic Council, September 12, 2019, https://www.atlan ticcouncil.org/in-depth-research-reports/report/russias-intervention-in-venezuela-whats-at-stake/ (accessed October 3, 2021).

65. Matt Ferchen, "China-Venezuela Relations in the Twenty-First Century: From Overconfidence to Uncertainty," U.S. Institute of Peace, September 2020, https://www.usip.org/sites/default/files/2020-09/20200924-sr_484-chi na-venezuela_relations_in_the_twenty-first_century_from_overconfi dence_to_uncertainty-sr.pdf (accessed October 3, 2021).

66. Derek Scissors, "China Global Investment Tracker," American Enterprise Institute, https://www.aei.org/china-global-investment-tracker/ (accessed October 3, 2021).

67. Brent Sadler, "Effective Naval Statecraft Can Prevent Communist Chinese Naval Bases in Africa," Heritage Foundation, March 10, 2022, https://www .heritage.org/defense/report/effective-naval-statecraft-can-prevent-commu nist-chinese-naval-bases-africa (accessed March 24, 2022).

68. Eklavya Gupte, "Mounting Piracy off Gulf of Guinea Unsettles Tanker Owners," S&P Global, November 16, 2020, https://www.spglobal.com/platts /en/market-insights/latest-news/oil/111620-mounting-piracy-off-gulf-of-guinea-unsettles-tanker-owners (accessed October 3, 2021).

69. Joyce Karam, "US to Move Giant Floating Sea Base to Greece Sparking Doubts over Turkish Airbase," *National News*, September 30, 2020, https:// www.thenationalnews.com/world/the-americas/us-to-move-giant-floating-sea-base-to-greece-sparking-doubts-over-turkish-port-1.1085732 (accessed October 3, 2021).

70. Dorian Archus, "US Navy Sends ESB Hershel 'Woody' Williams to Gulf of Guinea," *Naval Post*, August 7, 2020, https://navalpost.com/us-navy-sends-esb-to-gulf-of-guinea/ (accessed October 3, 2021).

71. *World Drug Report 2019* (UN Publication, Sales No. E.19.XI.8), pp. 16–17, https://wdr.unodc.org/wdr2019/prelaunch/WDR19_Booklet_1_EXECU TIVE_SUMMARY.pdf (accessed October 3, 2021).

72. Channing May, "Transnational Crime and the Developing World," March 2017, pp. 3–11, https://secureservercdn.net/50.62.198.97/34n.8bd.myftpu pload.com/wp-content/uploads/2017/03/Transnational_Crime-final.pdf (accessed October 3, 2021).

73. R. D. Alles, "Counter-drug Operations: Fiscal Year 2020 Report to Congress," Department of Homeland Security, August 14, 2020, pp. 2–3, 5, https://www .dhs.gov/sites/default/files/publications/uscg_-_counter-drug_operations .pdf (accessed October 3, 2021).

74. Public Law 99–658, "Palau Compact of Free Association," November 14, 1986, title 3, article 2, secs. 312, 321, 322, https://www.govinfo.gov/content /pkg/STATUTE-100/pdf/STATUTE-100-Pg3672.pdf (accessed October 3, 2021); Public Law 99–239, "(Marshall Islands and Federated States of Micronesia) Compact of Free Association Act of 1985," January 14, 1986, https:// www.doi.gov/oia/about/compact (accessed October 3, 2021).

75. "US Military Lands C130 on Newly Renovated Angaur Airfield in Palau" (press release), U.S. Embassy Palau, September 5, 2019, https:// pw.usembassy.gov/us-military-lands-c-130-on-newly-renovated-angaur-airfield-in-palau/200906-usarpac-anguar-airfield-release/ (accessed October 3, 2021).

76. Ben Wan Beng Ho, "The Strategic Significance of Manus Island for the US Navy," U.S. Naval Institute *Proceedings* 144, no. 12 (December 2018), https:// www.usni.org/magazines/proceedings/2018/december/strategic-signifi cance-manus-island-us-navy (accessed October 3, 2021).

77. "The Pacific Patrol Boat Project," Royal Australian Navy, https://www.navy .gov.au/media-room/publications/semaphore-02-05 (accessed October 3, 2021).

78. Martin Manaranche, "Austal Australia Delivers Guardian-Class Patrol Boat for the Republic of Vanuatu" (press release), Austal, August 2, 2021, https:// www.navalnews.com/naval-news/2021/08/austal-australia-delivers-guard ian-class-patrol-boat-for-the-republic-of-vanuatu/ (accessed October 3, 2021).

79. Karl Schultz, "Illegal, Unreported, and Unregulated Fishing Strategic Outlook," USCG, September 2020, p. 3, https://www.uscg.mil/Portals/0/Images /iuu/IUU_Strategic_Outlook_2020_FINAL.pdf (accessed October 3, 2021).

80. "USCG Intercepts Illegal Fishing Vessels Off Guam and Hawaii," *Maritime Executive*, February 24, 2020, https://maritime-executive.com/article/uscg-intercepts-illegal-fishing-vessels-off-guam-and-hawaii (accessed October 3, 2021).

81. "Fishing in the Blue Pacific," New Zealand Foreign Affairs and Trade, https:// www.mfat.govt.nz/de/aid-and-development/our-aid-partnerships-in-the-pacific/case-studies/fishing-in-the-blue-pacific/ (accessed October 4, 2021).

82. David Gootnick and Oliver Richard, "American Samoa: Economic Trends, Status of the Tuna Canning Industry, and Stakeholders' Views on Minimum Wage Increases," Government Accountability Office, June 2020, pp. 19, 26–28, 31, 33, https://www.gao.gov/assets/gao-20-467.pdf (accessed October 4, 2021).

83. Nick Blenkey, "USCG FRCs Could Be Based in American Samoa," MarineLog, October 26, 2020, https://www.marinelog.com/shipping/safety-and-security/uscg-frcs-could-be-based-in-american-samoa/ (accessed October 4, 2021).

84. "Coast Guard Commissions 3 Fast Response Cutters in Guam," U.S. Coast Guard, July 29, 2021, https://www.dcms.uscg.mil/Our-Organization/Assistant-Commandant-for-Acquisitions-CG-9/Newsroom/Latest-Acquisition-News/Article/2713364/coast-guard-commissions-3-fast-response-cutters-in-guam/ (accessed October 4, 2021).

85. Standing NATO Maritime Group Two, https://mc.nato.int/SNMG2 (accessed December 28, 2020).

86. "UN Salutes New Libya Ceasefire Agreement That Points To 'a Better, Safer, and More Peaceful Future,'" United Nations, October 23, 2020, https://news.un.org/en/story/2020/10/1076012 (accessed October 5, 2021).

87. Wes Rumbaugh and Shan Shaikh, "The Air and Missile War in Nagorno-Karabakh: Lessons for the Future of Strike and Defense," Center for Strategic and International Studies, December 8, 2020, https://www.csis.org/analysis/air-and-missile-war-nagorno-karabakh-lessons-future-strike-and-defense (accessed October 5, 2021).

88. Jack Detsch, "The US Army Goes to School on Nagorno-Karabakh Conflict," Foreign Policy, March 30, 2021, https://foreignpolicy.com/2021/03/30/army-pentagon-nagorno-karabakh-drones/ (accessed October 5, 2021).

89. "Where Russia Markets and Sells Advanced Conventional Weapons," RAND Corporation, June 11, 2021, https://www.rand.org/nsrd/projects/russian-arms-sales-and-sanctions-compliance/where-russia-markets-and-sells-military-equipment.html (accessed October 5, 2021).

90. Rachel S. Cohen, "Biden's Pentagon to Keep Turkey out of F-35 Program," Air Force Magazine, February 5, 2021, https://www.airforcemag.com/bidens-pentagon-to-keep-turkey-out-of-f-35-program/ (accessed October 5, 2021).

91. "Territorial and Urban Aspects of Migration and Refugee Inflow," European Regional Development Fund, December 15, 2015, https://www.espon.eu/topics-policy/publications/maps-month/territorial-and-urban-aspects-migration-and-refugee-inflow (accessed October 6, 2021).

92. "Migrant Crisis: Migration to Europe Explained in Seven Charts," BBC News, March 4, 2016, https://www.bbc.com/news/world-europe-34131911 (accessed October 7, 2021).

93. Jacob Poushter, "European Opinions of the Refugee Crisis in 5 Charts," Pew Research Center, September 16, 2016, https://www.pewresearch.org/fact-tank/2016/09/16/european-opinions-of-the-refugee-crisis-in-5-charts/ (accessed October 7, 2021).

94. Moira Fagan and Jacob Poushter, "NATO Seen Favorably across Member States," Pew Research Center, February 9, 2020, https://www.pewre search.org/global/2020/02/09/nato-seen-favorably-across-member-states/ (accessed October 7, 2021).

95. Jens Stoltenberg, "NATO and Europe's Refugee and Migrant Crisis," North Atlantic Treaty Organization, February 26, 2016, https://www.nato.int/cps /en/natohq/opinions_128645.htm (accessed October 6, 2021).

96. "Assistance for the Refugee and Migrant Crisis in the Aegean Sea" (press release), North Atlantic Treaty Organization, May 17, 2021, https://www .nato.int/cps/en/natohq/topics_128746.htm (accessed October 6, 2021).

97. Kristin Archick and Rhoda Margesson, "Europe's Refugee and Migration Flows," Congressional Research Service, March 20, 2019, https://sgp.fas.org /crs/row/IF10259.pdf (accessed October 7, 2021).

98. Robin Emmott, Sabine Siebold and Andrius Sytas "Lithuania, EU Say Belarus Using Refugees as 'Political Weapon,'" Reuters, July 12, 2021, https:// www.reuters.com/world/europe/belarus-using-refugees-weapon-must-face-more-eu-sanctions-lithuania-says-2021-07-12/ (accessed October 6, 2021).

99. "Declaration by the High Representative on Behalf of the EU on the First Anniversary of the 9 August 2020 Fraudulent Presidential Elections in Belarus" (press release), European Council, August 8, 2021, https://www .consilium.europa.eu/en/press/press-releases/2021/08/08/belarus-declara tion-by-the-high-representative-on-behalf-of-the-eu-on-the-first-anniver sary-of-the-9-august-2020-fraudulent-presidential-elections-in-belarus/ (accessed October 6, 2021).

100. Catherine Belton, *Putin's People: How the KGB Took Back Russia and Then Took On the West* (New York: Farrar, Straus and Giroux, 2020), 396–98.

101. Belton.

102. Mark Galeotti, "Crimintern: How the Kremlin Uses Russia's Criminal Networks in Europe," European Council on Foreign Relations, April 18, 2017, https://ecfr.eu/publication/crimintern_how_the_kremlin_uses_russias _criminal_networks_in_europe/ (accessed October 10, 2021).

103. Greg Miller, "How US Sanctions Take a Hidden Toll on Russian Oligarchs," *Washington Post*, October 5, 2021, https://www.washingtonpost.com/world /interactive/2021/us-russia-sanctions/ (accessed October 10, 2021).

104. Haley Ott, "Malta Government Responsible for Killing of Journalist Daphne Caruana Galizia, Inquiry Finds," CBS News, July 30, 2021, https://www .cbsnews.com/news/daphne-caruana-galizia-malta-government-responsi ble-death/ (accessed October 10, 2021).

105. "The Russian Laundromat," Organized Crime and Corruption Reporting Project, August 22, 2014, https://www.occrp.org/en/laundromat/russian-laundromat/ (accessed October 10, 2021).

106. Michael Peel, "Moscow on the Med: Cyprus and Its Russians," *Financial Times*, May 15, 2020, https://www.ft.com/content/67918012-9403-11ea-abcd-371e24b679ed (accessed October 10, 2021).

107. Office of the Spokesperson, U.S. Department of State, "Fact Sheet: United States Imposes Additional Costs on Russia for the Poisoning of Aleksey Navalny," August 20, 2021, https://www.state.gov/fact-sheet-united-states-imposes-additional-costs-on-russia-for-the-poisoning-of-aleksey-navalny/ (accessed October 10, 2021).

108. H. I. Sutton, "Russian Navy Seen Escorting Iranian Tankers Bound for Syria," USNI News, October 21, 2020, https://news.usni.org/2020/10/21/russian-navy-seen-escorting-iranian-tankers-bound-for-syria (accessed October 10, 2021).

109. Graham Hutchings, *Modern China: A Guide to a Century of Change* (Cambridge, MA: Harvard University Press, 2001), 166–71.

110. Center for Strategic and International Studies, Asia Maritime Transparency Initiative, "Mischief Reef," https://amti.csis.org/mischief-reef/ (accessed November 19, 2020).

111. Press statement by Michael A. Pompeo, Secretary of State, "US Position on Maritime Claims in the South China Sea," U.S. Department of State, July 13, 2020, https://www.state.gov/u-s-position-on-maritime-claims-in-the-south-china-sea/ (accessed November 19, 2020).

112. David M. Finkelstein, "Breaking the Paradigm: Drivers behind the PLA's Current Period of Reform," in *Chairman Xi Remakes the PLA: Assessing Chinese Military Reforms*, ed. Phillip P. Saunders, Arthur S. Ding, Andrew Scobell, Andrew N. D. Yang, and Joel Wuthnow (Washington: National Defense University Press, 2019), 45, 77, https://ndupress.ndu.edu/Portals/68/Documents/Books/Chairman-Xi/Chairman-Xi.pdf (accessed April 23, 2021).

113. U.S. Defense Intelligence Agency, *China Military Power: Modernizing a Force to Fight and Win* (Washington: U.S. Defense Intelligence Agency, 2019), 28–29, 33, https://www.dia.mil/Portals/27/Documents/News/Military%20Power%20Publications/China_Military_Power_FINAL_5MB_20190103.pdf (accessed April 23, 2021).

114. Office of the Secretary of Defense, *Annual Report to Congress: Military and Security Developments involving the People's Republic of China 2020* (Washington: U.S. Department of Defense, 2020), v, ix, 3, 6, 30–32, 94, 112, 159.

115. Robert D. Kaplan, *Asia's Cauldron: The South China Sea and the End of a Stable Pacific* (New York: Random House, 2014), locs. 725, 895.

116. Veasna Kong, Steven G. Cochrane, Brendan Meighan, and Matthew Walsh, "The Belt and Road Initiative—Six Years On," Moody's Analytics *Analysis*, June 2019, p. 3, https://www.moodysanalytics.com/-/media/article/2019/Belt-and-Road-Initiative.pdf (accessed November 19, 2020).

117. Derek Grossman, "China Refuses to Quit on the Philippines," RAND blog, July 22, 2020, https://www.rand.org/blog/2020/07/china-refuses-to-quit-on-the-philippines.html (accessed April 24, 2021).

118. "Najib: A Lot Has Been Achieved through Blue Ocean," *The Star*, February 24, 2018, https://www.thestar.com.my/news/nation/2018/02/24/najib-a-lot-has-been-achieved-through-blue-ocean/ (accessed October 12, 2021).

119. W. Chan Kim and Renee Mauborgne, *Blue Ocean Strategy* (Boston: Harvard Business Review Press, 2015), 15–16, 22–26.

120. Cal Wong, "After Summit, ASEAN Remains Divided on South China Sea," *The Diplomat*, May 3, 2017, https://thediplomat.com/2017/05/after-summit-asean-remains-divided-on-south-china-sea/ (accessed November 19, 2020).

121. Catherine Wong, "Golden Period of China-Philippines Friendship Loses Its Shine," *South China Morning Post*, July 25, 2020, https://www.scmp.com/news/china/diplomacy/article/3094393/golden-period-china-philippines-friendship-loses-its-shine (accessed November 19, 2020).

122. Liu Zhen, "Thailand Puts Chinese Submarine Order on Hold to Fund Coronavirus Fight," *South China Morning Post*, April 23, 2020, https://www.scmp.com/news/china/military/article/3081308/thailand-puts-chinese-submarine-order-hold-fund-coronavirus (accessed August 25, 2020).

123. Dzirhan Mahadzir, "Malaysian and Singapore Drill with U.K., Australia and New Zealand in Bersama Gold 2021," USNI News, October 8, 2021, https://news.usni.org/2021/10/08/malaysian-and-singapore-drill-with-allis-u-k-australia-and-new-zealand-in-bersama-gold-2021 (accessed October 12, 2021).

124. Euan Graham, "The Five Power Defence Arrangements at 50: What Next?," IISS, December 10, 2020, https://www.iiss.org/blogs/analysis/2020/12/five-power-defence-arrangements (accessed October 12, 2021).

125. "Mission, Vision, Values," Defense Security Cooperation Agency, April 2021, https://www.dsca.mil/mission-vision-values (accessed October 11, 2021).

126. Siemont T. Wezeman, "Arms Flows to Southeast Asia," SIPRI, December 2019, pp. 11, 14–17, https://www.sipri.org/sites/default/files/2019-12/1912_arms_flows_to_south_east_asia_wezeman.pdf (accessed October 11, 2021).

127. China Power, "How Dominant Is China in the Global Arms Trade?," CSIS, May 27, 2021, https://chinapower.csis.org/china-global-arms-trade/ (accessed October 11, 2021).

128. Prashanth Parameswaran, "US Launches New Maritime Security Initiative at Shangri-La Dialogue 2015," *The Diplomat*, June 2, 2015, https://thediplomat.com/2015/06/us-launches-new-maritime-security-initiative-at-shangri-la-dialogue-2015/ (accessed October 11, 2021).

129. "Security Cooperation FY2021 President's Budget," Department of Defense, pp. 27–28, https://comptroller.defense.gov/Portals/45/Documents/defbudget/fy2021/fy2021_Security_Cooperation_Book_FINAL.pdf (accessed October 11, 2021).

130. Ryan D. Martinson, "East Asian Security in the Age of the Chinese Mega-Cutter," Center for International Maritime Security, July 3, 2015, https://cimsec.org/east-asian-security-age-chinese-mega-cutter/ (accessed April 24, 2021).

131. Philip Heijmans, "Chinese Navy Chases Philippines' News Crew in Disputed Sea," Bloomberg, April 9, 2021, https://www.bloomberg.com/news/articles/2021-04-09/filipino-reporters-chased-by-armed-chinese-ships-in-disputed-sea (accessed April 24, 2021).

132. Thomas A. Shugart III, "Trends, Timelines and Uncertainty: An Assessment of the Military Balance in the Indo-Pacific," statement in *Advancing Effective US Policy for Strategic Competition with China in the Twenty-First Century: Hearing before the Committee on Foreign Relations*, U.S. Senate, March 17, 2021, https://www.foreign.senate.gov/hearings/advancing-effective-us-policy-for-strategic-competition-with-china-in-the-twenty-first-century-031721 (accessed April 24, 2021).

133. Andrew S. Erickson, "The China Maritime Militia Bookshelf: Latest Data, Official Statements, Wikipedia Entry . . . and Now—Force Size!," December 19, 2020, https://www.andrewerickson.com/2020/12/the-china-maritime-militia-bookshelf-latest-data-official-statements-wikipedia-entry-now-force-size/ (accessed April 24, 2021).

134. Liu Xuanzun, "PLA Starts Maritime Drills Featuring 'Powerful Ammunition' on Doorstep of S. China Sea," *Global Times*, July 25, 2020, https://www.globaltimes.cn/content/1195595.shtml (accessed April 25, 2021).

135. Kristin Huang, "Exclusive: Chinese Military Fires 'Aircraft-Carrier Killer' Missile into South China Sea in 'Warning to the United States,'" *South China Morning Post*, August 26, 2020, https://www.scmp.com/news/china/military/article/3098972/chinese-military-launches-two-missiles-south-china-sea-warning (accessed April 25, 2021).

136. Table, "Major Naval Units," in Office of the Secretary of Defense, *Annual Report to Congress: Military and Security Developments involving the People's Republic of China 2020*, 49, https://media.defense.gov/2020/Sep/01/2002488689/-1/-1/1/2020-DOD-CHINA-MILITARY-POWER-REPORT-FINAL.PDF (accessed April 25, 2021).

137. H. I. Sutton, "Chinese Navy Expanding Bases Near South China Sea," USNI News, December 29, 2020, https://news.usni.org/2020/12/29/chinese-navy-expanding-bases-near-south-china-sea (accessed April 25, 2021).

138. Office of the Secretary of Defense, *Military and Security Developments involving the People's Republic of China 2020* (Washington: U.S. Department of Defense, 2020), 80, 101–2; and Center for Strategic and International Studies, Asia Maritime Security Initiative, "Still on the Beat: China Coast Guard Patrols in 2020," December 4, 2020, https://amti.csis.org/still-on-the-beat-china-coast-guard-patrols-in-2020/ (accessed April 25, 2021).

139. Robert G. Loewenthal, "Cold War Insights into China's New Ballistic-Missile Submarine Fleet," in *China's Future Nuclear Submarine Force*, ed. Andrew S. Erickson, Lyle J. Goldstein, William S. Murray, and Andrew R. Wilson (Annapolis: Naval Institute Press, 2007), 300–301.
140. Bill Gertz, "China Tests New Sub-Launched Strategic Missile," *Washington Free Beacon*, June 13, 2019, https://freebeacon.com/national-security/china-tests-new-sub-launched-strategic-missile/ (accessed April 25, 2021).
141. Michael A. McDevitt, *China as a Twenty-First-Century Naval Power* (Annapolis: Naval Institute Press, 2020), 27–40.

## Chapter 5. Posture, Presence, and Platforms

1. U.S. Department of Defense, Joint Chiefs of Staff, *Deployment and Redeployment Operations*, Joint Publication 3-35, January 10, 2018, pp. I-4 and I-5, https://www.jcs.mil/Portals/36/Documents/Doctrine/pubs/jp3_35.pdf (accessed November 22, 2020).
2. "Department of Defense Statement on Unified Command Plan Change," U.S. Department of Defense, January 15, 2021, https://www.defense.gov/News/Releases/Release/Article/2473648/department-of-defense-statement-on-unified-command-plan-change/ (accessed November 6, 2021).
3. Andrew Feickert, "The Unified Command Plan and Combatant Commands: Background and Issues for Congress," Congressional Research Service, January 3, 2013, pp. 12–13, https://sgp.fas.org/crs/natsec/R42077.pdf (accessed November 6, 2021).
4. "US Navy Resurrects Second Fleet in Atlantic to Counter Russia," BBC News, May 5, 2018, https://www.bbc.com/news/world-us-canada-44014761 (accessed November 6, 2021).
5. Adm. James G. Foggo III, "Change of Command Remarks," U.S. Naval Forces, Europe/Africa/U.S. Sixth Fleet, July 17, 2020, https://www.c6f.navy.mil/Media/transcripts/Article/2275980/adm-foggo-change-of-command-remarks/ (accessed November 22, 2020).
6. Transcript, *Senate Armed Services Committee Hearing on United States European Command and United States Transportation Command Defense Authorization Request for Fiscal Year 2021*, February 25, 2020, https://www.eucom.mil/transcript/40285/senate-armed-services-committee-hearing-on-un (accessed November 22, 2020).
7. Adm. Philip S. Davidson, U.S. Navy, Commander, U.S. Indo-Pacific Command, "On US Indo-Pacific Command Posture," statement before the Committee on Armed Services, U.S. Senate, February 12, 2019, pp. 3, 12, 16–18, https://www.armed-services.senate.gov/imo/media/doc/Davidson_02-12-19.pdf (accessed November 22, 2020).
8. Adm. Philip S. Davidson, "Transforming the Joint Force: A Warfighting Concept for Great Power Competition," address delivered at West 2020, San

Diego, California, March 3, 2020, https://www.pacom.mil/Media/Speeches-Testimony/Article/2101115/transforming-the-joint-force-a-warfighting-concept-for-great-power-competition/ (accessed November 22, 2020).

9. U.S. Indo-Pacific Command, "National Defense Authorization Act (NDAA) 2020, Section 1253 Assessment, Executive Summary: Regain the Advantage: US Indo-Pacific Command's (USINDOPACOM) Investment Plan for Implementing the National Defense Strategy, Fiscal Years 2022–2026," https://int.nyt.com/data/documenthelper/6864-national-defense-strategy-summ/8851517f5e10106bc3b1/optimized/full.pdf (accessed November 22, 2020).

10. Christine E. Wormuth, Management of U.S. Global Defense Posture (GDP), Office of the Under Secretary of Defense for Policy, DoDI 3000.12, May 8, 2017, pp. 4–6, 11, https://www.esd.whs.mil/Portals/54/Documents/DD/issuances/dodi/300012p.pdf (accessed October 3, 2020).

11. Daniel R. DePetris, "SMA Negotiations: Why Trump's Demand of $5 Billion from South Korea Is Wrong," *National Interest*, November 21, 2019, https://nationalinterest.org/blog/korea-watch/sma-negotiations-why-trumps-demand-5-billion-south-korea-wrong-98337 (accessed October 3, 2020).

12. Emma Chanlett-Avery et al., "Japan-US Relations: Issues for Congress," Congressional Research Service, October 19, 2018, p. 21, https://crsreports.congress.gov/product/pdf/RL/RL33436/91 (accessed October 3, 2020).

13. Jason Bair, "Defense Logistics Agreements: DoD Should Improve Oversight and Seek Payment from Foreign Partners for Thousands of Orders It Identifies as Overdue," Government Accountability Office, March 4, 2020, p. 5, https://www.gao.gov/assets/710/705110.pdf (accessed October 3, 2020).

14. G. James Herrera, "Military Construction: Authorities, Process, and Frequently Asked Questions," Congressional Research Service, November 26, 2019, pp. 2–7, 14, https://fas.org/sgp/crs/natsec/R44710.pdf (accessed October 3, 2020).

15. Michael Lopez, "NMCB-3 Assumes Lead of Naval Construction Force Operations in Indo-Pacific," Commander U.S. Pacific Fleet, July 22, 2020, https://www.cpf.navy.mil/news.aspx/130686 (accessed October 3, 2020).

16. Michael Lopez, "Naval Mobile Construction Battalion-3 Works around the Clock, Completes MOX and CPX," U.S. Indo-Pacific Command, September 2, 2020, https://www.pacom.mil/Media/News/News-Article-View/Article/2334422/naval-mobile-construction-battalion-3-works-around-the-clock-completes-mox-cpx/ (accessed October 3, 2020).

17. Matthew R. White, "30th Naval Construction Regiment Relocates to Guam," Commander U.S. Pacific Fleet, July 2, 2018, https://www.cpf.navy.mil/news.aspx/130347 (accessed October 3, 2020).

18. Sam LaGrone, "Paying the Price: The Hidden Cost of the 'Fat Leonard' Investigation," USNI News, January 25, 2019, https://news.usni.org/2019/01/24/paying-price-hidden-cost-fat-leonard-investigation (accessed November 7, 2021).

19. Craig Whitlock and Spencer Hsu, "Navy Contractor Returns to US to Face Charge," *Star and Stripes*, October 19, 2021, https://www.stripes.com/theaters/us/2021-10-18/frank-rafaraci-us-navy-contractor-bribery-scandal-charges-3293427.html (accessed November 7, 2021).

20. Testimony of Gen. Tod D. Wolters, USAF, Commander, U.S. European Command, and North Atlantic Treaty Organization Supreme Allied Commander Europe, in *Senate Armed Services Committee Hearing on United States European Command and United States Transportation Command Defense Authorization Request for Fiscal Year 2021.*

21. U.S. International Development Finance Corporation, "Our Products," https://www.dfc.gov/what-we-offer/our-products (accessed November 7, 2021).

22. Testimony of Gen. Steve Lyons, Commander, U.S. Transportation Command, in *US Transportation Command and Maritime Administration: State of the Mobility Enterprise. Joint Hearing, Subcommittee on Seapower and Projection Forces and Subcommittee on Readiness, Committee on Armed Services, U.S. House of Representatives*, March 7, 2019, https://armedservices.house.gov/2019/3/u-s-transportation-command-and-maritime-administration-state-of-the-mobility-enterprise (accessed January 4, 2021).

23. USTRANSCOM J37, *United States Transportation Command Comprehensive Report for TURBO ACTIVATION 19-PLUS*, December 16, 2019, p. 5, https://www.ustranscom.mil/foia/docs/USTRANSCOM%20Turbo%20Activation%2019-Plus%20AAR.pdf (accessed January 4, 2021).

24. Peng Guangqian and Yao Youzhi, eds., *The Science of Military Strategy* (Beijing: Military Science Publishing House, 2005), 463–65.

25. Bryan Clark, Seth Cropsey, and Timothy A. Walton, *Sustaining the Undersea Advantage: Disrupting Anti-submarine Warfare Using Autonomous Systems*, Hudson Institute, September 2020, https://s3.amazonaws.com/media.hudson.org/Clark%20Cropsey%20Walton_Sustaining%20the%20Undersea%20Advantage.pdf (accessed November 21, 2020).

26. Center for Strategic and Budgetary Assessments, "CSBA Fireside Chat with Secretary of Defense Mark Esper," October 6, 2020, https://csbaonline.org/about/events/csba-fireside-chat-with-secretary-of-defense-mark-esper (accessed January 4, 2021).

27. Bradley Martin and Michael E. McMahon, *Future Aircraft Carrier Options*, RAND Corporation, 2017, pp. 16, 40, 47–48, 53, 65, https://www.rand.org/pubs/research_reports/RR2006.html (accessed January 4, 2021).

28. Timothy A. Walton, Ryan Boone, and Harrison Schramm, *Sustaining the Fight: Resilient Maritime Logistics for a New Era*, Center for Strategic and Budgetary Assessments, 2019, pp. 64–70, https://csbaonline.org/uploads /documents/Resilient_Maritime_Logistics.pdf (accessed November 21, 2020).

29. Bryan Clark and Timothy Walton, *Taking Back the Seas: Transforming the US Surface Fleet for Decision-Centric Warfare*, Center for Strategic and Budgetary Assessments, 2019, pp. 59–60, https://csbaonline.org/research /publications/taking-back-the-seas-transforming-the-u.s-surface-fleet-for-decision-centric-warfare/publication/1 (accessed January 4, 2021).

30. Clark and Walton, 65–68.

31. U.S. Department of Defense, Defense Science Board, *2019 DSB Summer Study on the Future of US Military Superiority: Final Report*, Executive Summary, June 2020, https://dsb.cto.mil/reports/2020s/2019_Future_of_US _Military_Superiority_Executive_Summary.pdf (accessed January 4, 2021).

32. For *The Science of Military Strategy*, see n. 64 above; for Russia's General Gerasimov, see n. 9 above.

## Chapter 6. A New Model Navy

1. Deputy Secretary of Defense Bob Work, speech delivered to a Center for a New American Security Defense Forum, Washington, DC, December 14, 2015, www.defense.gov/News/Speeches/Speech-View/Article/634214/cnas-defense-forum (accessed October 30, 2021).

2. During the English Civil War (1642–46), Oliver Cromwell emerged as the leader of Parliament's army fighting the Royalists. Dissatisfied with the conduct of the war despite clear financial and manpower advantage, Parliament in 1645 established and Cromwell led the New Model Army of professional soldiers, who unlike past practice were not tied to particular districts allowing execution of an effective national war. A focus on military proficiency, rather than nobility, for officer promotions was revolutionary for its time.

3. CNO Adm. Michael Gilday, memorandum titled "Project Overmatch" to Rear Adm. Douglas W. Small, October 1, 2020, and memorandum titled "A Novel Force" to Vice Adm. James Kilby, October 1, 2020, https://news .usni.org/2020/10/27/navy-focused-on-strengthening-networks-to-support-unmanned-operations (accessed April 8, 2022).

4. Megan Eckstein, "Navy Remains Mum on Project Overmatch Details So China Won't Steal Them," *Defense News*, February 25, 2022, https://www .defensenews.com/naval/2022/02/25/navy-remains-mum-on-project-overmatch-details-so-china-wont-steal-them/ (accessed April 8, 2022).

5. Bryan Clark, Dan Patt, and Harrison Schramm, "Mosaic Warfare: Exploiting Artificial Intelligence and Autonomous Systems to Implement Decision-Centric Operations," Center for Strategic and Budgetary Assessments, 2020, pp. ix, 23–25, 48–55, https://csbaonline.org/uploads/documents/Mosaic_Warfare_Web.pdf (accessed April 8, 2022).

6. Jeffrey Engstrom, "System Confrontation and System Destruction Warfare," RAND Corporation, 2018, pp. 15–22, https://www.rand.org/pubs/research_reports/RR1708.html (accessed April 8, 2022).

7. Jason Hall and Jesse Mink, "SEWIP AN/SLQ-32(V) Electronic Warfare System Overview and Program Status," Naval Sea Systems Command, January 13, 2022, https://www.navsea.navy.mil/Portals/103/Documents/Exhibits/SNA2022/SNA2022-CAPTJasonHall-SEWIP.pdf (accessed April 8, 2022).

8. Tyler Rogoway and Brett Tingley, "Navy's New Shipboard Electronic Warfare System is Being Shrunk Down for Smaller Ships," The Drive, January 15, 2022, https://www.thedrive.com/the-war-zone/43824/navys-new-shipboard-electronic-warfare-system-is-being-shrunk-down-for-smaller-ships (accessed April 8, 2022).

9. Brian Kerg and Gary Lehmann, "The Information Environment Is Primed for Maneuver Warfare," U.S. Naval Institute *Proceedings* 148, no. 2 (February 2022), https://www.usni.org/magazines/proceedings/2022/february/information-environment-primed-maneuver-warfare (accessed April 13, 2022).

10. Pavel Aksenov, "Stanislav Petrov: The Man Who May Have Saved the World," BBC News, September 26, 2013, https://www.bbc.com/news/world-europe-24280831 (accessed April 13, 2022).

11. William J. Crowe, "Formal Investigation into the Circumstances Surrounding the Downing of Iran Air Flight 655 on 3 July 1988," Department of Defense, pp. 7–8, https://www.jag.navy.mil/library/investigations/VINCENNES%20INV.pdf (accessed April 13, 2022).

12. Scott Shane and David E. Sanger, "Drone Crash in Iran Reveals Secret U.S. Surveillance Effort," *New York Times*, December 7, 2011, https://www.nytimes.com/2011/12/08/world/middleeast/drone-crash-in-iran-reveals-secret-us-surveillance-bid.html (accessed April 13, 2022).

13. George Galdorisi and Sam J. Tangredi, *AI at War: How Big Data, Artificial Intelligence, and Machine Learning Are Changing Naval Warfare* (Annapolis: Naval Institute Press, 2021), 289, 291, 302–4.

14. Shelby S. Oakley, "Uncrewed Maritime Systems: Navy Should Improve Its Approach to Maximize Early Investments," GAO, April 2022, pp. 18–24, https://s3.documentcloud.org/documents/21580882/gao-22-104567.pdf (accessed April 14, 2022).

15. Gilday, "Project Overmatch" memorandum to Rear Adm. Douglas W. Small, October 1, 2020, https://www.documentcloud.org/documents/7276835-Project-Overmatch-Memos (accessed April 14, 2022).

16. Lars Jaeger, *The Second Quantum Revolution: From Entanglement to Quantum Computing and Other Super-Technologies* (Switzerland: Springer Nature, 2018).

17. William M. McBride, "Technological Revolution at Sea," in *America, Sea Power, and the World*, ed. James C. Bradford (Chichester, U.K.: John Wiley & Sons, 2016), 84–85.

18. In marketing strategy, first mover advantage is gained by the initial significant occupant of a market segment. This advantage may be gained by technological leadership or early purchase of resources. Marvin B. Lieberman and David B. Montgomery, "First Mover Advantages," *Strategic Management Journal* 9 (Summer 1988): 41–58.

19. Michael J. Mazarr, "The Revolution in Military Affairs: A Framework for Defense Planning," Army War College, June 10, 1994, https://publications .armywarcollege.edu/pubs/1550.pdf (accessed November 6, 2021).

20. Ray Kurzweil, *How to Create a Mind: The Secret of Human Thought Revealed* (London: Penguin Books, 2012), 249–64.

21. Drake Baer, "Google's Genius Futurist Has One Theory That He Says Will Rule the Future—and It's a Little Terrifying," *Business Insider*, May 27, 2015, https://www.businessinsider.com/ray-kurzweil-law-of-accelerating-returns -2015-5 (accessed February 24, 2020).

22. Bill Ibelle and Allie Nicodemo, "The Next Big Breakthrough in Robotics," *phys.org*, January 24, 2018, https://phys.org/news/2018-01-big-breakthrough -robotics.html (accessed January 18, 2020); Courtney Linder, "Bad News for Dads: Robots Can Grill Hot Dogs Now," *Popular Mechanics*, December 23, 2019, https://www.popularmechanics.com/technology/robots/a30298216 /hotdog-cooking-robots/ (accessed January 18, 2020).

23. Peter B. Allen, Zin Khaing, Christine E. Schmidt, and Andrew D. Ellington, "3D Printing with Nucleic Acid Adhesives," *ACS Biomaterials Science and Engineering* 1, no. 1 (2015): 19–26, https://pubs.acs.org/doi/10.1021 /ab500026f (accessed August 3, 2022); Michael J. Ford, Cedric P. Ambulo, Teresa A. Kent, Eric J. Markvicka, Chengfeng Pan, Jonathan Malen, Taylor H. Ware, and Carmel Majidi, "A Multifunctional Shape-Morphing Elastomer with Liquid Metal Inclusions," *Proceedings of the National Academy of Sciences* 116, no. 43 (2019): 21438–44, https://www.pnas.org/doi/full/10 .1073/pnas.1911021116 (accessed August 3, 2022).

24. Sam Kriegman, Douglas Blackiston, Michael Levin, and Josh Bongard, "A Scalable Pipeline for Designing Reconfigurable Organisms," *Proceedings of the National Academy of Sciences* 117, no. 4 (January 2020): 1853–59, https:// www.pnas.org/doi/pdf/10.1073/pnas.1910837117 (accessed August 3, 2022).

25. Amy Nordrum, "China Demonstrates Quantum Encryption by Hosting a Video Call," IEEE Spectrum, October 3, 2017, https://spectrum.ieee.org/tech -talk/telecom/security/china-successfully-demonstrates-quantum-encryp tion-by-hosting-a-video-call (accessed February 21, 2020).

26. "First Chip-to-Chip Quantum Teleportation Harnessing Silicon Photonic Chip Fabrication," University of Bristol, December 24, 2019, https://phys.org/news/2019-12-chip-to-chip-quantum-teleportation-harnessing-silicon.html (accessed February 21, 2020).

27. Edwin Cartlidge, "Quantum Sensors: A Revolution in the Offing?," *Optics and Photonics News*, September 2019, https://www.osa-opn.org/home/articles/volume_30/september_2019/features/quantum_sensors_a_revolution_in_the_offing/ (accessed January 18, 2020).

28. Carl von Clausewitz, *On War* [*Vom Krieg*], ed. Michael Howard and Peter Paret (1832; repr., Princeton, NJ: Princeton University Press, 1984).

29. "How Is Robotics Changing the Maritime Industry and What Kind of Robots Are Being Used in Shipping?," *Marine Digital*, https://marine-digital.com/article_robotics_in_maritime_industry (accessed November 13, 2021).

30. John Burrow, Philip Cullom, and Michael Dana, "Additive Manufacturing Implementation Plan," Department of the Navy, May 4, 2017, pp. 4, 8, 12, https://apps.dtic.mil/sti/pdfs/AD1041527.pdf (accessed November 12, 2021).

31. Joint Defense Manufacturing Council, "Department of Defense Additive Manufacturing Strategy," Under Secretary of Defense for Research and Engineering, pp. 11–12, https://www.cto.mil/wp-content/uploads/2021/01/dod-additive-manufacturing-strategy.pdf#page19 (accessed November 12, 2021).

32. Williamson Murray and Allan R. Millett, *Military Innovation in the Interwar Period* (Cambridge: Cambridge University Press, 1996), 403–15.

33. Sam LaGrone, "Navy Names First Director of Unmanned Weapon Systems," USNI News, June 26, 2015, https://news.usni.org/2015/06/26/navy-names-first-director-of-unmanned-weapon-systems (accessed January 18, 2020).

## Chapter 7. Fleet Design 2035

1. Jimmy Cornell, *World Cruising Routes* (London: Adlard Coles, 2019), 764–68.

2. "Smooth Sailing for East China Sea Fishing," Asia Maritime Transparency Initiative, November 30, 2017, https://amti.csis.org/smooth-sailing-east-china-sea/ (accessed October 18, 2020).

3. Cornell, *World Cruising Routes*, 730, 736, 740, 743–44.

4. Gregory B. Poling, "Illuminating the South China Sea's Dark Fishing Fleets," Center for Strategic and International Studies, January 9, 2019, https://ocean.csis.org/spotlights/illuminating-the-south-china-seas-dark-fishing-fleets/ (accessed October 18, 2020).

5. Bonnie Glaser and Matthew P. Funaiole, "China's Maritime Gray Zone Operations," in *China's Maritime Gray Zone Operations* (Annapolis: Naval Institute Press, 2019), 189–201.

6. Kenneth Allen and Morgan Clemens, "The Recruitment, Education, and Training of PLA Navy Personnel," CMSI Red Books, Study No. 12 (August 2014), 15–17.

7. Office of the Secretary of Defense, *Annual Report to Congress: Military and Security Developments involving the People's Republic of China 2020* (Washington: U.S. Department of Defense, 2019), v, ix, 3, 6, 30–32, 94, 112, 159, https://media.defense.gov/2020/Sep/01/2002488689/-1/-1/1/2020-DOD-CHINA-MILITARY-POWER-REPORT-FINAL.PDF (accessed September 21, 2020).

8. Cornell, *World Cruising Routes*, 55, 366.

9. Cornell, 1427–29.

10. Duncan Cook and Sally Garrett, "Somali Piracy and the Monsoon," American Meteorological Society, October 2013, https://journals.ametsoc.org/wcas/article/5/4/309/882/Somali-Piracy-and-the-Monsoon (accessed October 19, 2020).

11. Cornell, *World Cruising Routes*, 1141–46.

12. "Persian Gulf Weather—Shamal," Global Security, https://www.globalsecurity.org/military/world/iran/shamal.htm (accessed October 19, 2020).

13. Cornell, *World Cruising Routes*, 293.

14. UNODC, *World Drug Report 2010* (UN Publication, Sales No. E.10.XI.13), 70, 100–101, 233–35, https://www.unodc.org/documents/wdr/WDR_2010/World_Drug_Report_2010_lo-res.pdf (accessed October 19, 2020).

15. Mark Godfrey, "Chinese Overfishing Threatens Development of West African Fishing Sector," Seafood Source, June 26, 2020, https://www.seafoodsource.com/news/environment-sustainability/chinese-overfishing-threatens-development-of-west-african-fishing-sector (accessed October 19, 2020).

16. U.S. Department of Defense, "Military Units: Navy," https://www.defense.gov/Experience/Military-Units/Navy/#1283.296875 (accessed November 20, 2021).

17. U.S. Department of the Navy, Office of the CNO, "Optimized Fleet Response Plan," OPNAVINST 3000.15A, November 10, 2014, pp. 3–6, https://www.secnav.navy.mil/doni/Directives/03000%20Naval%20Operations%20and%20Readiness/03-00%20General%20Operations%20and%20Readiness%20Support/3000.15A.pdf (accessed November 23, 2020).

18. Megan Eckstein, "US Fleet Forces: New Deployment Plan Designed to Create Sustainable Naval Force," USNI News, updated January 20, 2016, https://news.usni.org/2016/01/19/u-s-fleet-forces-new-deployment-plan-designed-to-create-sustainable-naval-force (accessed November 23, 2020).

19. David B. Larter, "The US Navy's Vaunted Deployment Plan Is Showing Cracks Everywhere," *Defense News*, February 7, 2020, https://www.defensenews.com/naval/2020/02/07/the-us-navys-vaunted-deployment-plan-is-showing-cracks-everywhere/ (accessed November 23, 2020).

20. Sam LaGrone, "Navy, DoD Conducting Parallel Reviews of OFRP," USNI News, January 16, 2020, https://news.usni.org/2020/01/16/navy-dod-conducting-parallel-reviews-of-ofrp (accessed November 23, 2020).

21. Coast Guard News, "Coast Guard Cutter Stratton to Depart for Western Pacific Deployment," June 11, 2019, https://coastguardnews.com/coast-guard-cutter-stratton-to-depart-for-western-pacific-deployment/2019/06/11/ (accessed November 23, 2020).

22. Dakota Wood, "2022 Index of US Military Strength," Heritage Foundation, October 20, 2021, pp. 339–54, https://www.heritage.org/military-strength/assessment-us-military-power (accessed November 20, 2021).

23. Commission on the National Defense Strategy for the United States, *Providing for the Common Defense: The Assessments and Recommendations of the National Defense Strategy Commission*, pp. 21–22, 35, 66, https://www.usip.org/sites/default/files/2019-07/providing-for-the-common-defense.pdf (accessed November 20, 2021). The commission's report is undated but was released in November 2018. "National Defense Strategy Commission Releases Its Review of 2018 National Defense Strategy" (press release), United States Institute of Peace, November 13, 2018, https://www.usip.org/press/2018/11/national-defense-strategy-commission-releases-its-review-2018-national-defense (accessed November 23, 2021).

24. Thomas Callender, "The Nation Needs a 400-Ship Navy," Heritage Foundation, October 26, 2018, pp. 3, https://www.heritage.org/sites/default/files/2018-10/SR205.pdf (accessed November 20, 2021).

25. Bryan Clark and Timothy A. Walton, *Taking Back the Seas: Transforming the US Surface Fleet for Decision-Centric Warfare*, Center for Strategic and Budgetary Assessments, 2019, pp. 26–30, https://csbaonline.org/research/publications/taking-back-the-seas-transforming-the-u.s-surface-fleet-for-decision-centric-warfare/publication/1 (accessed November 23, 2020).

26. Clark and Walton, 65–68.

27. Congressional Budget Office, *The US Military's Force Structure: A Primer*, July 2016, pp. 45, 47–48, 54–55, 62, https://www.cbo.gov/sites/default/files/114th-congress-2015-2016/reports/51535-fsprimer.pdf (accessed November 23, 2020).

28. Megan Eckstein, "Marines Look to Two New Ship Classes to Define Future of Amphibious Operations," USNI News, updated June 12, 2020, https://news.usni.org/2020/06/08/marines-look-to-two-new-ship-classes-to-define-future-of-amphibious-operations (accessed November 23, 2020).

29. John Keller, "Navy Places Order for 166,500 Anti-submarine Warfare (ASW) Sonobuoys in $219.8 Million Deal," *Military and Aerospace Electronics*, October 11, 2017, https://www.militaryaerospace.com/power/article/16726220/navy-places-order-for-166500-antisubmarine-warfare-asw-sonobuoys-in-2198-million-deal (accessed November 23, 2020).

30. Richard R. Burgess, "Navy's Future Carrier Air Wing Configuration Coming into Focus," *Seapower Magazine*, September 14, 2020, https://seapowermagazine.org/navys-future-carrier-air-wing-configuration-coming-into-focus/ (accessed November 23, 2020).

31. Richard R. Burgess, "Navy to Establish First MQ-25 Stingray UAV Squadron in 2021," *Seapower Magazine*, October 2, 2020, https://seapowermagazine.org/navy-to-establish-first-mq-25-stingray-uav-squadron-in-2021/ (accessed November 23, 2020).

32. Fact File, "MQ-8C Fire Scout," U.S. Navy, last updated February 21, 2019, https://www.navy.mil/Resources/Fact-Files/Display-FactFiles/Article/2159302/mq-8c-fire-scout/ (accessed November 23, 2020).

33. Norman Friedman, *U.S. Aircraft Carriers: An Illustrated Design History* (Annapolis: Naval Institute Press, 1983), 342–47.

34. Rear Adm. Michael A. McDevitt, "China's Navy Will Be the World's Largest in 2035," U.S. Naval Institute *Proceedings* 146, no. 2 (February 2020), https://www.usni.org/magazines/proceedings/2020/february/chinas-navy-will-be-worlds-largest-2035 (accessed November 23, 2020).

35. Michael Kofman, "A Year of Challenging Growth for Russia's Navy," U.S. Naval Institute *Proceedings* 146, no. 3 (March 2020), https://www.usni.org/magazines/proceedings/2020/march/year-challenging-growth-russias-navy (accessed November 23, 2020).

36. Clark and Walton, *Taking Back the Seas*, 65–68.

37. Bryan Clark, Timothy A. Walton, and Seth Cropsey, *American Sea Power at a Crossroads: A Plan to Restore the US Navy's Maritime Advantage*, Hudson Institute, October 2020, pp. 36, 43, and 52, https://s3.amazonaws.com/media.hudson.org/Clark%20Cropsey%20Walton_American%20Sea%20Power%20at%20a%20Crossroads.pdf (accessed November 23, 2020).

38. Eckstein, "Marines Look to Two New Ship Classes to Define Future of Amphibious Operations."

39. Ben Werner, "Navy Awards Boeing $43 Million to Build Four Orca XLUUVs," USNI News, updated April 17, 2019, https://news.usni.org/2019/02/13/41119 (accessed November 23, 2020).

40. PEO Unmanned and Small Combatants Public Affairs, "Navy Awards Contract for Medium Unmanned Surface Vehicle Prototype," U.S. Navy, Naval Sea Systems Command, July 13, 2020, https://www.navsea.navy.mil/Media/News/SavedNewsModule/Article/2272591/navy-awards-contract-for-medium-unmanned-surface-vehicle-prototype/ (accessed November 23, 2020).

41. Congressional Budget Office, "CBO's Interactive Force Structure Tool," last updated August 15, 2018, https://www.cbo.gov/publication/54351 (accessed December 22, 2020).

## Chapter 8. A National Maritime Program

1. U.S. Navy, Naval Sea Systems Command, "USS *Fitzgerald* Leaves Dry Dock, Continues Repairs Pierside in Pascagoula," April 17, 2019, https://www.navsea.navy.mil/Media/News/SavedNewsModule/Article/1816293/uss-fitzgerald-leaves-dry-dock-continues-repairs-pierside-in-pascagoula/ (accessed November 21, 2020).

2. Sam LaGrone, "USS *John S. McCain* Back to Sea after Completing Repairs from Fatal 2017 Collision," USNI News, updated October 28, 2019, https://news.usni.org/2019/10/27/uss-john-s-mccain-back-to/-sea-after-completing-repairs-from-fatal-2017-collision (accessed November 21, 2020).

3. U.S. Government Accountability Office, *Navy Shipyards: Actions Needed to Address the Main Factors Causing Maintenance Delays for Aircraft Carriers and Submarines*, GAO-20-588, August 2020, pp. 7–13, https://www.gao.gov/products/GAO-20-588 (accessed November 21, 2020).

4. Ronald O'Rourke, "Navy Force Structure and Shipbuilding Plans: Background and Issues for Congress," Congressional Research Service *Report for Members and Committees of Congress* No. RL32655, November 11, 2020, pp. 16–17, https://crsreports.congress.gov/product/pdf/RL/RL32665 (accessed November 23, 2020).

5. U.S. Department of the Navy, Office of Budget, *Highlights of the Department of the Navy FY 2021 Budget*, February 10, 2020, sec. 1, p. 11, and sec. 4, pp. 3–4, https://www.secnav.navy.mil/fmc/fmb/Documents/21pres/Highlights_book.pdf (accessed November 23, 2020).

6. Maiya Clark, "US Navy Shipyards Desperately Need Revitalization and a Rethink," Heritage Foundation Backgrounder No. 3511, July 29, 2020, https://www.heritage.org/defense/report/us-navy-shipyards-desperately-need-revitalization-and-rethink. For information on BRACs, see Christopher T. Mann, "Base Closure and Realignment (BRAC): Background and Issues for Congress," Congressional Research Service *Report for Members and Committees of Congress* No. R45705, April 25, 2019, https://www.everycrsreport.com/files/20190425_R45705_9e300ef394d6f4dabc78a7ef8fbbc33ef9bd01e7.pdf (accessed December 15, 2020).

7. Mann, "Base Closure and Realignment (BRAC)," 9–10, 12–13.

8. "Executive Summary to Naval Shipyard Recapitalization and Optimization Plan," USNI News, updated September 13, 2018, https://news.usni.org/2018/09/12/executive-summary-to-naval-shipyard-recapitalization-and-optimization-plan (accessed November 21, 2020).

9. Bryan Clark, Timothy A. Walton, and Adam Lemon, *Strengthening the US Defense Maritime Industrial Base: A Plan to Improve Maritime Industry's Contribution to National Security* (Washington: Center for Strategic and Budgetary Assessments, 2020), 19, 22–23, https://csbaonline.org/uploads/documents/CSBA8199_Maritime_Industrial_FINAL.pdf (accessed November 21, 2020).

10. Ellen Mitchell, "Navy to Scrap USS *Bonhomme Richard* after Days-Long Fire," *The Hill*, November 30, 2020, https://thehill.com/policy/defense/528026-navy-to-scrap-uss-bonhomme-richard-after-days-long-fire?rl=1 (accessed March 31, 2021).

11. David B. Larter, "Trump Just Made a 355-Ship Navy National Policy," *Defense News*, December 13, 2017, https://www.defensenews.com/congress/2017/12/14/trump-just-made-355-ships-national-policy/ (accessed April 7, 2021).

12. HR 2810, National Defense Authorization Act for Fiscal Year 2018, Public Law 115-91, 115th Cong., December 12, 2017, https://www.congress.gov/bill/115th-congress/house-bill/2810/text (accessed April 7, 2021).

13. Table 2, "FYDP Funding for Ship Building and Conversion Navy (SCN)," in Office of the CNO, Deputy CNO (Warfighting Requirements and Capabilities—OPNAV N9), "Report to Congress on the Annual Long-Range Plan for Construction of Naval Vessels," December 9, 2020, p. 5, https://media.defense.gov/2020/Dec/10/2002549918/-1/-1/1/SHIPBUILDING%20PLAN%20DEC%2020_NAVY_OSD_OMB_FINAL.PDF (accessed March 30, 2021).

14. U.S. Government Accountability Office, *Navy Shipbuilding: Past Performance Provides Valuable Lessons for Future Investments*, GAO-18-238SP, June 2018, pp. 8–9, https://www.gao.gov/assets/700/692331.pdf (accessed March 30, 2021).

15. U.S. Department of the Navy, Office of the Secretary, "Defense Acquisition System and Joint Capabilities Integration and Development System Implementation," SECNAVINST 5000.2F, March 26, 2019, https://www.secnav.navy.mil/doni/Directives/05000%20General%20Management%20Security%20and%20Safety%20Services/05-00%20General%20Admin%20and%20Management%20Support/5000.2F.pdf (accessed March 31, 2021).

16. 10 U.S. Code § 8685, https://www.law.cornell.edu/uscode/text/10/8685 (accessed March 31, 2021).

17. For a detailed discussion on the "Two-Pass, Seven-Gate" Navy acquisition process and how it relates to shipbuilding, see Brent Sadler, "Foundational Improvements for Better U.S. Navy Shipbuilding," Heritage Foundation, April 13, 2021, pp. 16–19, https://www.heritage.org/sites/default/files/2021-04/BG3609.pdf. According to the U.S. Government Accountability Office, "in an effort to increase leadership attention on program sustainment, the Navy updated its acquisition policy to add a Gate for sustainment, called Gate 7." U.S. Government Accountability Office, *Navy Shipbuilding: Increasing Focus on Sustainment Early in the Acquisition Process Could Save Billions*, GAO-20-2, March 2020, p. 55, https://www.gao.gov/assets/gao-20-2.pdf (accessed April 1, 2021).

18. Ronald O'Rourke, "Navy Ship Procurement: Alternative Funding Approaches—Background and Options for Congress," Congressional Research Service *Report for Members and Committees of Congress* No. RL32776, updated July 26, 2006, pp. 1–12, https://fas.org/sgp/crs/weapons /RL32776.pdf (accessed March 30, 2021).

19. "Advance Appropriations," in Executive Office of the President, Office of Management and Budget, *Appendix: Budget of the US Government, Fiscal Year 2018*, May 2017, p. 1241, https://www.govinfo.gov/content/pkg/BUD GET-2018-APP/pdf/BUDGET-2018-APP-2-2.pdf (accessed March 30, 2021). For the complete budget document from which this page is taken, see U.S. Government Printing Office, "Budget of the US Government, Fiscal Year 2018," https://www.govinfo.gov/content/pkg/BUDGET-2018-APP/pdf /BUDGET-2018-APP.pdf (accessed March 30, 2021).

20. See Ronald O'Rourke, "Navy Ship Procurement: Alternative Funding Approaches—Background and Options for Congress," Congressional Research Service *Report for Members and Committees of Congress* No. RL32776, updated July 26, 2006, pp. 10–11, https://fas.org/sgp/crs/weapons /RL32776.pdf (accessed April 1, 2021).

21. 10 U.S. Code § 2218a, https://uscode.house.gov/view.xhtml?req= granuleid:USC-prelim-title10-section2218a&num=0&edition=prelim (accessed March 30, 2021).

22. Lee Hudson, "Pentagon Shifts $630 Million to National Sea-Based Deterrence Fund," *Inside Defense*, October 24, 2017, https://insidedefense.com/ insider/pentagon-shifts-630-million-national-sea-based-deterrence-fund (accessed March 30, 2021).

23. "Document: National Sea-Based Deterrence Fund Reprogramming Action," *Inside Defense*, March 16, 2020, https://insidedefense.com/docu ment/national-sea-based-deterrence-fund-reprogramming-action ?destination=node/206834 (accessed March 30, 2021).

24. Frederico Bartels, "Cumbersome Defense Reprogramming Process Hampers National Defense and Should Be Streamlined," Heritage Foundation Back-grounder No. 3543, October 13, 2020, https://www.heritage.org/defense /report/cumbersome-defense-reprogramming-process-hampers-national-defense-and-should-be (accessed December 14, 2021).

25. Pat Towell, Kate McClanahan, and Jennifer M. Roscoe, "Defense Spending under an Interim Continuing Resolution: In Brief," Congressional Research Service, No. R45870, August 15, 2019, https://fas.org/sgp/crs/natsec/R45870 .pdf (accessed March 31, 2021).

26. Ronald O'Rourke, "Navy Ford (CVN-78) Class Aircraft Carrier Program: Background and Issues for Congress," Congressional Research Service *Report for Members and Committees of Congress* No. RS20643, updated January 21, 2020, p. 58, https://crsreports.congress.gov/product/pdf/RS/RS20643/220 (accessed March 30, 2021).

27. Drew DeSilver, "Congress Has Long Struggled to Pass Spending Bills on Time," Pew Research Center, January 16, 2018, https://www.pewresearch .org/fact-tank/2018/01/16/congress-has-long-struggled-to-pass-spending-bills-on-time/ (accessed March 30, 2021).

28. Gus Wezerek, "20 Years of Congress's Budget Procrastination, in One Chart," FiveThirtyEight, February 7, 2018, https://fivethirtyeight.com/features/20-years-of-congresss-budget-procrastination-in-one-chart/ (accessed March 30, 2021).

29. Heather Krause, Director, Strategic Issues, U.S. Government Accountability Office, "Budget Issues: Continuing Resolutions and Other Budget Uncertainties Present Management Challenges," in *Testimony before the Subcommittee on Federal Spending Oversight and Emergency Management, Committee on Homeland Security and Government Affairs, U.S. Senate*, GAO-18-368T, February 6, 2018, https://www.gao.gov/assets/690/689914.pdf (accessed March 30, 2021).

30. Adm. Jonathan Greenert, U.S. Navy, CNO, "Statement before the Committee on Armed Services on the Impact of Sequestration on the National Defense," U.S. Senate, November 7, 2013, pp. 11–12, https://www.armed-services.sen ate.gov/imo/media/doc/Greenert_11-07-131.pdf (accessed April 1, 2021).

31. Robert G. Keane, Barry F. Tibbitts, and Peter E. Jaquith, "The Navy's Ship Design Factory: NAVSEA—the 'Golden Goose,'" *Naval Engineers Journal* 131, no. 3 (September 2019): 61–78.

32. Ronald O'Rourke, "Navy DDG-51 and DDG-1000 Destroyer Programs: Background and Issues for Congress," Congressional Research Service, No. RL32109, updated November 10, 2020, pp. 23–24, 28, https://fas.org/sgp/crs /weapons/RL32109.pdf (accessed November 23, 2020), and "Navy Littoral Combat Ship (LCS)/Frigate Program: Background and Issues for Congress," Congressional Research Service, No. RL33741, January 5, 2016, pp. 49, 63, https://www.history.navy.mil/content/history/nhhc/research/library/online-reading-room/title-list-alphabetically/n/navy-littoral-combat-ship-lcsfrig ate-program.html (accessed November 23, 2020).

33. Norman Friedman, *U.S. Destroyers: An Illustrated Design History*, rev. ed. (Annapolis: Naval Institute Press, 2004), 424–25.

34. Jim Inhofe and Jack Reed, "The Navy Needs a Course Correction: Prototyping with Purpose," U.S. Naval Institute, *Proceedings* 146, no. 6, issue 1,408 (June 2020), https://www.usni.org/magazines/proceedings/2020/june/navy -needs-course-correction-prototyping-purpose (accessed March 31, 2021).

35. David B. Larter, "US Navy Takes Delivery of New, More Powerful RADAR," *Defense News*, July 20, 2020, https://www.defensenews.com /naval/2020/07/20/us-navy-takes-delivery-of-new-more-powerful-radar/ (accessed March 31, 2021).

36. John F. Schank, Cesse Ip, Frank W. Lacroix, Robert E. Murphy, Mark V. Arena, Kristy N. Kamarck, and Gordon T. Lee, *Learning from Experience*, vol. 2: *Lessons from the US Navy's* Ohio, Seawolf *and* Virginia *Submarine Programs* (Santa Monica: RAND Corporation, 2011), 43–46, https://www.rand.org/content/dam/rand/pubs/monographs/2011/RAND_MG1128.2.pdf (accessed March 18, 2021).

37. Keane, Tibbitts, and Jaquith, "The Navy's Ship Design Factory," 66.

38. Ronald O'Rourke, "Navy Ford (CVN-78) Class Aircraft Carrier Program: Background and Issues for Congress," Congressional Research Service *Report for Members and Committees of Congress* No. RS20643, updated March 17, 2021, https://crsreports.congress.gov/product/pdf/RS/RS20643/245 (accessed March 31, 2021).

39. Gregory V. Cox, "Lessons Learned from the LCS," U.S. Naval Institute *Proceedings* 141, no. 1 (January 2015), https://www.usni.org/magazines/proceedings/2015/january/lessons-learned-lcs (accessed March 31, 2021).

40. "Fleet Review Panel of Surface Force Readiness Findings," SailorBob 3.0, p. 2, http://www.sailorbob.com/files/Attachment%202%20-%20Systemic%20Findings.pdf (accessed March 31, 2021). For the complete final report, see *Final Report: Fleet Review Panel of Surface Force Readiness*, February 26, 2010, http://www.sailorbob.com/files/foia/FRP%20of%20Surface%20Force%20Readiness%20(Balisle%20Report).pdf (accessed March 31, 2021).

41. Sam LaGrone, "NTSB: 'Unexplained' Course Change Was 'a Critical Error' in Fatal USS *Fitzgerald* Collision," USNI News, September 3, 2020, https://news.usni.org/2020/09/03/ntsb-unexplained-course-change-was-a-critical-error-in-fatal-uss-fitzgerald-collision (accessed March 31, 2021).

42. Keane, Tibbitts, and Jaquith, "The Navy's Ship Design Factory," 68–69.

43. Ronald O'Rourke, "Navy Virginia (SSN-774) Class Attack Submarine Procurement: Background and Issues for Congress," Congressional Research Service *Report for Members and Committees of Congress* No. RL32418, April 16, 2019, https://crsreports.congress.gov/product/pdf/RL/RL32418/170 (accessed March 31, 2021).

44. John F. Schank, Mark V. Arena, Paul DeLuca, Jessie Riposo, Kimberly Curry, Todd Weeks, and James Chiesa, *Sustaining US Nuclear Submarine Design Capabilities* (Santa Monica, CA: RAND Corporation, 2007), https://www.rand.org/content/dam/rand/pubs/monographs/2007/RAND_MG608.pdf (accessed March 31, 2021).

45. Megan Eckstein, "Navy Awards $9.47B Contract for First *Columbia*-Class SSBN, Advance Work on Second Boat," USNI News, November 5, 2020, https://news.usni.org/2020/11/05/navy-awards-9-47b-contract-for-first-columbia-class-ssbn-advance-work-on-second-boat (accessed March 31, 2021).

46. Office of the CNO, Deputy CNO (Warfighting Requirements and Capabilities—OPNAV N9), "Report to Congress on the Annual Long-Range Plan for Construction of Naval Vessels," December 2020, p. 6.

47. Figure II-3-2-4, "Transition of the NDPG Annex Tables," in Government of Japan, Ministry of Defense, *Defense of Japan 2020*, p. 219, https://www.mod.go.jp/en/publ/w_paper/wp2020/DOJ2020_EN_Full.pdf (accessed March 31, 2021).

48. Naval Sea Systems Command, "Engineering and Technical Authority Overview," January 15, 2019, https://www.navsea.navy.mil/Portals/103/Documents/Exhibits/SNA2019/Eng_TechAuth-Lind.pdf?ver=2019-01-15-165059-767 (accessed March 31, 2021).

49. "Statement Submitted by John F. Lehman, Jr. to the Subcommittee on Seapower of the Senate Armed Services Committee, July 17, 2017," https://www.armed-services.senate.gov/imo/media/doc/Lehman_07-18-17.pdf (accessed November 23, 2020).

50. John F. Lehman, *Oceans Ventured: Winning the Cold War at Sea* (New York: W. W. Norton, 2018), 143–44.

51. Adm. Karl Schultz, Commandant, U.S. Coast Guard; Adm. Craig S. Faller, Commander, U.S. Southern Command; Rear Adm. (Ret.) Tim Gallaudet, Assistant Secretary of Commerce for Oceans and Atmosphere; Dr. Benjamin S. Purser III, Deputy Assistant Secretary for Oceans, Fisheries, and Polar Affairs, Bureau of Oceans and International Environmental and Scientific Affairs; and Dr. Whitley Saumweber, Director, Stephenson Ocean Security Project, "Online Event: Strategic Perspectives on Illegal, Unreported, and Unregulated Fishing," Center for Strategic and International Studies, September 17, 2020, time: 7 min. 10 sec., 11 min. 30 sec., 37 min. 36 sec., and 48 min. 30 sec., https://www.csis.org/events/online-event-strategic-perspectives-illegal-unreported-and-unregulated-fishing (accessed November 23, 2020).

52. Appendix A, "Planned NSC, OPC, and FRC Procurement Quantities," in Ronald O'Rourke, "Coast Guard Cutter Procurement: Background and Issues for Congress," Congressional Research Service *Report for Members and Committees of Congress* No. R42567, updated November 16, 2020, pp. 29–35, https://fas.org/sgp/crs/weapons/R42567.pdf (accessed November 23, 2020).

53. Ronald O'Rourke, Specialist in Naval Affairs, Congressional Research Service, statement in hearing on "Future Force Structure Requirements for the United States Navy," Subcommittee on Seapower and Projection Forces, Committee on Armed Services, U.S. House of Representatives, June 4, 2020, pp. 17–19, https://crsreports.congress.gov/product/pdf/TE/TE10057 (accessed November 23, 2020).

54. Maritime Administration, "Vessel Calls in US Ports, Selected Terminals and Lightering Areas," U.S. Department of Transportation, 2015, https://www.maritime.dot.gov/data-reports/data-statistics/data-statistics (accessed November 13, 2021).

55. Maritime Administration, "Consolidated Fleet Summary and Change List," U.S. Department of Transportation, July 20, 2021, https://www.maritime.dot.gov/sites/marad.dot.gov/files/2021-08/DS_USFlag-Fleet_2021_0720_Bundle.pdf (accessed November 13, 2021).

56. "Fact Sheet #14: Merchant Fleet," UNCTAD Handbook of Statistics 2020—Maritime Transport, https://unctad.org/system/files/official-document/tdstat45_FS14_en.pdf (accessed November 13, 2021).

57. U.S. Commission on Merchant Marine and Defense, "Second Report Recommendations," December 30, 1987, p. 9.

58. The Merchant Marine Act of 1920, commonly referred to as the Jones Act, is a federal statute that aims to promote domestic shipbuilding and the merchant marine. It does this by requiring that shipping between U.S. ports be conducted on U.S.-flagged, -built, and -manned ships. Following the lessons of World War I, the intent is to support an adequate U.S. shipping industry that can sustain the nation in wartime. The law has been revised several times, most recently in 2006. Despite best efforts and protections to domestic shipbuilding, there have been numerous waivers allowed to facilitate trade and disaster response, notably following Hurricane Katrina in 2005; for getting emergency fuel supplies to Nome, Alaska, from Russia in 2012; and following several 2017 hurricanes impacting Texas, Florida, and Puerto Rico.

59. Clark, Walton, and Lemon, *Strengthening the US Defense Maritime Industrial Base*, 9–13, 48.

60. Colin Grabow, Inu Manak, and Daniel J. Ikenson, "The Jones Act: A Burden America Can No Longer Bear," 6; Colin Grabow, "Rust Buckets: How the Jones Act Undermines US Shipbuilding and National Security," 27; and Daniel J. Ikenson, "Dragging the Anchor: A Look at the Myriad Costs of the Jones Act," 43, all in *The Case against the Jones Act*, ed. Colin Grabow and Inu Manak (Washington: Cato Institute, 2020).

61. Clark, Walton, and Lemon, *Strengthening the US Defense Maritime Industrial Base*, 50–52.

62. National Defense Authorization Act for Fiscal Year 2021, "Limitations on Use of Funds in the National Defense Sealift Fund for Purchase of Foreign Constructed Vessels," 116th Congress, H.R. 6395, sec. 1022, https://www.congress.gov/116/bills/hr6395/BILLS-116hr6395enr.pdf (accessed November 14, 2021).

63. Grabow, "Rust Buckets," 25.

64. Clark, Walton, and Lemon, *Strengthening the US Defense Maritime Industrial Base*, 26–27.

65. Tim Johnson, "The US Merchant Marine Fleet Is Dying—and It May Hurt America's Ability to Wage War Abroad," *Task and Purpose*, May 15, 2018, https://taskandpurpose.com/analysis/us-mercant-marine-fleet-military (accessed November 23, 2020).

66. US Department of Transportation, *Goals and Objectives for a Stronger Maritime Nation: A Report to Congress*, February 2020, p. 8, https://www.maritime.dot.gov/sites/marad.dot.gov/files/2020-07/Final_2_25_Stronger%20Maritime%20Nation%20Report_.pdf (accessed November 23, 2020).

67. Testimony of Mark H. Buzby, Administrator, U.S. Maritime Administration, in "Subcommittees on Seapower and Projection Forces and Readiness Joint Hearing: 'Sealift and Mobility Requirements in Support of the National Defense Strategy,' Committee on Armed Services, U.S. House of Representatives" (video), March 11, 2020, https://armedservices.house.gov/2020/3/subcommittees-on-seapower-and-projection-forces-and-readiness-joint-hearing-sealift-and-mobility-requirements-in-support-of-the-national-defense-strategy (accessed November 23, 2020). See also Mark H. Buzby, Administrator, U.S. Maritime Administration, U.S. Department of Transportation, statement for *Hearing on Sealift and Mobility Requirements in Support of the National Defense Strategy, Subcommittee on Seapower and Projection Forces and Subcommittee on Readiness, Committee on Armed Services, U.S. House of Representatives*, March 11, 2020, https://www.congress.gov/116/meeting/house/110720/witnesses/HHRG-116-AS28-Wstate-BuzbyM-20200311.pdf (accessed November 23, 2020).

68. Jude Blanchette, Jonathan E. Hillman, Maesea McCalpin, and Mingda Qiu, "Hidden Harbors: China's State-Backed Shipping Industry," CSIS, July 2020, pp. 2, 4–7, https://csis-website-prod.s3.amazonaws.com/s3fs-public/publication/207008_Blanchette_Hidden%20Harbors_Brief_WEB%20FINAL.pdf (accessed November 14, 2021).

69. "Disputes by Member," World Trade Organization, https://www.wto.org/english/tratop_e/dispu_e/dispu_by_country_e.htm (accessed November 14, 2021).

70. Clark, Walton, and Lemon, *Strengthening the US Defense Maritime Industrial Base*, 11–13.

71. Mark Buzby, Administrator, Maritime Administration, U.S. Department of Transportation, statement for *Hearing on "Review of Fiscal Year 2020 Budget for the Coast Guard and Maritime Transportation Programs," Subcommittee on Coast Guard and Maritime Transportation, Committee on Transportation and Infrastructure, U.S. House of Representatives*, May 21, 2019, https://www.transportation.gov/testimony/review-fiscal-year-2020-budget-coast-guard-and-maritime-transportation-programs (accessed November 23, 2020).

72. Clark, Walton, and Lemon, *Strengthening the US Defense Maritime Industrial Base*, 48.

73. William Roper, "Can Market Bridges Speed to New Naval Fleet Capabilities?," Heritage Foundation Events, October 28, 2021, https://www.heritage.org/defense/event/can-market-bridges-speed-new-naval-fleet-capabilities (accessed November 14, 2021).

74. Richard Whittle, "Agile Change in Air Force 'Agility Prime' Launch Pays Off," Electric VTOL News, July–August 2020, https://evtol.news/news/agile-change-in-air-force-agility-prime-launch-pays-off (accessed November 14, 2021).

75. U.S. Department of Transportation, Maritime Administration, U.S. Maritime Transportation System National Advisory Committee, *Maritime Workforce Working Group Report*, U.S. Maritime Transportation System National Advisory Committee, approved September 27, 2017, pp. 26–32, https://www.maritime.dot.gov/sites/marad.dot.gov/files/docs/mariners/1026/mwwg-report-congress-finalr3.pdf (accessed November 23, 2020).

76. U.S. Department of Transportation, Maritime Administration, *Opportunities and Challenges to Increasing the Number of United States Coast Guard Credentialed Mariners: Report to Congress*, May 22, 2020, pp. 23–29, https://www.maritime.dot.gov/sites/marad.dot.gov/files/2020-07/Mariner%20Opportunities%20and%20Challenges%20Report%20%28002%29.pdf (accessed November 23, 2020).

## Chapter 9. Developing Leaders for Great Power Competition

1. John F. Lehman, *Oceans Ventured: Winning the Cold War at Sea* (New York: W. W. Norton, 2018), 46, 49, 53–55, 58–59, 61, 70, 73, 85–87, 92, 99, 103–4, 107, 112, 119, 129, 145–46, 153–54, 173, 194–95, 225, 228, 235, 255.

2. See Ronald O'Rourke, "Statement before the Subcommittee on Seapower and Projection Forces, Committee on Armed Services, U.S. House of Representatives, Hearing on Future Force Structure Requirements for the United States Navy," June 4, 2020, https://www.congress.gov/116/meeting/house/110772/witnesses/HHRG-116-AS28-Wstate-ORourkeR-20200604.pdf (accessed December 6, 2020), and Ronald O'Rourke, "Navy Force Structure and Shipbuilding Plans: Background and Issues for Congress," Congressional Research Service Report for Members and Committees of Congress No. RL32665, December 1, 2020, https://fas.org/sgp/crs/weapons/RL32665.pdf (accessed December 6, 2020).

3. U.S. Navy, "Executive Summary: 2016 Navy Force Structure Assessment (FSA)," December 15, 2016, http:/static.politico.com/b9/99/0ad9f79847bf8e8f6549c445f980/2016-navy-force-structure-assessment-fsa-executive-summary.pdf (accessed December 6, 2020).

4. U.S. Navy, Office of the CNO, *A Design for Maintaining Maritime Superiority, Version 2.0*, December 2018, https://www.sdmac.org/media/uploads/a_design_for_maintaining_maritime_superiority_ver_2.0.pdf (accessed December 6, 2020).

5. U.S. Navy, Office of the CNO, *A Design for Maintaining Maritime Superiority, Version 2.0,* 9.

6. Sam LaGrone, "SECDEF Esper Holds Back 30-Year Shipbuilding Outlook, New 355-Ship Plan Ahead of HASC Testimony," USNI News, February 25, 2020, https://news.usni.org/2020/02/25/secdef-esper-holds-back-30-year-shipbuilding-outlook-new-355-ship-plan-ahead-of-hasc-testimony (accessed November 21, 2020).

7. See, for example, U.S. Department of the Navy, . . . *From the Sea: Preparing the Naval Service for the 21st Century,* September 1992, https://www.hsdl.org/?view&did=484786 (accessed December 6, 2020), and U.S. Marine Corps, U.S. Navy, and U.S. Coast Guard, *A Cooperative Strategy for 21st Century Seapower,* March 2015, https://www.globalsecurity.org/military/library/policy/navy/21st-century-seapower_strategy_201503.pdf (accessed December 6, 2020).

8. U.S. Department of the Navy, Office of the CNO, *Report to Congress on the Annual Long-Range Plan for Construction of Naval Vessels,* December 9, 2020, https://media.defense.gov/2020/Dec/10/2002549918/-1/-1/0/SHIPBUILDING%20PLAN%20DEC%2020_NAVY_OSD_OMB_FINAL.PDF/SHIPBUILDING%20PLAN%20DEC%2020_NAVY_OSD_OMB_FINAL.PDF (accessed January 4, 2021). See esp. table A1.1, "Force Structure Comparison," 9–10.

9. U.S. Navy, U.S. Marine Corps, and U.S. Coast Guard, *Advantage at Sea: Prevailing with Integrated All-Domain Naval Power,* December 2020, https://media.defense.gov/2020/Dec/17/2002553481/-1/-1/0/TRISERVICE STRATEGY.PDF/TRISERVICESTRATEGY.PDF (accessed January 4, 2021).

10. Department of the Navy FY2023 President's Budget, March 2022, p. 5, https://www.secnav.navy.mil/fmc/fmb/Documents/23pres/DON_Press_Brief.pdf (accessed April 2, 2022).

11. "CNO NAVPLAN," January 2021, https://media.defense.gov/2021/Jan/11/2002562551/-1/-1/1/CNO%20NAVPLAN%202021%20-%20FINAL.PDF (accessed April 2, 2022). "CNO NAVPLAN," July 2022, https://media.defense.gov/2022/Jul/26/2003042389/-1/-1/1/NAVIGATION%20PLAN%202022_SIGNED.PDF (accessed August 3, 2022).

12. U.S. Naval Academy, "Strategic Plan: Qualifications of a Naval Officer," https://www.usna.edu/StrategicPlan/archives/2011-2020/naval_officer_quals.php (accessed December 13, 2020). The source reflects that it was "compiled by Augustus C. Buell from letters written by John Paul Jones."

13. Adm. Michael M. Gilday, CNO, "FRAGO 01/2019: A Design for Maintaining Maritime Superiority," December 2019, https://media.defense.gov/2020/Jul/23/2002463491/-1/-1/1/CNO%20FRAGO%2001_2019.PDF (accessed January 4, 2021).

14. U.S. Department of the Navy, *Strategic Readiness Review 2017*, p. 5, http://s3.amazonaws.com/CHINFO/SRR+Final+12112017.pdf (accessed November 22, 2020).

15. Mark D. Faram, "Navy Sees Recruiting Challenges on the Horizon," *Navy Times*, November 2, 2018, https://www.navytimes.com/news/your-navy/2018/11/02/navy-sees-recruiting-challenges-on-the-horizon/ (accessed November 22, 2020).

16. The Honorable Thomas B. Modly, Acting Secretary of the Navy; Adm. Michael M. Gilday, CNO; and Gen. David H. Berger, Commandant of the U.S. Marine Corps, "Statement before the Committee on Armed Services, U.S. Senate, on Fiscal Year 2021 Department of the Navy Budget," March 5, 2020, p. 25, https://www.armed-services.senate.gov/imo/media/doc/Modly--Gilday--Berger_03-05-20.pdf (accessed November 22, 2020).

17. Joshua Taylor, "FAOs Lead the Way," U.S. Naval Institute *Proceedings* 145, no. 4 (April 2019), https://www.usni.org/magazines/proceedings/2019/april/faos-lead-way (accessed November 11, 2021).

18. Remarks by Secretary Carter and Q&A at the Shangri-La Dialogue, Singapore, June 5, 2016.

19. Shannon Tiezzi, "US, Japan Put South China Sea at the Forefront of Asia Summits," *The Diplomat*, November 18, 2015.

20. "Quad Joint Leaders' Statement," White House, May 24, 2022, https://www.whitehouse.gov/briefing-room/statements-releases/2022/05/24/quad-joint-leaders-statement/ (accessed August 3, 2022).

21. "AUKUS Leaders' Level Statement," White House, April 5, 2022, https://www.whitehouse.gov/briefing-room/statements-releases/2022/04/05/aukus-leaders-level-statement/ (accessed August 3, 2022).

22. Robert C. McFarlane, *Special Trust* (New York: Cadell & Davies, 1994), 28, 372–80.

23. Adm. Scott H. Swift (Ret.), foreword, xiv; Andrew S. Erickson and Ryan D. Martinson, "Introduction: 'War without Gun Smoke,'" 7–8; and Ryan D. Martinson and Andrew S. Erickson, "Conclusion: Options for the Definitive Use of US Sea Power in the Gray Zone," 293–98, all in *China's Maritime Gray Zone Operations*, ed. Andrew S. Erickson and Ryan D. Martinson (Annapolis: Naval Institute Press; Newport, RI: China Maritime Studies Institute, U.S. Naval War College, 2019).

24. Hunter Stires, "Win without Fighting," U.S. Naval Institute *Proceedings* 146, no. 6 (June 2020), https://www.usni.org/magazines/proceedings/2020/june/win-without-fighting (accessed November 23, 2020).

25. Fact Sheet, "Active Denial Technology (ADT)," U.S. Department of Defense, Joint Intermediate Force Capabilities Office, Non-lethal Weapons Program, updated August 2020, https://jnlwp.defense.gov/Portals/50/Documents/Press_Room/Fact_Sheets/FACT%20SHEET_ADT_AUG20.pdf (accessed January 4, 2021). "The Department of Defense Non-Lethal Weapons

Program stimulates and coordinates non-lethal weapons requirements of the US Armed Services and allocates resources to help meet these requirements. The Commandant of the Marine Corps serves as the Department of Defense Non-Lethal Weapons Executive Agent. Located at Marine Corps Base Quantico, Va., the Joint Intermediate Force Capabilities Office serves as the Department of Defense Non-Lethal Weapons Program Executive Agent's day-to-day management office." U.S. Department of Defense, Joint Intermediate Force Capabilities Office, Non-lethal Weapons Program, "Organization," https://jnlwp.defense.gov/About/Organization/ (accessed January 4, 2021).

26. "US Navy Delays Test of Future Force Concepts due to COVID-19," *Maritime Executive*, March 25, 2020, https://www.maritime-executive.com/article/u-s-navy-delays-test-of-future-force-concepts-due-to-covid-19 (accessed November 22, 2020).

27. U.S. Navy, Office of Naval Research, Corporate Strategic Communications, "Unmanned Capabilities Front and Center during Naval Exercise," April 22, 2021, https://www.navy.mil/Press-Office/News-Stories/Article/2582101/unmanned-capabilities-front-and-center-during-naval-exercise/ (accessed July 14, 2021).

28. David Axe, "The Pentagon's Robot Warship Just Fired Its First Missile," *Forbes*, September 8, 2021, https://www.forbes.com/sites/davidaxe/2021/09/08/the-pentagons-robot-warships-just-fired-their-first-missiles/?sh=2afe964e3c78 (accessed November 7, 2021).

29. Joseph Trevithick, "New Navy Task Force Will Be All about Bringing Unmanned Capabilities to the Middle East," *The Drive*, September 8, 2021, https://www.thedrive.com/the-war-zone/42302/new-navy-task-force-will-be-all-about-bringing-unmanned-capabilities-to-the-middle-east (accessed November 7, 2021).

30. U.S. Navy, Navy Recruiting Command, "About the Navy Reserve," https://www.navy.com/forward (accessed November 22, 2020).

31. Vice Adm. Luke M. McCollum, U.S. Navy, Chief of Navy Reserve, "Statement before the Subcommittee on Defense, Committee on Appropriations, U.S. Senate, on Fiscal Year 2021 National Guard and Reserve," March 4, 2020, pp. 4–5, https://www.appropriations.senate.gov/imo/media/doc/03.04.20--McCollum%20Testimony.pdf (accessed November 22, 2020).

32. McCollum, "Statement on Fiscal Year 2021 National Guard and Reserve," 8, 11.

33. McCollum, "Statement on Fiscal Year 2021 National Guard and Reserve," 11–12.

34. Albert A. Nofi, *The Naval Militia: A Neglected Asset?* (Alexandria, VA: Center for Naval Analyses, 2007), 12–20, https://www.cna.org/CNA_files/PDF/D0015586.A1.pdf (accessed November 22, 2020).

35. U.S. National Guard, "State Partnership Program: Partner Focused, Strategically Aligned," https://www.nationalguard.mil/leadership/joint-staff/j-5 /international-affairs-division/state-partnership-program/ (accessed November 23, 2020).

## Conclusion

1. Nathaniel Bowditch, *American Practical Navigator: An Epitome of Navigation*, vol. 1 (Washington: Defense Mapping Agency Hydrographic/Topographic Center, 1984), 340-44.

2. Terry L. Deibel, *Foreign Affairs Strategy: Logic for American Statecraft* (New York: Cambridge University Press, 2007), 16-17.

3. Using inflation rates provided by the Bureau of Labor Statistics, a baseline Navy budget starting with the Navy's 1989 budget of $97.675 billion was calculated. DoD and Navy budgets were accessed from Naval History and Heritage Command and World Bank data on reported DoD budgets. See U.S. Navy, Naval History and Heritage Command, "Budget of the US Navy: 1794–2014," August 23, 2017, https://www.history.navy.mil/research/library /online-reading-room/title-list-alphabetically/b/budget-of-the-us-navy-1794-to-2004.html (accessed November 19, 2020); and Macrotrends, "US Military Spending/Defense Budget 1960–2020," https://www.macrotrends .net/countries/USA/united-states/military-spending-defense-budget (accessed November 19, 2020).

4. Kyle Mizokami, "The US Navy Won't Bring Back Mothballed Ships to Boost the Fleet," *Popular Mechanics*, February 21, 2019, https://www.popularme chanics.com/military/navy-ships/a26448230/navy-wont-bring-back-moth balled-ships/ (accessed November 24, 2020).

5. Evan Munsing and Christopher J. Lamb, *Joint Interagency Task Force–South: The Best Known, Least Understood Interagency Success*, National Defense University, Institute for National Strategic Studies, Center for Strategic Research, *Strategic Perspectives*, no. 5, June 2011, https://ndupress.ndu.edu /Portals/68/Documents/stratperspective/inss/Strategic-Perspectives-5.pdf (accessed November 24, 2020).

6. Testimony by Elbridge A. Colby in *Senate Armed Services Committee Hearing on Implementation of the National Defense Strategy*, January 29, 2019, pp. 4–6, 11, https://www.armed-services.senate.gov/imo/media/doc /Colby_01-29-19.pdf (accessed December 30, 2020).

# BIBLIOGRAPHY

## Selected Books

Andrew, Christopher, and Vasili Mitokhin. *The Sword and the Shield*. New York: Basic Books, 1999.

Arena, Mark V., Cesse Ip, Kristy N. Kamarck, Frank W. Lacroix, Gordon T. Lee, Robert E. Murphy, and John F. Schank. *Learning from Experience*, vol. 2: *Lessons from the US Navy's Ohio, Seawolf and Virginia Submarine Programs*. Santa Monica, CA: RAND Corporation, 2011.

Baker, James E. *In the Common Defense: National Security Law for Perilous Times*. Cambridge: Cambridge University Press, 2007.

Barnett, Thomas P. M. *The Pentagon's New Map: Blueprint for Action*. New York: G. P. Putnam's Sons, 2003.

Belton, Catherine. *Putin's People: How the KGB Took Back Russia and Then Took On the West*. New York: Farrar, Straus and Giroux, 2020.

Bowditch, Nathaniel. *American Practical Navigator: An Epitome of Navigation*. Vol. 1. Washington: Defense Mapping Agency Hydrographic/Topographic Center, 1984.

Bracken, Paul. *The Second Nuclear Age: Strategy, Danger, and the New Power Politics*. New York: Henry Holt and Co., 2012.

Brooks, Stephen G. *Producing Security: Multinational Corporations, Globalization and the Changing Calculus of Conflict*. Princeton, NJ: Princeton University Press, 2005.

Brose, Christian. *The Kill Chain: Defending America in the Future of High-Tech Warfare*. New York: Hachette Books, 2020.

Brynjolfsson, Erik, and Andrew McAfee. *The Second Machine Age: Work, Progress and Prosperity in a Time of Brilliant Technologies*. New York: W. W. Norton & Company, 2014.

Colby, Elbridge A. *The Strategy of Denial: American Defense in an Age of Great Power Conflict*. New Haven, CT: Yale University Press, 2021.

Cole, Bernard D. *Asian Maritime Strategies: Navigating Troubled Waters*. Annapolis: Naval Institute Press, 2013.

Cooley, Alexander. *Base Politics: Democratic Change and the US Military Overseas.* Ithaca, NY: Cornell University Press, 2008.

Cooper, John F. *China's Foreign Aid and Investment Diplomacy*, vol. 2: *History and Practice in Asia, 1950–Present.* London: Palgrave Macmillan, 2016.

Corbett, Julian Stafford. *Some Principles of Maritime Strategy.* London: Longmans, Green and Company, 1911.

Cornell, Jimmy. *World Cruising Routes.* London: Adlard Coles, 2019.

Deibel, Terry L. *Foreign Affairs Strategy: Logic for American Statecraft.* New York: Cambridge University Press, 2007.

De La Pedraja, René. *The Russian Military Resurgence.* Jefferson, NC: McFarland & Company, 2019.

Drew, Christopher, and Sherry Sontag. *Blind Man's Bluff: The Untold Story of American Submarine Espionage.* New York: Public Affairs, 1998.

Finkelstein, David M. "Breaking the Paradigm: Drivers behind the PLA's Current Period of Reform." In *Chairman Xi Remakes the PLA.* Washington: National Defense University Press, 2019.

Friedman, Norman. *U.S. Aircraft Carriers: An Illustrated Design History.* Annapolis: Naval Institute Press, 1983.

Friedman, Norman. *U.S. Destroyers: An Illustrated Design History.* Rev. ed. Annapolis: Naval Institute Press, 2004.

Friedman, Thomas L. *The World Is Flat: A Brief History of the Twenty-First Century.* New York: Farrar, Straus and Giroux, 2005.

Giles, Lionel. *Sun Tzu on the Art of War.* Tokyo: Tuttle, 2008.

Glaser, Bonnie, and Matthew P. Funaiole. "China's Maritime Gray Zone Operations." In *China's Maritime Gray Zone Operations.* Annapolis: Naval Institute Press, 2019.

Globke, Werner. *Weyers Flottentaschenbuch 2022/2022.* Bonn: Bernard & Graefe, 2020.

Gore, Lance. *The Chinese Communist Party and China's Capitalist Revolution: The Political Impact of Market.* London: Routledge, 2011.

Gorshkov, S. G. *The Sea Power of the State.* Oxford: Pergamon, 1979.

Gresh, Geoffrey F. *To Rule Eurasia's Waves: The New Great Power Competition at Sea.* New Haven, CT: Yale University Press, 2020.

Grygiel, Jakub J., and A. Wess Mitchell. *The Unquiet Frontier: Rising Rivals, Vulnerable Allies, and the Crisis of American Power.* Princeton, NJ: Princeton University Press, 2016.

Guangqian, Peng, and Yao Youzhi. *The Science of Military Strategy.* Beijing: Military Science Publishing House, 2005.

Guest, Robert. *Borderless Economics: Chinese Sea Turtles, Indian Fridges and the New Fruits of Global Capitalism.* New York: Palgrave Macmillan, 2011.

Gunitsky, Seva. *Aftershocks: Great Powers and Domestic Reforms in the Twentieth Century*. Princeton, NJ: Princeton University Press, 2017.

Haddock, Robert. *Fire on the Water: China, America and the Future of the Pacific*. Annapolis: Naval Institute Press, 2014.

Haynes, Peter D. *Toward a New Maritime Strategy: American Naval Thinking in the Post–Cold War Era*. Annapolis: Naval Institute Press, 2015.

Hendrix, Henry J. *To Provide and Maintain a Navy*. Annapolis: Focsle, 2020.

Holmes, James R., and Toshi Yoshihara. *Red Star over the Pacific: China's Risa and the Challenge to U.S. Maritime Strategy*. Annapolis: Naval Institute Press, 2010.

Hutchings, Graham. *Modern China: A Guide to a Century of Change*. Cambridge, MA: Harvard University Press, 2001.

Jaeger, Lars. *The Second Quantum Revolution: From Entanglement to Quantum Computing and Other Super-Technologies*. Switzerland: Springer Nature, 2018.

James, Lawrence. *The Rise and Fall of the British Empire*. New York: St. Martin's, 1994.

Kaplan, Robert D. *Asia's Cauldron: The South China Sea and the End of a Stable Pacific*. New York: Random House, 2014.

Kehn, Donald M. *In the Highest Degree Tragic: The Sacrifice of the US Asiatic Fleet in the East Indies during World War II*. Sterling: Potomac Books, 2017.

Khanna, Parag. *Connectography: Mapping the Future of Global Civilization*. New York: Random House, 2016.

Kim, W. Chan, and Renee Mauborgne. *Blue Ocean Shift: Beyond Competing—Proven Steps to Inspire Confidence and Seize New Growth*. New York: Hachette Books, 2017.

Kissinger, Henry. *Diplomacy*. New York: Simon & Schuster, 1994.

Kittrie, Orde F. *Lawfare: Law as a Weapon of War*. Oxford: Oxford University Press, 2016.

Klare, Michael T. *Rising Powers, Shrinking Planet: The New Geopolitics of Energy*. New York: Henry Holt and Company, 2008.

Kroenig, Matthew. *The Return of Great Power Rivalry*. New York: Oxford University Press, 2020.

Kuehn, John T. *Agents of Innovation: The General Board and the Design of the Fleet That Defeated the Japanese Navy*. Annapolis: Naval Institute Press, 2008.

Kurzweil, Ray. *How to Create a Mind: The Secret of Human Thought Revealed*. London: Penguin Books, 2012.

Leebaert, Derek. *The Fifty-Year Wound: The True Price of America's Cold War Victory*. Boston: Little, Brown, 2002.

Lehman, John. *Oceans Ventured: Winning the Cold War at Sea.* New York: W. W. Norton, 2018.

Loewenthal, Robert G. "Cold War Insights into China's New Ballistic-Missile Submarine Fleet." In *China's Future Nuclear Submarine Force,* edited by Andrew S. Erickson, Lyle J. Goldstein, William S. Murray, and Andrew R. Wilson, 286–301. Annapolis: Naval Institute Press, 2007.

Lynch, Allen C. *Vladimir Putin and Russian Statecraft.* Washington: Potomac Books, 2011.

Mahan, Alfred Thayer. *The Influence of Sea Power upon History.* Boston: Little, Brown and Company, 1894.

Mahnken, Thomas G. *Competitive Strategies for the 21st Century: Theory, History and Practice.* Stanford, CA: Stanford University Press, 2012.

Mankoff, Jeffrey. *Russian Foreign Policy: The Return of Great Power Politics.* 2nd ed. Lanham, MD: Rowman & Littlefield, 2012.

McBride, William M. "Technological Revolution at Sea." In *America, Sea Power, and the World,* edited by James C. Bradford. Chichester, U.K.: John Wiley & Sons, 2016.

McDevitt, Michael A. *China as a Twenty-First-Century Naval Power.* Annapolis: Naval Institute Press, 2020.

McFarlane, Robert C. *Special Trust.* New York: Cadell & Davies, 1994.

McGregor, Richard. *The Party: The Secret World of China's Communist Rulers.* New York: HarperCollins, 2010.

Mearsheimer, John J. *The Tragedy of Great Power Politics.* New York: W. W. Norton, 2014.

Murray, Williamson. *Strategy for Chaos: Revolutions in Military Affairs and the Evidence of History.* London: Taylor and Francis, 2005.

Murray, Williamson, and Allan R. Millett, eds. *Military Innovation in the Interwar Period.* Cambridge: Cambridge University Press, 1996.

Naim, Moises. *Illicit.* New York: Anchor Books, 2006.

Neustadt, Richard E., and Ernest R. May. *Thinking in Time: The Uses of History for Decision Makers.* New York: Free Press, 1986.

Nordenman, Magnus. *The New Battle for the Atlantic: Emerging Naval Competition with Russia in the Far North.* Annapolis: Naval Institute Press, 2019.

Nye, Joseph S. *Soft Power: The Means to Success in World Politics.* New York: Public Affairs, 2004.

O'Hanlon, Michael E., and James Steinberg. *Strategic Reassurance and Resolve: US-China Relations in the Twenty-First Century.* Princeton, NJ: Princeton University Press, 2014.

Paulson, Henry. *Dealing with China: An Insider Unmasks the New Economic Superpower.* New York: Twelve, 2015.

Posen, Barry R. *Restraint: A New Foundation for US Grand Strategy.* Ithaca, NY: Cornell University Press, 2014.

Rahim, Saad. "China's Energy Strategy toward the Middle East." In *China's Energy Strategy: The Impact on Beijing's Maritime Policies.* Annapolis: Naval Institute Press, 2008.

Renz, Bettina. *Russia's Military Revival.* Cambridge: Polity, 2018.

Rigger, Shelley. *Why Taiwan Matters: Small Island, Global Powerhouse.* New York: Rowman & Littlefield, 2011.

Rothkopf, David. *Running the World: The Inside Story of the National Security Council and the Architects of American Power.* New York: PublicAffairs, 2004.

Salvatore, Dominick. *International Economics.* 8th ed. New York: John Wiley & Sons, 2020.

Shambaugh, David. *Modernizing China's Military: Progress, Problems, and Prospects.* Berkeley: University of California Press, 2002.

Stopford, Martin. *Maritime Economics.* London: Taylor and Francis, 2003.

Walter, Carl E., and Fraser J. T. Howie. *Red Capitalism: The Fragile Financial Foundation of China's Extraordinary Rise.* Singapore: John Wiley and Sons, 2011.

Wise, David. *Tiger Trap: America's Secret Spy War with China.* New York: Houghton Mifflin Harcourt, 2011.

Zarate, Juan C. *Treasury's War: The Unleashing of a New Era of Financial Warfare.* New York: PublicAffairs, 2013.

Zeihan, Peter. *The Accidental Super Power: The Generation of American Preeminence and the Coming Global Disorder.* New York: Twelve, 2014.

## Monographs, Case Studies, and Reports

Acemoglu, Daron, and James A. Robinson. *Why Nations Fail: The Origin of Power, Prosperity and Poverty.* New York: Crown, 2012.

Ashta, Kartik. "China's Expanding Influence in the UN System." Gateway House, Report No. 4, May 2021, https://www.gatewayhouse.in/wp-content /uploads/2021/05/Chinas-Expanding-Influence-in-the-UN-System_Gate way-House_Report_2021.pdf (accessed January 2, 2022).

*Asia Maritime Transparency Initiative.* Center for Strategic and International Studies, https://amti.csis.org (accessed August 2, 2022).

Bachman, Elizabeth. "Black and White and Red All Over: China's Improving Foreign-Directed Media." Center for Naval Analyses, August 2020, https://www .cna.org/CNA_files/PDF/DRM-2020-U-027331-1Rev.pdf (accessed January 2, 2022).

Bassler, Chris. "Mind the Power Gap: The American Energy Arsenal and Chinese Insecurity." Center for Strategic and Budgetary Assessments, August 25, 2021, https://csbaonline.org/research/publications/mind-the-power-gap-the-american-energy-arsenal-and-chinese-insecurity (accessed January 2, 2022).

Bassler, Chris, Bryan W. Durkee, Thomas G. Mahnken, and Travis Sharp. "Implementing Deterrence by Detection: Innovative Capabilities, Processes, and Organizations for Situational Awareness in the Indo-Pacific Region." Center for Strategic and Budgetary Assessments, July 14, 2021, https://csbaonline.org/research/publications/implementing-deterrence-by-detection-innovative-capabilities-processes-and-organizations-for-situational-awareness-in-the-indo-pacific-region (accessed January 2, 2022).

Bellacqua, James. *The Future of China-Russia Relations*. Lexington: University Press of Kentucky, 2010.

Bhandari, Amit, Chaitanya Giri, and Kunal Kulkarni. "US Sanctions on Russia and Its Impact on India." Gateway House, Research Paper no. 14, September 4, 2018, https://www.gatewayhouse.in/wp-content/uploads/2019/01/Gateway_House_RUSSIA_PAPER_13_10_18_FONT_11.pdf (accessed January 2, 2022).

Blechman, Barry M., James A. Siebens, and Melanie W. Sisson. *Military Coercion and US Foreign Policy: The Use of Force Short of War*. New York: Taylor & Francis, 2020.

Bradford, John, and Jeffrey Ordaniel. "Advancing a Rules-Based Maritime Order in the Indo-Pacific." Pacific Forum, July 2021, https://pacforum.org/wp-content/uploads/2021/07/Issues-and-Insights-Vol-21-SR2-ver-3.pdf (accessed January 2, 2022).

Bricker, Mindy Kay, *The Fukushima Daiichi Nuclear Power Station Disaster*. London: Routledge, 2014.

Buszynski, Leszek, and Christopher B. Roberts. *The South China Sea Maritime Dispute: Political, Legal and Regional Perspectives*. New York: Routledge, 2015.

Caballero-Anthony, Mely, and Margareth Sembiring. "Resilience in the Face of Disruptions." S. Rajaratnam School of International Studies, February 19, 2019, https://www.rsis.edu.sg/rsis-publication/nts/resilience-in-the-face-of-disruptions-2/#.YdHyHi-B0Ts (accessed January 2, 2022).

Calfee, Sharif H. "Delivering Advanced Unmanned Autonomous Systems and Artificial Intelligence for Naval Superiority." Center for Strategic and Budgetary Assessments, May 25, 2021, https://csbaonline.org/research/publications/delivering-advanced-unmanned-autonomous-systems-and-artificial-intelligence-for-naval-superiority (accessed January 2, 2022).

Cevallos, Astrid Stuth, Arthur Chan, Michael S. Chase, Larry Hanauer, Michael Johnson, Bonny Lin, Logan Ma, Ivan W. Rasmussen, Andrew Scobell, Howard J. Shatz, Aaron Strong, and Eric Warner. "At the Dawn of Belt and

Road China in the Developing World." RAND Corporation, https://www.rand.org/pubs/research_reports/RR2273.html (accessed January 2, 2022).

Chandler, Nathan, Samuel Charap, John J. Drennan, Edward Geist, Bryan Frederick, and Jennifer Kavanagh. "Russia's Military Interventions Patterns, Drivers, and Signposts." RAND Corporation, September 27, 2021, https://www.rand.org/pubs/research_reports/RRA444-3.html (accessed January 2, 2022).

Chandler, Nathan, Christian Curriden, Bryan Frederick, Timothy R. Heath, and Jennifer Kavanagh. "China's Military Interventions Patterns, Drivers, and Signposts." RAND Corporation, September 27, 2021, https://www.rand.org/pubs/research_reports/RRA444-4.html (accessed January 2, 2022).

Chase, Michael S., Eric Heginbotham, and Kevin L. Pollpeter. "The Creation of the PLA Strategic Support Force and Its Implications for Chinese Military Space Operations." RAND Corporation, November 10, 2017, https://www.rand.org/pubs/research_reports/RR2058.html (accessed January 2, 2022).

Cheng, Calvin. "The Regional Comprehensive Economic Partnership (RCEP): What This Means for ASEAN and Malaysia." Institute of Strategic and International Studies Malaysia, November 17, 2020, https://www.isis.org.my/2020/11/17/the-regional-comprehensive-economic-partnership-rcep/ (accessed January 2, 2022).

Cordesman, Anthony H. "Chronology of Possible Russian Gray Area and Hybrid Warfare Operations." Center for Strategic and International Studies, December 8, 2020, https://www.csis.org/analysis/chronology-possible-russian-gray-area-and-hybrid-warfare-operations (accessed January 2, 2022).

Curriden, Christian, Rafiq Dossani, and Lynn Hu. "Implementing China's Grand Strategy in Asia through Institutions." RAND Corporation, November 29, 2021, https://www.rand.org/pubs/research_reports/RRA16531-1.html (accessed January 2, 2022).

Ditter, Timothy, Anthony Miller, Kevin Pollpeter, and Brian Waidelich. "China's Space Narrative Examining the Portrayal of the US-China Space Relationship in Chinese Sources and Its Implications for the United States." Center for Naval Analyses, October 2, 2020, https://www.cna.org/CNA_files/PDF/DES-2020-U-028472-Final.pdf (accessed January 2, 2022).

Eaton, Derek, David R. Frelinger, Victoria A. Greenfield, John Halliday, Michael J. Lostumbo, Michael J. McNerney, Patrick Mills, Bruce R. Nardulli, Eric Peltz, and Stacie L. Pettyjohn. "Overseas Basing of US Military Forces." RAND Corporation, 2013, https://www.rand.org/pubs/research_reports/RR201.html (accessed January 2, 2022).

Erickson., Andrew S. *Chinese Naval Shipbuilding.* Annapolis: Naval Institute Press, 2016.

Erickson, Andrew S., and Ryan D. Martinson. *China's Maritime Gray Zone Operations*. Annapolis: Naval Institute Press, 2019.

Estes, Madison A. "Prevailing under the Nuclear Shadow: A New Framework for US Escalation Management." Center for Naval Analyses, September 2020, https://www.cna.org/CNA_files/PDF/CRM-2020-U-027973-Final%20(002) .pdf (accessed January 2, 2022).

Gabuev, Alexander, and Leonid Kovachich. "Comrades in Tweets? The Contours and Limits of China-Russia Cooperation on Digital Propaganda." Carnegie: Moscow Center, June 3, 2021, https://carnegiemoscow.org/2021/06/03/com rades-in-tweets-contours-and-limits-of-china-russia-cooperation-on-digi tal-propaganda-pub-84673 (accessed January 2, 2022).

Han, Eugeniu, Logan Mă, Andrew Radin, Clint Reach, Howard J. Shatz, Andrew Scobell, Elina Treyger, J. D. Williams, and Sean M. Zeigler. "China-Russia Cooperation Determining Factors, Future Trajectories, Implications for the United States." RAND Corporation, 2021, https://www.rand.org/pubs /research_reports/RR3067.html (accessed January 2, 2022).

Hannas, William C., James Mulvenon, and Anna B. Puglisi. *Chinese Industrial Espionage: Technology Acquisition and Military Modernization*. New York: Routledge, 2013.

Harold, Scott W., Logan Ma, and Lyle J. Morris. "Countering China's Efforts to Isolate Taiwan Diplomatically in Latin America and the Caribbean: The Role of Development Assistance and Disaster Relief." RAND Corporation, May 13, 2019, https://www.rand.org/pubs/research_reports/RR2885.html (accessed January 2, 2022).

Hashimova, Umida, and Michael McDevitt. "Views of China's Presence in the Indian Ocean Region: A Workshop Report." Center for Naval Analyses, March 2020, https://www.cna.org/CNA_files/PDF/DCP-2019-U-022222-1Rev%20(002).pdf (accessed January 2, 2022).

Ito, Nobuyoshi. "Britain and the Dissolution of the Mediterranean Fleet: Convergence of the End of Empire and Alliance Management." National Institute for Defense Studies, January 2021, http://www.nids.mod.go.jp/english/publica tion/briefing/pdf/2021/briefing_e202101.pdf (accessed January 2, 2022).

Kamphausen, Roy, David Lai, and Andrew Scobell. *Chinese Lessons from Other People's Wars*. Carlisle, PA: Strategic Studies Institute, 2011.

Kikuchi, Tomoo. "Financial Cooperation in East Asia." S. Rajaratnam School of International Studies, April 9, 2019, https://www.rsis.edu.sg/rsis-pub lication/cms/mn35-financial-cooperation-in-east-asia/#.YdHx1S-B0Ts (accessed January 2, 2022).

Kripalani, Manjeet. "Quad Economy and Technology Task Force: A Time for Concerted Action." Gateway House, August 2021, https://www.gateway house.in/wp-content/uploads/2021/08/Quad-Economy-and-Technology-Task-Force-Report_GH_2021.pdf (accessed January 2, 2022).

Landry, Pierre F. *Decentralized Authoritarianism in China*. Cambridge: Cambridge University Press, 2008.

Mapp, Wayne. "Military Modernisation and Buildup in the Asia Pacific: The Case for Restraint." S. Rajaratnam School of International Studies, November 21, 2014, https://www.rsis.edu.sg/rsis-publication/rsis/monograph31/#.YdHyiS-B0Ts (accessed January 2, 2022).

*The Military Balance*. International Institute for Strategic Studies, https://www.iiss.org/publications/the-military-balance (accessed January 2, 2022).

Monaghan, Andrew. "How Moscow Understands War and Military Strategy." Center for Naval Analyses, November 2020, https://www.cna.org/CNA_files/PDF/IOP-2020-U-028629-Final.pdf (accessed January 2, 2022).

National Institute for Defense Studies. *China Security Report*. http://www.nids.mod.go.jp/english/publication/chinareport/index.html (accessed January 2, 2022).

Nersisyan, Leonid. "Russian Combat Aviation: Procurement, Modernization and Future Outlook." Center for Naval Analyses, December 2020, https://www.cna.org/CNA_files/PDF/IOP-2020-U-028810-Final.pdf (accessed January 2, 2022).

Overfield, Cornell. "Diego Garcia: US and Allied Basing Rights in the Era of Great Power Competition." Center for Naval Analyses, July 2020, https://www.cna.org/CNA_files/PDF/CCP-2020-U-027652-Final.pdf (accessed January 2, 2022).

Pacatte, William C. "Competing to Win: A Coalition Approach to Countering the BRI." Center for Strategic and International Studies, December 2019, https://csis-website-prod.s3.amazonaws.com/s3fs-public/publication/191219Pacatte_Countering_BRI_WEB_FINAL.pdf (accessed January 2, 2022).

Sadler, Brent. "Rebuilding America's Military Project: United States Navy." The Heritage Foundation, February 18, 2021, https://www.heritage.org/defense/report/rebuilding-americas-military-the-united-states-navy.

Schwab, Klaus. *The Fourth Industrial Revolution*. Geneva: World Economic Forum, 2016.

Searight, Amy. "Countering China's Influence Activities: Lessons from Australia." Center for Strategic and International Studies, July 31, 2020, https://www.csis.org/analysis/countering-chinas-influence-activities-lessons-australia (accessed January 2, 2022).

*Strategic Survey*. International Institute for Strategic Studies, https://www.iiss.org/publications/strategic-survey (accessed January 2, 2022).

Tallis, Joshua. "Maritime Security and Great Power Competition: Maintaining the US-Led International Order." Center for Naval Analyses, May 2020, https://www.cna.org/CNA_files/PDF/DOP-2020-U-025085-Final.pdf (accessed January 2, 2022).

Tanner, Travis, and Ashley J. Tellis. *China's Military Challenge*. Seattle: National Bureau of Asian Research, 2012.

Volkov, Denis. "Russian Elite Opinion after Crimea." Moscow Center, Carnegie Endowment for International Peace, March 23, 2016, https://carnegiemos cow.org/2016/03/23/russian-elite-opinion-after-crimea-pub-63094 (accessed January 2, 2022).

Williams, Ian. "More Than Missiles: China Previews Its New Way of War." Center for Strategic and International Studies, October 16, 2019, https://www.csis .org/analysis/more-missiles-china-previews-its-new-way-war (accessed January 2, 2022).

Zysk, Katarzyna. "Russia's Military Build-Up in the Arctic to What End?" Center for Naval Analyses, September 2020, https://www.cna.org/CNA_files/PDF /IOP-2020-U-027998-Final.pdf (accessed January 2, 2022).

**Interviews and Correspondence**

Braithwaite, Kenneth, Secretary of the Navy (2020–21)

Cheng, Dean, Senior Research Fellow on Chinese Political and Security Affairs, Heritage Foundation

Clark, Bryan, Director, Chief of Naval Operations Strategic Actions Group (2011–13), and Senior Fellow, Hudson Institute (2020–)

Coffey, Luke, Director, Douglas and Sarah Allison Center for Foreign Policy

Cole, Bernard, Professor, National War College

Cullom, Philip, Vice Admiral (Ret.), U.S. Navy; Deputy Chief of Naval Operations for Fleet Readiness and Logistics (2012–17)

Egel, Daniel, developmental economist

Filler, Lukas, Director, China Strategic Focus Group at U.S. Indo-Pacific Command (2019–21)

Finkelstein, David M., Vice President and Director, China and Indo-Pacific Security Affairs Division, Center for Naval Analyses

Fireman, Howard, Deputy Director, Programming Division, Naval Architect of the Navy (2009–14)

Foggo III, James G., Admiral (Ret.), U.S. Navy: Commander Naval Forces Europe and Africa (2017–20)

Klinck, Heino, Deputy Assistant Secretary of Defense for East Asia (2019–21)

Lehman, John, Secretary of the Navy (1981–87)

Malavet, Joaquin F., Major General (Ret.), U.S. Marine Corps: Director, Strategic Planning and Policy U.S. Indo-Pacific Command (2017–19)

Martin, William, Executive Secretary, U.S. National Security Council (1985–86); Special Assistant to the President for National Security Affairs (1983–85)

Mazarr, Mike, Professor and Associate Dean, National War College (2002–14)

McFarlane, Robert, U.S. National Security Advisor (1983–85) and U.S. Deputy National Security Advisor (1982–83)

Middendorf, J. William, Secretary of the Navy (1974–77)

Nesheiwat, Julia, U.S. Commissioner at U.S. Arctic Research Commission (2020–)

Roper, Will, Assistant Secretary of the Air Force for Acquisition, Technology and Logistics (2018–21), Director of DoD Strategic Capabilities Office (2012–18)

Selby, Lorin, Rear Admiral, U.S. Navy: Chief of Naval Research (2020–)

Stilwell, David R., Assistant Secretary, Bureau of East Asian and Pacific Affairs (2019–21)

Stires, Hunter, Fellow, John B. Hattendorf Center for Maritime Historical Research (2017–)

Swift, Scott, Admiral (Ret.), U.S. Navy: Commander, Pacific Fleet (2015–18)

Switzer, Rick. Economic Affairs Chief, East Asia Pacific Bureau (2004–20)

Vandroff, Mark, Deputy Assistant to the President and Senior Director for Defense Policy (2020–21)

Weitz, Rockford, Professor of Practice and Director of Maritime Studies, Fletcher School at Tufts University (2015–)

Wills, Steven, research analyst at Center for Naval Analyses and author

### Archives, Congressional Hearings, and Official Files

"Defense White Paper: China's National Defense in the New Era." State Council Information Office of the People's Republic of China, July 24, 2019, http://english.scio.gov.cn/2019-07/24/content_75026800_5.htm (accessed January 2, 2022).

Department of the Navy. Budget Materials. https://www.secnav.navy.mil/fmc/fmb/Pages/Fiscal-Year-2020.aspx (accessed January 2, 2022).

"Global Security Challenges and Strategy." U.S. Senate Armed Service Committee, March 2, 2021, https://www.armed-services.senate.gov/hearings/21-03-02-global-security-challenges-and-strategy (accessed January 2, 2022).

International Tribunal for the Law of the Sea. Cases. https://www.itlos.org/en/main/cases/list-of-cases/ (accessed January 2, 2022).

Millennium Challenge Corporation of USA. *Our Impact.* https://www.mcc.gov/our-impact (accessed January 2, 2022).

Ministry of Defence of the Russian Federation. https://eng.mil.ru/en/index.htm (accessed January 2, 2022).

Ministry of Foreign Affairs of Japan. *Diplomatic Bluebook.* https://www.mofa.go.jp/policy/other/bluebook/index.html (accessed January 2, 2022).

Ministry of Foreign Affairs of Japan. *Free and Open Indo-Pacific.* https://www.mofa.go.jp/policy/page25e_000278.html (accessed January 2, 2022).

Ministry of Foreign Affairs of the People's Republic of China. https://www.fmprc.gov.cn/mfa_eng/ (accessed January 2, 2022).

Ministry of Foreign Affairs of the Russian Federation. "Government Decisions." http://government.ru/en/docs/ (accessed January 2, 2022).

Ministry of Foreign Affairs of the Russian Federation. "Description." http://gov ernment.ru/en/department/92/events/ (accessed January 2, 2022).

National Institute for Defense Studies. Military Archives (Japan). http://www.nids. mod.go.jp/english/military_archives/index.html (accessed January 2, 2022).

National Oceanic and Atmospheric Administration. Weather and Climate Resources. https://www.noaa.gov/tools-and-resources/weather-and-climate-resources (accessed January 2, 2022).

Naval History and Heritage Command. Archives. https://www.history.navy.mil /research/archives.html (accessed January 2, 2022).

Naval History and Heritage Command. "US Ship Force Levels." https://www .history.navy.mil/research/histories/ship-histories/us-ship-force-levels.html (accessed January 2, 2022).

NAVSEA Shipbuilding Support Office. Naval Vessel Register. https://www.nvr .navy.mil (accessed January 2, 2022).

"Nomination—Aquilino" (video). U.S. Senate Armed Service Committee, March 23, 2021, https://www.armed-services.senate.gov/hearings/21-03-23-nomi nation_aquilino (accessed January 2, 2022).

Oceans and Law of the Sea, United Nations. "Convention and Related Agree-ments" and "Settlement of Disputes." https://www.un.org/Depts/los/index .htm (accessed January 2, 2022).

Office of Management and Budget, Executive Office of the President. "Statisti-cal Programs of the United States Government." https://www.whitehouse .gov/omb/information-regulatory-affairs/statistical-programs-standards/ (accessed January 2, 2022).

Office of Ocean and Polar Affairs, U.S. Department of State. Limits in the Seas. https://www.state.gov/limits-in-the-seas/ (accessed January 2, 2022).

"Open/Closed: The Posture of the Department of the Navy in Review of the Defense Authorization Request for Fiscal Year 2022 and the Future Years Defense Program" (video). U.S. Senate Armed Service Committee, June 22, 2021, https://www.armed-services.senate.gov/hearings/the-posture-of-the-depart ment-of-the-navy-in-review-of-the-defense-authorization-request-for-fiscal -year-2022-and-the-future-years-defense-program (accessed January 2, 2022).

"Open/Closed: United States Indo-Pacific Command" (video). U.S. Senate Armed Service Committee, March 9, 2021, https://www.armed-services.senate.gov /hearings/21-03-09-united-states-indo-pacific-command (accessed January 2, 2022).

Parliament of Australia, Parliamentary Library. https://www.aph.gov.au/About _Parliament/Parliamentary_Departments/Parliamentary_Library (accessed January 2, 2022).

Permanent Court of Arbitration. Cases, https://pca-cpa.org/en/cases/ (accessed January 2, 2022).

President of Russia, Russian Federation. *Documents Signed.* http://en.kremlin.ru /acts/news (accessed January 2, 2022).

"Review of the FY 2022 State Department Budget Request." Senate Foreign Relations Committee, June 8, 2021, https://www.foreign.senate.gov/hearings /review-of-the-fy-2022-state-department-budget-request (accessed January 2, 2022).

Russian Federation. *2021 National Security Strategy.* http://static.kremlin.ru /media/events/files/ru/QZw6hSk5z9gWq0plD1ZzmR5cER0g5tZC.pdf (accessed January 2, 2022).

"Strength through Partnership: Building the US-Taiwan Relationship." Senate Foreign Relations Committee, June 17, 2021, https://www.foreign.senate.gov /hearings/strength-through-partnership-building-the-us-taiwan-relation ship-061721 (accessed January 2, 2022).

"Subcommittee on Seapower and Projection Forces Markup of H.R. 4350— National Defense Authorization Act for Fiscal Year 2022." House Armed Services Committee, July 28, 2021, https://armedservices.house.gov /hearings?ID=3F53B7A4-C0CB-43C9-B774-C51BA76B2E13 (accessed January 2, 2022).

"To Receive Testimony on United States European Command and United States Transportation Command in Review of the Defense Authorization Request for Fiscal Year 2022 and the Future Years Defense Program." U.S. Senate Armed Service Committee, April 13, 2021, https://www.armed-services.senate.gov /hearings/-to-receive-testimony-on-united-states-european-command-and- united-states-transportation-command-in-review-of-the-defense-authori zation-request-for-fiscal-year-2022-and-the-future-years-defense-program (accessed January 2, 2022).

Under Secretary of Defense (Comptroller), U.S. Department of Defense. *DoD Budget Request.* https://comptroller.defense.gov/Budget-Materials/ (accessed January 2, 2022).

"The United States' Strategic Competition with China." U.S. Senate Armed Service Committee, June 8, 2021, https://www.armed-services.senate.gov/hear ings/the-united-states-strategic-competition-with-china (accessed January 2, 2022).

U.S. International Development Finance Corporation. *Our Work.* https://www .dfc.gov/our-impact/our-work (accessed January 2, 2022).

U.S. Navy. Fact Files. https://www.navy.mil/Resources/Fact-Files/ (accessed January 2, 2022).

World Bank. Open Data. https://data.worldbank.org (accessed January 2, 2022).

# INDEX

tanks, xi–xii

Tariff Act (1930), 242, 243, 244, 270

task forces: counter-piracy missions, 93; Eastern Mediterranean task force, 130–31, 148–49, 202–3, 270–71; focus of fleet on mission purpose task groups, 161; joint exercises and exercises between task forces, 270–71; Persian Gulf task forces, 148–49; South China Sea task force, 146, 148–49, 201–2, 270–71

Taylor, Gavin, 174

Taylor, Josh, 257

technology: advances in and naval missions and warfare, 34, 179–85; consequences of late adoption of revolutionary capabilities, 177, 185; factors and trends in global trade and maritime commerce related to, 73–74; Mighty Trio incorporation into fleet structure and platforms, 176–85, 323n18; offset strategies and emerging and disruptive technologies, 170–71; risks related to novel technologies into a single hull, 177; Thousand Talents and acquisition of, 52

TeleGeography, 86

terrorism, 113–14

THAAD (advanced ballistic missile defenses), 53–54

Thailand, 20, 91, 118, 140, 271

Theater Reconnaissance and Antisubmarine Patrol Force, 205

theaters/decisive theaters of operations: advance and seize the initiative regions, 109, 130–47; build, strengthen, and bolster regions, 109, 122–29, 147, 154; focusing limited national power and resources on, xii, 108–9; hold and respond regions, 109–22, 147; initiatives for planning for the future, 248–49; map of areas of naval activity, 106; positioning force in, 30, 72, 147, 148–54, 194–201; security of decisive theaters and national security, 105

theory of victory: alienation of U.S. from allies and partners as basis for, 8–9; Chinese and Russian theories, 8–9; contesting and denying victories for China and Russia, 9–10, 71–72, 265–66, 275–76; deterrence and, 8, 266; focus on decisive theaters key to theories of victory, xii, 108–9; Navy capabilities and strength as basis for, xvi, 6–7, 8–9, 275–76

third front strategy, 90

thirty-year shipbuilding plan, 210–11, 227, 229, 231, 238, 253–54, 275

Thousand Talents, 52

Tiananmen Square protests, 36, 37, 136

Tibet, 36, 52

titanium, 98, 99, 101

Title 10 U.S. Code, 157, 226, 263, 270, 275

trade. *See* commerce and trade

Trafalgar memo and Battle of Trafalgar, 108, 254–55, 269

Transportation, U.S. Department of, 114, 241, 250, 270, 271, 274

treaties and agreements, naval statecraft and, 30–31, 259–60

Trilateral Cooperative Agreement, xix

Trump administration and Donald Trump, 19, 64, 100, 254

tungsten (electron tubes), 97–98, 99, 101

Turbo Activation 19-Plus exercise, 161

Turkey, 102, 131, 132

"Two-Pass, Seven-Gate Process," 226, 329n17

Ukraine: aid for, xiii; border changes by Russia in, 8; NATO strength and invasion of, 113, 189; Russian invasion and war in, xi, xiii, xv, xvi, 26–27, 36, 39, 40, 43, 258; Russian military performance in, 132; Russian operations in, 39–40, 148; shipbuilding industry in, 44; titanium production in, 99; Western-supplied weapons to, 26–27. *See also* Crimea

undersea cables, 84–86, 96–97, 106, 112

Unified Command Plan (UCP), 149, 151

United Front (Central United Front Work Department), 51–54, 61, 72

United Kingdom/Great Britain: AUKUS membership, 258; colonial power in Pacific, 125; defense of maritime rules-based order by, 108; Five Powers Defense Arrangement role, 140–41; Joint Declaration and way of life in Hong Kong, xvi, 37, 89; North Atlantic operations of, 112, 113

United Nations Convention on the Law of the Sea (UNCLOS), 103, 111, 115, 116

United States (U.S.): AUKUS membership, 258; Chinese students and researchers in, 52; colonial power in Pacific, 125–26; decline in influence of, 2; geography of and trade and commerce, 102–5; machine tool production in, 99; maritime nation identity of, 74; Russian operations in water off coasts of, 42; titanium production in, 99; tungsten production in, 99

United States–Mexico–Canada Agreement, 91

Unmanned Carrier-Launched Multi-Role Squadron (VUK-10), 207

unmanned platforms: autonomous platforms, 171, 176–77, 178, 179, 181, 183–85; exercises with, 261–62; experimental ship

to refine unmanned operations, 184; extra-large unmanned submarines (XLUUVs), 146, 165, 198, 202, 205, 211, 215; fleet design and roles for, 198, 207–8, 209, 210; fleet recommendations and construction plan, 10, 215, 216; integration of inter-domain and interplatform architecture, 175–76; large unmanned surface vehicle (LUSV), 198, 204, 205, 211, 215; networked on-demand fleets, 181; reliability of and missions for, 198
unmanned systems office (N99), 175, 184
USAID (U.S. Agency of International Development), 22, 33, 159, 195
Uyghur population, 7, 36

Venezuela, 41, 46, 92, 123, 124
vertical launch systems (VLS), 167, 201, 204, 211
*Victorious*-class surveillance ships, 61, 211, 234–35
Vietnam: arms sales to by Russia, 70; defense budget and military inventory of, 141; importance of partnership with, 11, 137; Johnson South Reef confrontation with, 107; manufacturing and factory moves from, 91; manufacturing and factory moves from China to, 89–90; maritime disputes with China, 137; maritime militia encounters of, 63; transfer of military resources of, 142
*Virginia*-class submarines, 165, 221
Visiting Forces Agreement (VFA), 24–25

Wagner Group, 16, 40, 41, 46–47, 49, 134, 135
Walton, Timothy, 167, 200–201, 203–4, 211, 213
war games, 273
warships, xii, xv, 11, 34, 210–18
war/warfare/naval warfare: challenges from new types of warfare, xi; earning wealth by the sea in peace and ruling in, 1; flash-points and risk of, 8, 118–20, 122, 153;

fog of war, 180; force groupings for naval missions and to fight and win in war, 201–7; Navy force and capabilities to win, 11–12, 13, 74, 200–201, 266–68; operational planning for, 186–87, 199, 200–201; peace and war, blurring lines between, xvi, 2; preparation for winning, xi, 72, 187, 275–76; supreme excellence in, 6; systems approach to, 171; technological advances and, 34, 179–85
weapons/weapon systems: aging of, xi; area denial weapons and A2/AD capabilities, 8, 60, 72, 160, 206; Chinese arms sales, 142; contested operations, platforms and weapons for, 160–69; coproduction with partner nations, 27–28; energy weapons, 181; improved and new technologies for, xi–xii, xx; Russian arms sales, 131–32, 142; sales and transfers of U.S. equipment, 27–28
*West Capella* (Panama), 7, 17, 18–19, 33, 34, 143
World Bank, 5, 54, 56, 88, 118
World Trade Organization, 36, 91
World War I, 1, 74, 334n58
World War II (WWII): legacy infrastructure and U.S. relations in Pacific region, 126–27, 129; lessons from, 28, 153, 195; repair ships during Pacific campaign, 166

Xi Jinping: Belt and Road Initiative under, 54; China Dream of national rejuvenation under, 61; domestic challenges faced by, 38, 71; military modernization and reforms under, 59; removal of term limits on, 38; South China Sea island-building under, 136–37

Yellow Sea, 107, 118

Zhou Enlai, 52

# ABOUT THE AUTHOR

**Brent Droste Sadler** is a twenty-six-year Navy veteran with numerous operational tours on nuclear-powered submarines. He has been a member of personal staffs of senior Defense Department leaders and was a military diplomat in Asia. He writes about great power competition, advanced technologies, and building the Navy the nation needs.